More Praise for *The Age of Heretics*

"Art Kleiner has written a book that is both brilliant pop culture history and bible for business radicals. The perfect book for managerial martyrs who are prepared to be burned at the stake—but would prefer not to be."

—Michael Schrage, author, *Serious Play*

"I know of no other book that deals so completely and so effectively with the topic of recent corporate history in America. It is alive with fascinating information. The introductions to each chapter are absolute gems."

—Myron Stolaroff, author, *Thanatos to Eros* and *The Secret Chief*

"It took persistence on Art Kleiner's part to flush out the histories of the people at National Training Laboratories, SRI International, and the Shell planning group. And he has a wonderful way of explaining what they did, and why and how they did it. The book deserves a wide audience."

—Milt Moskowitz, author, compiler of the
"100 Best Places to Work" list in *Fortune*

"*The Age of Heretics* shows the insidious impact of the cult of numbers that gripped American management thinking after World War II. I like very much Art Kleiner's statement that the purpose of a corporation is, and always has been, to recreate the world."

—H. Thomas Johnson, author, *Profit Beyond Measure*

"Why would anyone bother with a book like this? Because it's terrific. *The Age of Heretics* offers one of the few compelling, intelligent, thoroughly researched histories of the field of organizational development. Kleiner proves particularly adept at summarizing an approach or technique succinctly, as if in passing, and all the while in the context of corporate change movements. *The Age of Heretics* is what the English like to call 'a rollicking good read': fast-paced, persuasive, and written for adults, not sixth-graders."

—Jonathan Leyrich, Linkage

"*The Age of Heretics* is almost unfairly engrossing (I read it in a single sitting). Its superb and nuanced documentation at times reads almost like an additional narrative. And Kleiner's wonderfully accessible writing makes this intellectual history of organizational development speak to those otherwise put off by the cerebral work."

—R. Michael Bokeno, Murray State University, Kentucky

"This book provides a brilliant and passionate intellectual trip through the history of corporate vitality today. Above all, it explores how business (that domain so many of us care deeply about) can regain its 'vernacular' roots—reaching back to recognize and re-form some of the meaningful 'community' ties it once had. I urge anyone who cares about business as a place where personal growth takes place, where work is more than a mere job, and where groups of people achieve great things, to read this book."

—Tom Ehrenfeld, author, *The Startup Garden*

"Anyone who works in the area of organizational design or development should read this book. Art puts the history into context and lets us know the people who shaped the ideas. I loved learning about Kurt Lewin, Ron Lippitt, Tom Peters . . . and so many others. The stories Art tells help me understand the events that shaped their lives and their thinking. I was truly sorry when I arrived at the last chapter. I wanted to hear more."

—Roger Breisch, founder, Midwest Organizational Learning Network

"Art has done a great job looking at leaders who have the attribute of going 'against the grain' of the times. It is a very interestingly different cut on leadership models at a time when we seem to be getting a new book on the topic each month that is not always that new."

—Charlie Seashore, Fielding Institute, American University/
NTL Institute

"Isn't the debate over layoffs, C.E.O. compensation, shareholder value, and corporate responsibility—if not about demons and chaos—really about the role corporations play in society? *The Age of Heretics* pushes that debate past good and evil into ambiguity, where it is really interesting."

—Barbara Presley Noble, *strategy+business*

"*The Age of Heretics* is a fascinating read, illuminating the roots of corporate culture changes that are still evolving today. Very informative and well grounded in history, and the storytelling style makes it a pleasure to read. Not only does it all hang together as an entire piece, but you can sample sections and still get a ton of value."

—Dan Simpson, vice president, Office of the Chairman, Clorox

"This is a journalistic history of an important chapter of the 20th Century that could easily have gone unwritten: a generation of attempts, more or less countercultural, to reform and reinvent the corporation. It's all here: unpredictable experiments in social engineering, weird tales of engineers dropping acid, computer programs predicting the future of the whole world, and the truly odd omnipresence of an Armenian mystic named G. I. Gurdjieff."

—Phil Agre, University of California at Los Angeles

"*The Age of Heretics* is great; beautifully written. I am especially enjoying learning about my unknown professional ancestors."

—Adam Kahane, author, *Solving Tough Problems*

"The heroes of Kleiner's book are concerned with reducing the psychic costs of work by better aligning the personal hopes and dreams of employees and the corporations they work for. For students of organizational development the book is full of fascinating insights into people like Douglas McGregor, Kurt Lewin, Chris Argyris, Saul Alinsky, and Warren Bennis."

—James McRitchie, publisher, Corporate Governance website (www.corpgov.net)

"I could not put it down, and when I had to, because I had finished it, I promptly ordered 35 more copies to give to my close circle of heretics in Hewlett-Packard. We are getting much needed energy, inspiration, and even direction in some right-brained way from this book."

—Barbara Waugh, author, *The Soul in the Computer*

"Art Kleiner reminds us that great innovation often originates with some of the most unlikely people, the heretics who have championed once unconventional ideas and used them to transform organizations—for customers, employees, as well as the bottom line. *The Age of Heretics* offers a compelling grand tour of some of the most important ideas and thinkers that have influenced leadership at its best."

—Andrea Gabor, author, *The Capitalist Philosophers*

A WARREN BENNIS BOOK

This collection of books is devoted exclusively to new and exemplary contributions to management thought and practice. The books in this series are addressed to thoughtful leaders, executives, and managers of all organizations who are struggling with and committed to responsible change. My hope and goal is to spark new intellectual capital by sharing ideas positioned at an angle to conventional thought—in short, to publish books that disturb the present in the service of a better future.

Books in the Warren Bennis Signature Series

Branden	*Self-Esteem at Work*
Mitroff, Denton	*A Spiritual Audit of Corporate America*
Schein	*The Corporate Culture Survival Guide*
Sample	*The Contrarian's Guide to Leadership*
Lawrence, Nohria	*Driven*
Cloke, Goldsmith	*The End of Management and the Rise of Organizational Democracy*
Glen	*Leading Geeks*
Cloke, Goldsmith	*The Art of Waking People Up*
George	*Authentic Leadership*
Kohlrieser	*Hostage at the Table*
Rhode	*Moral Leadership*
George	*True North*
Townsend	*Up the Organization*
Kellerman, Rhode	*Women and Leadership*
Riggio	*The Art of Followership*
Gergen, Vanourek	*Life Entrepreneurs*
Frohman, Howard	*Leadership the Hard Way*
George, McLean, Craig	*Finding Your True North: A Personal Guide*

THE AGE OF HERETICS

A History of the Radical Thinkers Who Reinvented Corporate Management

Second Edition

Art Kleiner

JOSSEY-BASS
A Wiley Imprint
www.josseybass.com

Published by Jossey-Bass
A Wiley Imprint
989 Market Street, San Francisco, CA 94103-1741—www.josseybass.com

Jossey-Bass books and products are available through most bookstores. To contact Jossey-Bass directly call our Customer Care Department within the U.S. at 800-956-7739, outside the U.S. at 317-572-3986, or fax 317-572-4002.

Jossey-Bass also publishes its books in a variety of electronic formats. Some content that appears in print may not be available in electronic books.

Library of Congress Cataloging-in-Publication Data

Kleiner, Art.
    The age of heretics : a history of the radical thinkers who reinvented corporate management / Art Kleiner ; foreword by Warren Bennis. — 2nd ed.
        p.   cm. — (Warren Bennis)
    Includes bibliographical references and index.
    ISBN 978-0-470-19070-8 (cloth)
        1. Organizational change—United States—Case studies.   2. Management—United States—History.   I. Title.
    HD58.8.K57   2008
    658.4'063—dc22

                                                          2008018501

Printed in the United States of America
SECOND EDITION
HB Printing   10 9 8 7 6 5 4 3 2 1
First edition published by Doubleday, 1996

CONTENTS

To the heretics, named and unnamed as such, who have given themselves to a grand dream; and to Faith, Frances, Elizabeth, and Constance, in honor of the dreams they have shared with me

FOREWORD

Warren Bennis

ART KLEINER'S *The Age of Heretics* is that rarest of books, one that is both important and a pleasure to read. Its subtitle—*A History of the Radical Thinkers Who Reinvented Corporate Management*—lets readers know at the outset that they are about to encounter something other than the standard cast of characters who write or star in most business books today, the exemplary leaders whose names we know almost as well as our own. This highly original history is devoted to the mostly forgotten pioneers, including the eccentrics and rogues, who have shaped American and increasingly world business and organizational life since World War II.

That is a huge swath of history to take on, and it is evidence of Kleiner's ambition. A comprehensive account of those sixty years would be invaluable, but it would also be too heavy to lift and all but unreadable. And so the author has made the wise decision to illustrate key events by telling emblematic stories featuring colorful, often unconventional individuals.

As Kleiner reveals, when postwar American business was a vast sea of gray flannel suits and tasteful ties, a few unorthodox individuals were not so quietly shifting the paradigm toward the breezier, Google-ier workplace of today. These change agents include a raft of idealistic social scientists as well as nonacademics, like labor organizer Saul Alinsky, who pioneered the use of shareholder activism to open Kodak's doors to more African Americans. Alinsky, who was literally willing to smash dishes to get attention, was the embodiment of the activist principle that behaving badly is sometimes necessary because, in the words of the civil-rights anthem, "The nice ways always fail."

Kleiner uses religious terms to title each of the chapters of his book— "Monastics," "Pelagians," "Mystics," and so forth. At first that seems an odd choice for a study of modern corporations and other secular institutions. But Kleiner is insightful to do so. Like the heretic whose rejection of religious orthodoxy might send him to the pyre, Kleiner's organizational heretic "is someone who sees a truth that contradicts the conventional wisdom of the institution to which he or she belongs—and who remains loyal to both entities, to the institution and the new truth." The person who is willing to make a great sacrifice to change an institution he or she loves is a hero as well as a heretic because, Kleiner writes, "the future of industrial society depends on our ability to transcend the destructive management of the past, and build a better kind of business."

One of the transformations that Kleiner's heretics brought about is a modern workplace that increasingly recognizes the centrality of work to a person's deepest needs and aspirations. The author uses the word "vernacular" to describe the sense of community and personal integration that so many of today's workers long for, a desire that is reflected in everything from corporate matching of employees' charitable contributions to the recognition by enlightened employers that workers want to do the right thing as well as put food on their tables. In this sense, Google's motto "Don't be evil" is an even more seductive lure to many gifted potential hires than its free gourmet meals.

At its heart, Kleiner's book is a history of ideas, some good, some less so. One of the trends he documents is the absorption into the Western mainstream of aspects of Eastern spirituality advocated by such once-influential gurus as G. I. Gurdjieff. It is fascinating to read how Pierre Wack helped prepare Royal Dutch/Shell decades ago for present-day oil politics in part because of his exposure to Gurdjieff and the wisdom of a Japanese master gardener, who taught Wack to see truly what was in front of him. Wack's consciousness seems to have genuinely expanded because of these teachers. But one wonders how many others have simply used the language of Eastern enlightenment to justify substituting gut instinct for a sounder, if more strenuous blend of intuition and old-fashioned Western-style analysis.

Kleiner writes with verve and a novelist's or filmmaker's appreciation for the value of a scene. The reader is unlikely to forget the image of a group of United States rear admirals on their knees trying to identify "their" lemon among a pile of lemons on the floor during a National Training Labs session. Equally memorable is the moment when my sometime coauthor and longtime friend Chris Argyris used a shocking demonstration to shatter the antibusiness bias of his Harvard education students.

One of the pleasures of this book is its expansive frame of reference. I cannot think of another volume that refers to Heloise and Abelard, Norwegian resistance fighters of World War II, my mentor Doug McGregor, consumer crusader Ralph Nader, *and* counterculture cartoonist R. Crumb (he of "Keep on Truckin'"). Moreover, the book is studded with delicious, unexpected factoids. Did you know that the term "scenario," now ubiquitous in corporate planning, was first suggested by a sometime writer for the Rand Corporation—Leo Rosten, later author of *The Joys of Yiddish*?

Although it is unsettling to discover how others see and write about you, I am happy to be one of the many heretical change agents who appear in this book. As Kleiner points out, all of us—heroes and outlaws alike—are the spiritual and intellectual children of the great social psychologist Kurt Lewin and, almost two millennia before him, of the heretical British monk Pelagius. Both believed in the perfectibility of humankind and helped us to believe in it as well. To a greater or lesser degree, each of us helped destroy, if not the Man in the Gray Flannel Suit, the soulless organization that stole his labor and his days. And in doing so, each of us contributed to a new organizational reality in which the personal and business are inextricably linked and success is measured in human terms as well as dollars and euros. That is a worthy history to have been part of, and this is a worthy account of that history.

Warren Bennis
April 2008

PREFACE

Steven Wheeler and Walter McFarland

THE NATURE OF EFFECTIVE MANAGEMENT has become increasingly clear in recent years. We now know, for example, that the leader of an organization has only a few years to make change succeed; that attention to people can make the difference between success and failure; that businesses run by the numbers alone, without a sense of purpose, tend to fail; that high-quality teams can operate with autonomy and be trusted with the future of the enterprise; and that organizations that treat people as fully invested participants, and themselves as full-hearted citizens, and become great places to work where people continually learn and improve are the companies and agencies that end up with competitive advantage.

These are simple ideas, taken for granted in many companies, but all of these were heretical not so long ago. This book is a history of those countercultural ideas and others, their grounding in World War II and then in the cultural changes of the 1960s and 1970s, and the ways in which they may be influential in the future. This book was written by our colleague Art Kleiner, the editor-in-chief of *strategy+business,* the management magazine published by Booz & Company. Art wrote the first edition between 1990 and 1996, after a stint helping Peter Senge develop *The Fifth Discipline* and *The Fifth Discipline Fieldbook.* And he revised it while working with us on an article on strategic leadership that appeared in the winter 2007 issue of *s+b.* We have had a number of conversations among us about the nature of leadership in times of change and its importance to the organization of the future, and we see the evolution of Art's thinking, and the continued impact of his journalism and research, in this second edition.

To Art Kleiner, a heretic is someone who sees a truth that contradicts the conventional wisdom of the organization and remains loyal to both that truth and the organization he or she works for. In our lexicon, that definition of *heretic* could just as easily apply to leadership in general. As advisers to large mainstream companies and large government agencies on effective strategies for human development, from the executive suite on down, we are keenly aware of the value of unconventional wisdom. Organizations get stuck in counterproductive ways of doing things, and it often takes a heretical point of view to get past the deadlock and move forward.

Heretics matter because leadership matters. In case after case, in organizations and in society at large, when the single individual at the top is replaced, everything else changes—for the better or the worse. But more than is generally realized, the effectiveness of leaders depends on the context around them. The best leaders pay a great deal of attention to the design of elements around them: they articulate a lucid sense of purpose, create effective leadership teams, prioritize and sequence their initiatives carefully, redesign organizational structures to make good execution easier, and, most important, integrate all of these tactics into one coherent strategy.

They do this because they know that the success of their enterprise will depend on it. They have that knowledge because the heretics in large mainstream corporations have made that understanding clear over the past fifty years.

Some of the stories in this book were familiar to us, and no doubt will be familiar to you: those of W. Edwards Deming, Kurt Lewin, Saul Alinsky, General Electric's Work-Out program, and Amory Lovins. Some of them are little-known aspects of eminent careers. How many people know, for instance, that Paul Hawken got his start managing a macrobiotic foods business, or that the pioneers of scenario planning traced some of their intellectual heritage back to the Sufi mystic G. I. Gurdjieff? And some of the people in this book are forgotten, but they made immense contributions at the time or represented (like John Mulder at Kodak) impulses toward decent and high-quality management that rise again and again from within corporations. There are also links between the heretical ideas of the past and the most prominent issues of our time: scenarios and the end of apartheid in South Africa, or organizational development and the need for diversity in the modern global corporation.

These fascinating stories describe success and failure in riveting ways. But underneath them is a deeper question: What is known, and yet to be known, about the quality of effective leadership and practice in the large mainstream organization? It's not enough to manage by the numbers anymore; that has been clear for at least a decade. But how then do you run a large company or a large government agency? And how can you make strategic changes while running a company (or part of one), as every leader seeking sustainable competitive advantage is forced to do these days?

The stakes couldn't be higher, because the world runs through its corporations and governments; improve those, and you improve not just the economy but the social and political prospects for everyone. And if we care about the dream of human fulfillment, we need to pay attention. Not only has the world become a world of organizations, but more and more human time, effort, and emotion are invested in them. Great organizations and great leaders give more than a good living: they contribute to a good life.

If you agree, then you will find in this book an invitation—not just to appreciate the stories but to consider becoming a heretic yourself. And you will find, both implicit and explicit, the guidance needed to take on that challenge (and survive) and have some impact.

Finally, we think you will discover in these pages, as we have, an argument that management knowledge does advance (albeit fitfully, and not always smoothly for the people involved). The world is getting wiser, and we who pay attention to that wisdom are more capable as a result.

Here is some of that story.

Steven Wheeler, Senior Vice President, Booz & Company
Walter McFarland, Vice President, Booz Allen Hamilton

TO THE READER

THIS BOOK, while it is fact-checked and historically accurate to the best of my ability, makes no attempt to be comprehensive. Many people who deserve coverage are omitted from these stories, only for the sake of coherent narrative. Personally I don't subscribe to the "great person" theory of history, but focusing on a few people makes it much easier to tell the story.

My model is not typical business journalism, but the mythic literature of destiny and integrity. Myth holds its characters to a higher ethical standard than they can possibly fulfill and yet shows us how to love them when they slip—or at least it forces us to recognize that slippage is inevitable. All of the characters in this book are real people, with lives outside these pages. If any of them have been misinterpreted here, that responsibility is mine.

I welcome comment from readers. I can be reached either through strategy+business, at kleiner_art@strategy-business.com, or at http://www. ageofheretics.com.

Art Kleiner
April 2008

THE AGE OF HERETICS

MONASTICS

CORPORATE CULTURE AND ITS DISCONTENTS, 1945 TO TODAY

Heresy: Business is always personal.

The historian John P. Davis tells us that the great-great-grandfathers of today's large, mainstream corporations were the monasteries of the early Christian Church.[1] Organized during the dissolution of the Roman Empire, they were built as isolated communities, cut off from worldly villages and barbarian raids. Monks shared every aspect of their lives together. On a trip to town, they wore the community's best robes and returned them to the community's closet, exchanging them for everyday muslin. Rituals governed every moment of the monks' days. Uncertainties of the outside world, from the preparation of meals to their sense of life's purpose, were serenely controlled within. They learned to control their impulses for the sake of the monastery's greater goal, and their membership gave them an elite status that few other people enjoyed. For their time, their culture and position were not unlike the culture and position of many corporate managers today.

Some monasteries evolved into great European ecclesiastical universities, such as the University of Paris and Oxford University, places of learning chartered by kings. These in turn became the models for great mercantile stock companies. Expeditions across the Atlantic or around the Cape of Good Hope were too expensive for sea captains to finance themselves. If a ship failed to return, the owner might go to debtors' prison. Thus, European kings and queens chartered corporations—creatures of legal sovereignty, named after *corpus,* the Latin word for "body." The stock company had no human body, but it was corporeal in every other sense. It was an engine for creating material. It could own property, outlive its human members, and borrow or lend money (a neat maneuver around the Christian law against usury). The monarchs had designed these new institutions to carry out the policies that they found too risky to undertake themselves. To each successful corporate appli- cant, the Crown said, as Isabella might have said to Columbus: *Go now. I judge you responsible to return with gold and spices. You are free to take a risk in our name; you are free to fail.*

Corporations evolved further in 1783 when the new American republic won its independence from England, and the states took over the royal role of granting charters. In that era of budding indus- try, thousands of would-be railroad magnates and factory builders beleaguered the legislatures with applications to start companies. In 1811 the New York State legislature changed the rules of the game. Instead of tediously sorting through individual requests, they estab- lished a blanket corporate charter: anyone who met the legal criteria was automatically granted the powers of a company: to own prop- erty, to outlive human members, and not to burden any individuals with their debts or liabilities. Nascent entrepreneurs flocked to New York, and then to other states such as Delaware and New Jersey, that strove to outdo the leniency of the others' laws.

Through the rest of the 1800s, the form of the corporation took shape. Gilded Age entrepreneurs known as robber barons (both unscrupulous extortionists and merely ruthless empire builders) tested the limits of public sentiment, defrauding shareholders and squeezing out competitors. These abuses led to new regulations, which sent businessmen scurrying for new ways to get around them. Meanwhile, new types of technological webs—railroads, steamships, electric power, telegraph and telephone lines—broadened corporate reach. They also required larger and larger companies to run them.

By 1945, the mainstream corporation had come to dominate the culture of the world. Like patrons of immense crystal gardens, industrial leaders had built up great latticeworks of thrumming wires and churning highways. They had cultivated, with indifference to any value but the growth of their own enterprises, the banking empires needed to finance those infrastructures. They had put forth new packaging and refrigeration methods that had freed the hungry from the tyranny of seasons—and then, to move that food around the world, they had created a distribution and transport system that would have boggled the imagination of a Renaissance-era trader. Through broadcasting, they had made real the age-old fantasy of seeing distant events reflected through magic mirrors; through advertising, they had created a new kind of creative sales vehicle that affected the habits of millions; through the aircraft industry, they had brought into reality the miracle of flying. All of these boons, and many more, were commonplace by the 1960s, to the point where no one praised them; it would have meant voicing a self-evident cliché.

The large mainstream firms of the twentieth century also redefined popular images of success and achievement, of human worth and value. Decision makers at desks overlooking cityscapes plotted elaborate diagrams of authority and signed off on allocating money, while secretaries brought coffee and the afternoon mail. Men measured themselves by the size of their paychecks and option plans or by the number of tiles in the ceilings of their offices. Women judged their worth by the cumulative growth of their husbands' and fathers' careers.

Corporate culture was a vast wave, comforting to those whose natures fit with it, splashing across all competing desires for power and fulfillment, carrying progress and industry to every other culture. It struck with such immense, captivating grandeur that there seemed to be no escape.[2]

But the greater the wave, the stronger the undertow.

○

THIS BOOK IS THE STORY OF THAT UNDERTOW. It started small; it built up greater and greater influence, until now, the heretical ideas of the corporate past are the business mainstream of the present and (especially) the near future. We live in an age of heretics: an age where unconventional ideas become conventional wisdom rapidly. And that's a good thing, because the future of industrial society depends on our ability to transcend the destructive management of the past and build a better kind of business.

That doesn't mean embracing every unconventional idea. Nor does heresy mean flouting authority. A heretic is someone who sees a truth that contradicts the conventional wisdom of the institution to which he or she belongs and remains loyal to both entities—the institution and the new truth. Heretics are not apostates; they do not leave the "church." Instead they try to influence the larger institution to change for its own sake, because they think that its survival, and their own role within it, depends on meeting truth halfway.

Heretics tend to pay a price. In medieval times, they often paid the ultimate price. Today's heretics are not burned at the stake, but they may be relegated to backwaters or pressured to resign. They see their point of view ignored or their efforts undermined. They see others get credit for their ideas and work. Worst of all, they see the organization decline as they predicted it would; they may see the leaders of that organization exploit or perhaps sell it, and profit accordingly, while the truth that the heretic fought to bring to the surface, the truth that might have led to a robust, sustainable company, remains unarticulated and lost.

In the meantime, the skills all of us are going to need, as citizens and private individuals, have to do with learning to be responsible for large-scale endeavors without being in control of them. Corporate heretics have pioneered the use and understanding of these skills.

Like all other heretical movements, the movement to reform corporations from the inside came into being because the prevailing institutions left a need unfilled. Despite the power of corporate practice, something desperately desirable had been lost in everyday corporate life, and without it, corporations could not truly perform. This lost quality, unnoticed and yet desperately needed, was the vernacular spirit of everyday life.

Or so we might call it. As the writer Ivan Illich pointed out, there is no better word than *vernacular* for the quality of relationships and culture that dominated community life before the advent of the industrial age, when most work was unpaid and the workplace was indistinguishable from the hearth and commons. The word originally came from the Latin word for "homespun" or "home-grown"—anything rooted in village culture, where goods were made not to be sold but to be consumed by the maker.[3] Vernacular life was the way of life that still exists in the villages of our dreams (and television programs and in a few preserves where indigenous cultures are maintained). In a vernacular culture, the best things in life *are* free, economic and personal life are mixed together, children are always underfoot in the workplace, and every exchange of goods is not just an economic transaction but an expression of the community's spirit. A barn raising is a vernacular event because the new building exists as an expression of the community's needs. It has not been paid for with money. Thus, it has not been distilled through the universality of the marketplace—which, after all, doesn't care where a building might be most needed but reflects only the expectation of profits and returns.

In the preindustrial world, before the advent of the giant corporation, mainstream business had been a vernacular affair. To be sure, it was global, and currency was involved; indeed, every merchant was part of a web of commerce that extended throughout Europe and the Near East, interlaced with markets, fairs, shopping districts, and sailing routes. But commerce was also intensely personal, in a way that lasted through the centuries. There was no alternative, because the pace of global commerce was so slow. A sixteenth-century trader would borrow the money to finance an import-export trip between, say, Portugal and Java; that trip might take eleven years or more, with stops along the way to lend and borrow more money and exchange goods en route.[4] Even if all went well and the trader returned to port a wealthy man, the books on the trip would be closed only a half-generation after they were opened.

With that kind of rate of return, trust had to be based on something, and the most reliable foundation was the merchant's family. A family name was the individual's bond. The family also took care of all the merchant's domestic concerns; it educated his children and cared for his elders. Work and family could not be separated. No one would have thought of separating them.[5] If you were the scion of a merchant family, you could not choose your mate or your career, because the family's line of succession, and all the people supported by its business, depended on your playing your part.

Then the world sped up.[6] By the 1800s, thanks in part to the telegraph and the railroad engine, the feedback loop of commerce had been dramatically accelerated.[7] Now, if you borrowed money for a long-distance enterprise, you could return it within perhaps a quarter of a year. You did not need to buttress your credit with your personal relationship with a trader's family or guild. Individual capitalists could now set out on their own without being held back by their families. The bold entrepreneurs of the robber baron era could build larger, more comprehensive enterprises than had ever existed before, and on an international scale. They believed that the sheer size of their expanded enterprises would insulate them from the whims and vagaries of their customers and suppliers. The corporations they built became living monuments to their intent to control the uncontrollable marketplace.

The new form of the corporation evolved quickly. By 1940 the age of the great monopolists like J. P. Morgan was over. The modern corporation was a hive of well-trained people (gradually labeled "managers") with overlapping responsibilities and channels of command (called "functions" and "divisions"), who all sat in judgment on each other (through a form of mutual persecution called a "performance appraisal"), acting together to comprise a single sentient entity, with powers and capabilities that the same number of trained people acting as individuals could never have equaled.

To outsiders, corporate leaders might have seemed like supremely powerful individuals, projecting their personalities on the global canvases of their companies. But with very few exceptions, chief executives tended to be unremarkable men. Most of them, as the economist John Kenneth Galbraith noted, tended to retire into "Stygian darkness." Their power stemmed from the power of the company, not the other way around.[8] As with the medieval monasteries whose culture still subtly influenced theirs, the power came from something innate to the enterprise, some understanding that was available only to people within the walls. It was as if every company were a living being, giant and invisible, offering great material rewards in exchange for fealty, seeking a kind of impersonal love and devotion that was all the more compelling because no one ever talked about it in public.

o

If no one controlled it—no entrepreneur, no robber baron, no banker, no investor, no legislator, and no king—then where had the power of the corporation come from? It came, in a very real sense, from magic. Magic, as the medievalist Jeffrey Burton Russell suggests, is a system of practice, uncanny to those who don't understand it, that attempts to manage, instead of simply accepting, the forces that shape human life.[9] Magic is a craft of rituals, often based on some scientifically provable truth, but expanded into assumptions that could never be tested.

Consider, for instance, the priests of the Nile in ancient Egypt, who lived in a temple far upstream, near the junction of its tributaries. Every spring they would check the color of the water. If the water ran clear, the Nile would flood mildly that summer, and the crops would be meager. If it ran brown, there would be overflooding, and the country would be impoverished. But if it ran blue, there would be ample water to irrigate the fields; there would be prosperity, and the pharaoh could raise taxes and go to war. The priests may or may not have known the reasons that the rituals worked each year; they may or may not have known that a different tributary, the Blue Nile or the White Nile or the brown Atbara River, controlled the river's flow each year.[10] It didn't matter. All that mattered was the ritual, and the lives of the priests depended on the fact that their predictions continued to work, season after season. Meanwhile, they guarded the secrets of the temple as closely as they could.

In corporations, the secrets of the temple were, simply enough, the magic of the numbers. The everyday rituals of financial analysis and operations control were so effective at managing life on a large scale, and so impenetrable to outsiders, that in any other age, the wielders of these methods would have been known as sorcerers or priests.

The practices of this "magic" had emerged through years of trial and error. In the salad days of the industrial age, every company was a laboratory for new methods of counting and measuring work. From the New England textile firms of the early 1800s came the formulas of "cost per pound": a way to compare the speed and skill of every worker who spun cloth rather than simply depending on observation. From the early railroads came elaborate analyses of the costs per mile of track—a way, for the first time in history, to meaningfully compare one manager's overall performance with another.[11] From the great mail-order store Sears, Roebuck came a method for scheduling the paths of goods at a distribution center, as if they were railway cars in a freight yard. And from Henry Ford came an adaptation of the same inventive scheduling to the automobile assembly line.[12]

From DuPont and Procter & Gamble came the innovation of diversification; when they produced a variety of products, managers were insulated from the inevitable ebbs and flows in the demand for any single item.[13] And from the gangsters of the 1930s, particularly Dutch Schultz's legendary financial handler, Otto Berman (whose nickname "Abbadabba" was derived from "abracadabra"), came a recognition of exactly how the numbers could be manipulated; Abbadabba used quadratic equations and probability formulas to rig his boss's illegal gambling rackets, increasing gross profits by more than 50 percent.[14]

One pivotal moment for the numbers came in the 1880s when the famous industrial engineer Frederick Taylor, studying the movements of immigrants loading pig iron at a steel mill, began to calculate ways of pacing human labor, so that manual work could be handled more effectively. Eventually these calculations were standardized down to the hundredth of a minute, covering the time it took to climb a ladder, walk to a desk, or read a gauge. A delusion took hold that "scientific management," the name given to this rigorous, formulaic oversight of human activity in the workplace, would yield boundless miracles of performance.

An even more influential (but less known) application of numbers was the invention of "return on investment." In the 1920s, a self-effacing Delaware farm boy turned management genius named F. Donaldson Brown moved up in the ranks at the DuPont Corporation, which was still family-owned and managed, despite the fact that his family had been feuding with the DuPonts for generations. He secretly married a DuPont daughter, and when the marriage was finally exposed, Brown was shunted off to a new Detroit company where DuPont executives had an interest—a collection of formerly independent automotive firms, now combined under the name General Motors. Both DuPont and General Motors were diversified businesses with a variety of product lines, and Brown put into practice at both companies a method for comparing divisions (or any business action) based on the money invested, the costs incurred, and the gap between expected and actual returns. Later, working closely with GM's brilliantly practical CEO, Alfred Sloan, Brown developed a way to compare the relative value of short-term and long-term investment with equally dispassionate clarity. These formulas allowed managers of vast enterprises like GM to think of all their far-flung divisions (Chevrolet, Cadillac, Buick) as components of a single system instead of as rivals within the firm.[15]

By the mid-1950s, nearly every large company had emulated Brown's formulas, Sloan's structures, Taylor's strictures, and most of the other management systems of the industrial era. At General Electric, AT&T, Procter & Gamble, and General Foods, encyclopedic manuals (sometimes called "blue books") dictated every aspect of workplace practice, from the layout of stamping machines to the format of quarterly reports to the placement of pencils on a secretary's desk. Formulas like these may have seemed rigorous and deadening to outsiders, but philosophically they represented nothing less than a breakthrough in human capability. Like incantations, the numbers gave names to elements of the world that had previously been vague, abstract entities; the value of human effort and the way that value might change over time could now be translated into "break-even points," "market sensitivities," "net present values," and the all-purpose measuring tool of "earnings per share."[16] A manager, through the numbers, could keep track of hundreds of people spending millions of dollars on dozens of thoroughly different projects. The marketer, through the numbers, could set a product's distribution and advertising patterns with the determination and strategic overview of a general plotting a war.[17] The financier, through the numbers, could build an explicit model of the forces of the future, forces that people from more traditional cultures could comprehend only through concepts like "karma," "hubris," and "destiny."

Profit itself, in this context, did not represent the company's gains extracted from its workers' labor, but the firm's capacity to generate more projects, more investments—more magic. With this type of power inherent in it, the magic of corporate finance overwhelmed all other considerations.

It no longer mattered that General Motors made cars or General Electric made electric appliances, except as means to the end of maintaining desirable numbers.

And the benefits of vernacular culture seemed to diminish by comparison as modernity came in. Few people mourned at first. Vernacular culture was unrelentingly local and parochial; it was slow and inefficient; it stultified ambitious people, and it condemned "worldliness." Moreover, the builders of industrial culture didn't have to reject vernacular culture; they merely ignored it or destroyed it in passing, while the power of finance and operations, the power of the numbers culture, undermined the relationships that vernacular culture depended on.[18]

In a preindustrial town, if you had been a grain miller, you would not have conceived of selling your grain overseas for a better price than you could get at home—not while people in the village were hungry. But once you knew the numbers, you gave up your loyalty to the village for loyalty to an impersonal exchange that, you knew in the abstract, would better serve everyone in the long run—even if it seemed disloyal now.[19] (The same logic would later enable managers to shut down plants in rust belt communities, where families had depended on their employment for decades.)

Even as businesspeople were attracted to the numbers culture because of the enormous new capabilities it brought them, they also found it psychologically compelling. Managers, with their engineering and finance backgrounds, knew how treacherous words and emotions could be. (That might be why they had gone into fields like engineering and finance in the first place.) But a number felt reliable; it made people feel secure. It could be compared to other numbers and brought to scale. Sure, the numbers could be misinterpreted and manipulated, but not for long. Good managers could read a table of costs, sales, profit margins, and earnings, alongside a table of budget forecasts, and patterns would leap off the page to confront them, with the force of a villain's grimace in Kabuki theater.[20] A great manager could almost smell subterfuge and pending problems in the same way that a great stock trader could smell when the market was about to rise or fall based on the rhythm of the tape. This was the skill that they taught in business school—the skill that made twenty-four-year-old holders of an M.B.A. so desirable as corporate minions.

A focus on the numbers also made managers feel that they were accomplishing something. If you worked to get the best scores you could, you did not have to think too carefully about the reasons underlying the choices you made. Nor did you have to think about the world outside the company—or the people within it. Like monks, the managers of corporations in the 1950s and 1960s began to systematically, and unconsciously, cut themselves off from any sense of responsibility for the rest of the world, even as their influence over it grew broader. Armed with the knowledge that they gleaned from the numbers, industrial people could say, in good conscience, using a slogan borrowed from gangsters like Abbadabba: "Don't feel bad that I won this round. It's just business. Nothing personal."

○

Unfortunately the ability to use the numbers to seek greatness, or even great results, is always ready to atrophy. In all too many companies, the numbers were used to make people look good or to reinforce the comforts of a complacent position.[21] People from the CEO on down lost sight of the purpose of their enterprises. They fixed their attention on the trappings of the rituals instead: the business plans, job descriptions, quarterly results, and performance appraisals, all of which had originally meant nothing in themselves. These decision makers had cornered the market on "know-how," said the architect and visionary Buckminster Fuller, but they lacked "know-why."[22]

Fuller had plenty of stories on which he based this claim. Again and again during his long life as an inventor and would-be entrepreneur, he had seen the "numbers" lead to corporate decisions that didn't make sense—decisions that screwed not just outsiders but the company's own long-term interest. In 1934, Fuller had interested auto magnate Walter Chrysler in financing his Dymaxion car, a durable, three-wheeled, aerodynamic land vehicle modeled after an airplane fuselage. Fuller had built three models that drew enthusiastic crowds wherever they appeared. Like all of Fuller's other projects (he was responsible for developing and refining the geodesic dome, the first practical dome structure), it was inexpensive, durable, and energy efficient; Fuller worked diligently to cut back the amount of material and energy used by any product he designed. "You've produced the exact car I've always wanted to produce," the mechanically apt Chrysler told him. Then Chrysler noted, ruefully, that Fuller had taken one-third the time and one-fourth the money that Chrysler's company usually spent producing prototypes—prototypes that Chrysler himself often hated in the end.

For a few months, it had seemed that Chrysler would go ahead and introduce Fuller's car. But the banks that financed Chrysler's wholesale distributors vetoed the move by threatening to call in their loans. The bankers were afraid (or so Fuller said years later) that an advanced new design would diminish the value of the unsold motor vehicles in dealers' showrooms. For every new car sold, five used cars had to be sold to finance the distribution and production chain, and those old cars would not sell if Fuller's invention made them obsolete.[23]

And in a very real sense, who could blame the bankers? Their reasoning was correct: the risk inherent in every innovation was threatening; especially risky was any innovation that threatened the stability of the corporate system, with its sunk expenses that had to be paid back. (As the Segway and the hydrogen-powered car would demonstrate in the early 2000s, genuinely innovative new products often clash with the existing infrastructure and consumer habits around them.) Nor was it fair to force all those new costs, all that added expense, on customers who had already bought cars and were satisfied with them. (This fact of life, years later, would force personal computer makers to shortchange their products by making them backward-compatible.) As long as the numbers supported decisions based foremost on protecting the corporate finances (and how could they not?), then projects like the Dymaxion car would continue to fail.

The safe, numbers-driven view had unanticipated consequences. In R&D labs, factories, and marketing departments, the numbers culture had the effect of diminishing corporate ambition. People got in the habit of discouraging products that broke new ground or demonstrated genuine public service. Instead they tried to sell products based on styling details and the moods of the mass buying public, and anything that did not threaten their past success. Engineers held back their highest-quality technical work (and gave it the name *overengineering,* a synonym for extravagant waste), particularly when it meant greater up-front costs.

When an organization's collective ambitions erode, the love of power and privilege rushes eagerly to fill the void. In a very real sense, fulfilling the trappings of success for its own executives became the primary purpose of many corporations. For a long time, in those flush years, they could afford it. In the 1960s, the rewards for people at the top of the corporate hierarchy increased disproportionately, setting a pattern that would continue for the next fifty years. James Roche, the chairman of General Motors, the highest-paid CEO in the country, made more than $900,000 per year in 1967—$200,000 plus bonus and stock options.[24] Even when converted into 2008 dollars (which would have made it, perhaps, equivalent to $6 million), it would have seemed downright meager compared to the top CEO salaries of our time, but it wasn't bad for a guy with no university degree, who had worked his way up from a sixty-cent-per-hour statistical research job for Cadillac. Any CEO salary was enough, in effect, to establish an aristocratic dynasty—with grandchildren who would never have to work.

The salaries, moreover, were supplemented by a wide variety of perks, most hidden from outside eyes. Many CEOs and senior managers went days without having to open their wallets; their meals, laundry, transportation, and entertainment simply arrived when needed. A retiring Royal

Dutch/Shell chief executive was asked what he would miss most: "The man who meets me at the plane," he said, "and takes care of everything." Sometimes "taking care of everything" meant chauffeuring a customs official from, say, Kennedy Airport to a smaller private airport in White Plains, New York, or southern Connecticut—a two- or three-hour round trip—while the CEO and his guests sat inside the company's private plane sipping wine.[25] And even the largest capital expenses moved around the top officers' convenience, as William H. Whyte, the author of *The Organization Man*, learned in the 1970s. Whyte studied corporations that had moved their headquarters out of New York. In every case, the new headquarters was located within eight miles of the CEO's home.[26]

With all of these rewards, was it any wonder that managers fought so bitterly over the chance to rise to the CEO position? Like a monarch's court, the structure of power in a corporation encouraged backbiting, sniping, and hiding information because those strategies helped people rise. Every step up the ladder had the effect, intentional or not, of isolating the manager further from the immediate consequences of his or her actions. At many organizations, no one was seen as powerful unless it was almost impossible to reach that person by phone or unless that person had found a way to balkanize and bully staff or keep them spinning, always a bit off balance, for favors and approval. After all, if they treated you as a colleague or if they couldn't produce the right numbers on demand, that showed that they (and you) were "out of control." It showed you had no mastery of the magic after all.

―――――――― o ――――――――

Beginning in the 1950s, a few heretical managers saw—or, rather, felt—the erosion of corporate purpose and the dangers of the numbers culture. They particularly felt the loss of community feeling, but many of them had no name to give to it. At heart, though they had no easy way to articulate it, they wanted to keep the best of the vernacular culture, the concern for relationships and quality, without losing the best of corporate culture either. This yearning could be vaguely heard in the taunts that managers made to each other or dimly seen in the way that executives leaned down for the scotch bottles in their bottom desk drawers. Every year a few more managers felt spurred to risk their jobs—to capture some kind of contact, some feeling of being in touch. Every year a few more managers acquainted themselves with the ferment going on outside the walls of their companies, which in the 1960s became the ferment of the counterculture. And gradually their attitudes began to change.

That was the beginning of the age of heretics. Slowly, tentatively, and with a variety of sources, new ideas began to emerge. They were simple ideas that ran against the grain of conventional management wisdom— for example:

○ People are basically good at heart; they are fundamentally trustworthy. Only workplaces that give their members the chance to learn and add value through their work will succeed in the long run.

○ Aim for the quality of work, and money will follow.

○ Industrial growth is not always desirable. Sometimes it can be destructive.

○ Predictions and forecasts are mechanistic substitutes for awareness, and substitutes for awareness lead to bad decisions.

○ There is no such thing as "just business, nothing personal." Business is always personal, even if it isn't supposed to be. And we are better off recognizing that.

○ Everything in business is connected to everything else. Business is a complex living system with many interconnections. No one can control the system; one can only learn to influence it.

Many of these ideas were based on a body of intellectual work that emerged after World War II. These ideas had roots in Western and Eastern spiritual traditions, in the new types of engineering and social science practice, in humanistic psychology and role-playing theory, in the experiences of anti-Nazi resistance fighters, in the models of systems engineers, and in the counterculture of the 1960s.

At various times, the promoters of these ideas—the heretics within corporations—have been reviled on political grounds. Critics on the left see them as ineffectual apologists for a corporate system that is so corrupt it ought to be destroyed, not reformed. Critics on the right see them as disloyal, effete, snobbish, and maybe communistic. Both sides have seen them as utopian, Pollyannaish, deluded, unrealistic, silly, pretentious, or self-serving. And there's a case to be made that many heretics are snake-oil salesmen (and saleswomen) of one sort or another, putting forth ideas about, say, leadership and management that don't pan out and charging enormous (or at least significant) fees in the process.

And yet corporate heretics may be the closest thing we have, in our self-contradictory time, to a true conscience of large organizations. Many of them have lost their jobs or failed to reach their potential because they would not turn back from the truth they saw. Despite all of these frustrations, it is better to be a heretic than to have one's soul wither through the denial of a truth. And in the end, the corporations of our time are much, much better because the heretics existed.

------------------ o ------------------

Outsiders to business, including quite a few pundits, artists, politicians, and journalists, have never really understood the importance of corporate heretics. In part, that's because they didn't get the magic of the numbers and the impact it has had, through corporations, on the world at large. Instead, seen from the vantage point of an outsider, the corporate world is purely a monstrous place—manicured, self-sealing, and vicious. Women, black people, non-American-born people, aging people—in, short, anyone who did not look, think, and act like bright, fresh-faced engineering college graduates—could never rise to the top. Or so the criticisms went. But who wanted to rise to the top anyway? Who wanted to work where you could not choose the focus of your work and where everyone around you continually sought to undermine your dreams?

From this perspective, business knowledge seemed like a fundamental evil, as usury had seemed evil to Christians for centuries. Look at all the frustration and suffering it caused. Politicians discovered during the 1960s, for the first time since World War II, that they could win votes by accusing giant corporations of villainy. People in the street increasingly blamed these giant companies, so visible in brand names and skyscrapers, for war, pollution, and the deadening squareness of modern life. The great French historian of economic life, Fernand Braudel, provided a good example of this attitude. He closed his three-volume explication of civilization and capitalism in European history with a complaint: big corporations, with their big production units, had squeezed out the small, vibrant companies that represented the lifeblood of the marketplace. "Public hostility," he wrote, "is accurately and rightly directed at the top."[27]

But corporations, even the largest and most closed, exist because they are necessary: they can provide the wherewithal for life, the food and electricity and transportation and communication, that people can get no other way. It's not their power that is dangerous, but the inhumanity in their culture—the lack of awareness, attentiveness, and life. To say that they are incapable of being benevolent is to overlook the many, many contributions that large, mainstream corporations have made and (more important) to overlook the fact that many, many people make their contributions to the world through the medium of large mainstream corporations.

And yet there is a dilemma: as long as the numbers culture holds sway alone, neither the companies nor the people in them can realize their potential.

One of the first writers to articulate this, if only obliquely, was Michael Maccoby, a Harvard-educated American psychologist who began in 1968 to investigate the personality of corporate winners. Maccoby had just returned from three years in Cuernavaca, Mexico, where he had worked closely with the psychologist Eric Fromm. Since Ivan Illich was a neighbor there, Maccoby had been exposed in depth to Illich's theories about how professionalization and industrial development had destroyed vernacular culture. And Maccoby had seen evidence of that himself. For his research with Fromm, he had spent hours in Mexican villages where corporations were due to build a factory, getting to know the farmers who lived there. Before the factories came, they spent their free hours playing guitar, talking, and playing basketball. Then the factories opened. Suddenly the villagers turned into automobile assembly-line workers who did nothing during their time off except watch television.[28]

Maccoby began to wonder about the psychology of corporate people. What went on inside people who created and sold this devastating technology? And then, by extension, what went on inside people who designed technologies for mass warfare—bombs, missiles, and the computers that guided them? Did these technologists realize the impact they had on the world? Did they care?

Maccoby got funding from Harvard for a study to answer his question.[29] But he couldn't find a corporation that would let him in to talk freely to its people. Then, in 1969, Maccoby gave a talk near Stanford that eventually led to his introduction to John Young, a junior manager at Hewlett-Packard. H-P, since its birth in 1934, had been known as a quintessential engineers' firm. But Young, who would later become CEO of H-P, was interested in understanding the human effects of corporate work. He wanted to know how to hire people at H-P who would become entrepreneurial risk takers, not just corporate bureaucrats. Almost immediately, he approved Maccoby's study for H-P. He helped organize the study, even writing some of the survey questions. More important, he insisted that Maccoby include other companies as well and arranged introductions to executives at Intel, Texas Instruments, and IBM.

During the next few years, from 1971 to 1974, Maccoby and a small research team visited ten corporations, administering surveys and showing managers Rorschach blots. The managers, after all the times they had been forced to appraise their performance, were remarkably good at describing themselves and each other. They could dispassionately pick apart others' strengths and weaknesses, attitudes toward work, sensitivities, goals, and the things that made them angry. In these interviews, many of them felt fully recognized for the first time. "I have more people working under me than ninety percent of the mayors in America," one manager said, "but nobody has ever heard of me. This interview, for me, is like being on the cover of *Time* magazine."

At that time, there was a theory in the air, taken for granted by anyone who studied corporations, that most managers were primarily "organization men"—driven by the need to belong and conform, dedicating their lives to fitting in to a hivelike whole. This theory came in large measure from the popular book *The Organization Man,* written in the mid-1950s by sociologist-journalist William H. Whyte.[30] Sponsored at first by *Fortune* magazine, Whyte had led a team of academic researchers who conducted dozens of interviews with managers at companies like General Electric, American Telephone and Telegraph, Richardson-Vicks, and Ford, along with their wives, who were solidly entrenched in suburban enclaves. Organization man culture, Whyte argued, had pushed out the previous Protestant ethic culture of independent individualism; it had fostered an atmosphere where people chose to deny their own individuality because they didn't value it highly.

But Maccoby (fifteen years after Whyte) concluded that the organization man culture was dead—even in the corporate world. There were still "company men" (as Maccoby called them) in most firms, striving to fit into a bureaucratic mind-set. But they did not rise to the top of the hierarchy anymore. The dominant people were motivated primarily by the desire to win—not at someone else's expense but in the sense of winning a game. They had little interest in understanding the world or figuring out which game to play; getting a big quarterly result gave them more joy than producing a product. They were the natural aficionados of corporate magic, the people who delighted in making the numbers sing. Maccoby called these people "gamesmen."

Before his research had gotten underway, Maccoby had expected most managers to be "ambitious but neurotic failures," as he put it—"petty bureaucrats who have been so humiliated and discouraged by life . . . that they have chosen to use the little power they have to make others squirm." But the gamesmen Maccoby interviewed were likable people. Their companies might be ruthless places, but as individuals, they had a strong sense of benevolence and justice toward the people around them. They drew enclaves around themselves, symbolized by the steel and glass structures that required visitors to run a gauntlet of security guards and receptionists to get in. The atmosphere within these enclaves was hard driving but warmhearted. Gamesmen looked after their own people, at the same time that they relentlessly competed with each other.

The gamesmen were unconcerned with morality or with restrictions. They used the sexual revolution as a playing chip; the stylized attention of stylish young women was just one of the prizes in the office, one of the many ways to keep score. Miniskirted secretaries were encouraged to mildly flirt with the managers in their departments, creating an atmosphere where everyone felt a little bit charged up, a little bit pushed forward, a little bit high on the job. The bosses flattered the secretaries by telling them how they helped control the men's moods. One secretary at Hewlett-Packard took the day off when her fiancé broke their engagement. "I didn't want to make a lot of people feel down just because I wasn't smiling," she told Maccoby.[31]

Despite the low-level singles-bar atmosphere, there was something innocent about the places that gamesmen set up. Divorce rates were low; the managers obviously cared about their children and families as much as they cared about their coworkers. "It felt to me like Santa Claus's workshop," recalled one of Maccoby's researchers. At the same time, he felt there was something tragically immature about the gamesmen, "as if playing to win was all that life was about."[32]

One of Maccoby's questions asked, "Is there any technology you would oppose on moral grounds?" In this post-Vietnam moment, the question triggered a distaste for the military. At electronics companies, managers consistently replied, "We would never work for a chemical company. *They* produce napalm." Meanwhile, executives at Dow Chemical said, "We would never work for an electronics firm. They make bombs." And at both, managers (even the most senior managers) consistently underreported the percentage of their company's business that went to military contracting. At the same time, all of this self-justification was conducted on an intellectual level, close to the surface, with little feeling behind it. Few of the gamesmen cared much about the uses to which their work was put. Few of them felt much responsibility to the people outside the enclave, whoever they might be.

Outsiders were losers. They were "sick" or "weak," deserving of exploitation. They didn't have the knowledge that corporate people had, the knowledge of how the world works through the financial perspective. Indeed, Maccoby himself didn't have that knowledge. In the eyes of his own gamesmen, he too was an evolutionary failure—an ineffective intellectual with no impact on the real world: the magical business mainstream.

But Maccoby, with his psychoanalytical training, also saw images of shame, self-betrayal, guilt, and despair come up again and again in the gamesmen's dreams. One manager dreamed of being buried alive, with a telephone in his casket. Another dreamed of shattered test tubes (symbolic of an early dream of being a chemist, which wasn't a lucrative enough career). Another dreamed of wandering through a city of slimy skyscrapers, with corpses peering out of the windows. Many, who did not remember their dreams saw bugs, worms, and rats in the Rorschach blots.[33]

One detail was so peculiarly disturbing that Maccoby left it out of his 1976 best-seller on this research, *The Gamesman*. Yet this detail was evident at all ten companies, not just H-P, and for all four managerial types. Maccoby's team had asked managers to name the historical figure they most admired. The answers, almost without exception, fit into a very short list: Abraham Lincoln, John F. Kennedy, Robert Kennedy, Martin Luther King Jr. It was an odd list—Why would predominantly white managers select King?—and it took a while to notice the one thing those heroes had in common: all had been assassinated.

Did businesspeople feel betrayed in some fundamental way, as if they had given so much of their life to their jobs that they too had been murdered? Did they lack examples of heroic figures who had survived? Or did they believe that anyone who broke through the mold of conventional office politics, who actually managed to accomplish something within the system, would be slain?

PELAGIANS

NATIONAL TRAINING LABORATORIES, 1947–1962

Heresy: People are basically trustworthy; you cannot understand a system unless you try to change it; people can rise to fill their highest potential; and small groups hold the key to beneficial change.

From the remote northern province of Britannia, around the year 390, came Pelagius: a fat, self-possessed cleric who landed footloose in Rome, preaching about the human capacity for redemption. God did not choose who was saved, he said. Salvation was the result of human effort. If we could reach within ourselves and draw forth the core of natural purity that God had put there—for why would He create us without it?—we could remake the world within our lifetimes. The role of the Church, Pelagius said, was to help its members fruitfully exercise the will to be good.

Followers gathered around the British monk. He often stood quietly on summer evenings as small groups of passionate would-be reformers of the Church, including several of the younger bishops, talked excitedly about doing away with baptism or encouraging good works. He attacked the nonsensical idea, as he called it, that Adam's sin had been transmitted to the rest of humanity. He argued that people were perfectible; that human actions and human will, guided by God, could create a kind of echo of heaven on earth.

The prayer groups that gathered to hear Pelagius were like reflecting pools in which the members could see their faith and aspiration echoed in the shape of the conversation.

Far away, in his cell outside Carthage, the brilliant bishop Augustine of Hippo turned his attention to the Pelagian gatherings. He had spent his life branding and fighting heretics; Pelagius would be his last great opponent. He was a supreme logician, who had spent his life exploring the relationship between thought and faith, and he rested his argument against Pelagius on the innate corruption twined within the animal core of human nature. We are all fundamentally flawed—all tagged with our own limited view of the world. Every time we think that we have turned the corner and mastered our fate, our pride contains the seeds of its own collapse. How can we presume to declare that we will create heaven when we can't even predict the effects of the everyday exercise of our will?

Saint Augustine won the ear of the emperor, the pope, and church leaders. Some say they found his doctrine more palatable because it legitimized their authority; if humans were innately damned, then they needed the Church to intervene. Others say Augustine's strictures fit the spirit of the times. And still others say simply that Augustine was right. Though they have free will, people do not oversee their destinies because they cannot be trusted to do so. Fearing for his life, Pelagius fled to Jerusalem. Twenty years later, he was finally tried for heresy there. Despite Augustine's objections, he was acquitted, but he died shortly after. His death inspired riots in Rome. All followers of Pelagianism were banished from Christian lands.

That was fifteen centuries ago. Ever since, Augustinians and Pelagians have battled for the soul of Western human beings. How arrogant, say the Augustinians, to presume that we can draw forth our full potential without God's direction. How hopeless, say the Pelagians, to deny our inner beauty and our capacity to help ourselves. ("There are no bad children, only bad parents" is a Pelagian sentiment.) The arguments echo today in the dilemmas that every management team faces. Can our colleagues be trusted? Will they rise to meet our trust or betray it? How much can we have faith in ourselves? And in our efforts to avoid evil and failure, if we can't control other people, how we can have confidence in our success?[1]

IN THE YEARS AFTER WORLD WAR II, businessmen were readier than anyone realized to be influenced by the Pelagian imperative. It quelled the ache that people felt when the vernacular spirit was dormant. Even in the hardest-driving, most authoritarian businesses, many managers wanted to believe that they could come to work, achieve the performance required by the numbers, and still feel welcomed and recognized as people. They wanted a chance to do something important beyond just making money.

The promoters of this view didn't call it Pelagianism; they called it group dynamics at first, and later they would call it organization development, the human potential movement, and organizational learning.[2] In its earliest days, it was a stepchild of the panic people felt after the end of World War II. Even in the late 1930s, before the full story of the Holocaust was known, the example of Nazi Germany raised profoundly disturbing questions. Were its obscene atrocities rooted in some evil aspect of the German character? Or was there some fundamental evil at the core of human nature? In either case, was there a way to organize society that would naturally draw people away from totalitarianism, and toward democracy instead?

In the late 1930s and early 1940s, one of the most influential people concerned about these issues was a German-Jewish social psychology professor named Kurt Lewin. Lewin had left Germany in 1933, after a fortuitous teaching sabbatical in America the year before, and settled into a teaching position at the University of Iowa. His mother, who remained in Germany, died in a Nazi gas chamber.[3] Photographs of him show a small, wiry, sharp-featured, and witty man, with spectacles and a sardonic smile, looking a little like one of the Marx Brothers out of makeup. Although he couldn't speak English well at first, he was a fervent, open-hearted, good-natured, and compelling teacher; his ideas were simultaneously lofty and resonant with everyday experience. He developed a circle of lifelong associates, many of them former students.

Kurt Lewin was never a businessman, and yet the distinctions and methods he taught (and the institute he cofounded, the National Training Laboratories) have become embedded in thousands of companies years after his death. Nearly every sincere effort to improve organizations from within can be traced back to him, often through a thicket of tangled, hidden connections. His work spread from mentor to student, from consultant to manager to colleague, always through the medium of small groups. He believed in the Pelagian ideal: that people have something innately valuable to offer the world. His work showed how this offering emerges, or is held back, depending on the groups in which people operate.

Lewin and his followers were social psychologists, but they abandoned conventional academic research methods such as surveys and dispassionate interviews. Instead they developed a concept that became central to organizational reform: you cannot know an institution until you try to change it. This meant studying companies with full immersion in their cultures, in partnership with managers who wanted to make changes— typically managers of some pilot project within the firm.

The tricky part was persuading senior managers to support such unorthodox research. Lewin found only one workplace willing to experiment with his ideas in full: a pajama factory in North Carolina, where the manager in charge was Alfred Marrow, one of Lewin's students. Marrow's experiments with shop-floor group meetings in the 1940s, with Lewin as a continual adviser, were unusual enough to inspire a Broadway musical and then a Hollywood movie, both called *The Pajama Game*.[4]

Lewin coined the now famous line, "Nothing is so practical as a good theory." He also developed a theory of human personality that synthesized Freudian insights—that subconscious echoes of past traumas drive our deep feelings—with the behaviorist's observation that people could be programmed to respond predictably to stimuli. Lewin argued that these were only two out of the many factors that could affect an individual's behavioral "force field" (as Lewin called a person's mental and emotional state at any given moment).[5] Other factors might include relationships with family members.

On blackboards, Lewin would sketch the topology of a given individual's force field as a big egglike oval, pressed by helpful and harmful forces from all directions: the person's marriage and family relationships, fears and hopes, neuroses and physical health, work situation and network of friends.[6] From earliest childhood, Lewin proposed, people have aspirations and goals. At first, they're as simple as wanting some chocolate or wanting to sit up without falling. Gradually they become more complex—for example, they aspire to a new job or a new career. Some factors help us move toward our goals, and others push us backward. The diagram laid all these out in relation to the person's goals, to show which forces produced the most important resistance and which offered the most leverage for an individual to grow and learn.

Social groups, Lewin believed, were particularly high-leverage forces for influencing behavior.[7] In the 1940s, the heady early years of social psychology, there was ample reason to think so. At Brandeis University, Solomon Asch was finding how people could be influenced by the opinions of strangers to deny the evidence of their own eyes—even about something as simple and self-evident as the length of lines drawn on a piece of paper. At Yale, Stanley Milgram was demonstrating that most people, when told by an authority figure to administer what they thought were painful and death-dealing electric shocks, would overcome their own distress and horror to carry out sadistic orders.[8] And in Iowa City, Lewin and his graduate student Ron Lippitt demonstrated how leaders of a group, by changing the character of the atmosphere, could dramatically help people grow and learn.[9] This work, which still provides powerful lessons for anyone trying to organize corporate teams, was conducted with boys' clubs, a venue that Lippitt knew well. Starting as a teenager, he had worked with Boy Scouts, the YMCA, and a succession of summer camps and orphanages. His high forehead and glasses made him look cerebral and shy (which he was), but he was also savvy, inventive, and people-wise, in a tart midwestern way. For the experiments with Lewin, he and a fellow researcher named Ralph White organized some public school, middle-class eleven year olds into "G-Man Clubs," with five boys in each and a carefully trained college student leader.

Some of these collegiate club leaders were told to become autocratic. They gave detailed directions to the boys, telling them exactly how to paint their clubhouse signs or build model airplanes. Other, the laissez-faire leaders, stayed out of the way, and in the third group, "democratic" leaders helped the boys execute their own ideas, with as much noncoer-cive guidance as possible. While the boys played indoors, a group of researchers, haggard from intensive note taking, observed them from a darkened corner of the room, while Kurt Lewin filmed them with a movie camera. ("Those people are just interested in how a good club goes," Lippitt murmured to the boys. "They won't bother us, and we won't bother them."[10])

Laissez-faire leadership, letting the boys do whatever they wanted, bred frustrated cynicism. Under authoritarianism, some boys became extremely obedient ("unnaturally good," Lippitt wrote), while others fought, bullied each other, and destroyed their own toys. In the democratic groups, boys gradually become more conscientious, more tolerant of each other, less selfish, and more adult. "Eddie really did a swell job on that, didn't he?" said one eleven year old about his former rival. "I couldn't do as good as that." Most intriguing, when the democratic group switched to an author-itarian leader, or vice versa, after a day or two of transition, the boys changed their behavior to match the new dynamics. The structure of a group determined the character of its members at least as much as the members determined the values of the group.

o

This was not an easy message to get across in the individualistically minded United States. Lewin and Lippitt were still pondering it when the United States entered World War II. The war was generally an immense catalyst for social science in the United States (and England) because it pulled university researchers from their isolated posts. They worked together on real-world problems: keeping up military morale, developing psychological warfare techniques, studying foreign cultures, training counterinsurgency forces, and coordinating civilian activities that needed military self-discipline in a democratic country. All of these war activities vindicated Lewin's action research idea: researchers *did* learn more from being involved, and the pace and colloquy were exhilarating. A researcher might find himself (in rarer cases, herself) working on several projects at once, with different groups of colleagues from around the country. (Lewin and Margaret Mead collaborated on a project in which housewives were convinced, through small-group dynamics, to eat more "poor people's meat," like kidneys, livers, and pork, to preserve more beef for the boys at the front.)

During the war years, Lippitt's path regularly crossed with two other young psychologists from the Midwest. Their names were Ken Benne and Leland (Lee) Bradford, and eventually they would form the founding triumvirate of the National Training Labs. Benne was a charismatic young political theorist who had been one of John Dewey's last graduate students. He was the son of an old-time Kansas populist, from whom he inherited a steadfast mistrust of capitalist competition. He was equally mistrustful of communism—or any other system in which democratic principles were suspended, even temporarily.[11]

Bradford was not a theorist but a natural organizer. Everywhere he went, even at temporary jobs, he brought people together into freewheeling volunteer discussion groups. Dedicated to the idea of adult education (and believing that learners, not an authoritarian teacher, should control the courses), he took a job at the National Education Association, the educators' professional and lobbying group. That concept of self-directed learning became an essential factor in his life after World War II, beginning with an event still known, in group dynamics circles, as the "Connecticut Workshop."

In 1946, amid a flood of returning GIs and the winding down of defense industries, racial tensions began to flare in some northeastern cities. A Connecticut state agency, with sponsorship from the National Conference of Christians and Jews, called Kurt Lewin to ask for help. Together with Lippitt, Bradford, and Benne, he planned a two-week workshop in creating better ethnic relations, particularly between blacks and Jews.

It was held in July in the small working-class city of Bridgeport, southwest of New Haven. There were fifty participants: about fifteen schoolteachers; an equal number of social workers; a smattering of businesspeople and real estate dealers; a few volunteer housewives; several organizers from community groups, labor unions, and veterans' groups; and a few young men who had grown up in street gangs and in their late twenties had become community leaders. Most of the time was spent in small discussion groups, role-playing some of the troubling aspects of interracial life—like the tough time social workers had getting white and black teenagers to accept each other's company. Role play was an accepted therapeutic device: a white social worker might play herself, trying to get a thirteen-year-old black girl to come to a mixed-race event: "Did you know we have a folk dancing group every Wednesday night, Nancy?" Another white social worker would mimic the girl's reply: "My friends wouldn't want to come. It's not really their gang." Then the group would talk through the implications. It must have been a wrenching experience for some of the nervous social workers, whose real concern (it was obvious, when they repeated the dialogue back) was making sure everyone appeared to get along. Given that frame of mind, how could they reach any teenagers, let alone teenagers struggling with moving from a black to a white culture? These adults believed in rationality; they felt they had to instill, in their troubled charges, a respect for the orderly, rational life. But the role play had suddenly confronted them with the huge wave of blocked fear, anger, and suspicion pent up within themselves, behind the wall of their stiff, well-meaning squareness.

The pivotal moment of the conference came one night during the second week. Four participants, wandering back to their hotel rooms, passed the open door of Lewin's room and asked to listen in as the trainers talked over that day's session. Lewin agreed. Sitting in the corner, one participant, a social worker named Mrs. Brown, began to recognize herself in Lippitt's description of a participant "who is customarily the most backward and hesitant" but had suddenly become "a very active and verbal leader" in a role play, even after the exercise ended. What did that mean? Was she unconsciously adapting the role-play personality into her own?

Before a social scientist jumps to a hypothesis, the observations must be verified. So Lippitt turned to a graduate student named Murray Horwitz, who concurred: Yes, Mrs. Brown *had* changed—and then he broke the frame. "I think she is here," he said, "so why don't we ask her if she noticed it too?" Lippitt agreed, and the attention of the group turned to Mrs. Brown. "Are we all off the beam here in our hunches?" Lippitt asked.

No, said Mrs. Brown. "I was aware too that I was much more in the swim of things this afternoon than I had been before." And then she started analyzing herself—a bit creakily at first, but the passion crept into her voice: "I surprised myself several times the way I spoke up and found myself enjoying it." She even complained—Lippitt had cut off the role play before she was ready!—and the evening group broke into good-natured laughter.

Kurt Lewin, the elder statesman of participative psychology, was delighted. Here was a simple, obvious solution to an eternal experimental problem: trying to guess a subject's thoughts. Sure, you could ask them, but the interviewer's biases (and the subject's) made the answers unreliable. Now, in groups like this, answers would have much more validity. "We may be getting hold of a principle here," Lewin said, "[with] wide application in our work."[12]

Indeed, as the staff and participants continued their talk about the day's session, the barriers between them dissolved; they were all now just people, mutual participants in the inquiry, comparing notes and disagreeing, just like members of a vernacular community. When the social scientists got it wrong, the participants corrected them; when the participants lost sight of the larger perspective, the social scientists gently drew them back to equanimity.

Word spread fast, and the next night, all fifty participants showed up for the evening critique. There at Bridgeport they had invented a powerful new kind of conversation, in which the flow of conversation is also the subject of the same conversation and in which people's understandings of themselves and each other seem to flow naturally to the surface. It wasn't a therapy group; its point was to understand social dynamics, not individual neuroses. Lewin, Lippitt, Bradford, and Benne called it the "T- Group" ("T" standing for training).

Within a few months, the Connecticut T-Group discovery was famous in psychology and education departments. Lippitt, Bradford, and Benne published their findings on it almost immediately and made plans to convene a regular series of groups the following summer. The National Education Association (through Bradford) and the Office of Naval Research (through Lewin and Lippitt) granted them money to continue experimenting. (Ironically, neither of the two original sponsors, the Connecticut State Interracial Program or the National Conference of Christians and Jews, ever funded a T-Group again.) To submit the applications, the researchers needed to form an institute, and they chose a name in a hurry: the National

Training Laboratories for Group Dynamics. Most people would simply call it NTL; Bradford, throughout his life, would call it the "labs."

Lewin suggested holding the T-Groups in a "cultural island," far from anyone's homes or daily cares, so participants could, in effect, enter into an isolated world together. After looking in Massachusetts, Bradford found the Gould Academy, a traditional New England school in Bethel, a small town in western Maine. They rented the classrooms for the summer and began looking for housing for the two hundred people—one-quarter of them staff—whom they expected to descend on Bethel.

In February, midway through this planning phase, Kurt Lewin abruptly died in his sleep of a heart attack. He was only forty-seven years old. The timing of his death gave NTL's birth a mythic stature, even for people who never knew him. Lewin had been a prophet. He had articulated the theoretical foundations of social psychology. He had inspired a world-wide community of practitioners to use a new set of tools and methods. And then he had passed away just before reaching the promised land.

○

It was left to Lewin's disciples—especially Lee Bradford, Ken Benne, and Ron Lippitt—to settle the new territory. At first they had difficulty attracting participants. They almost got thrown out of Bethel the first year when a party spilled out into the town streets after midnight—drinking (in a liquor-free town), singing, and driving one man's car around the Gould Academy's footrace track.[13] But by the mid-1950s, a series of grants from the Office of Naval Research (and later from the Carnegie Foundation), a solid business in training fees for nonprofit organizations, and an ongoing official existence as a division of the National Education Association had given NTL a relatively stable financial existence.[14]

All three of the principals found influential winter jobs. Lippitt moved Lewin's Institute for Group Dynamics Research from MIT to the University of Michigan (where it eventually formed the nucleus of a more general Institute for Social Research).[15] Benne got an appointment at Boston University, and Bradford maintained a permanent post coordinating adult education programs at the National Education Association (NEA). The NEA leaders barely tolerated the labs, whose suspicious group methods threatened conventional teaching styles. Nonetheless, the melancholy but stubborn director made NTL his first priority. He became the labs' center of gravity, the person around whom the whole enterprise revolved. As a child, while peddling newspapers on the Evanston-to-Chicago train, Lee Bradford had fallen off and broken his arm. It never healed right, and that, plus his thin drawl, gave him a lifelong quality of melancholy frailty, as if he were always about to burst into tears.[16] Bradford was proud of his unpretentiousness and his eagerness to help other people shine. In a way, he was proud of his lack of pride. He liked to tell the story about how, at the start of a conference he was leading, the audience waited patiently while a mumbling janitor fooled around with some microphone cables on the stage. Finally, the janitor turned around, announced he was Leland Bradford, and began to speak to the crowd.

This personality was perfect for the role Bradford had to play at NTL. In his mild-mannered way, he could get some of the most egocentric and self-aggrandizing people in the psychology and social work fields to return, year after year, to collaborate wholeheartedly. Thanks, perhaps, to his low-key gift for bringing out the best in people, NTL was never caught up in any cultlike episodes of charismatic leadership. Anyone who knew Bradford could see that leadership was supposed to emerge not from stars but from a collaborative group.

Throughout the 1950s, a growing number of faculty members and graduate students—in social psychology, psychiatry, education, and social work programs from around the United States—came year after year to Bethel, giving T-Group "laboratory sessions" at the Gould Academy.[17] The emphasis on "laboratories," with its research connotations, was deliberate. NTL was not governed by "partners," as in a typical consulting firm, but by "fellows"—about fifty of the leaders in the new academic field of human relations. T-Groups were not going to be management training workshops; they would train "change agents": expert community leaders who would promote egalitarian, democratic, participatory organizations in communities across the country.

Making a significant alteration in an attitude or belief, Lewin had said, required three stages: an unfreezing process to get rid of the old outmoded beliefs, a learning process to become familiar with the new idea, and a refreezing process, so that the new attitudes and practices would stick and take root. The NTL people didn't quite understand how to refreeze, but T-Groups were clearly the most effective unfreezing device anyone had ever seen. Anyone who had been through a T-Group could easily imagine city and country governments unfreezing out of their repressive, overly bureaucratic forms into collaborative "perfect communities."[18] Trainers began to show up at places like the United Nations, buttonholing delegates: "Don't you see? If we could just get the military leaders to sit down and do T-Groups, then there would be no war!" (Anna Freud had said the same thing about psychoanalysis, and years later the followers of W. Edwards Deming would say the same about total quality projects.) In their enthusiasm, who could blame them for losing sight, every now and then, of the fact that no one can force others to unfreeze their cherished beliefs?

————————o————————

T-Group sessions at Bethel typically began on Sunday night. Arriving late in the afternoon, participants would rush to the meeting room and be seated at a big round oak table with ten or so other strangers, all with faces composed in a polite mask of attentiveness. The politeness wouldn't last long.

There would always be two trainers, typically psychology or sociology Ph.D.s or Ph.D. candidates. The trainers were sharp, earnest men who had developed the art of being very good listeners. They had a great deal of latitude in the design of their group; only the opening moment was predictable. "We'll be together for many hours," a trainer would say to the people in the room. "We will learn by examining whatever happens as we meet together. And I won't be your leader." Then he would stop. Dead. Silent. And look impassively at the group.

"Could you repeat that, please?" someone might finally ask. The leader would offer the same few words. And again, silence.

"Well, what are we supposed to work on, then?" someone else might demand. "How are we supposed to get started?"

"You tell us," the second trainer might say. "These decisions will be made by the group."

Yet another silence. Then someone from the corner of the room might snap or growl, "This is a waste of time. Let's get started so we can accomplish something. I propose we talk about the problems of communicating in a large bureaucracy, and we can vote to pick a group leader. Who wants to vote?"

More silence. The faces would still be polite, but tense and a bit agonized. Some of them wouldn't have attended a meeting without an agenda since they were children. Finally, they'd begin introducing themselves. They might make it all around the table, each person telling his or her title and organization's name, and then a trainer would break in: "Why are people introducing themselves in terms of their organizations? Don't you think it's safe enough to talk more personally?"

A couple of people might make excuses or muse about their own shyness, and then one of the group members might snap at the trainers: "You have given us no help. You've just let us drift. Either tell us what to do, or stop criticizing us."

Now the atmosphere in the room would develop an enervated, stifling quality, as if the air were laden with ozone before a storm. Another member would jump in to defend the trainers: "That wasn't criticism; it was helpful." Others would chime in to describe the conversation the way *they* saw it, and the storm would break: the group would be off and running. For the next two weeks as they continued talking, they would pause every minute or two to consider their own progress. "Why isn't John speaking?" someone might ask. Or, "It seems to me that Sally answered a different question from the one Mike posed. Do others agree?" Or, "We're now in three factions. How did *that* develop?"[19] It was wonderful and terrifying to see remarks and gestures held forth for study, as if frozen in the air, a few moments (or a few days) after they were made. The group members would pore over their memories of each other's remarks, interpreting and responding, and possibly critiquing tapes of their own sessions. (NTL had a cabinet full of audiovisual apparatus, rare and expensive in those years.)

Morning sessions would go on for three weeks, punctuated by other types of workshops in the afternoon. In skill sessions, participants would learn techniques for leading their own groups. In fishbowl workshops, one group would watch another talk and then critique its openness and behavior. Participants might take part in a massive role-play session called "Regional City," lasting one or two days, in which all eighty or ninety people at Bethel would be given parts in mock unions, school boards, PTAs, chambers of commerce, and police departments. Through all of these exercises, they would see the value of experiential learning—how conducting their own experiments and seeing the results produced a much clearer understanding of human and organizational behavior than, say, listening to a lecture by an expert.

But there were lectures too: short ones, dubbed lecturettes by the trainers, about the dynamics of group behavior.[20] The T-Group participants would hear how their struggles over authority mirrored similar dynamics in workplaces and personal relationships everywhere. Meanwhile, participants in the groups would begin asking each other to serve as their mirrors, offering what NTL trainers called "personal feedback"— reflections on how they came across, moment by moment. T-Group participants became extraordinarily sophisticated at seeing and hearing each other. They could now see how falsehood and doubt hung in the air sometimes—invisible problems, created by no one and everyone, forceful enough to block people from fulfilling their goals and dreams. They could tell each other why they came across as having a poor attitude or a self-pitying demeanor and how to change it.[21]

There were also remarkably effective methods, available only at NTL because they had been invented there, for redesigning meetings. These included one of the mainstays of meeting management: the use of flip-chart paper for notes. One story placed the genesis back at the

Connecticut Workshop; Kurt Lewin needed some paper for his egg-shaped force-field diagrams, and someone (perhaps Ron Lippitt), looking in vain for a stationery store, passed a print shop, and bought some newsprint from the ends of the press rolls. With the papers taped to the wall, the room itself suddenly became a living memory for the group.[22] By the second week of a typical T-Group session, the rooms were a labyrinth of paper-covered walls, almost impenetrably dense with scribbled arrows, diagrams, and sentences.

Finally, toward the end of the two weeks (or three, or one), something wonderful and unfathomable would happen. It was rarely written down in the voluminous scholarly literature that NTLers created about T-Groups, but it kept drawing people back, session after session, and it prodded some participants to drop out of their management jobs to become educators and psychologists. After two or three weeks of soul baring in a group of soul barers, each person in the room discovered some core of redemption, some inner worth, deep within. The same feeling surged in those moments that perhaps surged when crowds gathered around Pelagius in Rome and that surge whenever people gather to understand the deepest ties they hold in common.

Some of the NTL participants described the experience as "unconditional love"; others as "pure joy"; others as a kind of mystical breakthrough or what psychologist Abraham Maslow labeled a "peak experience." They returned, at least for a moment, to what Maslow described as the state of mind of a child, free of fear and anxiety, spontaneous and simple, and thus naturally open to personal growth and deeper understanding.[23] (Maslow, who never spent much time at NTL but was closely associated with several prominent people there, was just then developing his famous hierarchy of needs; the highest stage of aspiration, he asserted, was "self-actualization," or the need to achieve one's full potential, and peak experiences were both a sign of getting close and an enabler.) In the final days of a T-Group, people saw firsthand that the unconscious (whether it was their own or that of another person) was not a Freudian cesspool spewing forth bitter legacies of childhood traumas. It was a source of Pelagian grace and hidden value, terrifying in its power and yet delightful in its beauty. It emerged naturally when people learned, in the group's trusting, empathetic environment, how to talk and think openly and freely.[24]

A few NTL participants never felt the Pelagian grace rise within them. They sat in their T-Groups, puzzled and mildly disappointed, while everyone around them was swept up in a contact conversational high.

○

NTL's researchers had inadvertently created an art form. Now they proceeded to dissect it. Like a newborn animal, each young laboratory group developed in distinct but predictable ways, ripe for study and analysis. If you were a young social psychologist, Bethel was the most coveted place in America to spend your summer, and you could get in only through the recommendation of an NTL fellow. "It would be a lot easier to get into the Burning Tree Country Club," one former research associate reminisced years later. And that was only the beginning of years of exciting but grueling apprenticeship. You would run T-Groups in collaboration with some of the best process facilitators in the world, gaining in skill year after year. Eventually you might become a fellow yourself—*if* you were valued enough to be approved by the existing fellows, in a ballot so secret that nominees never knew they were being considered. Once you passed that hurdle, your income was probably assured, for NTL did not take most of the consultation work that came its way. Instead, it referred business to fellows, who also referred business to each other.

NTL trainers and academicians lived for the days between T-Groups, when the "customers" were gone and the really humming, inventive work took place. In the evening, associates and fellows alike would present their theories in the Gould Academy gym, while the whole NTL community sat up on the running track, passing judgment. Kurt Lewin had theorized, back during the Connecticut Workshop, that the observations of an ordinary Mrs. Brown might be as significant as those of a trained social scientist. But Mrs. Brown could never have held her own in *this* crowd. "By God, you had to present good theory," one former associate recalled, "because it was thumbs up or thumbs down. Before my first big presentation one of the fellows took me aside and said, 'You see all of us acting spontaneous and unrehearsed. But we have gone over our presentations again and again before the mirror. So if I were you I'd get busy.'"

During NTL's first decade, T-Group attendees had mainly been teachers, academics, social workers, and church group members. A few executives had trickled in as Episcopal lay priests, but only in the mid-1950s did a corporate audience emerge en masse. The reason was simple: in short supply of funds, NTL went trolling. In 1956, Lee Bradford invited a *Business Week* reporter to visit Bethel—over the objections of some staff members. (Until then, reporters who wanted to peek under the T-Group tent had to be approved by the whole community.) Several large grants, which had sustained the labs for years, had run out. And NTL had bought a thirteen-room Victorian mansion in Bethel, at the extraordinarily low price of fifteen hundred dollars; the former owner, a reclusive young heir named William Bingham, had stipulated in his will that the house be sold to a medical or educational institution. Because of its NEA affiliation, NTL had qualified. Located at the end of a quiet cul-de-sac, surrounded by elegantly arranged trees and plants, the cream-colored house added dramatically to the labs' cachet. But furnishing and maintaining it cost thousands of dollars each year, a significant part of the NTL overhead.

The *Business Week* article fulfilled most of Bradford's hopes: it was cheerful, it treated NTL as a research institution instead of a cult (the word that a journal for educational librarians had applied to NTL), and it mentioned that the labs were looking for industrial grants to conduct research on group dynamics.[25] Grants were not forthcoming, but business attendance began to increase dramatically in 1956, particularly as some of the trainers began tailoring "management work conferences" especially for them, where they would not have to mix with the other types of attendees— and could be charged higher rates. Since businesspeople couldn't generally spare three weeks, Bradford and some of the other senior fellows decided to cut the laboratories from three weeks to two. That decision was a baby step on the road away from innocence. Three weeks had once been called essential so participants could experience all phases of group development. Now, it turned out, two weeks would have been optimal all along.[26]

Businessmen thronged to the two-week workshops—more than twenty thousand, at a fee of eight hundred dollars each, by 1966.[27] They were interested in anything that would give them an edge in communicating and negotiating, and some signed up just because T-Groups were the latest, hottest management fad. (They were, in fact, the first major human relations–oriented management fad since the war and the first to satisfy that invisible, yearning ache for the vernacular.) Rather than drag people up to Bethel, NTL's "industrial" session organizers generally held them at Arden House, an opulent castle in the Hudson Valley town of Harriman, about sixty miles northwest of New York City.

As T-Groups became more popular, the emphasis shifted from research to helping individuals grow—or, as the trainers began to call it, "therapy for normals." This approach naturally lent itself to organizational consulting, and trainers began collaborating on a wide range of exercises, games, and workshop formats.

Ron Lippitt, for instance, developed the idea of a "preferred vision" during his consultations with YMCA teams in Michigan. In a T-Group-like forum, he would ask them to brainstorm a list of the problems they faced. As the list grew longer, the vigor in the room deflated. People blamed each other or grew despondent. So Lippitt started asking teams instead to imagine a picture of the future they preferred: "Let's say it's twenty years from now, and you're flying over this region in a helicopter. What do you see down there?" The more detailed and sincere that people were in envisioning a desired future, the more energized and excited they felt. Suddenly they began coming up with mutual solutions to problems that had seemed insoluble before. A variety of corporate vision and mission-setting exercises would later descend from this practice.

Another exercise, called the Johari window, titled whimsically after the first names of its inventors (Joe Luft and Harry Ingham), is still in frequent use today. Like most other NTL inventions, it came alive in the meeting room but looked drab and prosaic on the printed page: a four-box matrix. First, participants took a quiz, working their way through a list of fifty-five human qualities ("able, mature, reflective, adaptable") and attributing them to themselves and others in the room. Then the group sorted out the attributes to match those that people had assigned to themselves against those assigned to others. Quadrant 1 (the arena) represented all freely available information that everybody in the T-Group knew ("Everyone, including Joe, says that he's open"). Quadrant 2 (the blind spots) represented the facts about people known to everyone else but them ("Everyone describes Harry as logical, but he thinks he's spontaneous"). Quadrant 3 (the facade) contained information individuals keep secret about themselves ("I am powerfully attracted to Joe, and I don't want anyone to notice"), and quadrant 4 contained the attributes that no one had applied to that individual, including that person ("I guess no one thinks you're energetic, Harry—not even yourself"). Of course, as soon as that conversation unfolded, people might recognize that Harry *was* energetic after all, but no one had realized it before. The more of that hidden material that came to the light, the more people dug out the feelings held deep within themselves and talked about them, the more powerful the T-Group seemed to get.[28]

The Johari window was unusual in one respect: its inventors were credited. There were dozens of other exercises without credit to those who developed them. People used them routinely, adapted and changed them freely, reported back on the results, and watched the cycle of innovation spiral from one trainer to another. In such a spirit of mutual invention, nobody could ever quite remember who had created what. Nothing was copyrighted, and no one was charged fees. Ideas were written up as informal, mimeographed notes and trainers' guides that were likely to change and improve from one week to the next. In 1957, one of the most popular trainers at NTL, Edie Seashore, took the Graduate Record Exam in Psychology. When her test scores bombed, the New York University professor who had encouraged her to get a doctorate asked her why it was so difficult. After all, she was acquainted personally with many of the researchers named in the questions. But giving people credit for specific work, she told him, was not easy. "If you knew these people as well as I do," she said, "you couldn't pass the test either."

Incoming attendees at a T-Group session for businesspeople often regarded it at first as an amusing, impractical diversion—a sort of summer camp with communication skills, paid for at company expense. But as the two weeks unfolded, they were often swept away, in part by the sheer freedom of speaking plainly and directly. Most of them worked normally in an atmosphere of power politics that determined their every move, which they could not discuss openly. Some managers talked freely at T-Groups for the first time since childhood, and that feeling alone—a feeling that humanities-oriented people usually took for granted—was a revelation to them. Just as business finance translated karma and hubris into numbers, the T-Group translated the "just-business, nothing-personal" imperatives of the numbers back into the personal sphere. Moreover, to some of the business attendees, the practices of NTL revealed an entirely new way to think about the task of managing people.

The man who gave voice to that shift in attitude was Douglas McGregor, who was the head of the organizational studies department at MIT's Sloan School. McGregor was a playful and charismatic man who had been at MIT twice in his career. In the late 1940s, as the founder of the industrial relations program at the School of Economics and Social Science, he had brought Kurt Lewin to MIT's faculty. Then he had left Cambridge in the early 1950s to become president of Antioch College, a well-known liberal arts college in western Ohio. And then he had returned to MIT's still relatively new Sloan Business School. Like many other MIT business professors, McGregor moonlighted as an industrial consultant—in his case, often with oil companies. At his suggestion in the early 1950s, some executives wandered into T-Groups from Standard Oil of New Jersey, where McGregor held a position on the board for a while and where a subculture of second-layer managers had rebelled during the 1930s against the legacy of unscrupulous harshness left by the company's founder, John D. Rockefeller. McGregor was enthusiastic about T-Groups, but he didn't lead them frequently; he was known at Bethel for pulling anyone he could find, eminences and newcomers alike, over to the piano to sing gospel songs. And then in the late 1950s he began to be known for his theories of human behavior. In part through his experiences at NTL, he had discovered a relationship between the structure of organizations and their managers' deepest attitudes.

Essentially, McGregor said (first in speeches during the late 1950s and then in his 1960 book, *The Human Side of Enterprise*) there were two possible attitudes that a manager could hold about people. Whether or not they admitted or realized it, these attitudes affected managers' decisions in a thousand unseen ways and colored the atmosphere of every conventional corporation. The first, and by far the more prevalent, was theory X. It was an Augustinian theory, professing that human nature is fundamentally corrupt—or that people are "gullible, not very bright, the dupe of the charlatan and the demagogue." Theory X said that people basically hate to work. They are motivated primarily by fear and desire, they will get away with shoddy work or laziness whenever possible, and a manager's task is to force them to perform, as if they were recalcitrant machines.

Unfortunately, McGregor said, theory X was false: "The findings which are beginning to emerge from the social sciences challenge this whole set of beliefs about man and human nature." Yes, people might behave passively and selfishly on the job, but not because of their inner nature. Lack of productivity was an effect, not a cause, of the way that conventional management treated people.

So McGregor would ask his audience to consider theory Y—another way of looking at people, closer to the truth (as he saw it), but harder for most people to accept. Work, in its noblest sense, is built into human nature. People can't be goaded, cajoled, threatened, or even bribed with money into giving their hearts and souls to an enterprise. But if they are placed in a situation that honestly calls for a commitment, they will rise to the occasion. Or, as McGregor put it, "The motivation, the potential for development, the capacity for assuming responsibility . . . are all present in people. Management does not put them there."[29] Pelagius couldn't have said it any more strongly.

It was quite an article of faith, this theory Y. It contradicted the prevailing structure and culture of most corporations: the hierarchy, the labor relations tradition, the curricula at most business schools (including MIT), and all those devices like performance appraisals that measured one person against another. Adopting theory Y would mean giving up both the stick (threatening to fire people) and the carrot (bribing them or being paternalistic). Without those two weapons, what leverage did a manager have? Only the ability to spark other people's involvement and commitment by giving them opportunities to do good work—hardly a strong incentive by conventional standards.

Yet McGregor had noticed, in a decade of corporate consultation, that the most effective managers always seemed to hold theory Y in their hearts. Many of them had seen firsthand—and this was the factor that made some managers in the audience take McGregor seriously—the obvious bankruptcy of both the carrot and stick. They could discipline workers and make them show up, but the old methods never managed to get people to act with care and commitment.

Unfortunately if only one manager in a company believed in theory Y, that manager would be impotent. No change could be put into practice until the whole company—indeed, most of industrial society—became more congenial to it. Thus, McGregor devoted more and more of his time to teaching a wide range of people about his concepts. He chose the names theory X and theory Y to avoid obvious bias, so managers could talk about their past attitudes without hearing them labeled as, say, "Theory Troglodyte." And he became more and more enthusiastic about T-Groups. Skeptical managers could simply be sent to a T-Group, where they'd feel their own intrinsic potential welling up inside them—and they could see firsthand how other people acted more powerful, free, and involved. They'd begin to think about harnessing a similar level of enthusiasm on the job, and suddenly theory Y would feel right to them.

———— o ————

McGregor's father had been a midwestern clergyman; he came out of the great American Protestant liberal tradition, the tradition of Quaker meetings, community barn raisings, and Ralph Waldo Emerson. It was no coincidence, perhaps, that so many other NTLers—including Lee Bradford, Ken Benne, Ron Lippitt, and the eminent T-Group advocate Carl Rogers—had similar backgrounds.[30] Somehow these ecumenical WASPs knew how to bring forth mutual understanding—which explained, perhaps, why the black and Jewish community leaders of the original Connecticut Workshop had called in three of these white-bread characters. It also may have explained why NTLers seemed to feel responsible for developing a better world—perhaps from noblesse oblige, perhaps from a deeply inbred sense of populist egalitarianism, or perhaps simply because they didn't feel alive unless they were improving the world.

Whatever the source of that feeling, its force gave the NTLers a sense of confidence that bordered on hubris at times; they knew they had a set of answers to the paralysis that people felt when tough questions like racism came up. But they didn't know why their technique was effective. Did it speak to a general condition within the human heart? Was it simply well suited to tweak the spirit of a mid-twentieth-century American? Or was it, as critics began to charge in the mid-1950s, a pernicious form of social control and brainwashing? That suspicion had been voiced every

now and then by anticommunists in the McCarthy era. T-Groups, like
communist cells, were small groups of people; they seemed deliberately
designed to "unfreeze"—to break down the individual's will and
resistance.[31]

Inside NTL, these accusations were taken seriously—but not in the
way they were intended. NTLers believed that *all* controlled environments (including families, churches, and corporations) created the conditions for brainwashing.[32] People were always being manipulated; whether
anyone felt manipulated depended on how angry they were about the
content of the message. T-Groups provided an antidote by giving people
a safe way to inquire: Did others feel the same pressures that they did?
What did those pressures mean?

As it happened, there was an expert on brainwashing within the NTL
community. A young psychologist named Edgar Schein, who came to
McGregor's department at MIT in the late 1950s, had gone to Inchon at
the end of the Korean War to help repatriate American prisoners of war.
Many of these POWs had been in captivity for more than a year, and the
U.S. Army leaders believed that the Chinese Communists in North Korea
had brainwashed them. (The word *brainwashing*, in fact, emerged from
this episode, as a translation of a Chinese phrase meaning "to cleanse the
mind"—in this case, of bourgeois concepts.) To an American audience in
the McCarthy era, there had to be some awfully powerful indoctrination
at work to induce well-trained American soldiers to renounce their patri-
otism, inform on other soldiers, march in Communist parades, and make
false confessions of germ warfare.

Stranded in Inchon for several weeks, Schein had interviewed some of
the returning soldiers, who were relieved to talk about their time in captivity. The Chinese social control had taken place without drugs, hypnosis,
Pavlovian conditioning, or even torture; all they had used was peer pressure. Just as in a T-Group, the Communists had put the POWs in a cultural island, cut off from all contact with outsiders, and surrounded them
with friendly Chinese "big brothers" (who had been promised a reward
for reforming their Western cellmates). There was always the threat of
brutality and even death; the prisoners were continually reminded that
collaborating with each other was the only way to survive. The "big
brothers" harangued, insulted, reviled, humiliated, and pleaded the case
of Communist values for days or months on end—an incredibly powerful
"unfreezing" effort. Less than 10 percent of the soldiers held out, resisting
to the end. Another 10 percent embraced the Communist line so fervently
that it stuck with them. The vast majority fell in the middle. Their
attitudes changed in Korea, but they changed back again without much

stress once they returned to America. It's not hard to persuade someone, Schein ultimately concluded, "if you can physically constrain them to remain in a setting over which you have milieu control."[33]

That was the difference from the NTL experience; people came to Bethel freely and left of their own volition. But Schein *did* see an analogue to the Korean POW camps in America. He had visited some of the most influential management training programs at GE's Crotonville and IBM's Sand Point. Isolated students in small groups analyzed "case studies," gave their guess about the correct answer, and were graded on how closely their answer matched the instructor's party line, with their grades sent back to their bosses.[34] Most important, they couldn't leave without risking their jobs.

If the corporate world represented a kind of brainwashing, then T-Group leaders had not just an invitation, but a responsibility, to enter the business world. Or so they thought. Then, in 1958, the techniques of NTL received their first full-scale test in a mainstream corporation.

o

New Jersey's factories and refineries stand far from the roadways and truck routes, visible only distantly, like metallic castles half cloaked in the thick marshland mists. Perhaps the largest of these sites is the Bayway refinery. Currently owned by ConocoPhilips, it had been an Exxon site until 2001. Its seven hundred labyrinthine acres of furnaces, tanker docks, and chemical processing plants, located on a small peninsula jutting out into the harbor from Elizabeth, comprise the largest provider of petroleum, natural gas, and related chemicals to the U.S. East Coast and the largest refinery of its kind (employing a technology called catalytic cracking) in the world.[35] In 1958, when Exxon's East Coast operations were still called Esso, a major labor contract was up for negotiation at Bayway.[36] The independent union of refinery workers had demanded concessions worth $3 million per year—enough, the managers felt, to put the refinery permanently in the red. Worse still, the union was flirting with joining a national affiliate—and not just any affiliate, but the national Teamsters union, whose president was Jimmy Hoffa. To Esso's managers—and the executives of their parent company, Standard Oil of New Jersey—this would put a critical production facility, one that controlled much of the energy supply of the East Coast, under the control of organized crime. The memory of Bayway's unruly, militant strikes from the 1930s still lingered in the viscera of both the managers and the union men.[37] Each side routinely referred to the other's leader as "that son of a bitch." Anywhere the managers looked, they saw an unbridgeable impasse.

Except when they looked at NTL. As it happened, a few Bayway managers had been to T-Groups, thanks to Esso's long-standing involvement
with Douglas McGregor. And in 1958, the Bayway general manager
urged two NTLers to join him at Bayway. They agreed, on the condition
that they could keep all their conversations discreet; they didn't want
anyone to open up to them and find themselves disciplined or fired as a
result. The first consultant was Herb Shepard, an MIT professor of industrial economics, a McGregor protégé, and an elegant, theatrical man who
loved to quote poetry. Shepard had an insouciant grace that reminded
people of Fred Astaire and such an innate flair for T-Group dynamics that
he could make them perform tricks. On the third day of a Shepard-led
T-Group, you could count on the members spontaneously throwing the
leaders out so they could organize themselves, unaware that the previous
half-dozen Shepard-led groups had done the same thing.

The other NTLer who came to Bayway, Robert Blake, was a professor
of social psychology at the University of Texas at Austin. He and Shepard
were good friends, but they couldn't have been more different in temperament. Blake was dour, moody, cheerfully acerbic, and seemingly indiffer-
ent to people's opinions of him. The inner circle at Bethel considered him
competent but uninspired, pedantic, and guilty of the worst possible sin:
he didn't know how to listen well. In the NTL pantheon, he seemed cast
as a sort of peevish, saturnine figure, a Caliban to Shepard's Ariel. "I'll
hit 'em high," Shepard once said to him. "You hit 'em low." Yet Blake's
blunt manner belied a far-reaching intellectual background; he had studied or worked with some of the most eminent luminaries in social psychology and semantics research. He had spent a year and a half in
London at the Tavistock Institute of Human Relations, a British counterpart to NTL that was seen as more rigorous, more strictly organized, and
more closely connected to the psychoanalytical tradition; it had been
founded by the noted group psychoanalyst Wilfred Bion, who had studied with Freud's associate Melanie Klein. It was also the home of a group
of work redesign researchers like Elliot Jaques and Eric Trist, who would
ultimately become well known for theories of hierarchy and team-based
management, respectively. At Tavistock, a group might last not three
weeks but a year and a half. The group's research would be rigorously
channeled toward in-depth studies of its own power and authority patterns. Tavistock leaders didn't care, as NTL leaders did, about building
"peak experiences" and helping people express themselves—or, as Blake
put it scornfully, assuaging their feelings of "morale and cohesion."

NTL seemed to bring out Blake's bitter side. But at the Bayway refinery, he was a thoughtful adviser who could listen just fine and who

managed to build confidence on both the labor and management sides. He ended up devoting two years of his life to the project, taking an unpaid leave of absence from his faculty position to do so. Shepard came in as a consultant, and Blake also brought in a third person: his chief collaborator, Jane Srygley Mouton.

Mouton had been a mathematician, and then one of Blake's graduate students at the University of Texas. Now she was a professor there and one of a handful of women in the 1950s to lead T-Groups. A fiercely intellectual woman, known for her composure, her devotion to work, and her outdoorsiness, she had married an investor named Jack Mouton. She and her husband lived on a ranch they owned outside Austin, where Mouton was an avid horsewoman. When she was working, she spent much of her time inventing and researching with Blake.[38] In their outpost far from the Bethel/Cambridge/Ann Arbor NTL axis, they had developed their own variation on the T-Group, a form that ultimately would become the template for a new type of organizational development practice.

In ordinary T-Groups, Blake and Mouton realized, no matter how nondirective the facilitator tried to be, he or she was still subtly dictatorial, even more dictatorial (because of its subtlety) than the harshest CEO, because all of that control was hidden—as in Shepard's manipulation of his T-Group's third day. But what if the T-Group was autonomous, without an assigned expert trainer? What if there were no change agents but only participants ready to change themselves?

Blake and Mouton were well steeped in the techniques of devising "instruments" (as social scientists called them)—questionnaires that people could grade for themselves, which sparked conversation that led them to learn. (To get the flavor of these questionnaires if you've never seen one, imagine the sorts of "self-assessment" tests that appear in magazines like *Cosmopolitan*. Now imagine one that was truly challenging, and that measured your competence in a range of tough areas like business knowledge and ability to manage people. Imagine that you never had to show anyone else the results but were told to use the group to talk through any of the issues that the questionnaire raised.)

One year in the mid-1950s, when two hundred University of Texas undergraduates wanted to enroll in a course on T-Groups, Blake and Mouton tried breaking the course into sections and having each section more or less run itself. Remarkably enough, it worked. Students gleaned the same understandings of group power and authority, and even the same peak experiences, as if Blake and Mouton had led the groups themselves. So they tried it next with a group of Esso managers (on an off-site location in a Baptist church in Bella Vista, Arkansas). Instead of a leader, participants who walked into the room found a set of questions, beginning with: "What is the ideal working relationship?" It turned out they all, unbeknown to each other, had a similar ideal. "Why then," asked the next questions, "is it so hard to reach that ideal?"

While the managers deliberated, Bob and Jane sat in the next room, worrying. What if the group exploded into a fight? Or, worse, what if they drifted into boredom? Every now and then, they sent in an undergraduate on a pretext such as looking for a piece of paper. Then they grilled the student relentlessly: Was everything really okay in there? "No problem," the student would say. "They're doing great." In truth, hard as it was for an expert consultant to accept, the groups seemed more charged up, and yet more benign, when people could lead themselves.

When Blake, Mouton, and Shepard began to work at the Bayway refinery in 1958, they planned on using similar instrumented groups. But the Esso leaders wanted in-depth counseling, most of which fell to Blake because he had moved to New Jersey to work at Bayway full time. Every night he recorded his observations and field notes onto a tape, which he sent to Jane Mouton, who was pregnant that year, back in Austin. She would listen to the tapes, and the two of them would talk at length once a week about exactly what was going on at Bayway. Today this would all seem commonplace, but in 1958 no corporation had ever invited a group dynamics expert so completely into its offices. The three NTLers recognized, almost from the beginning, that they were inventing a kind of therapeutic counseling that would not be aimed at helping individuals improve (or, if they did improve, it would only be a by-product). They were there to further the organization's development as a whole. Almost from the beginning, they referred to their work with a term that would soon become jargon: *organization development.*

Blake had to be flown in by helicopter for some of his early meetings; the plant was on strike, and since he would have to talk in depth with the union, the managers didn't want him to be seen crossing the picket line. In his journal entries (which were published in the mid-1970s), the impression comes through again and again of how squeezed everyone felt on both the union and management sides.[39] More than once a manager made a promise to the unions in a meeting—for instance, a promise to name Bayway as a union shop so that workers would be required to join the union—only to have it undone, or denied, in the most humiliating way possible, through a pronouncement from Houston.[40]

In his earliest sessions with managers, held off-site in hotels, Blake often posed the question, "How can the union become an effective unit of the company?" "They can't," was the first answer. The union leadership was composed of thugs, thieves, and crooks. "How could you cooperate with such a rat pack?" The only solution (other than "killing off the leaders," which some of the managers joked they wanted to do) was to secretly (and illegally) try to influence union politics to reveal the current elected officials "in the true phosphorescent light of their putridity, so that when the wage people come to ballot again, they'll do a better job."[41]

Gradually, as often happens in group dynamics, the managers' own attitudes came to the light. They said they were open and fair, but they bullied and humiliated the union people constantly. They called meetings in midday so "these bums will have to change in and out of their work clothes." They held last-minute meetings late, so the union reps would miss their carpools. They insisted on meeting in the administration building, where the union people felt uncomfortable. And they never said in advance what they wanted a meeting to achieve; instead, they sat as stony-faced as poker players, giving in on each concession only at the last possible minute. Finally, after getting the venom out of their system, the managers realized, "We can only move forward by learning how to stop saying 'no.' That doesn't mean we say, 'yes.' But when the union raises a point, we need to learn how to talk about it."

Meeting more informally with the union leaders, Blake asked about one of their biggest gripes: accidents and safety hazards. Here too there was a knee-jerk answer: it's management's fault: "Those penny-pinching bastards take away the safety inspectors, cut corners, and make us work faster. Pretty soon, they get accidents." Blake patiently heard them out— arguably the first time anyone from the management side had done so—and let them reach their own conclusions about what to do next. "I see somebody out on the platform," a union leader might say, "and he's walking through grease. I say to myself, 'He's gonna fall and bust a hip.' Sure enough, he falls, and I say to myself, 'I knew that would happen.'" In other words, they could get the accidents under control only if the hourly workers started speaking up ahead of time instead of waiting for managers to handle it.

Over the next few months, the safety problems were cleaned up. The labor problems, albeit in fits and starts, began to diminish. The managers treated the union with respect; the union remained independent from the Teamsters and organized crime. The next year, Bayway managers had to close down part of the refinery. Instead of clamming up and insisting on layoffs, they walked the union leaders through the rationale for the shutdown. "Now that you know why we're doing this," they asked, "what do you think of it?"

Flush with success, the Bayway executives sent two thousand of their managers, from refinery foremen to market researchers, through instrumented groups—five teams of ten people each per session. During the summer of 1959, Esso took over part of the Thayer Hotel at West Point to handle the crowds. And to focus their attention, Blake and Mouton devised a framework that they called the management grid (Figure 2.1).[42]

It looked like a nine-square-by-nine-square checkerboard, but actually it was a map of management attitudes with which people could identify their own behavior or attitudes around them. Those who cared about production and efficiency fell further to the right (toward number 9). Those who cared greatly for people moved closer to the top (again, toward number 9). You could fit any managerial style onto this chart by

Figure 2.1. The Management Grid

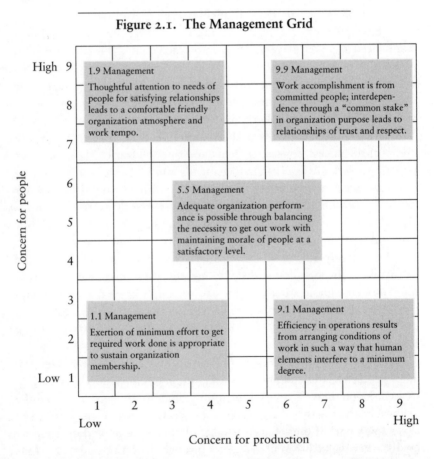

High 9

1.9 Management
Thoughtful attention to needs of people for satisfying relationships leads to a comfortable friendly organization atmosphere and work tempo.

9.9 Management
Work accomplishment is from committed people; interdependence through a "common stake" in organization purpose leads to relationships of trust and respect.

5.5 Management
Adequate organization performance is possible through balancing the necessity to get out work with maintaining morale of people at a satisfactory level.

1.1 Management
Exertion of minimum effort to get required work done is appropriate to sustain organization membership.

9.1 Management
Efficiency in operations results from arranging conditions of work in such a way that human elements interfere to a minimum degree.

Concern for people

Low 1

1   2   3   4   5   6   7   8   9
Low   High

Concern for production

Source: *The Management Grid is reprinted with permission; copyright ©1964, 1995, Robert Blake and Scientific Methods, Inc.*

putting the two numbers together. The "theory X" that McGregor had identified seemed to fit best around 9,1: lots of attention to performance and production but little attention to human relationships or needs. Paternalistic "people pleasers," who in Blake's view were just as destructive, hovered around 1,9. Most damaging of all (Blake and Mouton argued) were the people who spread themselves out around the chart, bouncing inconsistently between paternalistic benevolence and threatening autocracy. It was remarkable how many backstabbing, paternalistic, duplicitous types of behavior there were in organizations, behaviors that could be named now, all with the relatively noncommittal language that Blake and Mouton had written into the chart. "Martin's being awfully 5,5," you could say; or you could say, "He's balancing performance and morale concerns in equilibrium," instead of saying, "Martin cares only about covering his ass."

The grid concept was very successful: managers loved it, and performance in the refinery noticeably improved. Yet the Bayway experiment ultimately ended ignominiously. The plant manager who had approved all the "organization development" training was recognized by being placed in charge of the Eastern Hemisphere at Esso operations. His successor was a more hard-edged rationalist manager who tried immediately to show how he could squeeze the union. Within twelve weeks, as one NTL observer, Dick Beckhard, later remembered it, the plant's union had signed on with the Teamsters. The NTL people would see this sort of thing happen again and again through the 1960s; it took months and years to develop positive change and only a few weeks to kill it.

———————— o ————————

After Bayway, Bob Blake and Jane Mouton continued to develop the grid system. They redesigned it into a year-long management development course, covering all the NTL group process skills—giving productive feedback, sharing a vision for the future, bringing hidden assumptions to the surface, plus fine-grained business skills.[43] Over the course of the six modules, managers would meet at length with their own direct coworkers to plan workplace changes, take part in companywide in-depth visioning sessions, and ultimately adopt a set of rigorous practices based on the business practices of General Motors's Alfred Sloan. The course used Alfred Sloan's just-then-published memoir, *My Years with General Motors,* as a mirror. Managers would compare their solutions to Sloan's and discuss the differences in groups. The purpose was to create a company full of managers with Sloan's dual commitments to people and business results simultaneously. And they would have succeeded, except that in many organizations, the enthusiasm for the grid dropped off somehow. Rare was the company that made it all the way to the Alfred Sloan material, partly because Blake and Mouton could never find enough session trainers who knew both business strategy and group dynamics.

The more interested they became in implementing change throughout large companies, the more compelled they felt to leave the university. To academics, implementing change precluded "real" research. Blake and Mouton were too busy, enmeshed in the messy day-to-day lives of thousands of corporate patrons. This left them no time or attention for conducting the sorts of narrow, well-defined, self-contained management studies—measurement of a cognitive shift in how people perceive systems in a training process—that would lead to a respectable journal article. The academics were great at diagnosis but lousy at treatment. Blake and Mouton wanted to treat.

Before long, Blake and Mouton split with NTL as well—or, rather, NTL split with them. The NTLers could never reconcile themselves to Blake and Mouton's "T-Group in a box." To them, the grid system was merely Bob Blake's way of cashing in on the techniques he had learned at Bethel. The grid gave a false impression, they said, that anyone could lead a T-Group by following a few simple recipe steps. Worse still, Blake and Mouton had broken the unwritten sharing code. Unlike Ron Lippitt, who also created instruments on paper, they had copyrighted their materials. When managers in companies around the country called NTL to ask for the grid system, the staff in Washington had to sorrowfully say no. No NTL trainer, and none of the new "OD" consultants, could use the grid except by becoming a Blake franchiser. Blake had violated no overt NTL rule, but the trainers and faculty members were furious. They complained about the danger of letting managers lead their own T-Groups. "This will be the end of Bethel," Lee Bradford told Blake. "Why would people come here if they can transfer training into the organization?" Blake excused himself early in the summer of 1960 and never returned.[44]

Blake, of course, had his own view. He had copyrighted the material only to keep it from being degraded by trainers who wanted to "borrow" an exercise or two, with no regard for its careful whole-system design. Moreover, he now believed, NTLers wanted managers to remain dependent on them. Maybe they even wanted organizations to remain sick, for that way they could keep their roles as vitally necessary therapists, with entire groups of people who needed their talents to remain healthy.

Maybe that was true, but Robert Blake's system dealt a blow to NTL's spirit of freewheeling experimentation, from which it never recovered. Once he had shown that it was feasible, and far more lucrative, to offer programs on your own—and arguably better for clients—everyone else realized, sooner or later, that they were foolish unless they followed his example. Bit by bit, the vitality drained out of the labs as trainers took their innovations into other venues.

In 1968, NTL's community spirit was tested still further when two trainers named Bill Pfeiffer and John Jones published a workbook of exercises that had been introduced at the labs.[45] If Blake was a black sheep, then Pfeiffer and Jones were out-and-out traitors, but other NTL faculty members reasoned, logically enough, that if they couldn't beat the copyrighters, they might as well join them. Instead of being researchers engaged in mutual inquiry, they were now primarily paid consultants, looking for an edge over each other. Suddenly no one wanted to show their best techniques up in Bethel, any more than a comedian will use the very best jokes when other comedians are in the room, pencils poised to write them down.

More and more, NTL-based trainers eschewed the long trek to Bethel altogether. They returned only occasionally, ostensibly to recharge their facilitation skills or rekindle conversations with old colleagues. Mainly, they came to feel, even for a few hours, some of the old T-Group spirit. No one who had been exposed to that spirit could forget it.

Nevertheless, Robert Blake was correct: the Pelagian spirit is not enough in itself to recreate an organization. Some structure or plan had to be designed that would not just carry that spirit into the fabric of the enterprise, but reshape the habits of the people who worked there. It isn't enough to give people more control; they must be systematically trained to act with humility and grace, time after time, to look after themselves and each other, continually alert for their own imperfections, hating the errors while loving those who commit them, and thus becoming better and better each day, without falling prey to the kind of debilitating pride that leads people to overshoot and fail. The grid system had tried to instill that awareness at a massive scale, and in the end, it too failed. It is still in use today, but its popularity and influence have diminished since Mouton and Blake passed away (in 1987 and 2004, respectively).

Somehow the very process of capturing, distilling, and disseminating Pelagianism seemed to diminish any group that tried. But how then, could an organization be developed into a more capable enterprise? How could anyone make Pelagianism prosper in an Augustinian society?

3

REFORMISTS

WORKPLACE REDESIGN AT PROCTER & GAMBLE AND
THE GAINES DOG FOOD PLANT IN TOPEKA,
1961–1973

---

*Heresy: Self-managing teams, in a well-designed operation,
with oversight and awareness from the bottom up, are far more
productive than any other known form of management.
And they exalt the human spirit.*

Why does Galileo Galilei have the reputation of a heretic, while his seventeenth-century fellow scientist Johannes Kepler does not? Because Kepler evaded the Church. Galileo sought to change it. The professor from Pisa spent the last third of his life arguing, with increasing fervor, that the Christian doctrines and even Bibles should be rewritten to conform to the realities he had seen through his telescope. Many of the cardinals and Church officials who censured and imprisoned him recognized the validity of the new cosmology and physics that Galileo championed, but they didn't want to shake up their system too quickly. Too many monks and village priests clung to Ptolemy and Aristotle. The "people" would rebel at any sudden revision of the "truth."

Galileo didn't care. Like many other heretics, past and present, he thought at first that the truth would set the institution free. He only had to show people what he had seen, and they would naturally adapt. When people doubted observations that to him were obvious, he lost his tact. He made enemies (some said needlessly) of the Jesuits, who fought bitterly to see him condemned, and he closed one of his notorious tracts, the *Dialogue on the Great World Systems,* with a snide lampoon of the views of Pope Urban VIII. Until then Urban had been his patron and champion. Ten months after publication in 1633, Galileo was on trial in Rome.

Even under house imprisonment, Galileo continued researching and writing, developing and articulating his theories of physics and the heavens. Perhaps he was comforted by the knowledge that people outside the Church hierarchy had carried forth his research and were building on his theories. Or perhaps he spent much of his time in his cell in mourning for the institution of the Church and the beacon that it might have been—if only he could have found a way to get the point across.

○

THAT WAS AKIN, IN A WAY, TO ERIC TRIST'S lifelong heartbreak. In the mid-1940s, he began to articulate a better way of managing the workplace, a democratic approach that would clearly lead to unparalleled performance. He spent his life testing and preaching his vision, building a worldwide network of devoted colleagues and correspondents (including Kurt Lewin, whom he first met in 1933, and Douglas McGregor) whose work laid the groundwork for the management innovations of the 1980s. The movement inspired many successes, including a series of secret but dramatic workplace design reforms at Procter & Gamble, a passionate experiment at a dog food plant in Topeka, Kansas, and significant change at such companies as DuPont, Volvo, and Crown Zellerbach. But it never got the mainstream public acceptance that its performance record probably deserved; it never became the corporate norm. Like Galileo and many other reformists throughout history, Trist was mournfully aware that the prevailing institutions of his world did not live up to the great destiny he saw for them.

Trist was a small, almost frail man, with a shy smile, prone to bouts of depression and long periods of melancholy, and yet thoroughly gregarious.

Although he made his living as an academic and wrote in impenetrable academese, he talked like a British laborer—with working-class outrage, sly irony, and quiet profanity. His morose spirit, like that of Robert Blake, may have stemmed in part from his background at the Tavistock Institute of Human Relations. While National Training Labs took its cue from sunny Pelagianism, Tavistock was guided by the brooding Augustinian spirit of psychoanalysis.[1] Tavistock's practitioners were well aware of the dark side of human nature—the visceral "death instinct" of primordial envy and hatred that could crop up in even the most idealistic personality. They believed that group dynamics in itself could not deal effectively with the hidden rage, frustration, and viciousness that inevitably emerged when people began to work together. It would take a redesign of the channels of power within the workplace. In the numbers-ridden industrial age, there was no persuasive model for how that redesign might look.

And then Eric Trist stumbled into one. In 1947, a postdoctoral student at Tavistock casually invited him to visit a British coal mine at Haighmoor. Nearly all British coal mines had been industrialized into an assembly-line approach since the nineteenth century, but Haighmoor was an exception; it was based in a rich seam that assembly-line-style equipment couldn't reach. Therefore, the miners had developed their own system. It was part vernacular, part industrial—a hybrid of mining traditions from generations past and new postwar technologies. Instead of being set up as interchangeable parts, cogs on the assembly line of the mine, these miners worked in teams they organized themselves. Each man might handle a half-dozen jobs. The teams ran the job and sold the coal—even taking care of their members' families if someone was hurt or killed.[2] They also competed vigorously against each other—to the point where fights sometimes broke out between members of rival teams.

The results, as Trist discovered, were remarkable. Haighmoor was far safer and far more productive than any other mine. In fact, since the rewards were based on tonnage per cycle and the miners felt some influence over their work, they all continuously added innovations to the work. They had no incentive, as long-wall miners did, to "screw the next shift" by cutting corners on maintenance or safety. To Trist, Haighmoor provided a glimpse of how the best of vernacular and business culture could be designed to fit together—anywhere.[3]

The British government agency that managed the mine let Trist study it at first—until Trist, following Lewin's tradition of learning through experimentation, wanted to see if some of the same techniques might help the beleaguered workers at other mines. Then the managers balked. Why try to instill freedom when mines were becoming even more controlled and mechanized? Why set up false expectations? They even forbade Trist to include the name "Haighmoor" in his reports.

So Trist devoted himself to conducting workplace experiments and seeking ways to broaden the intellectual base of his insights. From the 1960s through most of the 1990s, Trist and his wife, Beulah, were the unofficial center of an international community of experimenters and theorists. A key group of his colleagues were Norwegian, with roots in the resistance movement of World War II. Norway had beaten back the Nazis through small groups of eight to ten people, somewhat like the teams of Haighmoor. There was no central command. Each group chose its own immediate objectives and tactics, acting with greater persistence, commitment, and skill than they would ever have gained by taking orders. When the Nazis captured a team, the members could reveal no one's plans but their own. During the 1950s and 1960s, the resistance veterans spread through Norway, gradually becoming directors of its state-owned industries and government agencies, helping each other set up self-managing teams in wire companies, lumber mills, the electric utility Nørsk Hydro, and elsewhere.[4]

Trist and his closest colleagues, particularly the Australian researcher Fred Emery, adopted several terms for their work: "industrial democracy," "open systems," and "sociotechnical systems." They believed that corporations were analogous to ecosystems, subject to the same sorts of interrelationships that governed prosperity and survival in the wild. As business environments became more turbulent, top-down hierarchies would cease to be effective, just as they were ineffective amid the disorder of nature. (Emery and Trist had hit on this theory during a turbulent plane trip to Norway, when Trist was forced repeatedly to use the airsickness bag and realized that his feeling was an analogue for the way managers often felt.[5]) Living systems coped with this turbulence by generating their own order from the bottom up. A living creature can take its shape even from a damaged fetus or ovum (this had been proved with sea urchins), without any external control. In fact, attempts to control a living creature's growth too harshly would make it wither and die. Why couldn't the same be true for organizations?[6]

———— o ————

Nearly all factories of that time were, like the British coal mines, set up as elaborate machines. Work was broken up into disparate, specified tasks. Workers were programmed, through stringent rules and elaborate pay scales, to specialize in those tasks. Expert engineers designed the jobs, set the pace, and inspected the products. Workers who followed the rules got pensions. Workers who slackened or faltered got disciplined or fired, unless their unions, explicitly or implicitly, arranged to protect them.[7]

The overall approach, often dubbed "scientific management," owed its compelling power to the systematic practices devised by Frederick Taylor, the first industrial-era management consultant. In the early 1880s, Taylor began clocking the movements of workers—from burly immigrant steelworkers to young girls inspecting ball bearings—hoping to establish, once and for all, the most efficient methods of working. The productivity gains in the short run were enormous. One ball bearing factory, following Taylor's advice, cut the number of inspectors from 120 to 35, nearly doubled wages, dropped two hours from the workday, tripled production, and improved accuracy by two-thirds.[8] But Taylor's methods also ossified industrial work in the long run. Living inside a machine ultimately leads to deep, inbred malaise and resentment, the atrophy of creativity and productivity, and the propensity to sabotage.

What if, as Eric Trist and his colleagues did, you saw the dangers of the machine approach and wanted to try an alternative? Then you would have to establish your factory as a community. Every part of the assembly line would be managed by self-governing teams of, say, ten to twelve people. The teams would have a task at hand—a product to get out—and they would care about the results of their labors. If they found a way to improve the work, they would have the power and the interest to bring that improvement to life, without going through a lot of bureaucratic approval, and they would be rewarded in ways that touched their wallets and their pride. Despite the seeming lack of control, the community as a whole would run itself much more smoothly than any machine—through the interplay of dozens of teams of people, all acting in sync, with everything from the machine setup to the maintenance schedule designed to reinforce their collegiality.

In an open system or industrial democracy, control would rest with the people on the bottom—teams of people who handled the frontline work of making a product or providing a service. Their "bosses" would then actually be "servants," making sure the work teams had whatever they needed and coordinating information so everyone had a view of the organization as a whole. The results, as with the Haighmoor mines, would be unprecedented performance gains, and Trist managed to interest a few corporations, including Royal Dutch/Shell, in his ideas. But sooner or later, most managers retreated queasily, as if they had just discovered that Trist was trying to kill them off. And in a sense, he was. "Their opinion had a modicum of correctness in it," he said, years later.

"They'd had all the power and did what they liked, and they didn't want
to share power."

o

The most prominent mainstream corporation that practiced open systems
during the early 1960s was so secretive that even Eric Trist couldn't learn
much about what it was doing. That company was Procter & Gamble,
the Cincinnati-based manufacturers of soap, detergent, toilet paper, and
other household products. For P&G, open systems was a kind of magic
formula, as precious as a patented cleaning formula, and it wanted to get
the most it could from it.[9]

In 1962, Procter & Gamble had just celebrated its 125th birthday.
There was much to celebrate. It was the predominant company in American
marketing; P&G managers had originated not just packaged soap and
laundry detergent, but the structure of the advertising business (including
its mainstay, brand management), the soap opera, the profit-sharing plan,
and (just the previous year) the disposable diaper. P&G (or "Procter," as
its managers routinely called it) had also consistently doubled its annual
sales every ten years since it had started, an operational mission that the
company had held since its beginnings.

At the same time, some of P&G's manufacturing people were beginning
to discover firsthand the problems of scientific management. Workers
were rigorously measured, sometimes in hundredths of a minute, against
the optimum time that the rule books said it should take to climb a ladder, walk to a tank, or read a gauge. Maintaining this tangle of rules
required so much time and caused so much frustration that a group of
quiet rebels began to gather in the upper echelons of the manufacturing
functions. Led by David Swanson, the manufacturing manager for the
paper division, the rebels were determined to find a way out from under
Procter's rigid constraints. They knew it would mean fighting the corporate hierarchy, whose members were deeply committed to scientific management; they would have to master the art of keeping a low profile,
hiding their innovations from their own corporate chiefs.

They began by bringing in Douglas McGregor from MIT.[10] McGregor
had just published *The Human Side of Enterprise,* and his visits represented the first time anyone in manufacturing at P&G had been allowed to
"examine our navels," as one plant manager later put it.[11] At first glance,
McGregor's ideas seemed like a major shift for managers at Procter, who
expected reliably high performance from themselves and everyone around
them. In the Procter lexicon, the worst thing you could be called was a

"tinkerer" or an "experimenter"; that meant you weren't sure about your results. By contrast, McGregor was the ultimate advocate of learning from experimentation and accepting uncertainty.

But in another way, P&G was well suited to hear McGregor's message. Unlike many other "organization men," Procterites valued the plain-speaking, brutally frank, fiercely engaged management style that McGregor championed. They particularly appreciated what he told them about Eric Trist's work. They used those ideas when developing a new Tide detergent plant in Augusta, Georgia, in 1963.

The Augusta managers abandoned some of P&G's most cherished practices. They banned incentive pay schemes, production quotas, and job classifications. There would be no more operators who ran the lines, mechanics who fixed them, electricians who handled the wiring, or machinists who tooled new parts. There would be only "technicians" working in teams, rewarded not for performance within the defined boundaries of their jobs but for the skills they possessed. If the packing insulation around pipes leaked out, the operators wouldn't have to wait around for a mechanic who was allowed to carry a wrench. The opera-tors would carry wrenches, blueprints, and slide rules or calculators. Together the technicians would gradually develop all the expertise they needed to keep the plant going and improve it. They spent an unprece-dented four hours per week in training and two more hours per week meeting together to solve problems. The idea of these technicians was central to the new design, so manufacturing manager Dave Swanson dubbed the plants "high-performance technician systems."

Augusta and its successors were so successful that by 1967 every new P&G plant was required to operate under the technician system. At the same time, with the rationale that they represented a competitive advantage—but at least in part because the approach seemed so damn weird—P&G main-tained rigid secrecy. No one was allowed to see the plants; even most peo-ple inside Procter never learned much about them. Some P&G managers were subtly threatened with being fired when they tried to learn more.[12] On the outside, labor leaders and sociotechnical experts would hear only vague, whispered rumors about the experiments going on.

Thus, in the most progressive manufacturing circles, the P&G plants acquired a mythic, legendary reputation, bolstered by the exotic names of the prosaic places where they had been located. There was Mehoopany, located in rural Pennsylvania, where Douglas McGregor came to consult on labor relations in 1963 and brought in his MIT colleague Dick Beckhard to conduct a thorough work systems overhaul. (Beckhard, a former theater director, was an early and important leader of the new field of organization development, and one of the first to reshape T-Groups into new forms tailored to corporate managers.) There were Modesto, in central California; and Albany, in Georgia, which made paper products like toilet tissue and disposable diapers. (Mr. Whipple, that emasculated mockery of authoritarianism, made his first television warnings against "squeezing the Charmin" just as P&G was decreasing the authoritarian nature of its factories.) Albany was notable because Procter's managers, responding in 1970 to the civil rights imperative then becoming briefly influential in business, deliberately placed it in a fiercely segregated Georgia city. They wanted to see if the technician system would improve race relations within the plant, and they concluded that it did. One reason may have been the attentiveness to staff: every employee had four hours of training and an hour and a half of team meetings per week.

And then there was Lima, Ohio, which made Downy fabric softener when the plant started up, with Biz detergent added soon after. It was the first plant designed from the ground up to incorporate the technician system instead of having the new structures merely grafted onto an existing factory design. Twenty years later, the management writer Robert Waterman would hold up Lima as the primary example of "what America does right" on the factory floor and as probably the best-managed plant in the United States.[13] It was a wonderful place to work, and not just because wages were high (so high that P&G managers from corporate grumbled about "giving away the store"). Yet production costs were said to be half the costs of a conventional plant, and the true ratio was even lower; the Lima managers assumed that nobody would believe the real figures.[14]

Lima was a philosophical crown jewel for the technician system, and perhaps the single place in the world where sociotechnical ideas and practices had been given full rein. The chief philosopher there, the man who pushed Lima into its legendary status, was one of the great charismatic leaders in the history of American organizational change. Twenty years in the future, he would become (somewhat unfairly) labeled as a cult figure in a management scandal. But in 1967 he was simply a plant engineer, which is not very high in the Procter hierarchy, with a strong following among some of his P&G associates. They liked the way his conversation mixed nuts-and-bolts shop floor data with cosmological theories about the purpose of human life. His name was Charles Krone.

o

Charlie Krone was not a typical Procter production manager. Raised in Kansas, he had graduated from an experimental high school run by the psychologist Karl Menninger, a school where students were taught to study the processes of their own learning. He had an engineering degree from the University of Kansas and had done postdoctoral work in the philosophy of law at Northwestern. In the navy, he had been part of a group that rewrote the code of military justice. He had started his P&G career as an engineer at a fatty-alcohol plant, but as the technician system took hold, he had become increasingly committed to it. He was one of the first P&G people to attend a workshop at NTL in the early 1960s, in the days when Douglas McGregor was still consulting for Procter. After McGregor's death in 1964, he had become one of twelve "organization development consultants" within P&G sent for in-depth training to the University of California at Los Angeles, of eminent NTLers, sociotechnical researchers, and Eric Trist himself.[15]

But Krone also pursued his own studies. During one of his visits to UCLA, he had been introduced to some of the teachings of the spiritual leader G. I. Gurdjieff. Gurdjieff was perhaps the first twentieth-century figure to expound Tibetan and Sufi mysticism in the West—certainly of all mystic leaders, he has been the most influential in business circles. (In Chapter Five, we will see his influence on the scenario planners of Royal Dutch/Shell.) Gurdjieff and his followers, who lived together in Paris from the 1920s through his death in 1957, developed a worldwide community composed of small groups of people who practiced and studied self-observation, group mirroring, and reflective dances.

Mankind, according to Gurdjieff, had gone astray.[16] The "old world," the materialist and nationalist global civilization that had created wars and suffering, was on the point of dying. Either it would extinguish itself and humanity would perish, or it would be replaced by a more highly evolved epoch. To prevent the former, Gurdjieffians took on a mission of a life-long "war against sleep," a constant battle against the numbing complacency of everyday existence. Gurdjieff had discovered that an immense personal power was available through increasing awareness—not just through study and discussion but through dancing, movement, theater, and meditation. Like the NTLers, Gurdjieffians used small groups as a kind of mirror of inner life, bringing to the surface the behavior and thoughts of people in the room.

To follow Gurdjieff's path, you would have to learn to give up your habitual automatic knee-jerk reliance on your own gut feelings about right or wrong. Gurdjieff told a mythic story about the "kundabuffer"—an organ planted in the bodies of the earliest human ancestors, blocking them from fully experiencing reality. Though that organ had disappeared long ago, humans still carry the vestigial emotions that it spawned: self-love, vanity, swagger, pride, and arrogance. Any human being can be convinced of anything, Gurdjieff wrote. All you need to do is find a way to resonate with one of those vestigial misperceptions, buried so deeply within us that we are unaware of them. But if you could find a way to eliminate the automatic, learned, ego-driven responses within yourself, a void would be created, into which your true self could flow.

Charlie Krone would become linked, over the years, with Gurdjieffian thinking, but he also incorporated a variety of other sources into his thinking: Menninger the psychologist; Alfred Korzybski, the Polish American theorist of general semantics; Gurdjieff's student J. G. Bennett; and Lama Anagarika Govinda, the Buddhist monk and writer who founded the Pali Tibetan Buddhist order of the Arya Maitreya Mandala. This was leavened with a heavy flavor of Socratic questioning and Charlie's own cheerful, no-nonsense persona. He stood six foot six, with sharp features and shrewd, heavy-lidded eyes, and he weighed a rangy two hundred pounds. At meetings, he would hover silently in the corner like a benign giant, injecting questions every now and then that seemed to put everything into perspective. When he did speak, it was often to delineate a framework. This would typically be a conceptual sketch that showed how disparate factors fit together or introduced new ideas in a palatable way. Charlie distanced himself from corporate rituals and the trappings of authority, talking as easily to factory floor workers as to managers. He was the kind of guy who would sit down at a tense, confrontational union management meeting and say, "Let me show you how things would work if we could just operate as one system."

All of this gave him a rare ability to draw people out and draw them into his orbit. He inspired intense loyalty among his friends at Procter, as if he were not just their friend and colleague but a kind of in-house spiritual teacher. Other Procterites didn't care for him. They resented his cavalier approach to schedules, rules, and boundaries. In that tight, closely knit corporate culture where people were expected to keep their promises, Krone would schedule two or three meetings at once. Then, seemingly at the last minute, he would decide which one to show up at. Was he just being arbitrary and self-indulgent? Or (as his friends professed) was he deliberately acting as a trickster, to spur groups into stepping forward to think for themselves, without having to rely on himself or any other inspirational leader?

———— o ————

In 1966 Procter & Gamble chose Krone to form a team to plan a new demonstration factory. They selected a site at Lima, a half-day's drive north of Cincinnati, just far enough away to escape the pull from headquarters. Krone was already talking to his closest associates at P&G

about the need to go audaciously beyond the achievements of previous plants at Augusta and Mehoopany—even beyond what sociotechnical leaders like Eric Trist thought was possible. This new plant would deal explicitly with the emotional and psychological issues—the spiritual issues, really—that the technician system had raised. Borrowing from all the schools of thought they knew—Gurdjieff, Trist, NTL, systems design, and Tibetan and Sufi mysticism—he and the other Lima designers argued that the whole plant should be an "open system." This did not mean democracy in any representative sense; if policy at Lima were decided by taking votes, then each person would only have one vote out of three hundred. To accomplish anything, they'd have to join a power bloc or special interest group; they'd spend their time politicking instead of taking part in the plant as a whole.

Instead Krone argued that the whole plant should embody learning. It would never be finished; it would never stop evolving during its lifetime. In addition, it would be conceived as a coherent whole. Not only would most people at the plant work at a variety of tasks (as in Augusta), but everyone in the plant would be aware of all the stages of the work.

As commonsensical as this approach might seem today, it was the opposite of the conventional way that factories were engineered, in which each stage was treated separately, and often designed separately, with components imported from different places.[17]

"Remember," Krone said, "people are learning this process one stage at a time. People really learn the technology. And then they start putting in variations. They manage the thing rather than just turning buttons. When they really have a conceptual grasp for how the plant is put together, what it is designed to do, how to manage the variances, how to analyze all of that, and they are doing a lot of head work at the same time, then the work goes a lot better."[18]

Krone encouraged technicians from the assembly line to explore every phase of corporate life, even such seemingly far removed functions as marketing. Tracking shelf turnover statistics from grocers, the technicians figured out how to raise the quality of the "market basket": the likelihood that people with Biz and Downy in their shopping carts would also spend more money on other products. They did this in part by increasing quality; products that genuinely improve consumers' lives tend to inspire other purchases. Gradually this improved the deals that P&G could cut with its retailers. As Lima manager Carol Sanders later recalled, "The reason Charlie was doing this was to increase the scope of the mind of the people in the operation. If they could conceive of where the product was going and improve the life of the consumer, that would change their minds—and then they'd do better overall."

The distinctive capabilities of the Lima system, like its capacity for groundbreaking innovation, were inseparable from the plant's overall culture. Suppose you were a technician with an idea for a machine that would place empty plastic bottles onto the conveyor belt instead of having someone place them by hand. You would raise the issue in your own team, knowing that nobody else would steal it, take credit for it, or dismiss it as dumb. Instead, they would challenge it: if they liked the idea, some would champion it with you, adding features of their own. The members would then take it to their other teams, and gradually the idea would filter through the plant.

If interest lasted long enough, a team of enthusiasts might form around this project; since you had proposed it, you might lead the team. You would rotate between time on the assembly line and time in this special project. All your fellow team members (including some engineers) would get an education available nowhere else, because your investigations would not be bound by the preconceptions of professionals. According to established engineers, for instance, a bottle-placing machine was technically impossible. But the team at Lima invented one. Procter ordered it, an industrial supplier built it (after meeting with various key participants in the plant), and it runs in Lima today.

Lima's technicians soon became famous for the speed and ingenuity with which they handled difficult problems. In 1969, for instance, the state of Michigan outlawed phosphates in detergent. Ordinarily P&G's product development engineers would have turned that change into an expensive, time-consuming, bureaucratic endeavor. But for Biz, the technicians sent a delegation to the supplier's plant site to help develop a new material that could fit their process. They managed the changeover of formulation and packaging and ended up producing the only detergent that replaced phosphates without jacking up costs, reducing quality, affecting performance, or facing shortages of supplies.

And the rewards the technicians got? They were not paid as highly as managers, but the salary structure was set up to encourage team collaboration and individual learning. For example, the amount of pay was based not on seniority but on the number of "qualified blocks of skills" that a technician mastered. There was very little overtime at Lima; teams managed their own weekly schedule, and pay rates were high enough that they never got in the habit of sacrificing weekends for extra pay. Unlike at other plants, though, pay was not the only incentive at Lima. There was also an intangible kind of satisfaction from both the process of creation and the fact that Lima had no team leaders; everyone rotated in and out of the leadership positions, so that everyone had a stake in the whole operation. Krone dubbed this approach the "flowering organization" and drew an organization chart on the wall composed of interlocking circles, like an unfolding flower. Power rested not at the top but at the center, in each individual's core leadership, and it filtered out to related areas of interest as needed.[19]

In place of consensus or democracy, there was a kind of jazz-like creativity. Initiatives were carried out when someone championed them and nobody else came up with good reasons to get in the way. Real authority should be based, Krone would say, not on who had the highest rank, the best skills, or the most charisma but on who was ready to play a solo: who cared the most about that particular initiative and could act most effectively on it. To make the organization live up to that notion, the salaried managers had to take on a leadership role that was unfamiliar to most of them. Did they have enough faith in the process to let a problem go unsolved for as long as it took for someone to step forward to assume leadership? And would they have enough self-awareness—and this was the truly hard part—to recognize when it was appropriate for them to be the leader because they cared more than anyone else?

Hard as it was for the Lima managers, it would have been even tougher if they'd had to buck headquarters at the same time. Therefore, Lima's leaders, despite some reservations, never protested the strict secrecy policy that all the technician plants had to adopt. Today, thirty years later, Procter & Gamble is one of the few companies that has built its manufacturing expertise into a long-standing source of competitive advantage.[20] But for all the value of its knowledge in this field and all the management lessons it has had to offer America over the years, P&G's innovations remain largely invisible to the public eye. In the late 1960s, it fell to a few heretical managers at an obscure division of a far more troubled company to introduce sociotechnical practice to the public eye.

○

One morning in 1966, in an isolated warehouse at a dog food plant in Kankakee, Illinois, a twenty-year-old night shift worker was discovered bound to a column with packaging tape. He was unhurt, but he could not get free. He furiously kicked against the tape because his shouting could not be heard. Once found, he was easily cut away, but figuring out what to do with him, or with the workers who had tied him up, was not so simple.

At that time, this plant, which made Gainesburgers and Gravy Train, belonged to the grocery products conglomerate General Foods: one of the oldest food manufacturers in the world, and at the time, as recognizable a company by name as its fellow behemoths General Motors and General

Electric. That did not mean that its managers felt powerful. For instance, they were bound by strict regulations for hourly workers that had been negotiated with GF's unions over the previous thirty years. At the Gaines dog food plant, a manager couldn't sack workers outright without triggering a grievance from the Federated Grain Millers local. Depending on how hard the union fought, the manager might win the right to hire a replacement, but the manager might also find himself in a long drawn-out arbitration dispute. Even for an offense like taping a twenty-year-old man to a pole, firing or disciplining people was hardly worth the trouble. A manager who cared would have to find some other way of preventing that problem from happening again.

In this case, that task fell to the third-most senior person at the plant, engineering manager Ed Dulworth. He was thirty-one years old, a burly, boyish-looking man with wavy blonde hair and a genial, plain-spoken style. He had a volatile temperament and was prone to both enthusiasm and anger, but he also had a knack for making people feel comfortable. Of all the managers at Kankakee, Dulworth had the best rapport with hourly workers, which was why he was often tapped to deal with these sorts of problems. He stayed late the next night and called the boy's coworkers together in an impromptu meeting. Why had they taped this kid to the pole? "We didn't," one of them said. "We found him there. We were trying to get him down." Dulworth just stared at them. Amiably but persistently, he drew the truth out of them.

The kid, who had been hired a few days before, was working too hard. If he kept up his pace on the line, the rest of them would have had to speed up. They tried to warn him to slow down, but he couldn't stop. He was too charged with nervous energy. So they taped him up there.

Dulworth had been through dozens of similar situations (indeed, they were endemic to American factories), and he knew what would happen: nothing. He was damned if he disciplined them harshly; they would just ignore any punishment he was allowed to give them. And yet he was damned if he laughed it off and let them go back to work. Unofficially he knew who was guilty, but officially, he couldn't hold a hearing. Nobody, not even the kid, would testify. He couldn't even move the kid to another locale or shift. Like everything else in the plant, the kid would just stay put.

That burned him. In a sense, Ed Dulworth had been running away from systems that "just stayed put" all his life. He had grown up in rural Michigan and then trained as a production engineer at General Motors. He had left GM when he saw that no matter how well he performed, he would have to "sit in the goddamn chair," as they called the low-level supervising jobs, until he paid his dues as a manager. So in 1961 he'd come to this

Gaines plant, and he'd advanced to become the youngest engineering manager in the entire General Foods system. He'd fulfilled his dream, or so he felt, of working in a place where people were judged on their performance, not on company politics. And his performance, in turn, depended on his geniality and open-mindedness. He had gotten in the habit, years before, of asking for help and advice from people who worked on the assembly lines he designed, and his systems tended to work better than those of engineers who thought they knew all the answers themselves.

Over the years, he'd also come to realize the value of looking at things from the other person's point of view. The line workers who strapped up that kid, for instance, were reacting to the pressure that the whole plant felt. Semimoist dog foods, the generic name for cellophane-wrapped, pressed-together, semidry pellets like Gainesburgers, had surged in popularity during the last year or two. The new Gaines dry dog food, Gravy Train, was also extremely popular. Demand for both had grown fourfold in four years.

But at the GF headquarters in White Plains, New York (thirty miles north of New York City, a thousand miles from Kankakee), Gaines pet food was a low-prestige product. GF was a conglomerate, formed through a half-century's worth of mergers. There was continual, bitter turf conflict among the divisions, or (as managers called them) "mafias": glamorous Maxwell House versus household name Jell-O (the Jack Benny sponsor), versus technologically innovative Birds Eye (inventors of frozen foods), versus the profit center of Post cereals. Meanwhile, there was also an ongoing cross-divisional battle between the old-time production and sales people—gritty, matter-of-fact engineers and salesmen trained at municipal New York colleges—and the younger newcomers in marketing— arrogant and aggressive with Ivy League M.B.A.s. Nobody ever talked about that rivalry publicly, which made it all the more deadly. Since most managers shifted jobs every three years, anyone might land under a boss from another faction, who could block his advancement or fire him.

For the moment, a production man named Tex Cook was CEO, so the production guys had the upper hand. But the war had made both sides hunker down, avoid mistakes, and play strictly by the rules and procedures. Occasionally managers rebelled in small ways; one used footage of the GF corporate hallways in a mock-horror film: "Here is where the brain-dead sleep."

Gaines, with its little dog food business, was not even a full division. None of the experts at headquarters expected it to develop a miracle product. When Gainesburgers took off, they didn't quite believe it. They called it a fad, underestimating demand and underbudgeting investment, while the Kankakee facility struggled to keep up with its mushrooming orders.

Only a few years before, five hundred people had worked at Kankakee. Now seventeen hundred were packed into spots on the assembly line. Supervisors were under constant pressure to boost production, which meant haranguing the workers to move faster in a plant that was crowded, damp, and prone to temperature extremes. (Part of the plant, converted from a warehouse, had never been insulated.) People had to struggle with new equipment designed for a complex Gainesburger packaging process that was still being broken in. More than half the plant's workforce was under twenty-eight years old; they'd been hired right out of high school and seemed angry to be there at all. Sensing the hostility of the supervisors, they retaliated with inarticulate, frustrated, and sometimes dangerous pranks. Some workers, for instance, nearly killed one unpopular manager by dumping a bucket of water on him while he was a hundred feet in the air, holding on to a vertical chain-link conveyor belt called a "man-lift."

Dulworth also understood the resentment that supervisors and production managers felt. They too were mostly in their late twenties; the plant sometimes looked like a dank, subterranean city full of men just past their teenage years. The young managers usually came to Kankakee just out of business school, where they had studied the formulas for financial analysis and operations control. But they never learned the more crucial skills (as Dulworth saw them): how to listen to people or how to think on their feet. Those who learned these vernacular skills on the job soon got promoted elsewhere; Kankakee was a development arena, feeding managers to other plants in General Foods.[21] The more inept managers stayed put. They complained regularly to Dulworth and the other senior managers about not being backed up when there was "trouble in the ranks." They wanted Dulworth to "kick ass and take names": to give harsher orders and punish the worst offenders.

Maybe that approach would have worked in the past, but now, in the mid-1960s, Dulworth thought it would create more bitterness and trouble than it solved. In effect, he felt stalemated, and he was thinking about leaving the company when, in 1966, a new operations manager arrived at Kankakee. (At the four biggest General Foods plants, which were Battle Creek, Hoboken, Dover, and Kankakee, the top executive had the title "operations manager" to distinguish him from mere "plant managers" at smaller facilities.) The new boss's name was Lyman Ketchum, but people called him Ketch. In his late forties, bespectacled and grizzled-haired, he was a natural mentor for Ed Dulworth, and in fact soon came to regard him as a favored nephew.

Ketchum understood both the hourly workers and the low-level managers. He was the son of a fervent union man. His father, a carman for the Santa Fe Railroad, had lost his job when he led a bitter, violent railroad strike in the early 1920s. Ketch had gone to Kansas University on a football scholarship and then put himself through engineering school, determined never to feel the resentment of the system that he saw in his father. He had worked at a variety of jobs in the grocery and food industry, including plant management for Quaker Oats Company, the U.S. Naval Reserve, Safeway Stores, Staley Milling Company (a small feed manufacturer), and then General Foods. Like Dulworth, he knew how capable and motivated factory workers could be, and he had been somewhat influenced by a few management professors who had pushed, during the 1940s and early 1950s, for what they called participative management—giving workers influence over their work.[22]

But while Ketch remained convinced of the value of worker participation, he hadn't thought much about it for several years. Beginning in the late 1950s, he had begun to work his way successfully out of the production track at General Foods and into marketing and regional sales. Then he had been tapped in 1965 for a dream job, the first that would really use his intellectual gifts: strategic planning for Gaines pet food. His first project had been a major report on the future of American consumers, influenced by a few farsighted people in the market research department. The mass audience was going to fragment into dozens of smaller, less homogeneous audiences, with vastly different tastes. Subcultures would appear among pet owners; for instance, there would be "anthropomorphists," who treated their animals like people and relied on them for companionship. Ketchum argued that GF should produce multiple flavors for dogs whose owners thought they craved variety.

As far as Ketchum ever heard, the study was well received at GF, but his sympathizers in marketing heard differently: the Ivy Leaguers who ran that function mocked them. "Treating a dog like people? That's sick!"[23] A plan to redesign Gaines Biscuits and Bits packages to emphasize companionship was turned down because the corporate plan said it wasn't time yet to change the package. (The marketing man who proposed the plan left the company in disgust; when his redesign finally went through two years later, it received the Pet Food Institute's Package of the Year award and probably quadrupled sales.)[24]

Ketchum, meanwhile, spent only four months in planning. A reshuffling at the top had led to a battle over who would head the Kankakee plant.

As the only candidate acceptable to both sides, he was drafted in what was seen as a great career break. "Going to Kankakee is like going to the bank," one GF executive told him. If he could run the plant effectively, he was slated to become general manager of the pet food business.

But Lyman, from the moment he got to Kankakee, could see the Gaines problems all too clearly—and their roots in the corporate investment policies. During his many visits back to White Plains (for he had purchasing, inventory, manufacturing, and engineering responsibilities for all of Gaines), he began to speak out about the stresses on the plant. Salespeople would ask him to fill new orders, and he would say, "All right, but which of our old customers do you want to ask to wait?"

------------ o ------------

In the early 1960s, the GF human resource staff began promoting NTL T-Groups to help ease tensions among the "mafias." Ketchum's turn came up, as it happened, a month before he left for Kankakee. A year later, after hearing about it from Ketchum, Ed Dulworth signed up.

Both men were impressed with T-Groups, but Dulworth in particular felt an awakening within himself. In his session, which took place in a hotel on the Jersey shore, one man convincingly portrayed himself as an outstanding management expert. But the group's conversation broke through the man's veneer and revealed him to be (as Dulworth later recalled it) "the biggest schmuck in the group." The "schmuck" finally confessed that his marriage was falling apart and he was in danger of losing his job because he kept fighting with his fellow managers. Seeing this man's defenses, Dulworth understood a little better what drove the many self-appointed experts at GF, whose arbitrary-seeming judgments had stymied him throughout his career.

When he saw his wife after the session, he began immediately raving about the fabulous insights he'd felt and about what it meant to be a more open person. She stiffened, so he began to probe into her responses, to draw her out as the T-Group leaders did. She burst into tears. He saw, then and there, how threatening all this talk about "being remade" could be to someone who wasn't prepared for it with two weeks of camaraderie, and he resolved to keep a low profile around the plant about this group dynamics stuff.

Nonetheless, the T-Group had left him with a more philosophical perspective. He still had to deal with rigorous paperwork, but it no longer made him fume. It was just a symptom of deeper problems in the system, and he began to talk more freely with Ketchum and a few other managers at Kankakee about performance and sabotage problems: "There's something wrong here. What on earth is going on?" They could admit they had no answers, at least to each other, without the constant fear most managers have of appearing not to be in control of the situation. They thought more coherently about the welfare of everyone in the plant, as if everyone were part of a single community. Ketchum would catch himself, as he drove to work, musing about the other people who worked there. "What is each one of them thinking right now?"

The two men began to treat people more judiciously, to set up opportunities to talk through problems, and to invite involvement, to some small degree, from workers.[25] And by 1967 behavior began to change a little. First-line supervisors were a little less likely to blame the workers; workers were a little less likely to sabotage their work. Ketchum had time to put together a long-range facility plan, a project most GF managers never got to because they were too busy dealing with crises. Yet when he looked at the Kankakee plant as a whole, he despaired: there were too many people, too entrenched, with too many constituencies at White Plains or in the union to change just because a senior manager was promoting a new crusade. Ketchum wished he could start Kankakee over from scratch.

That fall, when the senior executives at General Foods finally began to talk seriously about expanding Kankakee, Ketchum argued instead for designing a new plant. Typically launching a new factory was a cumbersome, rushed process in which cadres of construction engineers, financial controllers, and personnel managers battled with the specs and regulations. The plant manager and his staff, let alone the workers, were never asked for advice about the building in which they would spend their days. This time, Ketchum said, let us "unlearn" every traditional practice, and design the plant as a single effort. We'll spend six months researching how the most farsighted, high-performance plants in the world are organized. Then we'll develop a plan for the site, the management, the adaptation of machinery from Kankakee, and the labor force all simultaneously, all working together, as if we were creating them all from scratch on a blank sheet of paper.

Ketchum knew vaguely, from people he had met at NTL, that dramatic innovations were taking place in factories at Procter & Gamble, at Westinghouse, at AT&T, and in Sweden. He began to think that his little dog food division could learn from these examples and design a plant where people treated each other with grace and civility, and in turn set an example for others. It would be a daring deed for General Foods—a mission into uncharted territory. Nothing like this had ever been written into a rule book. He and Dulworth knew already, for example, that they would have to organize the factory's work around collaborative teams, but they had no idea how to compose the teams, how to set up pay scales, or how to fulfill a thousand other needs and details. They would have to figure all this out as they went along while still creating a profitable dog food factory.

For more than a year, the division managers of Gaines pet food, as well as the GF corporate executives, resisted Ketchum's idea. They relented only after a strike erupted in October and another was narrowly averted the following August. The grievances in both cases were the same: intolerable working conditions and long hours. By the end of the summer of 1968, Ketch had preliminary approval to scout around for a new site for a $12 million facility. Looking near Kansas City, to be close to freight lines and sources of grain, they finally found a site a few miles outside Topeka on a desolate, windswept stretch of prairie next to the railroad tracks.

Dulworth, in addition to his job at Kankakee, worked nights developing a technical design for this new plant in Topeka. He continued that work even after January, when Lyman appointed him manufacturing and engineering manager—the second-highest post at Kankakee. Lyman, meanwhile, persistently battled with senior executives at the Post division, where Gaines had been assigned during a reorganization. The Post corporate engineer insisted on putting engineers in every senior position; Ketchum argued back that it was more important to assign sophisticated managers of people. Meanwhile, for the all-important job of plant manager, the Post division president suggested an advertising and merchandising veteran who had never run a production facility before. When he heard that, Ketchum could barely control his temper. He still didn't know many of the details of this new plant, but he knew that it would require far more invention and sensitivity than an ordinary start-up. If it didn't have experienced and enthusiastic managers of people at the helm, it wouldn't fly. Unfortunately Ketchum didn't have any suitable candidates of his own to suggest.

Finally, one night early in 1969 at a bar in Kankakee, Ketch confessed his despair to Ed. How would they ever find a plant manager in time for the start-up date? "Look," Ed said, "if you want me to, I'll take the job." Both of them knew that Dulworth was one of the few candidates whom Ketchum and the White Plains executives could agree on. Nonetheless, Lyman said no at first; he was reluctant to gut Kankakee by removing Ed, and he wasn't sure it was Ed's best possible career move. Dulworth had to convince him that Topeka had become his baby too.

In April 1969, Ketchum and Dulworth were allowed to assemble a planning team. They felt some urgency because Kankakee was already overburdened and the new Topeka plant was overdue. But they took a few months to educate themselves. They read management books; visited consultants to ask about pay systems, facilities, and motivation studies; and tracked down every facility they could find that had tried something better than the conventional authoritarian approach.

Ketchum and Dulworth didn't realize that they were about to create the first major factory showplace of the postindustrial era. Nor could they foresee that their own careers would become a visible warning of how large corporations can martyr their visionaries. All that was still in the future. For the moment, they were simply asking: Had anyone, anywhere in America or around the rest of the world, ever created a plant like the one that Lyman and Ed imagined in their hearts?

Here they were extraordinarily lucky. One of their long-standing consultants was Purdue University professor Richard Walton, who was moving that year to the Harvard Business School. Walton had been a trainer at NTL, a labor negotiation specialist, and an expert on conflict resolution. He already saw that his own reputation could be bound up with this new General Foods project. He spent many hours helping with the plans for the new plant and began writing about it for management journals before the plant opened. Walton had also spent some time at UCLA, where he had gotten to know Charlie Krone. He offered to introduce the Gaines people to the seer from Procter & Gamble.

The General Foods people flew to meet Krone in his Cincinnati office and came away impressed on several levels. "He talked about Augusta, Lima and Mehoopany," Dulworth later recalled. "Jeez! These were big-time, total designs, committed to a radically different approach." It was also noteworthy how the Lima designers balanced their commitments to the new management philosophy and the old attitudes back at P&G headquarters.

Almost unwittingly, Krone and Dulworth had slipped under the Procter "soapsuds curtain." Charlie grandly dismissed all concerns about secrecy. "Procter has a social responsibility to share what we're doing with others," he told Ketchum and Dulworth. They assumed that he meant openness was Procter's policy; they didn't know he was speaking only about his *own* policy. Krone was also helping managers at the British chemical company ICI and at DuPont. He believed that open systems in general had more to gain by sharing their techniques than bottling them up. True, he forswore writing or speaking publicly about Lima, but only because he thought no one could do the concept justice except through in-depth consultations. He had a Zen-like belief that seekers should find masters only when they were ready to learn in depth, not when they wanted a quick answer. Ketchum and Dulworth were clearly eager to learn in depth.

They learned that the rest of Procter was not so open when they tried to verify what Krone told them. Somehow they obtained the design document for the Mehoopany plant. They figured they would follow up by going to Mehoopany, but no one let them inside. Instead they hung around the town's bars and bowling alleys, collaring plant workers to ask them what was going on. "It was a major learning experience," Dulworth said later, "to hear that it was alive, and not just words. It gave us lots of confidence."

○

Meanwhile, the Topeka project continued to ruffle feathers back at White Plains. Ketchum deliberately asked nobody from the powerful Post engineering and financial staffs to join the five-person Topeka planning group.[26] He had enough trouble with staff people as it was. Someone from personnel would pull out a policies and procedures book, and Ketchum would drawl, "Well, we're not going to have one." What about a controller? A personnel department? A quality control department? "No, we don't need any of those either."

They had also decided not to invite a union to organize the plant. This was in part a selling point at White Plains, and it meant they could experiment with shifting work rules far more easily. Later this would be a point of academic criticism against the plant. It wasn't an exercise in "workplace democracy," but an impossible showplace whose successes could never be duplicated in, say, Kankakee. Hourly workers, in particular, belong to a different class from the managers; they don't want involvement or improved performance because they don't share any ownership. They want the egalitarianism that comes from union membership, where they know that everyone with equal seniority is paid the same and they don't have to compete with each other. They want the relief of not having to live in fear, not having to deal with the kind of political battles that were starting to irritate Ed Dulworth and Lyman Ketchum. Or so the critics claimed.

For their part, Dulworth and Ketchum had talked to many shop floor workers who wanted more involvement as long as management could be trusted to keep its word. And neither Dulworth nor Ketchum felt the visceral, venomous resentment of unions that colored many managers' attitudes. Ketchum still maintained a close relationship with his labor organizer father, and one of the moments that Dulworth found most disturbing, during the research phase, was a visit to a "work redesign" team at Westinghouse that went into action only when there was wind of a union organizing campaign.

To help ensure that Topeka would be different, Dulworth invited onto the design team an hourly worker named Don Lafond, a maintenance craft foreman from the Kankakee shop floor. Lafond, insightful and thoughtful, was an unofficial counselor to other workers in the plant and had put himself through night school to learn electrician skills. He had also been a union shop steward and local president, which made him indispensable for understanding potential grievances that the rest of the design team would otherwise miss.

At first the rest of the team had trouble getting used to him. Lafond wasn't articulate in the way a college-educated General Foods–assimilated manager would be. He didn't know how to prepare and package his thoughts before he spoke. He would see something in the Topeka plans that didn't make sense—a design where workers could change the arrangement of work flow only by plugging in a preprogrammed cartridge, for instance—and he would shyly raise his hand and launch into an interminable preamble about how he was just a farm boy and people on farms learned to be jacks-of-all-trades. That would all be a warm-up for his main point: "You guys are trying to make everything idiot-proof again. I don't want there to be only one person in the plant who knows how to program the line."

In December the design team faced its biggest test: a series of presentations of the detailed Topeka plan to GF headquarters. One presentation stuck in Dulworth's mind for years. It came at a tough moment: the president of the Post division had recently told Lyman Ketchum that he would never be promoted again. Apparently Ketch had ruffled too many feathers in assembling the Topeka team. "This was at the height," he later recalled, "of the most creative work I had ever done in my life. Once I realized that my career was in jeopardy, that made me all the more determined. If I was going to go down in flames, I would go down my own way."

Dulworth had not yet been tagged with a negative label, and he handled most of the presentation. The pitch was based on the point that workers, even assembly-line workers, aren't in it just for the money. "People have 'ego' needs," Dulworth argued. "They want self-esteem, a sense of accomplishment, autonomy, increasing knowledge, and skill and data on their performance. People invest more when they have these things."[27]

The new plant would be designed to capitalize on that aspect of human nature, he said. It would have a minimum workforce, in which teams measured their own work and set their own goals. The managers, without the need to watch over people so closely, would be free to develop innovations. Dulworth and Ketchum estimated, on the basis of their research, that the new factory might expect productivity gains of 50 percent.

Sitting at the end of the table that winter morning was Jim Stone, the vice president of operations for all of General Foods.[28] Despite the lofty title, Stone's was a staff position; he advised, rather than controlled, the divisional managers of the GF "mafias." But he spoke for the organization as a whole, not just for the pet food division. To move forward, they needed his support. And Stone was sympathetic: he had long been interested in finding ways of making manufacturing more efficient and using insights from people on the assembly lines.[29] He saw that the Topeka plant would give General Foods an opportunity to experiment firsthand.

In the carefully orchestrated corporate meetings of the mid-1960s, senior managers did not speculate or join in any presenter's enthusiasm. Instead Stone sat there—not antagonistically but impassively, as if marking time—while Ed Dulworth grew progressively more nervous. Finally, the vice president for operations gave his judgment: "I don't think this is going to work." He then added a benediction that Dulworth had never heard before during his professional life: "But you are free to fail."

———— o ————

Being free to fail seemed to make Lyman promotable after all. In early 1970, he became the first operations manager for the Gaines pet food business overall. He interpreted the appointment as a vote of confidence in the new Topeka approach and as an unofficial opportunity to become an organizational change agent for all of General Foods, helping plants convert to the team system. Ketchum's move was a blow for Dulworth, however; he hadn't quite imagined life at Topeka without Ketchum right there, and now he had to run interference with headquarters. Instead of being protected, he was now the buffer.

Meanwhile, the first skeleton members of the Topeka crew moved into the plant, including Don Lafond and six people slated to be leaders of the Topeka teams when it opened. They were deliberately chosen to be diverse: a recent college graduate, a former auto plant supervisor from Ford, a college coach, a graduate of the U.S. Naval Academy, and a Food and Drug Administration inspector who also owned and ran a farm. Topeka was originally due to open in September of that year, but construction delays pushed the date back to January 1971. In the meantime, from a makeshift office in a storefront, the team leaders hired sixty-three plant staffers. At first, they ran applicants through an elaborate set of tests, but after a while they realized that they only needed to give them a plant tour. "We don't know exactly what this job is going to be," Dulworth would tell the applicants, "but you can pretty much make it what you want. The more you want to do, the more you'll be able to do." People who responded eagerly were probably Topeka material.

Within a few months of opening, the plant began to show the same kind of results that had been so impressive at Lima. Production costs were 40 percent below Kankakee's, and absenteeism held at a remarkable

2 percent rate (Kankakee's was 15 percent). Total production rose to three hundred tons of dog food per day, the plant's target, and it never fell below.

The plant found its first in-depth critic that year. A doctoral student of Dick Walton named Mike Brimm, researching his dissertation for the Harvard Business School, spent the summer of 1971 on the shop floor; Dulworth wouldn't admit him unless he agreed to work all summer. Brimm took on the job wholeheartedly. He didn't just interview his subjects; he worked with them, went swimming with them, and drank with them at 7:00 A.M. (Night-shift crew members often gathered in a field outside for a sunrise after-work beer.) Afterward Brimm would hurry home to record what he remembered into a tape recorder. Trained in Marxist theory, Brimm had deliberately set up his dissertation to look at the plant from two perspectives. To a sociotechnical theorist, it was an unqualified success. To a socialist, it was a failed attempt to mollify the working class within a capitalist framework. Yet he had to admit that the feeling of democracy was palpable, particularly when compared to his earlier visit to Kankakee.

For one thing, the plant was modern and temperature controlled. The square, grooved, five-story gleaming white tower at the plant's center rose from the stark Kansas fields like the last rook on a giant chessboard. Inside (like every other pet food plant) it stank of tallow and grain, but in every other respect it was a comfortable place to work. Most factories are laid out horizontally, but Topeka was designed as a living silo. Starting in bins at the top of the building, grain dropped through the floors, propelled by gravity, traveling through successive stages of production as it fell. Sections of the plant were painted bright colors that showed the flow of work; meeting rooms became natural centers where teams gravitated to compare notes or argue. Instead of supervisors (the Kankakee word for *foreman*), there were "team members" and "team leaders" (the GF designers had decided against importing the sterile term *technician* from Procter & Gamble). Unlike Kankakee, the Topeka plant had no reserved parking places for managers, and there was only one lunchroom, where everybody ate together at large round tables. The break rooms had carpeting, table tennis, and (most incomprehensible of all to GF headquarters) a television set. There was no bathroom on the first floor, so managers and workers used the same facility, and there was only one entrance, so everyone used the same door. There were no fences, no guards, and no locks on the lockers. When large quantities of dog food were found missing, the teams of workers laid a trap and caught the thief in the act.

Pay scales, instead of being based on seniority or the boss's favor, were based on knowledge. Team members decided when their fellow team members were ready for more pay simply by trusting them to handle a particular task.[30] (The design team had considered hiring everyone on a salary basis, but Ketchum knew he couldn't sell that to the executives at White Plains. He didn't even try.) Teams also set their hours and breaks and dealt with their own problems in meetings. If you were regularly late, the people who had to cover for you might ask you to cut them some slack. If that didn't work, then the whole team would talk about it at the next meeting. All this felt controlling and cliquish at times, but it gave the factory a barn-raising atmosphere. When railroad boxcars showed up full of hundreds of hundred-pound bags of dog food ingredients, every team member (including the team leaders) dropped what they were doing and pitched in to unload them.[31]

Brimm himself worked at nearly every job in the plant, sometimes in teams that processed the dog food and sometimes in teams that packaged it. He examined railroad carloads of incoming grain for infestation by insects ("a job for neither acrophobes nor those with queasy stomachs"[32]); he worked the assembly line where dog food was injected into bags; and he was a "humper" at the end of the line, piling fifty-pound packages onto wooden pallets. Normally everyone took two-hour turns as humpers, but there was a six-hour first-day initiation that Mike, like all his fellow team members, endured. "When I first saw you come in the door," one of his coworkers told him that day, "I said, 'Here comes Joe College to snoop around and keep clean.' Now, I see that you're a regular guy."[33]

Most of all, Brimm was impressed with the ways in which team members learned the work from each other. They felt free to cause "some losses in short-run productive efficiency," he wrote, "to net an increase in learning." The team expert on a repair operation would typically stand a few feet back when training someone else and let the person fumble through repairs, jumping in only when the novice asked for help. In Kankakee, workers had deliberately tried to keep production down, for that was their only weapon against the system. Here, Brimm wrote, "It was not uncommon for a passing fork-lift operator to stop and offer me tips on an easier way to pack bales." Despite his many years as a student, he added, "I have encountered few teachers and colleagues who exhibit the patience, skill, and sensitivity which I observed and experienced among this work force. . . . My successes were rewarded with smiles and slaps on the back; my failures, with compassionate concern and assistance.'"[34]

Other workers were also impressed with the place. Many referred to Topeka as "us" and internalized the corporate goals: "Trucking the product to market will cost us $5,000 more a day," or "Our product has to have a rich, red color or the consumer will buy Purina next time."[35] Comments like that brought out Brimm's Marxist suspicions. After all, the plant did not belong to these workers, no matter how much they felt they owned it. Suppose they insisted on replacing that backbreaking humping job with expensive machinery, which the accountants had already rejected because the payback period was too long?[36] Suppose they wanted to stop making dog food and produce something else? Suppose they wanted to use the increased profits from the plant to raise their own pay or hire more workers? They'd soon see that they were free to make decisions only "as long as these yielded the same outcomes that the higher-level authority would have chosen (had he been there)."[37] The managers set the goals; the workers merely had a bigger voice in how to implement them.

And, indeed, when Brimm returned for follow-up interviews the following summer in 1972, many of the workers had discovered the limits of the system. The feeling of being pioneers had leveled off. Ketchum had lobbied to have a second plant (to make canned dog food) built on the site, and now there were disputes about who would be team leaders in the new plant. Most telling of all, the people who had talked about utopian dreams the previous years now said to Brimm, in effect: Don't get me wrong. My job here is the best I could find anywhere in Kansas—maybe anywhere at all. But it's still just a job.

"We were all in the clouds for a long time," one worker told him. "Sometimes I think the people out in the office still are. But 300 tons of dog food a day, every day, can bring you down to earth in a hurry—particularly if you're the one who's making it. Some of the guys really crashed down when they realized this."[38]

---------- o ----------

You might think just having a job is not that awful a fate, particularly when American manufacturers were beginning a twenty-five-year period of downsizing and shifting jobs overseas. But Ketchum and Dulworth, like Eric Trist and Charlie Krone before them, began to feel a bit messianic. Only by making the job more than just a job could you realize the incredible performance gains. But when Ketchum, in particular, tried to communicate this back to the people in White Plains, he encountered nonchalant skepticism instead of the enthusiasm he had hoped for.

Staff people calling from White Plains knew nothing of improved performance; they knew only that when they called Topeka for the quality control or pricing data they needed fast, they had to wait on the line, fuming, until someone rounded up Ed Dulworth or Don Lafond. "Well, we can get that data," Lafond might say. "But not within twenty-four hours. We have to get it from the teams."

"Well, who can I talk to right now?" the staff member would snap.

"Anybody in team A might be doing quality this week. We'll have to find out. Team B doesn't come on until eleven. Are you sure I can't call you back?"

A plant manager not knowing who was "doing quality" was like a commanding officer not knowing the name of his quartermaster. But when the staff member went to complain to Ketchum, he would simply say, "You don't need those measures in the first place. They don't really help production, do they?" Ketchum may have been right, but the word began to get around in White Plains that performance at Topeka was out of control. The plant couldn't even make its numbers.

It was a shame, you might hear in the Maxwell House or Jell-O office, because everyone had always liked Lyman, but ever since this Topeka project, he'd become unbearable. This sort of flak hit practically everyone at some time in their career. But it worried Ketchum. He called Charlie Krone, asking, "Where can I find an expert to help me talk to these engineers?" Krone referred him to Eric Trist, whom Lyman invited to speak to a conference of General Foods manufacturing managers. The two men, who had been only vaguely aware of each other, became lifelong friends that night; eventually they collaborated on a book together.[39]

Trist, as part of his research, had studied the diffusion of pilot projects like Topeka. He had concluded that they were a losing game. They almost never influenced organizations like General Foods, which were set up, almost as if by design, to discourage any single division from learning from any of the others. "Don't get stuck," Trist told Ketchum, "on changing General Foods." Topeka's success, he predicted, would eventually stimulate other projects around the world.

———— o ————

It was a prescient remark. In the early 1970s, hand-wringing over American worker discontent—"blue-collar blues," it had come to be called—was percolating through the federal government and some parts of academia. If corporations continued to set up their plants in the traditional manner, workers might erupt as blacks had in the early 1960s. At the same time, more voices like Dick Walton's were recognizing that the brutal atmosphere of most production plants might have an effect on productivity and performance. And a report commissioned by Elliot Richardson, the secretary of health, education and welfare under Richard Nixon, concluded that working conditions in the United States were harmful to physical and mental health.

The task force leaders, James O'Toole and Edward Lawler III, would go on to become two of the most influential leadership and management writers in academia. And the resulting wave of conferences and books, known loosely as the quality of working life (QWL) movement, would gather force for several years in the United States and England. They studied the examples of companies like W. L. Gore, which operated through groups of self-directed "associates," and harman/kardon, an audio equipment company with a high-performance plant in Bolivar, Tennessee, which Michael Maccoby helped design. (The CEO of harman/kardon, Sidney Harman, published several books on workplace improvement and later became a Washington philanthropist, married to Los Angeles congresswoman Jane Harman.) Eric Trist by this time was old enough to play the role of senior eminence; he spent years involved with a group of businesses in Jamestown, New York, that sought to use workplace reform to revitalize the entire economy of the region. The QWL movement was also noteworthy because it involved labor leaders, such as the United Auto Workers' Irving Bluestone and Donald Ephlin, and it led directly to great innovative experiments in the auto industry, like GM's Saturn division (for whom Ephlin helped organize flexible job structures in exchange for a guarantee of no layoffs). But in the end, neither the union nor management accepted the ideas. As O'Toole and Lawler later wrote, "U.S. automakers and the UAW turned their backs on promising efforts to adopt [high-involvement] practices . . . and are paying a heavy price today for that mistake."[40]

———— o ————

In the QWL context, Topeka was big news. General Foods at that time was the largest mainstream company willing to talk publicly about its success. So starting in 1971, Ed Dulworth, Lyman Ketchum, and their adviser Dick Walton were invited, more and more, to make presentations about the fundamental industrial shift going on at Topeka.

In November 1972, Richard Walton published an article on the Gaines plant in the *Harvard Business Review*.[41] The following February, the *New York Times* ran a front-page story on the plant. Then NBC-TV covered it; then *Newsweek, Business Week,* and *Reader's Digest*. The articles tended to mention experiments going on at other companies[42] and then single out Topeka as the prime example of the next generation of industrialism. "We fit with the times," Dulworth said later. "We had a demonstration of a different kind of working life, one that valued individuals and wasn't highly structured. You could wear a beard and tennis shoes."

Spurred by the news reports, other companies began sending emissaries to visit the Gaines plant. The Japanese Productivity Institute, for instance, sent forty people; they endured three days of intensive study amid the stench of dog food. Eventually tours became so numerous that Dulworth charged fees. The most senior General Foods executives blessed the idea of making Topeka a public example. (GF had just had to publicly write off a series of large losses and bad investments—the first such write-off in its history. Topeka provided welcome positive publicity.) After the NBC broadcast about Topeka, Dick Walton ran into General Foods president Arthur Larkin at a party at the Harvard Club in New York. "Art, do you really understand what you've got in that plant?" he asked the president. Shortly afterward, Ketchum's appointment to his internal consulting job was approved. He would now be able to work full time, helping other GF facilities follow Topeka's example. A community of people involved in this type of work design was emerging, and General Foods would be at the forefront.

o

The short happy life of Topeka's influence at General Foods ended in April 1973. That month, the *Atlantic Monthly* published excerpts from a forthcoming book, *Job Power*, by a writer named David Jenkins who described both Topeka and Lima. It was the first time Procter & Gamble's Lima had been mentioned in print. Jenkins wrote, inaccurately, that teams at Lima, without any direction from management, hired their own people and set their own salaries. He found, and quoted, the elusive Charlie Krone: "The plant was designed from the ground up to be democratic. The technology—the location of instruments, for example—was designed to stimulate relationships between people, and to allow people to affect their own environment."[43] No doubt Charlie had said something like this, but for his career, it was the worst possible quote. In the tough-minded P&G culture, "democracy on the shop floor," no matter how much it helped performance, was not a plus.

Meanwhile, Tex Cook, the chairman of General Foods, made a formal visit to Topeka. At lunch, as Ketchum later recalled it, he mentioned all the help Charlie Krone had given. Cook once had been a star executive at Procter & Gamble; he had left for General Foods in 1950. "I still know the chairman of P&G," he said. "Would you like me to mention this to him?" Ketchum eagerly said yes, thinking it would help his friend. But it was the worst possible help he could have given Krone. First, it revealed that Krone had broken the secrecy barrier, and the *Atlantic* leaks were not a fluke. Worse still, General Foods and Procter & Gamble were competitors; both companies, for instance, made coffee. Perhaps worst of all, Tex Cook was not a credible source at P&G. He had committed one of P&G's most heinous cultural sins: leaving the company and doing well elsewhere.

Suddenly outside manufacturing consultants were banned at P&G on the grounds that they learned more than they imparted. The ban would last almost a decade. Krone was put under a form of house arrest, limited (as best as he could be limited) to Ivorydale (P&G's oldest plant, in Cincinnati) and Lima, and especially forbidden to work with other companies. Surreptitiously, however, he continued to bring outside managers into his consulting meetings. The first visitors, from the British chemical company ICI, were grudgingly accepted at Ivorydale because ICI was a Procter supplier and customer. Then Krone began to visit DuPont, whose managers showed up occasionally at the informal breakfast meetings he conducted in Cincinnati. From them, he began to get an idea of how much he could earn as an independent consultant.

The group of Procter & Gamble managers who had built the Lima plant, along with their wives, was coalescing into a tightly knit group of friends during the 1970s, a kind of midwestern Bloomsbury. They spent weekends together in impromptu study groups, instigated by Charlie's wife, Bonnie, in which they talked about Gurdjieff's ideas and the ramifications of their new workplace philosophy. It was not just a vehicle for increasing performance. They were creating a new type of community, they decided: a habitat that could raise the awareness and capability of the community's members. They read up on the great communal experiments of nineteenth-century America: Robert Owen's New Harmony, Indiana, and the transcendentalists' Brook Farm. Ultimately they even chipped in to buy and restore a run-down cattle farm in southern Indiana by hassling through the knotty questions that come up when people share a common property. Some of the members had teenage kids; some didn't. Some members had skills directly usable on the farm; others had never picked up a shovel. Some were willing to drive a hundred miles on a cold winter morning to empty the silage into feed bumpers so the cows could eat. How could the partnership compensate all these people fairly? In long meetings, the eleven couples gradually evolved a semiformal system so complicated that they never fully wrote it down. It couldn't be written down, because it depended on the informal web of relationships and trust that they had built between them.

Krone himself became more and more remote at Procter & Gamble. With an entrée through some of his UCLA contacts, he had begun to spend time on the West Coast. One day Krone's boss dropped in to the office of Charlie Eberle, another long-standing champion of the technician approach. "You know," said the visitor, "Charlie Krone is going into business for himself."

"I hadn't heard," Eberle said.

They were going to let him go, the visitor said matter-of-factly. "He'll make a hell of a lot more than we can pay him. We're really stretching now to keep his compensation where it is."

Years later Eberle remembered that exchange as an early signal of how Charlie Krone's style was changing. In 1977, at the suggestion of some of his UCLA contacts, the Krones moved away from Cincinnati to Carmel, California, to a house on the ocean in which Carl Rogers had once lived. Rumors began to circulate back at the conservative Cincinnati Procter & Gamble headquarters: Charlie was living in an ashram on a cliff. He conducted meetings in white robes, burning incense, while devotees in the audience chanted ritualistic hymns.

The reality was more prosaic. Starting with several faculty members and students from Stanford and UCLA, as well as some disenchanted managers, Charlie Krone had begun to assemble a core group of consultants who were eager to try the sorts of techniques that had worked at Lima in a wide variety of settings. Krone was more aware than ever before of the need to train people to lead such efforts, so he began to convene training sessions for them every six weeks—one series on the West Coast and one on the East. He opened the sessions by putting up his abstract "frameworks," like the flower diagram. Each one described a relationship between the structure of power, authority, or process flow at a workplace, and the attitudes and goals of the people in the situation. And then everyone would talk through the frameworks.

Krone wore sweaters and jeans, not robes, to his meetings, which he conducted with the same friendly, matter-of-fact approach that had served him well at P&G. He drove an old Mercedes from his Carmel seaside home to market and back, like his wealthy neighbors. He talked of mysticism, but he still combined it with practical stories of results achieved at Lima and elsewhere. He talked frequently, with admiration, about the achievements at Topeka. But pilot programs, limited to a single workplace or factory, would always fall short of the ideal. Krone was beginning to tackle with his small group of colleagues the same problem that had inspired Robert Blake and Jane Mouton's package of managerial grid instruments. Any significant change in the corporate world would have to take place on a large scale, involving the organization as a whole. It would have to be planned, with the breadth of a political campaign and the depth of a personal epiphany.

This challenge represented the central problem of corporate change, and at the time it looked as if Charlie Krone's group, with its blend of systems understanding, spiritual practice, work design, and practical engineering theory, might have a chance of solving it. Meanwhile, back at P&G, despite the company's strengths in operations compared to competitors, it would never again be a source of the underlying idea that Charlie Krone had fostered: that the right kind of systems awareness and practice could change the world, one factory at a time.

<hr>

Ketchum and Dulworth were themselves more vulnerable starting in 1973, in part because their most prominent protectors disappeared. Jim Stone, for instance, was promoted to run GF's Latin America/Far East division. Repercussions began to move against Ketchum as inexorably as the denouement of a Greek tragedy. Once, he returned to find his horizons literally shrunk: he had been moved into a smaller office. Instead of directing new plants, his job was reduced to advising the new plant managers. He had set up a network of sympathetic managers from different plants to compare techniques, but managers were discouraged from attending by their bosses. Plant managers were not supposed to talk regularly across channels. The corporate industrial engineering group conducted a major performance analysis and discredited Topeka's breakthroughs. (Years later it was recognized that the study was biased against Topeka and flawed in its accounting—for instance, the way it amortized the costs of new equipment.)

The worst blow to Ketchum's credibility at GF came when he was told to report to Betty Duval, the vice president in charge of organization development and compensation. Ten years earlier, Betty Duval and Ketchum might have been allies. As one of the first vice president–level women in the Fortune 500, she had come up through the training department. In the 1960s, she had brought T-Groups to General Foods—in effect, helping start Ketchum on the path that led him to the Topeka work. She still saw her role as changing the GF culture by putting the managers through communications training, to help them work together better across the barricades of the General Foods mafias. To Betty Duval, Ketchum's ideas were applicable strictly to the shop floor, with no broader interest. He, meanwhile, saw her as a politically motivated meddler without real power. It was as if they had been brought together to undermine each other.

"She tried to get me to become part of her team of OD consultants," Ketchum later said, "helping traditional factory managers learn to communicate better. The only trouble was that, under my system, there wouldn't be traditional factory managers. We didn't want to get people to fit into the system; we wanted to change the system. And she didn't want to hear me talk about that."

It was true that Ketchum could never explain clearly enough what he was trying to do. When he tried, all Duval heard was jargon. He'd talk about a "total systems approach," or he'd offer comments like, "This is the only way." It came across as too academic, too theoretical, too mysterious. Finally, he began to talk about the "Topeka phobia" at General Foods. People were afraid, he said, of opening their minds to see what Topeka had accomplished. Now senior managers began to complain to Duval: Couldn't she do anything about this missionary guy?

Resolved to prove everyone wrong, Ketchum teamed up with the amenable manager of a coffee plant in Hoboken, a plant with all the problems of Kankakee plus a union said to be controlled by organized crime. They were just starting to make progress when the Maxwell House operations manager pulled Ketchum out of Hoboken and told him to focus instead on a new Jell-O plant in Lafayette, Indiana, with one of the most authoritarian managers in the corporation. "If you can make this plant work under him," Ketchum was told, "then I believe your strategy could work anywhere." Ketchum gamely set out, returning to Hoboken in his spare time, and achieved some minor success at both plants. But he had no freedom to redesign the work processes from scratch, and he bitterly missed the collaboration he had enjoyed with the people at Topeka.

Other members of the team were, if anything, worse off. Many of the team leaders still at Topeka were eligible for promotions elsewhere, but nobody else in GF wanted them. Instead of being sought after, they seemed to have a kind of intellectual virus that no one else wanted to catch. Ed Dulworth was profoundly disillusioned with General Foods. When he talked privately with other General Foods managers—men he respected—about the performance gains, they were apathetic. "My boss isn't really interested in performance," they would say. Their talk turned quickly to matters that Dulworth thought of as "kissing ass": whose approval to get, what sort of presentation to make, and how to create a good impression. He turned down a promotion to product manager in White Plains, preferring the autonomy of being a plant manager in the outpost that he had come to think of as their little monastery. Inside, its halls rang with hope and laughter, but it stood forlornly alone in the fierce wind of the Kansas prairie.

---

o

Ketchum quietly lost his job at age fifty-seven in 1975. The last straw was "that damned Jell-O plant," where no one on either the management or the union side seemed to take to his ideas and everyone hated the attention he got outside the company. To top it all off, the price of sugar was rising so fast that the plant might never be profitable again. Why bother to save it?

He retired on a meager pension and opened a consulting business of his own. His first years of consulting were melancholy. Ketch was used to being considered an expert. Now he had to sell himself, like dozens of other organizational consultants, and without the faculty posts that many of them used to bolster their credibility. Back at General Foods headquarters, he had lost his close contact with Topeka, so he didn't fully realize that the people back at Topeka still regarded him as their own George Washington, the father of their new system. But he did expect Topeka's reputation to guarantee him a steady stream of consulting business. It didn't happen. A recession was raging. Few plant managers were interested in experimenting right then, particularly when it meant up-front investments. They had all they could handle trying to meet their quarterly targets.

That same year, at a meeting with the top management of the Post division, Ed Dulworth was asked by his boss to make a five-minute presentation. It was a routine request. In the political context of General Foods, it was a compliment, an invitation to make Topeka palatable to the brass. Any normal manager would have eagerly assented. But Dulworth was sick of the "usual bullshit." In front of the entire senior management, he told his boss that it was a "dumb idea." Five minutes wouldn't be enough time to present the Topeka concept in any way that made sense. "If they're interested," he said, "they can read about it."

Four weeks later, he was summoned to White Plains again and told he would be demoted to second-in-command at another plant, where someone else could supervise him. He just hadn't delivered the results at Topeka, they said, and he wasn't trustworthy. Then they mentioned that people said he was drinking too much. "I lived in a corporate culture where there was lots of drinking," he recalled later. "If I had a problem, then I knew a great number of people with the same problem, including some of my bosses. They used it as a crutch to get me, and shame me. We all knew that drinking was not the issue here."

Dulworth asked if he had any other options. They said he could resign, although his salary might continue for a while. None of his supporters felt able, or willing, to help. Ketchum was already gone. Jim Stone, out in Latin America, was thinking about retirement. "It's too bad," he told Dulworth, "but I'm not involved." Dick Walton, the sociotechnical consultant at Harvard, continued to write about Topeka. It defined his career, but he felt he had no influence on the senior management of General Foods; he barely knew anyone higher up than Ketchum. His interest turned to other companies.

So Dulworth resigned, and other Topeka managers also left. Soon, of the original team, only Don Lafond, the former union representative, remained. Perhaps because Lafond had started as an hourly worker, his reputation remained unscathed. Indeed, GF sent him to Puerto Rico for a while to start up a Tang plant. When he came back, Ed Dulworth was gone. Dulworth went on to several further careers: an executive at the Topps chewing gum company ("I walked away from the sale of that company with a lot of freedom"), an adviser to Pennsylvania governor Harris Wofford, and then a planner of the mid-1990s National Performance Review, the "reinventing government" initiative that Al Gore had sponsored from the White House. Meanwhile, for twenty-five years, he served as chairman of the board of a health care center in Scranton.

It took twenty-five years for the high-performance team system to die at Topeka. Dulworth's replacement was a long-standing pet food division manager who was told, when he started, that his mandate was to "cut out this missionary crap." But the team system was too deeply ingrained to change. After several years of great results and big bonuses, he became a Topeka system missionary himself. And when the new canned dog food plant opened next door, it too used the same approach.

Through the 1970s and 1980s, Topeka was the most productive plant in the General Foods system according to just about every measurement, including the satisfaction of people on the line. In 1984, when General Foods sold its pet food business to the Anderson Clayton conglomerate, the team structure persisted in a state of benign neglect. In 1986, when Quaker Oats bought all of Anderson Clayton, the Gaines dog food plant was the crown jewel of the acquisition, but Quaker made no attempt to extend the Topeka system anywhere else in its organization.

In March 1995, when Heinz acquired Quaker, it looked as if the new owners might finally put the experiment to sleep. Heinz's initial reaction was to make the plant conform to its policies: management shut down half the plant, eliminated the team system, suspended all the costly ongoing training that made the team system viable, and cut 150 jobs. But the team-based structure refused to roll over and play dead.

Starting in early 1996, Heinz performed a public about-face to broadcast its faith in the "Topeka system," calling it a model of where the company wanted to go. Training budgets and team meetings came back; pay-for-knowledge remained intact, people still rotated jobs, and teams determined assignments.[44] Then in 2002, Del Monte bought the company and expanded the plant further, but by some accounts, it discarded the remnants of the old sociotechnical approach.[45] Few people in the area remember that the plant was once a showplace.

Eric Trist passed away in 1993. Often depressed in his later years, fearing that his legacy had been lost, he had also had to have his leg amputated. But he continues to be remembered in management circles. Sociotechnical systems never became a professional field in the same way that organizational development did. But Trist and his colleagues inspired not just a few heretics like Ketchum and Dulworth and Krone, but thousands of people in organizations around the world to recognize that hard and soft systems—technologies and human practices—could work effectively only when they are redesigned from the ground up, in an experimental vein. That message has grown more and less popular at various times, but it has never been completely lost. It has been proven true too many times. Even the Roman Catholic church eventually admitted that Galileo's cosmology was correct—after 359 years.

4

PROTESTERS

SAUL ALINSKY, FIGHTON, CAMPAIGN GM, AND THE
SHAREHOLDER ACTIVISM MOVEMENT, 1964–1971

---

*Heresy: A company can move itself forward only by
moving its community forward.*

Into a twelfth-century village in Poland, or France, or the Low
Countries, a protester against the Church would stride.
He would find a high spot not far from the local church's outer
wall. He would position himself so that members of a gathering
crowd could turn their eyes easily from his face to the spire and
back to his face again.

"We propose to give knowledge and understanding of the true
Church of God," he would say. And they would fall silent: they knew
he was drawing a contrast, as audaciously as he dared, between the
institution as it ought to be and the local priests who presided in
the building before them. "This Church," he would say, "is not made
of stones or wood, or of anything made by hand, for it is written in
the Acts of the Apostles that the Most High dwelleth not in houses
made by hands." As they listened, men in the crowd could feel the
calluses on their fingers, or hear again the stories of fathers or grand-
fathers who had carried stones to this building.

"This Church refrains from adultery and all uncleanness," the man would say, and one or two women in the crowd would feel their lips tighten as they remembered a piece of gossip they had heard about the rector—or a glance from him. "This Church refrains from theft or robbery," the protester would say, and the wine merchant would think of the triplefold tithe that he had paid, while others thought of the gold rings that the cardinals wore. "This Church refrains from lying and from bearing false witness," the man would say. "This Church refrains from oaths. This Church refrains from killing." With every line, bitter memories would disturb the faces in the crowd. And finally, in a reference to himself, "This Church suffers persecutions and tribulations and martyrdom in the name of Christ."[1]

By then the priest would have had time to hear of the protester's presence. An angry force of three or four men might arrive, ready to seize him for a trial. Or perhaps the speaker would merely slink away, his speech incomplete. In evenings in someone's home, in the privacy of a more ardent group, he would add to the sermon. The sacraments were not real, and did not count, he would say, if they were performed by immoral priests. The "ravening wolves in sheep's clothing" whom Rome had ordained could not rightly preside over baptism or communion.[2] The people should take back their Church.

"Are you saying," a voice might inject from the back of the room, "that the sacraments are so weak that a mere priest can corrupt them?" Augustine had used this question against the Donatists eight hundred years before. Authority, after all, does not come from the priests. It comes from the Church as a whole. If your priest, or any local administrator, is corrupt, then you need not fear, for the system is stronger than the abuses of any of its members. The system will take care of you.

But if your argument is with the authority as a whole, it is senseless to criticize the priest. The priest is just a tiny reflection of a corrupt institution. Having come this far, you must take the next step. You must criticize the establishment that put the priest in place and the sacraments that were given to him. But that is unfathomable and unthinkable, because those foundations come from God. To question them is to move into exile.[3]

○

ONE COULD ARGUE THAT THE MODERN American middle class was born
in January 1914 when Henry Ford dramatically raised his autoworkers'
minimum wage to five dollars per day. The wage hike was part of a larger
campaign that included sick leave, an eight-hour day, and protection from
such abuses as arbitrary dismissal by supervisors, which had the effect of
attracting higher-skilled employees, reducing turnover, and raising productivity.[4] Ford, then regarded as one of America's greatest industrialists,
was not doing all this just to help his own workers afford automobiles.
He publicized the idea in the hope that other companies would follow
suit and thus engender a far broader customer base for the automobile.
To meet the demand he was creating, he planned a great new "super-
plant" along the River Rouge plant, an all-inclusive automobile assembly
line that would create entire cars from raw iron, limestone, and glass.

But even as other businesses began to follow Ford's example, his shareholders rebelled. Two of them, the machinist brothers John and Horace
Dodge, sued him in 1916 for breach of fiduciary responsibility. He was
reducing his prices, increasing his wages, and expanding his plant, they
complained, rather than releasing dividends to them. The plaintiffs' lawyer pressed Ford on the witness stand: Hadn't he stated publicly that he
had as much money as he needed? Yes, he said, he was one of the wealthi-
est men in the country. Was it his conscience, sneered the lawyer, that
wouldn't let him make such "awful profits"?

"I don't know that my conscience has anything to do with it," replied
Ford. "It isn't good business." He wanted to enlarge his operations, he
said, "to do as much good as possible for everybody concerned." And
when the lawyer pressed him to say what he meant by that, Ford said:
"To make money and use it, give employment, and send out the car
where people can use it. . . . And incidentally to make money."

"*Incidentally?*" echoed the lawyer.

"That's right," said Ford. "Business is a service, not a bonanza."

The lawyer tried to put it in the worst possible light: "Your controlling
feature, then, is to employ a great army of men at high wages, to reduce
the selling price of your car so that a lot of people can buy it at a cheap
price, and give everybody a car that wants one?"

"If you give all that," said Ford simply, "the money will fall into your
hands; you can't get out of it." That remark added to Henry Ford's public luster, but it lost him the case. Making shareholders wealthy in the
short run, ruled the judge, should not be incidental to making everyone
wealthy in the long run. And he ordered $19 million in dividends paid to
the Dodge brothers.[5]

The perennial battle over corporate responsibility and accountability—the roots of a governance crisis that persists to this day—dates back to that exchange. In part, Ford was driven by his own grandiose ambition (he ran unsuccessfully for the U.S. Senate soon after this episode). But he also had an instinct for the purpose of his business—his biographers agree that more than anything else, he wanted, through his machine, to make a mark on the world—and he trusted his instincts more than he ever trusted the numbers. Ultimately his instincts failed him, and he famously lost market share through the 1920s to General Motors, which offered a greater variety of cars tailored to different customer needs. In 1930, at the dawn of the Great Depression, he tried his familiar tactic again. He cut car prices and raised wages to seven dollars per day. This time it didn't work; within a year, he had to drop his own minimum wage back below his once-sacrosanct five dollars.[6]

--------------------- o ---------------------

Ford may have outlived his prime as a business leader, but he understood one thing that many businesspeople tragically lost sight of after the 1950s: a corporation exists to return profits on shareholders' investments. But that leaves an enormous amount of discretion to managers. When should those profits be returned? Every quarter? Every year? Or, as Henry Ford suggested, is the return of profits to shareholders an "incidental" by-product of making life better for customers and employees in the long run?

Any manager continually balances the value that may come from a long-term investment against the time it takes to receive the returns.[7] Moreover, the responsibility of profit says nothing about the vagaries of fate. Is it acceptable to invest heavily on a risky future? And in the process of returning profits, does the company owe anything to the rest of the public, even if paying off that more evanescent debt makes the bottom line suffer this quarter?

A manager who thinks seriously about these issues will recognize after a while that defining a corporate purpose means balancing a group of loyalties.[8] True, the shareholder is guaranteed profit and control. But the corporate manager has also signed a contract with government—the corporate charter, dating back to the European monarchs—in which the manager agrees not just to respect public laws but to contribute to public welfare, in exchange for protections against legal liability. There are also contracts, implicit or explicit, with unions (which are organized to bargain for stable employment) and with customers (who want the cheapest, best product, without hidden hazards).[9]

Finally, there is an implicit contract, vaguest of all, with the community. It is much like the implicit contract in medieval times between a church and its village. The church had the power of its far-flung organization, its Inquisitorial police, and its accepted link with God. There could be no greater power. But if there were visible simony, lechery, or corruption among the priests, then in the long run, protests would overwhelm the church. Similarly, today, the community wants the corporation to act in an exalted fashion: to be a delightful neighbor, refrain from polluting, contribute to the common good, and employ people in good faith. In exchange, the community will act neighborly itself. It will meet corporate initiatives halfway—to improve the schools, for instance, or reconstruct regulations. It will hold protest in abeyance.

This bargain works as long as the corporation and the community coexist with the same basic values. But in the 1960s, the prevailing values changed in many parts of the United States. It happened first in the civil rights movement, which redefined the boundaries of community. Civic responsibility no longer meant paying attention to the needs of the "nice" part of the city alone; rather, the demands of the whole community had to be met. Corporations didn't immediately follow suit, and the contract between corporation and community fragmented.

○

Consider, for example, the fragmentation that overtook the Kodak Corporation in the mid-1960s. If ever a neighborly company existed, that was Eastman Kodak. It was founded by a nineteenth-century bachelor named George Eastman, who lived with his mother all his life in the city of Rochester, New York, and who deliberately promoted civic responsibility. Eastman founded the city's Community Chest, along with a renowned school of music and a community theater. Under his guidance and after his death, Kodak always contributed generously to the city's hospitals, schools, and charities: $22 million between 1954 and 1964. As far as civil rights were concerned, Kodak's boosters could imagine no reason for complaint; the company sponsored a fellowship program for black schoolteachers and contributed generously to the United Negro College Fund. Kodak had been an early participant in John F. Kennedy's Equal Employment Opportunity Plan for Progress program, and in 1964 it had recently expanded its recruitment efforts to include black colleges.

Internally the company was also benevolent. Kodak people participated in the rewards of the company's success (the Instamatic cartridge-film camera, a marketing triumph, had come out only a few years before).

They were paid high salaries and generous annual bonuses averaging two thousand dollars per employee—most of whom took for granted that once they were in the door, they were employees for life. The senior managers of the firm were all well educated and straitlaced. The president, William Vaughn (he was about to become CEO), was a tall patrician man, originally from Tennessee. He maintained the same strict rules of propriety that had existed since George Eastman's day. Executives who kept secretaries after 5:00 P.M. had to call in a chaperone, and no one was reimbursed for liquor on a Kodak expense account.[10]

But if people felt well rewarded and well protected, they also tended to feel disoriented, at least when they worked on the factory floor. The old joke about traditional management practice being like mushroom farming ("Keep them in the dark and feed them manure") was bittersweet at Kodak, where light-sensitive film was manufactured in total darkness. As if to add to their disorientation, the plant had staggered schedules; workers alternated among the day shift, the night shift, and the graveyard shift, always without light. (A union would never have permitted that, which was one reason that Kodak's senior managers felt so phobic about organized labor.)

And to those outside the company, particularly the black people of Rochester, the company was an object of seething resentment. It was the largest employer in Rochester, and it had never let them into the family. In 1964 twenty thousand black residents lived in Rochester, crowded into a few neighborhoods where landlords rented to them. Most of them had come up from the southern states in search of jobs; now they lived in tenements with twenty-four or twenty-eight families squeezed into houses designed for two. Their unemployment rate reached almost 15 percent, three times as great as the white neighborhoods.[11] Churches were weak; only three thousand residents of the area went to church regularly. Street gangs were strong and growing stronger. The major employer in the neighborhood, the Rochester Institute of Technology, was already making plans to move to the suburbs.[12]

The leaders of "old, monied, Episcopalian, upper-class Rochester" tended to pooh-pooh the city's racial problems.[13] Frederick Douglass had published his papers on the abolition of slavery there. It had been one of the key stops on the Underground Railroad. It had no machine politics, a strong tradition of Jane Addams-style settlement houses, and high average salaries.

Why had prosperity not reached the city's black underclass? No doubt all the familiar factors were responsible: suspicion and resentment between the races, ingrained inequities, the inherent erosion of capability built into an underclass lifestyle, the suburban exodus of the middle class, and the pitiless barriers built into Rochester's educational system, banking habits, and hiring structures. Automation had also begun to play a part; opportunities for high-paying unskilled factory work, which had been an essential enabler of upward mobility for thirty years, were increasingly scarce. A contingent from Rochester took part in the 1963 March on Washington for civil rights, where three hundred thousand people shouted not just "Freedom Now!" but also "Jobs Now!"[14]

o

Rochester's riots took place in July 1964. They started, as riots often did, when white police entered a black neighborhood. One Friday night, a canine squad came in to answer a call about a disruptive man at a neighborhood block party dance. Many people in that neighborhood believed that the Rochester police deliberately used dogs to harass blacks, and a group of men who had been at the dance began throwing rocks at them. As the violence escalated, the police were rapidly forced to retreat. Within three days, four people had been killed and hundreds hurt; scores of stores had been damaged and looted; nearly a thousand people were arrested; and the governor, Nelson Rockefeller, had sent in the National Guard.[15]

The riot paralyzed Rochester's aristocracy; they could no longer represent themselves as one of the most benevolent cities in the North. Into the void came Rochester's Third Presbyterian Church. Before the federal War on Poverty began, churches in northern cities had often bankrolled independent community organizing efforts—generally with tacit support from all of a city's varied interest groups, from businesses to unions to the ghetto. With twenty-five hundred members, Third Presbyterian was one of the largest, most established churches in the city. Faced with a shortage of pastors, it had recently hired a thirty-two-year-old (white) minister named Paul Long, a slim, brash man with the kind of rich, deep voice that a disk jockey might have coveted. Long had been arrested and jailed during civil rights demonstrations in Mississippi the previous summer, one of thousands of northerners arrested in southern protests in 1963. Now, in the wake of the riot, he convened a six-week study group, meeting Thursday nights, to talk about a book by *Fortune* magazine writer Charles Silberman. *Crisis in Black and White* traced the history of racism in the northern American cities, predicted the cities could explode in riots (a few months before they did), and featured, as the best hope for fighting poverty and forestalling turmoil, a community organizer named Saul Alinsky.

Saul Alinsky's organization, the Industrial Arts Foundation, had an unparalleled track record for teaching slum dwellers to improve their own neighborhood conditions, often beginning by winning over the neighborhood's delinquent gangs. In most Alinsky campaigns, a figure-head leader (often Alinsky himself) would berate established leaders in speeches and newspaper articles. Meanwhile, organizers would fan out into the neighborhoods, ringing doorbells, starting block clubs, and building trust through gatherings in churches and homes. They shared information (about which landlords, for instance, were the most negli-gent), planned tactics (about how to picket the landlords' homes), and provided day-to-day advice on coping with government services or cut-ting down electric bills. The central idea was to build up the savvy and self-esteem of leaders from the communities themselves. Industrial Arts Foundation–sponsored meetings, in fact, were a bit like T-Groups in the freewheeling quality of their conversation. But instead of focusing on the group's behavior, the meetings taught people how to make a solid impact on the forces of the world outside. Within a few months of an Alinsky campaign, these people, with only high school educations, knew how to track down obscure public hearings, show up at those hearings en masse, and ask the expert lawyers and planners whether they'd remember to get the right approvals for, say, a freeway they proposed building through a poor neighborhood.

Alinsky himself cultivated flamboyance. The son of a Russian Jewish tailor who had emigrated to Chicago, he had an immediately recogniz-able warmth, set within an acerbic, brassy bluntness and a talent for self-promotion. At a retreat for Stanford M.B.A. students, he boasted that he couldn't get a life insurance company to sell him a policy because he was too likely a target. He cheerfully walked a tightrope between the wealthy patrons whose grants he courted and the impoverished people whom his organizations had to galvanize. Most of his speeches were built around comedy routines. Arguing with the political leaders of a city, Alinsky would compare himself to Moses arguing with God about destroying the Jewish people: "Look, God, you're God. You're holding all the cards. Whatever you want to do, you can do and nobody can stop you. . . . What do you care if people are going to say, 'There goes God. You can't believe anything he tells you. You can't make a deal with him. His word isn't even worth the stone it's written on.'"[16]

Paul Long, the young Presbyterian minister, brought five white and three black Rochester church leaders to Alinsky's office in Chicago that November. He had met Alinsky once before, when he spent a summer with a Chicago community organizing group. But to the other Rochester people, Alinsky was a third choice; Martin Luther King's Southern Christian Leadership Conference and Whitney Young's Urban League had turned them down. Alinsky had offers from two other communities, and he put them through a screening. Were they sure that they wanted him to get the attention of their smug city leaders? Once he began, he said, life in Rochester would never be the same.

While they thought about it, he had them take him to lunch at an elegant restaurant in Chicago, where the church leaders had trouble flagging their waitress. Alinsky smiled at them. "Do you really want her attention?" he asked. They nodded. "No, listen to what I'm saying," he said. "Do you *really* want her attention?" They assented again. Alinsky took up a plate from the table, held it high for a moment, and smashed it on the floor. The waitress came running, flushed with anger, while the church leaders sat aghast, looking at him. "We got her attention," Alinsky said.

He finally offered to bring his organization to Rochester for two years, for the extraordinary sum of $100,000—up front, with no strings attached. He and the organization would account for it, but they would spend it as they saw fit. But he wouldn't come into the black community, he said, unless black churches and organizations, not just their white counterparts, invited him. He began to muse about possible tactics to make the Rochester ghetto problems impossible to ignore. They could buy four hundred tickets to the Rochester symphony for blacks, hold a giant baked bean dinner just before the event, "and then fart the symphony out of existence. How would that go over in Rochester? Wouldn't people love that?"[17] To make sure the farting incident never happened again, he explained, the city leaders would agree to anything that the churches wanted. People in power would make the right choices, he said, only for the wrong reasons.

Despite their misgivings—Would he make the community placid again or incite the violence further?—the church leaders raised the money. To this day, Reverend Long isn't quite sure what convinced some of the donors, especially since public opposition to Alinsky was mounting fast among Rochester conservatives. Almost immediately on signing the contract, Alinsky polarized things further, casting himself as a lightning rod of resentment and outrageousness. Reporters quoted him calling the city a "little Congo" and a "huge southern plantation transported North." Privately he cheerfully admitted that his accusations were unfair. "The one thing that is certain to get your enemy to react," he said, "is to laugh at him."[18] The white establishment wasn't laughing. Alinsky had soon collected many of the most prominent Rochester citizens as his enemies. Paul Miller, the president of the Gannett paper, became a bitter and visible enemy, including many members of the Presbyterian church where Paul Long gave impassioned sermons on Alinsky's behalf on Sundays.

Meanwhile, Alinsky and his organizers moved into the black wards. Their first step was to cultivate black leaders, who were frankly suspicious of him. ("I don't know if you can trust me," Alinsky agreed. "You'd better watch me."[19]) A stocky pastor at the Church of Christ named Franklin Delano Roosevelt Florence—a friend of Malcolm X's who had marched in Selma, Alabama, and spoken out against the arrest of Black Muslims in Rochester—emerged as the president of a new organization, which they christened FIGHT, to show that they expected battles. (It was an acronym for "Freedom, Integration, Honor, God, Today.")[20] Following Alinsky's methods, FIGHT was set up as a coalition of smaller groups, based in social clubs, churches, pool halls, and beauty salons, each with its own leaders—a community equivalent to the self-organizing teams of Topeka and Lima. Florence was a naturally gifted, albeit inflammatory, leader, who showed up at most meetings wearing bib overalls and routinely kept his white supporters waiting two hours or more at appointments. "Why do you put up with that?" Paul Long's friends would ask him. But as he later put it, the encounters were cathartic and exciting: "All of a sudden, a black guy was rubbing our nose in what we'd been rubbing his nose in for three hundred years."

Florence also attacked middle-class blacks, the Urban League, and (foreshadowing the racial crises of the late 1980s) FIGHT's Jewish supporters. In a public argument with a Jewish superintendent of schools, Florence snapped, "That's the trouble with you Jews when you get your color up." In the mini-furor that followed, Alinsky tried to defend him by arguing that Negroes were hostile to all whites. Jews were simply more visible in the ghettos.[21] Somehow the ugliness got smoothed over, but Florence always had to battle against the discomfort which many white citizens of Rochester felt around him.

His hard-liner's attitude served him, however, in the black wards. These were the years of nascent Black Power. To be black and young in the early 1960s was to feel completely, irredeemably, and undeservedly shut out of American opportunity. As the first large-scale coalition to be organized by blacks in Rochester, FIGHT was credible only when it gave voice to that resentment. Thus, white sympathizers were not allowed to join FIGHT—not the whites who had hired Alinsky or even Alinsky himself. The white churches, Alinsky agreed, were not supposed to be like colonial powers, "sending in missionaries whether they're invited or not."[22] To provide a place for the whites, Florence and the Alinsky co-organizers hurriedly set up an auxiliary called Friends of FIGHT.

The Reverend Long was one of its first presidents. Florence took over the central role, and Alinsky stepped a bit into the background to act as his adviser.

During the next two years, there were no riots. FIGHT's leaders lobbied for and won a city-funded public housing corporation, mandated to build housing on undeveloped land. They trained black people to pass civil service examinations and developed job training programs with Xerox, the second-largest Rochester company. Despite their inflammatory rhetoric (at their first major meeting, Florence refused to shake any of the Xerox executives' hands), the Xerox people felt that FIGHT's people acted with integrity. FIGHT leaders didn't leak, for instance, any of Xerox's confidential information.[23] And they followed through on their promise to be responsible for the trainees: "to prepare them for the world of work," as Florence said, "getting up on time, making sure they had transportation, following them on Friday to make sure they didn't drink all weekend."[24] While other cities were mired in rioting, FIGHT (and Alinsky) got much of the credit for Rochester's peace.

All along, Alinsky wanted FIGHT to go after Eastman Kodak. The company employed 13 percent of the city's labor force, but its forty thousand employees included only fourteen hundred blacks. More important, Alinsky said, Rochester was under Kodak's thumb. The company was more powerful than the government, particularly when factoring in its influence. "If we can get Kodak in line," the Reverend Florence preached, "every other business would follow."

Thus, on September 2, 1966, Franklin Florence walked into the company headquarters with fifteen other members of FIGHT and demanded to speak with "the top man." They were taken to meet the three highest officials of the company, including the president, William Vaughn. Florence gave an impromptu speech about the problems of blacks in Rochester's ghetto and asked the Kodak leaders to set up a job training program for people who couldn't meet the regular Kodak recruitment standards. Vaughn replied that Kodak already had one. But Alinsky and Florence kept returning with new proposals, which they couched as demands.[25] Over an eighteen-month period, Kodak should hire and train between five hundred and six hundred black people for entry-level positions. FIGHT, as the only mass organization of poor people in the area, should recruit them. Kodak resisted. Alinsky and Florence organized a letter-writing and publicity campaign. Kodak announced an end run: expanding its training programs through another organization, a competitor to FIGHT. Florence was enraged; he and Alinsky stepped up the media pressure.

In principle, Kodak managers agreed that opportunities for blacks should be increased, but they didn't see that this was Kodak's responsibility. Let the blacks pull themselves up, as every other ethnic group in America had done, to the point where Kodak would want to hire them. The blacks had rioted; they had destroyed their own neighborhood. Why should a private company like Kodak assume any greater share of their burden? And even if they did, why should they accept this group, FIGHT, as the vehicle for their contribution? Florence replied that Kodak already had the burden, like it or not, because of its size and influence. And he and his group were qualified, because of their track record and their engagement; they'd taken up the issue. Moreover, FIGHT would not stop the pressure, he insisted. Anyone who looked at both organizations could see that an impasse was inevitable. You could see it in their buildings: "FIGHT's shabby storefront," one writer put it, "versus Kodak's carpeted tower on State Street."[26]

Then that December, a miracle took place. With startling suddenness, Kodak agreed to hire six hundred people referred by FIGHT. The FIGHT trainers agreed in turn to provide counseling and support. A joint Kodak-FIGHT committee would nail down "job openings, specifications, and hourly rates"—as well as make announcements to the press. It was a ground-breaking agreement and a dramatic boost to FIGHT's credibility. It might have made a significant difference to the future of Kodak. But it lasted less than a day.

---------------- o ----------------

A heretic within Kodak named John T. Mulder engineered the agreement that December. Like Ed Dulworth of the Gaines dog food plant in Topeka, he was a manufacturing guy—assistant vice president of operations, in charge of the company's largest Rochester plant, which manufactured film. Mulder was a sandy-haired, quiet, good-natured man, with thirty years of service to Kodak behind him and a genuine affection for his company. He had a large house on Lake Ontario, one of the first to have a swimming pool. He and his wife, who taught Sunday school at the Third Presbyterian Church, were among the most dedicated, meticulous people that the Reverend Long had ever met.

Mulder was also one of a growing group of people within Kodak who were sympathetic to FIGHT's ideas. He and his wife were veteran settlement house volunteers. His wife was a member of Friends of FIGHT, and both Mulders had belonged to the discussion group for *Crisis in Black and White*—the group that had been so instrumental in contacting Alinsky in the first place. As a long-standing plant manager, Mulder had a visceral sense of the ways in which the company's doors were unofficially closed to black workers. And he had an innate understanding of how race made no difference to an assembly line, particularly one where the workers couldn't even see each other.

One night during the months when FIGHT was waging its publicity campaign against Kodak, Mulder met with a friend who was a FIGHT leader, a reverend named Marvin Chandler. Together they developed a plan, which Mulder drafted and submitted to his superiors. It suggested that instead of talking with senior leaders, the FIGHT team should negotiate with the operations managers, who were, after all, directly responsible for hiring and training. With a sense of genteel relief (we may imagine), Vaughn agreed. He deputized John Mulder to head the Kodak delegation and authorized him to agree on a program with FIGHT. Mulder and Florence began meeting on December 19 in a room at the Downtowner Motor Inn.

Mulder had a pragmatic problem solver's mind. When he heard what FIGHT wanted—jobs for a large number of people, with the community organization involved in recruitment—his response was simple: "We can handle that." In fact, the idea sounded like an enlightened operations manager's boon: a chance to open the doors of the plant and learn from FIGHT's community leaders, while they in turn gained a hands-on understanding of what Kodak really needed from its workforce. Perhaps they could find a way to convert uneducated people into high-quality Kodak workers en masse. If so, Mulder must have reasoned, then they would have a huge jump on competitors, particularly in those years when the supply of young workers had begun to dwindle (in part because of the Vietnam War draft). During his meeting with Florence, Mulder kept calling Vaughn's office, and each time he got an approval to increase the number of trainees. On the second day, they settled on six hundred. The number seemed so large that Reverend Florence repeatedly asked Mulder, "Are you sure you are authorized to sign this?" He insisted that he was.

Around three o'clock that afternoon, a high-level Kodak manager called Louis Eilers, the incoming Kodak president: "Mulder has signed an agreement with FIGHT." The manager had heard about it on the radio. It had been billed as a great victory for the black organization.

"The hell he has!" Eilers snapped. He sent for Mulder and the agreement and sharply dressed him down. The next day, the executive committee met and repudiated the agreement. They knew it would be awful to renege in public, but they believed it would be worse to let the deal go through. Officially, as William Vaughn related it to *Fortune* later, Mulder had misunderstood his charter. Kodak could not enter into a direct relationship with FIGHT "and still be fair to the more than 60,000 people who apply each year."[27]

Unofficially there were several problems. Mulder had misunderstood his charter: they had expected him to negotiate some cosmetic settlement, not give away the company's sovereignty. The company's chief counsel, summoned to Eilers's office, had taken one look at the agreement and said, "This is a hiring law. We're involved with the National Labor Relations Board if we agree to this." That would be outrageous, particularly for a nonunion company that had successfully repelled several successful labor-organizing attempts. It could even open the doors to a fierce battle with organized labor.

Moreover, FIGHT was (in their view) a rabble-rousing group whose leaders were interested in power, not constructive change. They made inflammatory speeches and embarrassed and threatened their white supporters, and they could do the same to Kodak at any time. Saul Alinsky admitted as much: "It's only when the other part feels threatened that he will listen," he would say. FIGHT also, in Kodak's eyes, inflated the size of their constituency. (The organization claimed, through 110 community groups, to have 75 percent of the black population of Rochester among their memberships.[28]) Preoccupied with rational objections like these, Kodak's leaders overlooked the essential nature of interest group power. At any time, it could be taken away when members withdrew their membership. Even if there were manipulators at the top, the fundamental power rested in the community behind them. Unlike a corporation, where leaders set an agenda, the direction of a community emerged from the fears and hopes of the whole.

------------------ o ------------------

Mulder's friend Marvin Chandler had planned a Christmas party that night, with Franklin Florence as one of the guests. Around ten-thirty, Mulder showed up, pale and distraught, announcing that Kodak was repudiating the agreement. "He looked," Florence said later, "like he'd been in the hands of the KGB." Eilers lost no time making a public statement; the partygoers saw it on the eleven o'clock news. Alinsky was out of town, but his associate Ed Chambers and Florence immediately called a community meeting the next morning, if only to forestall a riot. There, Florence preached to an overflow crowd, excoriating the whites for not backing FIGHT enough. It was getting harder and harder, he said, to convince his ghetto constituents that they had a chance for a better life. Tensions were so high that one white preacher hung himself that afternoon, convinced that the city would go up in flames. But it didn't. Being organized into small groups, people apparently didn't feel the need to riot. Florence met privately with Eilers three times in the next few days. For the first time, the FIGHT leader agreed not to call their agreement a contract. Or Kodak leaders could dispense with the agreement altogether if they would appear with Florence on television, promising joint cooperation. Florence knew that if he didn't get Kodak to keep its word, his own credibility in black Rochester was at stake. Perhaps Eilers had exactly that in mind when he refused.

Publicly Florence took the only course left that would give him political survival: he stiffened. He began to hold public press conferences, calling Kodak "institutionally racist" and saying that the company's dishonesty would produce "troubled times, grave times, for the total community."[29] Eilers, meanwhile, held his own press conferences, where he accused FIGHT of running a continuing war on Rochester's Community Chest and schools. During the next few months, whenever Kodak had a training or recruiting session, FIGHT members were there protesting.

Publicly Eilers said there would be no change in John Mulder's job, but Mulder's future within the company was destroyed. He was stripped not just of his negotiating role but of his vice presidency. Then he was moved into a backwater position at Kodak Park. In retrospect, Mulder might have expected the reaction. Another Kodak manager had been stripped of his security clearance simply for standing up at a church and voicing support for Alinsky. But Mulder had such an exemplary record that it took him by surprise; he hadn't known he would be branded as a heretic. He refused to speak to the press and bowed out of the public eye. He would remain at Kodak, a quietly tragic figure, until his retirement. Within a few days, the negotiations ceased.

In mid-January 1967, Stokely Carmichael arrived in Rochester, threatening a national Black Power boycott of Kodak. Alinsky was impatient with the idea. "You couldn't ask the country to stop taking pictures," he said. But they needed some vehicle to carry the battle outside Rochester. Alinsky toyed with the idea of bringing Kodak up on antitrust charges and then stumbled across a much more provocative idea: they would hold a grand demonstration at Kodak's annual meeting of shareholders. He didn't fully understand its implications, but it clearly had immense possibilities.

○

Decades before, a crusader had tried to organize shareholders to criticize management at annual meetings. Lewis Gilbert was a young heir who began showing up at shareholder meetings in the 1930s to press managers to take fewer bonuses for themselves. He later wrote a book about his efforts, *Dividends and Democracy,* in which he talked of making annual meetings into "a modern extension of the New England town meeting."[30] The Securities and Exchange Commission (SEC) bolstered his efforts in 1942 by ruling that corporations had to mail out shareholder-proposed resolutions in their proxy mailings (the mailings that invited shareholders to allow some proxy, typically the corporate management, to cast the votes for their shares). Despite his idealistic metaphor, Gilbert's concerns were entirely limited to financial matters. He was not unlike the Dodge Brothers in their lawsuit against Henry Ford. He tended to see managers as insidious thieves, frittering away the money they should have been returning to shareholders. Even if he had been interested in other concerns, he would have been fettered by SEC rules, which permitted only raising concerns about financial performance and corporate governance. No political resolutions were allowed.

Kodak's annual meeting was scheduled for April 23, 1967, in a public school auditorium in Flemington, New Jersey, about fifteen miles northwest of Princeton. Like many other corporate annual meetings, it was held in a relatively obscure location to discourage casual participation by minority shareholders like Lewis. FIGHT spent $1,442.65 to buy ten shares, which meant that ten people could enter and raise objections from the floor. But Alinsky had something else in mind: he wanted thousands of protesters to descend on that annual meeting, and he was prepared to use the next two months to lobby with Kodak's existing shareholders to let some FIGHT member attend in their place and cast their votes for management. "Remember, these are not hippies," he insisted, "but American citizens in the most establishment sense—stockholders! What could be more American than that?"[31]

Though Alinsky probably didn't realize it, structural shifts in the economy had made the time ripe for shareholder protest in a way it had never been before. Since the early 1950s, the predominant ownership of corporate stock had shifted from investment banks to new types of shareholding institutions.[32] A typical company had 40 percent of its stock owned by pension funds, and pension funds (through bonds) typically controlled 40 percent of most companies' debts.[33] After a stock slowdown in 1966, the pension fund managers began to compare notes on the performance of their investments more carefully.

"I don't think anybody really knew," an AT&T pension fund manager named John English recollected years later, "how well or how poorly funds were doing until 1967."[34] But now that they knew, they began to impose more pressure on managers of companies whose shares they held. They demanded meetings with senior officials, wrote letters asking for better share performance, and even made timid threats to vote against the management's proxies—the officially approved candidates for the company's board of directors.[35] Since some of the largest pension funds were for public employees, such as teachers or social workers, their managers often had political backgrounds. These funds, as well as church groups, were attuned to Alinsky's idea: using the power of their position to pressure Kodak—in this case, to reach a settlement with FIGHT.

There was no resolution about the FIGHT dispute before the Kodak shareholders, but that didn't matter. Alinsky embarked on a six-week campaign, calling as many people as he could reach, to get Kodak shareholders to sign their proxy ballots over to FIGHT's name. Within a few weeks, the national representatives of Presbyterians, Episcopalians, the National Church of Christ, and Unitarians all announced publicly (albeit hesitantly) that they were withholding their Kodak stock proxies from management.

Before, the Kodak senior executives had been irritated. Now they were shocked. William Vaughn and a Kodak in-house lawyer actually traveled to New York to try to dissuade (without success) two church groups from giving Alinsky their support. At first glance, the Kodak managers' distress seems out of proportion; after all, Alinsky's allies controlled only forty thousand shares out of eighty million—barely half a percent in a real vote.[36] However, the announcement of the proxy fight piqued the curiosity of news reporters and politicians. New York's Republican senator, Jacob Javits, contacted Kodak with an offer to help mediate, and the Democratic senator, Robert Kennedy, offered to engineer a Senate subcommittee hearing if Alinsky gave the word. Kodak's managers could see themselves hauled before Congress, or permanently pilloried, at least in business circles, as the executives who could not keep their own shareholders under control.

Still, nobody gave in. By early April, Alinsky, Florence, and the FIGHT leaders had organized buses to Flemington from Rochester and from several universities: Cornell, Dartmouth, Princeton, and Yale. Kodak bused in its own employees, apparently enough to fill the auditorium. On April 23, the night before the meeting, William Vaughn, who had just succeeded Eilers as company president, went down on his knees at the Princeton Inn, where he was staying, and prayed that everything would come out right. ("If Saul Alinsky had only known that he had, so to speak, brought Kodak to its knees," wrote Alinsky's biographer, Sanford Horwitt, "he would have been a very happy man."[37]) Alinsky spent the evening talking to reporters, chortling about the Kodak security guards in his motel: "Kodak's afraid that if somebody knocks me off, they'll get blamed for it." The town braced itself: streets were lined with a hundred state troopers along with local police officers, most of them expecting a riot. Many of the stores in Flemington were closed.

Seven hundred FIGHT supporters marched to the auditorium the next morning. Ten people, including Alinsky and Florence, were admitted, while a few shareholders in the audience murmured that they should be thrown out. Taking the measure of the room, Alinsky decided that they should make a quick statement and leave. So as soon as Vaughn's gavel hit the podium, Florence stood up and cried for a point of order. "We'll give you until two o'clock to honor that agreement," he shouted, and then walked out with Alinsky, the rest of the FIGHT delegation, and about twenty other sympathetic shareholders.

They remained outside the rest of the day, surrounded by television cameras and demonstrators. Inside Vaughn gently suggested that "FIGHT deserves credit for putting pressure on us." All of the officers supported by Kodak's management won their ballots. No one within raised a question about the demonstration. At two o'clock, the reverend reentered and asked Vaughn, again, whether he would honor the agreement with FIGHT. Vaughn simply said, "No." Florence marched out, back to the TV cameras, to denounce the company.

The meeting ended with that stalemate intact. When FIGHT's buses and Vaughn's limousines left Flemington, both sides must have wondered whether they had won or lost. And both sides had reason to wonder. Alinsky's church groups were shaky; they had never used their stock options as a political weapon before, and they weren't sure they liked the feeling of confrontation. Kodak's leaders saw summer coming, and Franklin Florence had warned there would be more protests. A candlelight march on the anniversary of the 1964 riots was planned. Alinsky had threatened them with a better-organized stock proxy battle the following year. When Daniel Patrick Moynihan, then at the Joint Center for Urban Studies at MIT and Harvard, offered to mediate a settlement, both sides jumped at the opportunity. Alinsky and Florence knew they wouldn't get Kodak to agree to a contract. Instead, after a week of secret meetings, Florence accepted a mutual "settlement" (Louis Eilers called it an "understanding") that allowed both sides to begin a long-standing mutual plan.[38]

Within a year, several new job development programs existed in Rochester. None were controlled by FIGHT, but Florence was mollified, because the understanding included Kodak guarantees to order parts from a new subcontracting company, which FIGHT could control. They called the company FIGHTON and located it in an old textile factory in one of the black wards. It made electronic and vacuum-cleaning equipment used for photocopiers, starting with orders and management advice from the Xerox Corporation, also based in Rochester. (Years later, the company Web site would list Xerox CEO Joseph Wilson as a founder.)

Contrary to the expectations of anyone at Kodak, FIGHTON continues to exist, to be profitable, and to be minority owned, with a focus on diversity. Now named Eltrex, the company has undergone a startling transition to mainstream effectiveness. In 1976, with a recent Harvard Business School graduate named Matthew Augustine as CEO, it reorganized to, as Augustine later put it, "transform into a typical well-run company similar to the Fortune 500." Eltrex's management embraced the quality movement in the 1980s and branched out in the early 2000s into brokering and evaluating outsourcing services. Augustine, as of 2008, is still CEO.[39] Eltrex's differences with Kodak are long since forgotten; it is now, for example, a supplier of packaging for Kodak chemicals.

As for Alinsky's Industrial Arts Foundation, it moved out of Rochester in 1968; by then FIGHT didn't need (or want to pay for) his help any more. Florence remained as FIGHT's leader; with Stokely Carmichael, he continued to press for national demonstrations against Kodak. But as he became more militant, he began to lose the support of local churches. In mid-1967, the Rochester Area Council of Churches, which had supported FIGHT until then, passed a resolution criticizing FIGHT for "intemperance."

The Reverend Long, who had first suggested recruiting Alinsky, was pressured to leave the Third Presbyterian Church around that time; its conservative elders could no longer ignore his dual role as pastor and activist. He escaped to a Presbyterian church in Cincinnati.

Alinsky would never organize another ghetto community again. He was captivated by what he called his "Wall Street Wonderland" technique. He found himself increasingly fielding inquiries from corporate executives who wanted to know how he would use the proxy techniques next and didn't believe him when he said he didn't know. At one corporate luncheon, an executive challenged him to approach them fairly and courteously, with goodwill and reason, instead of playing power politics. "I'll consider the idea," Alinsky said, "as soon as your corporations approach your competitors with cooperation, instead of going for the jugular." He told his friends that he had never seen the establishment so uptight. Shareholder activism was a whole new handle with which to get a chief executive's attention. Moreover, it was based on the principle of democracy: one share, one vote. It opened a crack in the facade of the impermeable corporation, and it bred instant notoriety, of the kind he found both useful and exhilarating.[40] He began to spell out these thoughts in speeches and conversation, hoping to start a

new type of social activist movement. But before he got very far, the
movement for corporate responsibility lurched in a different direction.
For a couple of years, insiders took it over.

○

In the nineteenth and early twentieth centuries, industrialists like Andrew
Carnegie and Henry Ford had seen themselves as social reformers. But as
Carnegie's biographer David Nasaw has pointed out, this usually took
the form of micromanagement and moralizing.[41] And usually only a few
visible corporate leaders took part, while everyone below them focused
on business as usual. But in the late 1960s, something perhaps unprecedented in corporate history happened. There was a presumption, in the
air among corporate executives and managers, that they too could make
a difference; they could do something about the abuses of the industrial
world. Inflation was insistent and growing; race war, seemingly imminent; pollution, dire; and Vietnam, increasingly visible on the news as a
deadly cesspool of folly and abuse. If any of these apocalyptic visions
failed to move a businessman, he need only go home for dinner, where he
could count on a confrontation from his college-age offspring. Or
he might see the explosive light of the women's movement shining out of
his wife's eyes. He would be caught in the middle, between the moral high
ground of his spouse and children, on one hand, and the fact that the
corporation paid the bills (including the kids' tuition), on the other.

A few executives found themselves making a stand, sometimes (to their
own surprise) risking their careers. In the late 1960s, a group of staff
planners at General Electric insisted that GE should get out of military
contracting. They were part of a massive GE effort to analyze the external business environment, and they had become convinced it was going
to dramatically change.[42] At the time, GE was one of the leading manufacturers of military aircraft engines (including the controversial B-1
bomber) and nuclear weapons components. Now, the planners said, antiwar sentiment would grow, and the munitions business would stop being
profitable. They brought in Seymour Melman, a Columbia University
industrial engineering professor who had written books decrying the
"war economy's" devastating effects on corporate efficiency and the economy as a whole. At their planners' prodding, GE's budget office established the Re-Entry and Environmental Services Division to investigate
peacetime industries like cattle feed lots, prefabricated housing, and mass
transit, to which the war-machine-making plants might convert.

Unfortunately they discovered (as GE had already discovered once,
after World War II), that experience with military materiel doesn't

transfer easily to the private sector. Defense contracting is a high-cost but low-investment business; once the technical specifications are set, the government guarantees the profits and pays them on an even schedule. These new ventures would bring in higher profits but at much greater risk. For instance, what if the prefabricated housing market failed? After a heady six months, during which it looked as if they might influence the corporate direction, the GE planners found themselves ignored. The overall planning effort moved in more conventional directions, such as technological forecasting; the planners were shifted laterally into backwater slots and gradually left the company.

Around that same time, one of the most prominent executives in the country found himself caught up, with vigor and clamor, in the cause of corporate responsibility to society. In 1967, Henry Ford II, president of the Ford Motor Company, was fifty-one years old. Like his close friend Lyndon Baines Johnson, he was a living symbol of everything that was right and wrong with his generation. Like his grandfather, Henry Ford I, he was drawn to use his company to make life better for others, with decidedly ambiguous results.

In the early 1940s, "Hank the Deuce" had rescued the ailing and moribund Ford Motor Company from the thuglike henchmen whom his grandfather had put in place to run the company. Then the younger Henry Ford had turned the company around, beginning with a heroic effort to meet its warplane obligations to the U.S. Air Force. He had established the company's first good working relationship with the United Auto Workers union, and his celebrated "whiz kid" managers, hired from the Air Force in 1948 and celebrated for their extraordinary prowess at numbers-based management, had brought the firm its first coherent financial and product-development practices. (One of those "whiz kids" was Robert McNamara, the archetypal postwar Ford finance man, who became secretary of defense under LBJ.) By the time of the shining victory of the Mustang in the early 1960s,[43] Henry Ford II had proved that even the most messed-up company could be rescued and made whole by the can-do spirit and scientific techniques of a Depression-bred management team.

Biographies of Henry Ford II describe him as a complex man: shrewd and unpretentious, distant but likable, raucous and secretive. He had grown up privileged; Frank Sinatra sang at his twenty-first birthday party. But even the reverent society columns of Detroit's society columns portrayed "Hank the Deuce" as a coarse carouser—known for diving, fully clothed and drunk, into pools at formal parties. He spent much of his life demonstrating, in one way or another, that he didn't give a damn what people thought of him.[44]

Despite all that, he readily took on the mantle of a public figure, specifically aiming to show the country how to cure society's ills. He seemed to feel that no problem was beyond his power to solve if he put his mind to it, and especially if he got a raft of other business managers working with him. They would reach a "better understanding," he began to say in speeches, "between the profit motive and the public welfare."[45] They would tackle "jobs for Negroes" first. There was a logic to this: the original Henry Ford had been a pioneer in hiring blacks for responsible positions, and Henry Ford II himself had grown up with a fairly egalitarian attitude about race. In his summer job on a Ford line during college, Hank the Deuce had reported to a black supervisor.

In 1966, Ford met Whitney Young Jr., the head of the National Urban League, during a tour of Europe sponsored by Time-Life. As it turned out, the original Henry Ford had given Young's father his first career break—hiring him as an electrical engineer at three hundred dollars a month. The two scions, Ford II and Young Jr., formed a long-standing friendship and planned the details of a massive job-training and minority-hiring program at Ford Motor Company.

When riots erupted in Detroit in the summer of 1967 (they were the most violent, costly race riots in American history), the flames were visible from the windows of the new Ford headquarters building, twenty miles from the city core. General Motors's headquarters, much closer in, was guarded by tanks. Ford had a 23 percent black labor force at the time (GM, by comparison, was 13 percent), but in the light of Detroit's black majority population, Henry didn't think it was enough.[46] He and Young stepped up the pace of the job program.[47] At Young's instigation, it quickly expanded into a national job-training organization, the National Alliance of Businessmen (NAB). It was formed in January 1968, and less than a year later, the group announced it had spent $180 million (one-third from government, two-thirds from business) to create eighty-four thousand jobs at twelve thousand firms. Sixty-one thousand of those people were still working.[48] The NAB did little training itself but contracted out to small ghetto-based training firms. Large companies like Boeing and General Foods sometimes lent their training executives to help.[49]

In early 1969, Henry Ford II was ousted from the NAB; as a friend of LBJ, he was a casualty of the 1968 election. But the CEO of PepsiCo, Donald Kendall, accepted the post in Ford's place. Nonetheless, the glowing numbers of the NAB were already being questioned.[50] The training was often meager and perfunctory; trainers tended to return to their host companies after a month or two. The trainees were supposed to be grateful for what they got; the idea never even came up of inviting them to suggest ways to improve their training. Many jobs didn't last. Others were unskilled jobs—short-order cook and maintenance jobs paying two or three dollars per hour. In still other cases, people were thrown into jobs after a few days of training that required weeks or months of intensive technical education. Far too many of the NAB's new workers failed and were banished back to the ghettos—proof to some that members of the black underclass couldn't be trained. Small businesses shied away from the program. By October 1969, disgruntled staffers in the U.S. Labor Department were leaking statistics showing that companies had bothered to pick up less than a fourth of the $245 million allocated for NAB training.[51]

Apparently there were some challenges, after all, that the "can-do" Depression-bred managers of the postwar period couldn't tackle effectively. Henry Ford II was only the most visible of many managers who quietly stepped back from their social responsibility efforts. The NAB became a backwater; even at Ford, nobody got promoted by directing a job training program for underclass black men. In short, the NAB was having exactly the same problem that hit corporations that tried to break free of the standard numbers approach to business. Having left their zones of expertise, they no longer found it possible to succeed. Managers knew how to fight for turf, but not how to unite with their rivals in a common effort. They knew how to present current performance statistics that looked good but not how to create actual lasting change that would yield good performance statistics forever.

Henry Ford II moved on. He spent much of 1969 and 1970 making speeches on how to change the world, aimed directly at the college-age generation. The whole civilized world, he said in one speech at Vanderbilt University, was facing a crisis of confidence Young rebels and hippies, he said, should stop dropping out or rebelling; instead, they should work within the system to make it better. The system deeply needed them.

"Many of the young people I have talked to," he said, "have doubts about whether this way is still possible. They look about and see a society composed of huge, impersonal, hierarchical institutions—big universities, big business, big labor, big government. [They] wonder if there is really any room left to be one's self and to affect the way things are." Yes, it was difficult, Ford said, to change the "complex web of rules and sanctions that hold a society together." But it wasn't impossible, and "the basic reason why reform comes slowly is *not* that it is blocked by the concentration of power in the hands of a reactionary establishment. The basic reason is exactly the opposite. . . . Nobody—not the chancellor of Vanderbilt or the chairman of Ford or the President of the United States—has enough power to set things straight in a hurry."[52]

They were prescient words. But neither he nor his audience fully realized the import of what he was telling them to do. He was counseling them to become heretics: to keep their loyalty to the truth they had discovered outside the system while moving to fix the organizations from within. That was an immensely difficult task, as John Mulder could have told him. The Ford Motor Company itself was full of legendary heretics who had proposed one great idea or another or had taken a stand within the company, only to see their ideas shot down mercilessly by rivals—and often, in the end, by Hank the Deuce himself.[53] *Come and become heretics within our firm,* he might as well have said—*but be prepared to be martyred.*

———————— o ————————

If you really cared about corporate social responsibility in those years, then Saul Alinsky's techniques—the outsider approach—seemed to have a better change of success. But it too was limited. In 1969 and 1970, antiwar organizers began showing up at Dow Chemical annual meetings protesting napalm, at United Aircraft of Hartford meetings protesting warplanes, and at the Bank of America annual meetings arguing that the bank should close its Saigon branch. In Minneapolis, Honeywell's chairman shut down the 1970 annual meeting after only fourteen minutes when demonstrators, who had bought stock to protest the company's weapons production, started to shout *"Sieg heil!"* from the floor.[54]

Even sympathetic executives fiercely resisted these kinds of protests. Dow's managers, for instance, had grown weary of the napalm business; the returns weren't worth the aggravation. But Robert McNamara had publicly praised Dow. Its senior managers were not going to demonstrate to customers, shareholders, managers (and unions!) that they could be pushovers for a few campus radicals and church groups. If you want to stop the use of napalm against civilians, Dow managers told the press, then stop the government, not us. Meanwhile, they quietly bid high on the next napalm contract and did not squawk when another company's bid was chosen.

The arbitrariness of the protests always seemed peculiar to managers. Certainly the protesters selected large, visible companies—but why Dow and not DuPont or American Electric? Why Bank of America and not Chase Manhattan? The truth was, some targets had more mythic power than others. The closer to a household name, the better, because the provocation for the protest, the death of vernacular values, was so large and ill defined. In 1970 and 1971, the anticorporation protests coalesced in a shareholder action against the largest, most mythic target of all: the giant defense contractor and enabler of American mobility, General Motors.

Four young District of Columbia lawyers decided, late in 1969, to carry Saul Alinsky's shareholder proxy tactics to a national arena. Their names were Philip Moore, Joseph Onek, Geoffrey Cowan, and John Esposito. Three of them had been active in civil rights; one of them, Jeff Cowan, had worked with Alinsky in Rochester. They chose GM not because it was particularly pernicious, but because it was big. No one could live in America and not be unaffected by the company. "We want corporate leaders," their first press statement read, "to be accountable to all people affected by corporate decisions." Corporate leaders, they added, "could do more to eliminate job discrimination or air pollution than any U.S. senator." If turning Kodak might mean turning Rochester, then turning GM could turn the entire country.

They started by buying twelve shares of stock in General Motors. They incorporated themselves as The Campaign to Make General Motors Responsible—Campaign GM for short. At the press conference they held in February 1970, they announced they were introducing nine share- holder resolutions for a vote at GM's annual meeting in May. One was rhetorical: adding language to GM's certificate of incorporation stating that no policy would be "detrimental to the public health, safety, or wel- fare." Another challenged GM's management control: establishing a shareholders' committee on corporate responsibility, which would make an independent, annual public report on the company's behavior. Another resolution demanded that GM allot more car dealerships to minority owners; a fourth demanded support for public transportation. Two of the resolutions focused on safety: that all GM vehicles be designed so that a crash at sixty miles per hour would not injure passengers wearing shoul- der straps and that GM offer a five-year warranty on its cars and a life- time warranty on defective parts.[55] Two other resolutions would commit GM to doing something about air pollution: designing, for example, a pollution-free car over the next five years.

A final resolution expanded GM's board of directors by three members. The purpose of this resolution, which made no mention of the public interest, was to allow Campaign GM to nominate three symbolic people for election to GM's board if the resolution passed. They knew it proba- bly wouldn't pass, but they chose their nominees carefully: world- renowned environmentalist and author René Dubos; Channing Phillips, a black minister and politician; and Betty Furness, who had been New York City's consumer adviser. The lawyers formally asked GM to include their resolutions in the shareholder's proxy mailing.

Interestingly, none of the resolutions mentioned the most difficult crisis going on at that moment within the company. At a GM assembly plant in

Lordstown, Ohio, outside Akron, some of the younger workers on the line had developed their own team-based style, akin to the sociotechnical systems of the Gaines Topeka plant and Procter & Gamble. Instead of having a manager champion their efforts, they'd simply doubled up themselves—working the shift in pairs, covering for each other, and redesigning the layout of their stations. This was a matter of survival. The plant, recently opened, was designed as an automated "factory of future" to produce the Chevrolet Vega, the much ballyhooed GM small car of the moment. But a state-of-the-art factory in 1970 was a brutal place to work. Jobs had been divided, for efficiency's sake, into the smallest possible units. In some cases, workers were driven to handle two cars a minute on jobs so depressingly simple and numbing that they were literally beyond human endurance. Meanwhile, supervisors tracked every detail of their performance, particularly speed. The workers had a choice: redesign the work themselves, or take out their frustration in sabotage and absenteeism.

When General Motors had cracked down on "doubling up" in 1970 and the national United Auto Workers had refused to defend the workers, the plant entered a state of siege. The local assemblers initiated one of the worst strikes of the decade, staged almost entirely by young workers in their twenties. And although the strike was eventually settled, labor unrest would continue in the plant through the next few years. (In response to Lordstown, some GM executives and UAW leaders would become interested in the Quality of Working Life movement, eventually paving the way for GM's quality initiatives, like the NUMMI plant and the launch of Saturn, in the 1980s. But all of that was still far in the future. At the moment, Lordstown was just another unrecognized opportunity for productive change in American manufacturing.)[56]

───────── o ─────────

As a publicity move, the Campaign GM organizers invited the company's most visible public enemy, Ralph Nader, to join them before the press. Nader wasn't directly involved in Campaign GM, except as an occasional spokesman, but he became the most prominent figure of the campaign. The organizers spent the next two years in his shadow.

Nader thought corporations were incapable of self-control. Instead, he said, government should keep watch over companies and be the source of their accountability—and the consumer movement, of which he was now a leader, would be the watchdog over government. He had come to this opinion in his battles with General Motors, which had made him famous, in the same way that the popes had made the success of Martin Luther inevitable.[57] By fighting him antagonistically and trying to discredit him before they understood his criticisms, they had boosted his credibility at the expense of their own. Or as Henry Ford II said scornfully, "If this industry of ours had been on its feet instead of its ass, Nader would never have surfaced."[58]

In the early 1960s, after graduating from law school and a few years of law practice, Nader had drifted into a career as a freelance writer and researcher on auto safety. He was an anomaly in leftist circles: most crusaders against corporations came from the labor movement; Nader had no ties and no socialist sympathy. He believed strongly in government regulation, but on behalf of consumers, not unions or workers. He worked as a behind-the-scenes technical adviser to Abraham Ribicoff, the Democratic senator from Connecticut, when Ribicoff questioned GM's CEO, James Roche, about the company's investments in traffic safety. Then in 1964 he published *Unsafe at Any Speed,* about the hazardous Chevrolet Corvair, a small GM car with its engine mounted in the rear. The book accused GM of deliberately shortchanging the car's safety; instead of padded dashboards, shoulder belts, and collapsible steering wheel columns, the company had spent its research money on flaring tailfins, a faux-Porsche design, and "creative obsolescence"[59]—the cavalier, almost deliberate policy of making the cars shoddier than they had to be because quality cost money.

GM's managers couldn't imagine that someone like Nader existed, so they hired a private detective, who in turn devised some startlingly clumsy efforts at entrapment. Young women walked up to Ralph Nader in stores and tried to lure him back to their apartments. (He stiffly walked away.) People who said they were prospective employers called his old acquaintances, asking if he was homosexual or had a drinking problem.[60] Ultimately they figured that he had to be a shill for ambulance-chasing liability lawyers, an accusation that would dog Nader all the way through his third-party presidential campaign in 2000.

Nader sued GM for harassment the following year. He also brought the matter back to Ribicoff's attention. On March 22, 1966, the Senate Subcommittee on Government Functions, which Ribicoff chaired, subpoenaed Roche again. The tall, reticent chairman, whose voice rarely rose above a whisper, was forced to admit that his company had hired the detectives (though without the knowledge of top management, he claimed, and without any of the sexual entrapment attempts). Roche then apologized to Nader before television cameras at the hearing.

o

Throughout his career, Nader would rely on a network of whistle-blowers within companies for much of his corporate data. But he did not convert many executives. Businesspeople didn't understand him, nor he them. To people who worked for companies and wanted to know how they could improve the corporate product, he offered only one implicit answer: "Leave the company, blow the whistle, and devote your life to public service."

It was easy for Nader. He had no children, no mortgage, and no love for creature comforts. He maintained the austere life of a perpetual graduate student, in a small apartment, wearing cheap suits as a badge of pride or, more likely, disinterest. His social life revolved around work; he was so intensely shy with strangers, in any case, that he came off at first as brusque. Only to people who knew him well did he reveal his natural, almost childlike warmth. All of this made him insensitive to the burden of keeping profits high and insensitive to the seduction of perks and salaries. (The failed investigators who had worked for GM back in 1966 had tried unsuccessfully to find some personal weakness of Nader's that they could exploit.)

In Detroit, some engineers originally looked on Nader as a potential savior. He was making some of the same points about auto safety that they had tried, and failed, to foist up the chain of command. They recognized defects in the Corvair that Nader originally missed: its tendency to snap in two when hit in the side (this had killed the comedian Ernie Kovacs) and its shoddy engine blocks that slowly disintegrated under fast driving conditions. (One Ford engineer, driving behind a Corvair on a freeway, saw its engine pop out of the bottom of the car, strike the pavement, and explode.)

Even after Nader included these points in his criticisms, he got the technical nuances wrong—an inevitable mistake, perhaps, because of his visceral dislike for automobiles. He did not drive, did not own a car, and visibly blanched when he was forced to ride in a convertible or sports car. He was hypersensitive to the fragility of those hurtling metal boxes, and the engineers could tell. Anyone who "came out of the closet" at Ford or GM and said something like, "You know, this guy Nader has a point," would be immediately hooted at by the other car guys. "Gee," the head engineer of that function might say, "I thought you knew more about cars than to agree with that asshole."

Worse still, from the point of view of the managers in the companies he fought, Nader didn't play the game of confrontation fairly. Instead of trying to negotiate directly with GM, he leaked his criticisms to the press. Saul Alinsky admired him for this; in Alinsky's eyes, Nader knew how to go for the jugular. But managers felt about him the way they felt about the industry reporters from local newspapers, who always got key business details wrong because they hadn't worked inside for twenty years.

Nader, for instance, didn't seem to know that Detroit had already tried safety. In the early 1950s, Ford designers had put out a line of cars with a range of supersafe features. The cars had bombed. Detroit managers had concluded that Americans didn't want safe cars; they wanted styling. As a result, as the management writer Peter Drucker wrote in 1967, "the automobile manufacturers bitterly resent as rank ingratitude that they are being blamed for unsafe cars, subjected to punitive legislation, and held up for public scorn." And yet, Drucker had written, nobody should feel sorry for managers of large firms like GM: "They are indeed not to blame for unsafe cars [or] polluted air in the sense that they caused it. Theirs is a greater blame: They have not lived up to the demands of leadership. It is the task of the leader to anticipate . . . to find the right way and to lead the crowd."[61]

<hr>

Originally the Campaign GM organizers had planned to run Ralph Nader for the company's board of directors. An enormous and gripping public relations carnival would have ensued if they'd gone through with it, and Nader flirted with the idea for several months before declining.[62] He was still enmeshed in his invasion-of-privacy lawsuit against GM (he was now claiming damages of $17 million), but he did not decline for legal reasons. Years later, he told a social investing historian that he saw the whole shareholder election process as rigged; after all, management controlled large blocks of institutional shares, and support for the management position was too entrenched to shift. He didn't want to invest that much of himself in a symbolic effort, where the dissent level would be "not much larger than a Kremlin-style election."[63] But he threw his support behind the campaign. So did Alinsky, who praised it to his colleagues and introduced Nader to one of his own benefactors: Gordon Sherman, the liberal Chicagoan who had inherited ownership of the Midas Muffler company and appointed himself president.

Other notables joined the Campaign GM effort. The antiwar activist and Nobel-prize-winning biologist George Wald made speeches on its behalf; so did a British activist named Hazel Henderson, who ran a nonprofit called Citizens for Clean Air from her Manhattan kitchen table. Henderson had rallied insurance executives and other corporate leaders around the clean air campaign. Later she would write an influential *Harvard Business Review* article about the implications of Campaign GM, arguing that henceforth, social activists should naturally try to influence corporations through their shareholders. She would ultimately become a noted author on environmentalism and social entrepreneurship.[64]

Another Campaign GM supporter was Robert Townsend, the former president of Avis and author of the best-selling business book *Up the Organization,* an antibureaucracy screed in which he recommended that every manager do his own secretarial work. Townsend argued that Roche should cut GM's advertising budget from $240 million per year to $40 million and spend that on one message about what they would do with the savings: "General Motors is going to spend four hundred million dollars in two years to wipe out pollution."[65]

The young lawyers used a Securities and Exchange Committee ruling—the same one that the old gadfly Lewis Gilbert had lobbied for back in the 1930s to force GM to include two of their resolutions in its mailing to all shareholders. The actual mailing, of course, mattered less to the Campaign GM strategists than the press coverage they got when they announced that GM would include their proxy forms. Then they set about trying to mobilize church and student support groups, hoping that these would influence big institutional and pension fund trustees to turn their proxies over to the campaign. At MIT these efforts led the school to hold a debate between Joe Onek, one of the campaign's organizers, and a senior GM official. The official happened to be the treasurer—a shy, bespectacled finance man named Roger B. Smith. (Later he would become CEO and a foil to filmmaker Michael Moore.) Onek was a better debater, but the MIT trustees voted their proxies to GM management anyway. Nonetheless, Campaign GM did get proxy support from Amherst, Antioch, Tufts, Boston University, and Iowa State and from pension funds in San Francisco, Iowa, Wisconsin, and New York City.[66]

In May 1970, three thousand people showed up at the GM annual meeting in Detroit's Cobo Hall. Roche presided over its full six and a half hours. This happened to come in the midst of the company's most turbulent year since World War II. First quarter earnings per share were down; they'd fallen from $1.82 to $1.21. The stock price had fallen to the lowest point since 1963. The president of the United Auto Workers, Walter Reuther, had died in a plane crash just a few days before, which threatened the company's stable relationship with the UAW. Coincidentally, the UAW was poised to strike over cost-of-living wage increases, which—even if the union lost its demands—would cost the company twenty-six cents more per person per hour.

If Roche felt extra pressure, he didn't show it. Instead, he lifted his gavel at 2:00 P.M. to begin and continued stolidly and even-temperedly through an afternoon of nominations, motions, countermotions, and impromptu speeches about General Motor's air pollution and racial hiring policies. His voice hardly rose above its customary whisper, even when a black UCLA law student named Barbara Williams confronted him: "You have failed not only the shareholders, but the country. Why are there no blacks and women on the board?"

To many observers, the most irritating comments came not from the Campaign GM protesters but from their opposition—long-time, eccentric gadfly shareholders who had been protesting for years that GM's managers wasted their money. One of them wore a black bathing suit and a sash reading "Miss Air Pollution." Another made rambling speeches about (for instance) how GM's "splendid" cars would be involved in fewer accidents if only Ralph Nader's followers would stop taking drugs.

To all these disparate curmudgeons, James Roche responded courteously. (The *New Yorker* called him "gallantry personified.") The Campaign GM people were equally polite. Donald Schwartz, the Campaign GM counsel, gave the organization's closing statement for the day: "Mr. Roche, we look forward to seeing you next year."[67]

o

On paper at least, Campaign GM produced results. Within the next three months, General Motors had put into effect several new policies intended, in one way or another, to satisfy the campaign's concerns. The company instituted a public policy committee, delegating five board members to make a report to shareholders. Its leaders added a post of vice president of environmental matters and hired a University of California professor, Ernest Starkman, whose specialization was air pollution, to fill the post. They also formed a committee of scientists to study the environmental effects of GM cars. All of this, ultimately, was window dressing; none of it had much effect on the practices of the corporation.

But a final response was more significant. GM added a slot on the board and filled it with the Reverend Leon Sullivan, a black minister from Philadelphia and an outspoken civil rights activist. He had cofounded a black-owned aerospace parts manufacturing company in Philadelphia and pressured other Philadelphia companies to adopt open employment policies. Like Rochester's Franklin Florence, he was skeptical of managers' motives, although he was somewhat less confrontational. When he accepted the job, he explicitly told Roche that he wouldn't be tied down to a traditional board role: "I'm more interested in human terms than capital terms. My main concern is helping to improve the position of black people in America. I want to be a voice from the outside on the inside."[68]

At that time, few people in corporate circles knew much about Sullivan, but he would become one of the key figures of corporate change during the 1970s and 1980s. He made his presence known publicly the following year, at the 1971 annual meeting, when Campaign GM returned with three new shareholder resolutions. This time, although they'd done much more legwork and gotten more proxies dedicated to them up front, they ended up with far fewer votes. Apparently in its shareholders' eyes, GM had already done enough to change. But alongside Campaign GM, the Episcopal Church filed a proxy resolution of its own: that General Motors should shut down its manufacturing facilities in the apartheid-dominated country of South Africa.

The resolution was voted down, but not before Leon Sullivan asked for the floor. He made a dramatic speech about U.S. corporations in South Africa—how they had essentially underwritten the continuing presence of apartheid there. "American industry can't morally continue to do business," he said, "in a country that so blatantly, ruthlessly, and clearly maintains such dehumanizing practices against such large numbers of people."[69] It was the first time a GM director had ever spoken out against the board's position at an annual meeting.

○

The person angriest about Campaign GM, at least to judge by the tone of his prose, was not associated with General Motors at all. He was the economist and writer Milton Friedman. Unlike most other economists, Friedman was a well-known figure, mainly because of the clearly written, acerbic columns that he had written for *Newsweek* since 1966. His bespectacled, smiling face appeared every three weeks above a page of text in the magazine.

One of the most famous articles of his career appeared in the *New York Times Magazine* in the fall of 1970. It was titled, "The Social Responsibility of Business Is to Increase Its Profits,"[70] and in case readers missed its topical significance, the editors illustrated it with photographs of Jim Roche, faced off against the Campaign GM leaders at GM's annual meeting. Corporations could only hurt society, Friedman argued in the text, if they tried to tackle social problems. Executives were too "short-sighted and muddle-headed" about matters outside their own business purview. What if their well-intentioned efforts went wrong? Specifically, Friedman was fuming about wage and price controls that President Nixon had not yet put into effect but that a number of large American corporations were lobbying the president to adopt. But he had a point. Most corporate efforts toward social responsibility, like Henry Ford II's halfhearted training initiatives in Detroit, had arguably made things worse. They had raised expectations, failed to meet them, and claimed (through the numbers) that they *had* met them, making managers and trainees more cynical about further job efforts down the pike. Even the best-designed effort was now more likely to fail because it would exist in an environment where people didn't believe in it.

Even if a social program effectively created jobs or curbed pollution, Friedman said, it constituted fraud. Executives on company time were the agents of shareholders. Shareholders, by definition, had only one goal: higher value for their stock. That could come only from higher profits. Those who wanted to make a social contribution should act through individual charities or through their vote. Most Americans were not interested in social goals, he said, but as customers or shareholders, they bore the added cost of corporate social responsibility efforts, as either higher prices or lower dividends. In that context, these efforts represented an unseen tax without representation: the exact form of tyranny that had prodded America into revolution almost two hundred years before. Friedman's message to managers who wanted to harness their companies' power for the common good was simple: "Forget about it. Just make profits. If your conscience troubles you, give more to charities yourself."

Even Henry Ford II had begun to agree. The man who a year before had lectured college students about getting involved to change the world now retracted. Perhaps his attention had turned to battles within the firm, particularly with his protégé-turned-rival, Lee Iacocca. At Ford's annual meeting in 1972, he spoke in terms that Friedman approved and that his grandfather had once gone to court to deny. "I believe social responsibility," he said, "is fundamentally the same as it has always been: to maximize profits for shareholders by serving consumer wants with maximum efficiency."[71]

And there the debate sat, thoroughly missing the point that John Mulder had seen: an effective program, working with social forces, would serve shareholders by making the corporation thrive in the long run.

---------- o ----------

In 1971, Saul Alinsky finished writing *Rules for Radicals,* a book of tactics for community organizers. He had been working on it, on and off, between campaigns, for ten years. It was, as befit its author, a cheerful, flamboyant book. Alinsky had been buoyed by the success of Campaign GM, whose progress he had followed closely. The FIGHT campaign against Kodak had convinced him that the future of organizing lay with the middle class. In addition, as his biographer Sanford Horwitt notes, Alinsky had nowhere else to go. With the rise of Black Power, there was no place for him, or any other white organizer, in black ghettos.[72]

But consider the opportunities for making a difference! The lower middle class, wrote Alinsky, felt threatened from all sides: their future pressed by inflation, their jobs threatened by cutbacks (and competition from the black labor force), their daily life victimized by interest on installment payments and misinformation about their choices in advertising. They were potential fodder for demagogues—unless smart, rebellious organizers could find a way to reach them. The upper middle class, better educated and more secure in their employment, thought that they needed only "a split-level house in the suburbs, two cars, two color TVs, country club membership, a bank account, children in good prep schools and then in college, and they had it made. They got it—only to discover that they didn't have it." He exhorted the activists reading his book to "return to the suburban scene of your middle class with its variety of organizations from PTAs to League of Women." Find areas of common agreement, he told them. Excite their imaginations. Introduce drama and adventure into their lives. Pitch major battles around the quality and prices of consumer goods.

And then there were opportunities within corporations themselves: "The corporations must forget their nonsense about 'private sectors.' Every American individual or corporation is public as well as private; public in that we are Americans and concerned about our national welfare. We have a double commitment and corporations had better recognize this for the sake of their own survival." Organizing executives around this principle, Alinsky suggested, would give them "a reason for what they are doing—a chance for a meaningful life."

To show how citizens could apply outside pressure in the meantime, Alinsky sketched out some ideas for brash, large-scale proxy campaigns. Instead of a few thousand shareholders, bring fifty thousand to a town like Flemington, New Jersey. Force corporations to ask for the National Guard to control their own shareholders. Or force them to hold their meetings in venues like Yankee Stadium. Set up computerized operations to coordinate study groups on corporate policies, so people could learn which corporations were worth investing in and what corporations needed to be pressured. He wrote that he expected to be with this campaign "full time, for its launching and its setting out to sea."[73]

Alinsky didn't live to see it happen. About nine months after his book was published, he died of a sudden heart attack. The corporate social responsibility movement, which essentially got its start with Alinsky, Ford, and Nader, continued to exhibit the mutual contradictions of these three very different forebears. It has devolved, some argue, to a kind of vehicle for grudging compliance: a program in which corporations give money to charity, or make other halfhearted efforts, to forestall public criticism and regulation. But although many people continue to predict that the movement will diminish and die out,[74] it continues to cling to life.

Corporations are, after all, responsible to others besides investors. The demands of customers, employees, and the rest of us cannot be ignored. In the end, it takes the artistry and skill of a Henry Ford—the *first* Henry Ford—in his prime, to understand the subtle relationships among all those demands and to figure out how to satisfy them all.

Alinsky could be credited (not alone) with three separate legacies. The first was putting those tensions and contradictions of social responsibility out before the public: making visible the hidden role of shareholders in setting a corporate agenda. His second legacy was the unforeseen political impact that his movement engendered. Fueled by church investment groups, it would gather steam during the 1970s. By the mid-1980s, proxy battles—modeled in part on Campaign GM, with Louis Sullivan as one of the most significant participants—would be a major component of the fight to keep multinationals out of South Africa and to push for better environmental policies. More recently, in the early 2000s, shareholder activism has been an ever stronger check on the runaway impulses of self-indulgent CEOs.

Alinsky's third legacy to corporations showed up only in the hearts of a few people who had seen him at work, or heard about the way he worked, or worked with people who worked with him. Community organizers like Alinsky and his confederates knew how to work with the vernacular, and they did so in dozens of settings—not just in urban neighborhoods but with (for example) the United Farm Workers, during the grape boycott campaigns led by Cesar Chavez. Community organizers brought skills and tactics to the campaigns. They coordinated theatrical performances that dramatized people's aspirations and anger. ("At Friday night meetings," recalls a community organizer who worked with Chavez, "the grandparents, parents and children would watch with rapt attention as El Teatro, with only masks, small placards, a pair of sunglasses, a crude picket sign, or a red bandanna, served as midwives to the birth of hope."[75]) They ran group dialogues, specifically designed to bridge gaps between ethnic groups that had traditionally mistrusted each other. They made a point of publicly honoring people's contributions. And they set up community suppers, sometimes over meals as simple as beans, where people could contribute just by bringing food, even if they didn't talk. (One veteran bean supper organizer, Juanita Brown, later became a corporate consultant who used that experience to coinvent the "World Café" dialogue format.)[76]

All of these skills would be remarkably useful for the heretics within corporations who were bold enough to use them. Suppose, for example, that you are one of the few people at your company who understands a piece of its potential to exalt the world. Suppose you see a way to serve the people, inside and outside the company, and have some fun and make a profit in the process. Chances are there are few venues inside the firm where you can mention your idea without being shunned or made irrelevant. But consider the effect you would have if you felt charged with a mission and you could summon up Alinsky's verve, acumen, care for people, and willingness to dance on the edge of tolerance.

You could bring people together over impromptu meals. You could convene study groups to teach each other the ins and outs of bureaucratic regulations. You could challenge authorities within the company by publicly holding them accountable for the promises they have made. You could find a way to talk to the William Vaughns and James Roches and Henry Ford IIs of the world to make them see themselves more clearly. (Some executive coaches have made their career doing exactly that.) You could, from time to time, drop plates of food on the floor. If you found a way to survive and if your attitude was open-hearted, you might become the most valuable member that the organization ever had.

MYSTICS

ROYAL DUTCH/SHELL'S SCENARIO
PLANNERS, 1967–1973

Heresy: Awareness must be cultivated, because the future cannot be predicted or planned in a mechanistic manner.

To be a mystic in fourteenth-century Europe was to be more devout than the faithful. You would embrace ritual and ceremony with a fierce, scrupulous, almost unworldly joy. But your goal would not be devotion or sacrament. You would seek, above all else, awareness. You would want to see more deeply into the world, more thoroughly into reality. In that time, this meant learning to see God directly, finding your way to the direct divine presence.

The journey would begin with the control and suppression of worldly desires. Through meditation, prayer, and strict observance, you would cultivate the spiritual self. After going as far as possible on your own, it was said, you might reach a point, like a stopping place on a journey, where you could pause and wait, alone. Then God would come and lift you the rest of the way.

Eventually you would have to return from the meditative journey. You would present yourself to the local abbot and villagers—to tell them about what they too could see if only they found the discipline to look past the blinders of their daily thoughts. As a mystic, you would have the desire—what human, coming down from your journey would not have it?—to see your own new comprehension of reality ripple out into the community around you. If only you could find the words to describe it.

Mystics never find the words to spell out everything they've seen. And yet communities ardently remember the mystics who lived within them. Ordinary people, nontravelers, have changed their lives, then as now, because of what a mystic said to them.

The Church establishment leaders did not admire the mystics, who made them appear weak or irresolute, but they recognized that they needed them. The mystics, for their part, had to be careful not to undermine the Church. It sheltered them and made their journeys possible. For centuries, the priests and the mystics lived in this uneasy truce.[1]

———— o ————

ON THE SOUTH BANK OF THE THAMES, just across the river from the tower of Westminster Abbey, stands the tower of Shell Centre: a twenty-four-story, boxy-windowed, sand-colored skyscraper. When it opened in 1963, Queen Elizabeth dedicated it,[2] while Prince Philip remarked privately that it looked like a Chinese flophouse. Tourists sometimes idly wonder which country has positioned its embassy so prominently near the Houses of Parliament—until the flags on the roof unfurl in the snapping wind and reveal the symbol of the Royal Dutch/Shell Group of Companies, a yellow stylized scallop, outlined in a frame of red.

In 1964, one of the most senior directors of Standard Oil of New Jersey, Shell's greatest and oldest competitor, visited Shell Centre. Sometime during the visit he casually asked, "What is Shell doing about the long-term future?" A few years before, he added, Standard had put together a long-range planning group to consider the Far East. Its investments in marketing to Japan and Korea were beginning to pay off, and its futures group was working on a twenty-five-year plan.[3]

The executives of Standard Oil of New Jersey and of Shell probably never talked to each other again about the future. Twenty years later, in 1988—after Jersey's name had changed to Exxon; after the once-stable price of oil had ricocheted through shocking gains and losses; after several giant oil companies had disappeared, and Exxon itself had endured the worst round of layoffs in its history; and a few months before Exxon's Valdez oil spill would become an international symbol of negligence and corporate arrogance—an Exxon manager would hear about that now-legendary plan and ask to see it. When it was finally unearthed, the Exxon manager would discover that it said very little, except, "We will meet every eventuality." This was the blind confidence with which companies like "Jersey" greeted the future back in 1964.

Shell managers, however, could not afford that blind confidence, and some of them knew it back then. At that time, Shell was the weakest of the "Seven Sisters"—the major oil companies that dominated the international petroleum business.[4] (*Forbes* had called it the "ugly sister."[5]) Shell had neither the huge reserves nor the exclusive relationships with Arab nations that other major oil companies enjoyed. Its traders had to be more canny than the competition, because Shell bought more oil than it drilled. Thus, the Jersey man's casual remark lingered with one or two of Shell's managing directors. They decided that Shell should have its own in-house studies on the long-term future. For one of those studies, they asked the personnel department to find "someone with imagination."

Ted Newland, the man they found, was a staffer in Royal Dutch/Shell's planning department. He was recently transferred from Nigeria, where he had been the administration manager—in effect, the de facto mayor of the Shell compound where five hundred expatriate families lived. Now, back in London, Newland found himself given a couple of assistants, a tiny budget, and the only job in the world that he could ever excel at and love. It was the job of pundit.

At that time, most large companies, particularly in the oil business, employed large forecasting departments to help their managers make day-to-day decisions. The very name of Shell's forecasting technique, the Unified Planning Machinery (UPM), reflected confidence in its mechanistic process. Under the UPM system, Shell's managers around the world fed in estimates of the next year's sales and costs, based on the performance of the previous year. Then armies of analysts in the planning department, armed with calculators and ledger pads (for spreadsheet software had not yet been invented), reshaped the estimates into intricate predictions of the expected price of crude oil and the growth of demand for new oil. With those data, it was believed, Shell executives could plan their next moves—how much to invest in a refinery or a tanker or how much to bid when they traded. If a contrarian like Newland tried to talk about any of the long-term issues that gave the figures meaning, the operating managers would typically cut him off: "I don't need to know that. Just give me the price."

The price, as it happened, was stable in those years. It had hovered (wholesale) around two dollars per barrel since World War II—longer than most Shell executives' careers. (A barrel was forty-two U.S. gallons, or about two tanks of gas in, say, a 1968 Buick.) As for the worldwide demand for oil, it rose steadily but surely. When plotted on paper, it produced a graph of easy growth, always a little better than the planners anticipated. At Shell, they called this the "horse's tail" graph, because it arced up like the tail of a cantering horse, from the past to the optimistic future (Figure 5.1).[6]

The smoothness of the graphed lines did not mean the flow of oil was stable. The source of most petroleum, the Middle East, had staggered for decades from one volatile political squabble to another, but none of the squabbles ever disrupted oil supply for long. A peculiar structure of checks and balances had evolved out of World War II, composed of rivalries, treaties, arrangements, and alliances among oil companies, countries with large oil fields—Saudi Arabia, Iraq, Iran, Kuwait, Libya, and Venezuela—and major industrial powers—the United States, the Soviet Union, Britain, Japan, and Europe. The system was like a giant, invisible, global-sized apparatus of pipes and pumps, controlled by the largest oil companies (the Seven Sisters). When pressure built up in one part of the system (as in 1967, when the Saudis cut world oil supplies to protest

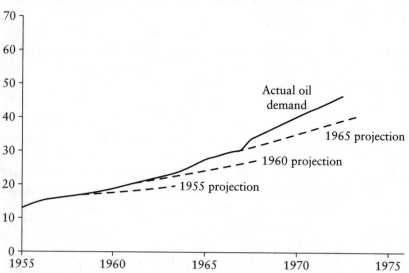

Figure 5.1. Estimates of World Oil Demand, 1955–1975

Source: *Adapted from J. S. Jennings, "The Energy Outlook—Its Implications for Upstream Oil and Gas" (paper presented at the Energy Policy Seminar, Sanderstolen, Norway, Feb. 9, 1989).*

Israel's victory in the Six-Day War), the Seven Sisters could relieve the pressure by turning a valve somewhere else (in that case, boosting production in Iran, Venezuela, and Texas).[7]

By the late 1960s, the leaders of most oil companies and nearly all the governments of the industrialized West behaved as if this machine could go on forever. The UPM forecasts concurred, almost as if they were specifically designed to tell oil managers around the world exactly what they wanted to hear. It was just one more example of how a numbers-based system could gradually devolve into meaningless, dangerous ritual.

Ted Newland was one of several people in the Shell planning department who suspected, as early as 1967, that the stable petroleum system was not going to last. UPM was hurting the company in the long run. A tall and reedy man, Newland was Anglo-Argentine by origin and still spent vacations on an Argentinean ranch that he had inherited. He had a cerebral temperament, but he had never completed a university degree; instead, he had been a Royal Air Force pilot in World War II before joining Shell in Venezuela. In Nigeria, he had been known for his iconoclastic style: he had integrated Shell's private hospital and made its subsidized housing available, for the first time, to locally born managers. He was also cheerfully pessimistic about human nature. During a 1964 strike, when a mob of Nigerians gathered nearby, Newland suggested turning an unfinished canal into a moat around the compound. The rioters, someone replied, would simply swim across. "Well," said Newland, "we can always put crocodiles in."

He was now going to have an opportunity, at corporate expense, to explore Shell's business environment with unprecedented depth and sensibility. He didn't do it alone. He would be part of a team of people. Like mystics, they would devote themselves to developing a new method for seeing the patterns around them more clearly. Like mystics, they would then have to communicate what they had seen in a way that would make the rest of the managers pay attention. Otherwise the corporation could face debilitating losses. Some Shell veterans still believe today that the survival of the enterprise depended in those years of crisis on its ability to cultivate its mystics.

—————— o ——————

Unlike other oil companies, Royal Dutch/Shell belongs to no nation in particular. Its history is half-Dutch and half-British. One of its early-twentieth-century founders was Henri Deterding, a financial prodigy and importer of kerosene from Sumatra who formed an alliance with the Rothschild family (the famous Jewish financiers) early in his career and later became an open supporter of Adolf Hitler. The other founder was Marcus Samuel, a seashell importer (hence the corporate name and logo) who switched to oil and joined the British aristocracy as Lord Bearsted after Deterding bought his company in 1907.[8]

After World War II, having eased Deterding out of the firm before the Nazis could take control of the company's oil reserves, Shell's managers established a tradition of rule by committee. The new Committee of Managing Directors (CMD) was put in charge of the company, usually with a membership of four or five people. The committee never voted on major issues; when there was a disagreement, they tried to come to a consensus on it, and if the disagreement persisted, they did not proceed. Other Shell teams imitated that style; the result was a culture in which Shell managers sometimes had to work by consensus, sometimes to obey orders, and sometimes to act alone. Other companies would have given managers a thick handbook of regulations for sorting through the resulting conflicts. At Shell, they followed unwritten rituals and unspoken hints, which they had learned to understand at either Cambridge or Oxford (where many of the British had gone to university) or in the equally closely knit Dutch university cultures of Delft and Leyden. (It has been called a company of "Scottish accountants and Delft engineers.")

International in scope from its beginnings, Shell evolved after World War II into a group of about two hundred separate firms (called "operating companies"). Most were centered in particular countries, each making its own decisions about (for instance) where to buy oil or how to set up a gas station franchise. This decentralized approach was accelerated in 1957 during an organizational equivalent of spring cleaning that took place roughly around the time Shell laid the cornerstone for its tower on the Thames. Too many relatively minor local decisions were being punted up to the CMD. In one celebrated case, the president of Shell Venezuela (Gerrit Wagner, later a member of CMD himself) had to fly to The Hague to argue for building a new storage tank. The top executives, with some irritation, granted Wagner his storage tank, but they also hired the McKinsey & Company consulting firm to study Shell's corporate structure.[9]

McKinsey's young M.B.A.s shrewdly picked up on the hunger within Shell for local autonomy; no national group, especially the Dutch and British, wanted to feel dominated by any other. They borrowed a matrix corporate structure from General Electric, whose scientific management wizards had adapted the concept from General Motors, which had learned to diversify from DuPont, which had more or less invented the idea in the 1920s. This new structure divided the Shell Group two ways: each activity was now part of a "function" and a "region," and every major request had to be approved by both chains of command. (At other companies, meanwhile, executives were growing tired of the contradictions and conflicts that matrix structures tended to encourage; another McKinsey team, at this same time, helped Mobil return to a centralized form. "They sold us Mobil's organization," some Shell managers later joked, "and Mobil bought ours.")

By the mid-1960s, the central operations, based in The Hague (in a building that looks like a palace) and London (in the embassy-like Shell Centre), were officially described as mere service providers—sources of such amenities as technical research, trading coordination, and the Shell gasoline brand name. Yet London and The Hague were still the only places from which a voice could speak for Shell with worldwide authority. An investor could not buy stock in Dänske Shell or Shell du Laos or even in the holding companies that owned them, but only in their owners, a Dutch and a British holding company with 60 and 40 percent of the stock, respectively. As a result of this peculiar structure, authority at Shell came not just from the top but from all directions; it filtered through the management by means of a kind of gravitational force, partly collegial, partly rigidly hierarchical, and partly based on the fact that sooner or later, its managers had worked at enough far-flung operating companies to become loyal to the group of companies as a whole and citizens of the world. (Decades later, Royal Dutch/Shell would reorganize into a somewhat more conventionally cohesive form, eliminating the matrix in the 1990s, bringing the operating companies more closely under central control, and merging the two holding companies of the Group into a single entity in 2005.)[10]

Its decentralized form and multinational history gave the Group a distinctive corporate culture. Although Shell executives came from every continent and background, they all seemed to be imbued with the same understated, pragmatic intellectualism. This was an era when oil executives were stereotyped as rough-and-tumble wildcatters, taking target practice from their hot tubs on weekends, like the oil cowboys of Larry McMurtry's *Texasville*. But Shell men (no oil industry executives were women in those years) were more likely to cultivate orchids and lead chamber music ensembles. One managing director, during the years of his tenure, published well-received histories of Nigeria and Turkey. To the rest of the industry in particular, Shell seemed uncommonly closely knit and insular. An observer of several meetings between the British government and oil company representatives during the 1970s noticed that men from Exxon, Texaco, BP, and Gulf tended to blurt out angry reactions on the spot. The Shell man would wait quietly, watchful and attentive, his position prepared. He would have talked over Shell's stance several times that week with colleagues back at the office. If he had to denounce someone or block a plan, he struck "not with a bludgeon, but with a rapier," the observer recalled. Shell men were like representatives of a secret service, he had decided—not people to oppose lightly.

In this type of organization, anyone like Ted Newland with an idea that the future might change could never simply convince one top boss or another to adopt the appropriate policies. Anyone who wanted Shell to change would have to find a way to make the future clearly visible, so a wide range of people within the company could see it coming.

o

Newland's assignment to look at the future was a minor task, one of many prospective papers and assignments handed to the planning department during the course of a year. But Newland took it seriously. He immediately began to look around for people who had found ways to think coherently about the future. The most interesting man he found was Herman Kahn, the founder-director of a freewheeling think tank, the Hudson Institute. Located north of New York City, the Hudson Institute specialized in a type of future stories that Kahn called "scenarios." These stories about the future aimed to help people break past their mental blocks and consider "unthinkable" futures, which would take them by surprise if they weren't prepared.

In those years, Kahn was best known for an idea that many people considered heretical: that the best way to prevent nuclear war was to think soberly and in full detail about what would happen if that war occurred. In his book *On Thermonuclear War,* Kahn described dozens of ways in which the nuclear powers might move into global confrontation.[11] There was one tit-for-tat exchange scenario, for instance, where the United States devastated Moscow after the Soviets destroyed New York City. In nearly all of these potential futures, society survived and had to cope with the results.

Kahn did sound detached, even jovial, when talking about these prospects; an acquaintance, movie director Stanley Kubrick, was said to have used him as part of the model for the title character in *Dr. Strangelove.* Kahn gleefully adopted his trademark phrase, "thinking about the unthinkable," from a bitter exchange of unpublished letters with the editor of *Scientific American,* after the magazine published a harsh review of his book. ("I do not think there is much point in thinking about the unthinkable," the editor, Dennis Flanagan, had written. "I should prefer to devote my thoughts to how nuclear war can be prevented." Kahn argued back that taboos like Flanagan's deflected awareness. Avoiding the subject of nuclear war would make it harder to cope rationally with finding a way to prevent it.)[12]

Kahn first began to "think the unthinkable" in the late 1940s, when he forsook an academic career to go to work at the RAND Corporation, the military think tank established just after World War II to research new forms of weapons technology.[13] RAND gave Kahn his first exposure to the war games of military strategy, which he began applying to technological prospects: "If a new weapon is developed, how will people respond to it?" He'd cloister a half-dozen RAND staff members in a week-long meeting,[14] and at the end they would emerge with a scenario about, say, India, written as if from a vantage point ten years hence: "In 1965, there was an uprising in Bengal . . . "

The term *scenario,* for these types of stories, was suggested by the sociologist, novelist, and screenwriter Leo Rosten (author of *The Education of H*Y*M*A*N K*A*P*L*A*N*). One night Rosten (who freelanced on RAND documents) poked his nose in on a group of physicists who were hunting for a name for alternative descriptions of how satellites might behave. "You should call them scenarios," he said. "In the movies, a scenario is a detailed outline of a future movie." Actually Rosten knew that the word *scenario* was already outdated in Hollywood; it hearkened back to the silent era. But to the RAND scientists, it sounded more dignified than *screenplay.*[15] Herman Kahn particularly loved the word, including its literary connotations. Scenarios, as Herman Kahn saw them, were supposed to be fictional and playful, not some sort of rigorous forecast. The point was not to make accurate predictions (although, like all other futurists, he gleefully loved being right), but to come up with a mythic story that brought the point home. That narrative quality was one of the things that impressed Ted Newland, one of the things he saw that he could bring back to Shell.

○

In the mid-1960s, Kahn left RAND to found the Hudson Institute, intending to court a broader range of clients. Military scenarios had become boring and repetitive; he and his staff of about twenty people wanted to look at culture and the economy. Kahn began by taking an assignment for the American Academy of Arts and Sciences to prepare background material for a series of inquiries on possible futures in the year 2000. Typically when Kahn was interested in something, he didn't let trivialities like the boundaries of an assignment stop him, and his small project quickly expanded into a full-scale set of scenarios for the world at the turn of the century. Most of them were variations on one full-scale, inexorable future: worldwide peace and financial boom. In the United States, prosperity would produce a permanent upper-middle class, taking on many of the habits and attitudes of the landed gentry of nineteenth-century Europe.[16] Kahn predicted that communism would collapse within twenty years, under the pressure of its own economic failures. He called this the "surprise-free" future: if it came to pass, it would not surprise anybody very much ("or at least not *me*," he said).[17]

Kahn himself made an impressive mythic figure. Over six feet tall and weighing three hundred pounds, he moved through his days with relentless energy. Colleagues remember him barreling through airports at top speed, bearing two shopping bags full of books he had bought en route, while a harried assistant scrambled frantically to keep up and passersby leaped out of his path to avoid collision. He spoke often in public, striding around stages in his shirtsleeves, cracking jokes and sweating with the exertion of getting his words out.

He was a fierce and unrelenting debater, but he also knew how to charm an audience. People could feel their place in the grand scheme of history as Kahn talked about the promise of the industrial revolution and how it was still in its infancy. They also recognized that his cosmic time frames made him treat facts loosely. Kahn didn't hide the point. It's not that he forgot facts; indeed, he had a photographic memory and could talk extemporaneously and accurately about subjects that ranged from the trajectory of ballistic missiles to the variations among translations of the *Rubaiyat* of Omar Khayyam. Nonetheless, he didn't think the specifics of the details were all that important. One of his favorite stories concerned the bloodthirsty Tuareg tribes of the Sahara. No matter what abuses they committed—rape, enslavement, burning villages—they never poisoned the drinking wells. They knew that once they started poisoning wells, they too would not survive. After saying that, however, Kahn would stand, shaking with silent laughter, while his mystified audience stared at him. "I have to tell you," he would finally say. "The other week, I met an anthropologist who had worked with the Tuareg. And he told me that they actually *did* poison the wells." Then he would pause again. "But it didn't happen *much!*"

Kahn tended to organize his thoughts in lists, and his list of the one hundred most probable scientific breakthroughs by the year 2000 included artificial moons, designed to light large areas of the Earth at night; individual flying platforms; human control of weather and climate; and extensive use of robot household slaves. (To be fair, he also predicted personal computers and superconductivity.) Because he was so willing to scatter hypotheticals, he was the first to hit some targets. For instance, Kahn was the first pundit to alert American corporate leaders about the need to watch the rise of economic rivals in Japan. "What will the Japanese do when they overtake the West?" he would ask. "I can't imagine a Japanese without a goal. Can they find one in organizing the political economy of Asia? Or, in the absence of a new fashion, will they turn to an old one—imperialism?"[18] He deflated one War Gaming Agency scenario, in which the United States emerged out of a nuclear skirmish victorious over the Soviet Union and with no other enemies, simply by asking, "If the U.S. massacres the Soviets that way, whose side will Japan be on?"

Beginning in 1966, pressed by the chronic financial straits that the Hudson Institute often landed in, Kahn began to hold meetings for corporate sponsors. Newland began to attend them regularly, jetting to New York as many as ten times a year, one of thirty corporate managers at a briefing. The others tended to be executive vice presidents and CEOs from companies like Corning, IBM, and General Motors—to Newland, the "top people of the world." But few of them seemed to take Kahn's material as seriously as he did. Like Kahn, Newland mistrusted idealists. He had seen, in South America and Nigeria, how a military coup could overrun a democratic government. The only effective counterweapon was economic growth, and plenty of it: enough not just to fill the pockets of the ruling class, but to create a broad middle class—as it had in the United States and was doing in Japan—everywhere in the world.[19]

Newland also realized that if economic growth continued (as Kahn seemed sure it would), then oil demand would reach astronomical figures. Newland figured a demand somewhere around 110 million barrels a day by the year 2000, more than double its levels at that time.[20] The world would need ten or twelve Saudi Arabias, all pumping full-tilt, to keep up. When Newland mentioned the possibility to some of his colleagues in Shell's planning department, even as a straw man, they shrugged it off: "We'll meet that need when we get to it." (In reality, demand would rise to 76 million in 2000, straining but not overtaxing the oil supply—at least not yet.[21])

———————— ○ ————————

A colleague from this era remembers Newland stopping him in the corridor to say, "I've just had an idea. What if the United States tried to close off the Western Hemisphere to the rest of the world? To corner the market on Venezuelan oil, for example?" The colleague spent a day or two researching the idea and then dropped into Newland's office to lay out the reasons why it wasn't plausible. Newland waved him aside: "You've shown that won't work. Let's look at something else, then."

This tolerance for speculative thinking was unusual at Shell. As at most other companies, people were expected to act as if they always had the answers. But Newland was protected by two influential advocates. The first was his boss, planning coordinator Jimmy Davidson. Davidson was a feisty former fighter pilot with a rakish moustache who, like Newland, had worked in both Venezuela and Nigeria. Then he had directed the economics and planning function for exploration and production. When the Royal Dutch/Shell planning department was reorganized, Davidson was appointed its head. He became one of several voices arguing, as early as 1967, against the use of the UPM. In 1968, Newland introduced him to Herman Kahn's scenario method, which Davidson saw as a possible alternative to UPM. It took several years, but by the end of 1969, the majority of the committee of managing directors became convinced, and they commissioned Davidson to manage the shift to a new set of planning methods.

Newland's other advocate was Lord Rothschild (Victor Rothschild), Shell's research coordinator and a member of the family that had bankrolled Henri Deterding. Rothschild was also a Cambridge-trained biophysicist, with a background in military intelligence from World War II.[22] He was impressed by Newland's first look at the future, and in 1970 he asked for an expansion, with a focus on the Middle East. This was controversial because Shell's exploration and production engineers, the most influential function in the Group, considered the Arab world their territory. Newland had never been there. As if that was not bad enough, the news he had to report was grim. The Western oil companies, including Shell, were about to lose control of their business. The UPM on which oilmen based their predictions gave no hint of the crisis to come.[23]

Yet anyone with a halfway sophisticated background in the industry could, if they cared to look, see the strain on the invisible pipes and pumps. The unthinkable, as Herman Kahn might put it, was about to happen: the balance of power in the Middle East was about to shift as world demand began to outstrip the abilities of the non-Arab oil fields to meet it. Americans overseas saw it. From Riyadh to Tripoli, local oil company office managers would send cables to their home offices saying, "This free ride is not going to last. Let's do something." They suggested new places to drill, new potential oil fields to invest in. They were ignored.

So was Newland. He sent a preliminary draft of his report to some Shell exploration and production managers, expressing his concerns. They returned it with a comment scribbled in the margin: "Arabs will never get together."[24] *Of course they won't,* Newland thought to himself. *They would compete with each other to see who could press the price of oil highest.*

In 1970, Libya's shrewd new dictator, Muammar al-Gadhafi, threatened to cut off supplies from his country. This drove the price of Libyan oil up 30 percent and forced Occidental Petroleum, which was locked into a contract there, to agree to give Gadhafi 55 percent of its Libyan profits instead of the standard 50 percent. When the news broke publicly about Libya's deal, all the other Arab countries insisted on similar terms. It was the first sign of an upheaval in the system.

Gerrit Wagner, the former general manager of Shell Venezuela who had once had to petition the CMD for a storage tank, was now a managing director himself and slated to become chairman. Wagner was an avuncular, genial amateur historian and a Dutchman who spoke five languages fluently (CMD business was always conducted in English). With planning finally slated to move away from its mechanistic system, he felt that it should take on a new mission: articulate the danger that might lurk in the Middle East. Shell managers needed to understand the forces that had produced this sudden upset. They needed an intellectual maverick who could speak to Shell managers throughout the world to help them learn how to be prepared before the crisis struck.

Ted Newland was too crusty and erratic to be the communicator that Wagner and Jimmy Davidson were looking for, but they knew of someone who would fit the job quite well. He worked in Paris as the director of economics research for Shell Française, the French operating company. He was unique within Shell: a former magazine publisher, trained in spiritual disciplines and government administration, familiar with Japan and India, and knowledgeable about Shell's business problems. He was also a magnetic man—the sort of man who people intuitively feel can understand them. His name was Pierre Wack.

○

Pierre Wack, then forty-eight years old, had been with Shell ten years. He had heavy-lidded eyes, a professorial air, a resonant voice that spoke English with a thick French accent, and the cosmopolitan quality of having grown up in two cultures at once. (He was from Alsace-Lorraine, the borderland where France and Germany meet.) He had graduated first in his class from the most prominent French university of public administration,

L'Ecole des Sciences Politiques. Then he had taken a job helping Alsace-Lorraine to rebuild after World War II. After growing disgusted with the bureaucratic mind-set of his government office, he had moved to Paris to become the editor of *Occident,* a magazine of current affairs.

Wack had a life-defining interest in spiritual practice that had started during World War II, when he was part of the circle of G. I. Gurdjieff, the philosopher-mystic whose ideas Charles Krone was studying so assiduously in Cincinnati. Gurdjieff, then in his late seventies, lived in Fontainebleau, near Paris. Wack was a university student at Sciences Politiques in Lyons, from which he sneaked into Paris regularly, sometimes across German lines. Years later, in conversation, he recalled his introduction to Gurdjieff:

> A friend of mine in Lyons told me, "Look, I met a very interesting chap, and I have an appointment at this address [in Paris] at four o'clock Friday, and you go in my place." So at four o'clock I rang the bell. I didn't know where I was or who I was seeing. I opened the door, and I saw the back of some armchairs in which a dozen people were sitting. I heard the voice of a woman speaking. This was Mme. Jeanne de Salzmann, a key associate of Mr. Gurdjieff's, and I was abruptly put in a quite advanced group.
>
> Very soon afterward—I think within four or five months—I was presented to Mr. Gurdjieff, alongside a quite famous man, Lanza del Vasto, who had written a best-selling book about walking across India. Happily, Gurdjieff started with him first. He really agonized del Vasto. We came back afterwards through the Metro, and del Vasto was so shattered [by Gurdjieff's gibes and questions] that he could hardly walk. I got a few tough remarks too, but after what I had witnessed, it was not much.

Throughout the war, Wack showed up at Gurdjieff's salons at least once a week. At times, the communal meals Gurdjieff cooked up from black market supplies were Wack's only source of food, and they may have been the deciding factor in his recovery from tuberculosis. Gurdjieff's spiritual influence on Wack was less direct. "I thought of him as a formidable, yet dangerous power," Pierre recalled in a memoir that he dictated to his wife, Eve, shortly before his death in 1995, and that she privately circulated some years later. "I do feel very grateful towards [Gurdjieff], because he was the first to make me see that higher states of consciousness could exist. . . . I did feel after several years that the road he took was not mine."[25] It was in his house that Wack began a lifelong preoccupation with the art of what he called "seeing." To *see,* Wack would later say, meant not merely being aware of an element of your environment, but seeing through it, with full consciousness.

He continued his spiritual explorations in Japan, Burma, and Thailand. In 1953, for example, he spent several weeks in Japan with a premier garden designer. Garden design is held in as much esteem in Japan as painting and sculpture are in the West, but the most renowned Japanese gardens have no exotic plants; rather, they are arranged to pull a visitor's mind past everyday mental chatter and past the expectations of what a garden should be, toward a more intense sense of being present. Instead of comparing the garden to other gardens, trying to learn names of plants, or admiring the work that went into the horticulture, "you see a branch, or a rock, or a leaf, very intensely. And when you see this way, you have an extraordinary feeling, that this is how I always should see." Wack sometimes told the story of his last day with the garden designer, who took him to a corner where vegetable brush had been piled. "'Look here,' he said. 'Look at it really. This is real. It *is.* And it is much more important than to be beautiful. Never forget. What is, is.' It was my first feeling of really seeing."

By "seeing," Wack meant a frame of mind beyond observation: the cultivated ability to connect patterns and causes that contradict our ingrained beliefs. "It is not common to see what is there," he would say. "Naturally, we 'look' with our minds—with interpretations, inferences, preconceptions, comparisons, expectations and through all our previous experience. To 'see' goes beyond 'likeing' or 'disliking.'" This wasn't an easy matter to learn: "By nature, I was not very predisposed to see," he recalled to his wife years later. "I would have been much more inclined to give myself over to interpretation and to mental constructions. Still, I launched myself into this activity with an enormous zeal."[26]

His preoccupation with seeing lasted the rest of his life, and it affected everything he and his colleagues did at Shell. For example, Wack made a point of seeking out "remarkable people" (as he called them) around the world. Acquaintances wondered if the "remarkable people" concept had been borrowed from Gurdjieff, who had written a book called *Meetings with Remarkable Men* and who defined a "remarkable man" as someone who "stands out from those around him by the resourcefulness of his mind"—someone who was not susceptible to corrupting influences like the kundabuffer.[27]

But Wack meant something different. The phrase "remarkable people" in French means not so much gifted people but people with unconventional insight: acute observers with keen, unending curiosity, who pay constant attention to the ways the world works. Meeting with them became, as Wack put it, "an addiction; my own luxury." When *Occident* folded, he became a consultant, specializing in marketing and economic policy studies; he arranged many of his assignments to take him overseas for months at a time, to Japan, Guatemala, Sri Lanka, Burma: "You find that a remarkable person usually has remarkable friends. It was a good preparation for what I had afterwards to do at Shell."

Among the people Wack became close to was a spiritual teacher in India named Svamiji Prajnanpad who ran an ashram a two-and-a-half-hour walk across rice fields from the nearest train station. Wack had studied with many masters since Gurdjieff, but he felt that Svamiji was unique among spiritual teachers. For example, Svamiji never spoke to more than one disciple at a time, not even to a small group, which allowed him to work closely and individually as a teacher in dense and intense sessions with his followers. In his sessions with Wack, he emphasized the responsibility of communicating awareness to others, or as Wack put it, "to be able to transmit this wisdom into personal and operational terms."[28] In other words, Pierre's work itself would become a test of his perceptiveness. He had the task of not just learning himself to see, but to make others see as well.

———————— o ————————

Under French law, people who began working for an organization after age thirty-nine were not guaranteed a pension. Thus, when he reached age thirty-eight in 1960, Wack took a full-time job. "My two favorite customers [as an economics consultant] were Shell and Michelin," he later recalled. "And I knew Michelin better than Shell. But [at Michelin] I heard to my amazement that I had to take my holiday when the whole company shuts its door—in August." In August, Japan and India are unbearably hot and humid, and Japan is overrun with insects. When Wack learned that he could schedule his own holidays at Shell Française, he agreed to join it.

This was typical of Wack's style. To his colleagues, he often seemed to extract extravagant perks where others didn't even dare ask, somehow bending the system to his will—not because he was manipulative but because he knew his own priorities. Wack had a distaste for small talk and pettiness, and he was a master at snubbing people whom he considered lightweight. But he was also a gifted listener, with the ability to remember, word for word, conversations that he had taken part in years earlier. Most of all, he was self-possessed; even in his moments of indignation, he seemed always aware of details around him.

After a few years as a marketing planner, Wack became the director of economics at Shell Française. At this time, a few operating companies had been asked to experiment with new planning approaches as part of the CMD's drift away from the UPM. Wack leaped to the bait. Like Ted Newland, he had gotten to know Herman Kahn ("an enormously stimulating man," he later said), and he experimented with Kahn's approach in looking at the future of Shell's heating oil business in France. How ample would supplies of the primary competitor, natural gas, be? "Only an idiot," Wack said, "or a god would pretend to know the answer."

Wack generated four obvious futures for heating oil. Then a hapless staff member, someone with no direct contact on the ground with the day-to-day business of providing that oil, spent weeks calculating projected forecasts for each future—calculating, for example, the expected number of oil-heated homes in each of France's regions. It took enormous effort to crunch the numbers, and the results, Wack realized, merely confirmed the strategies that Shell Française already followed. But the process of coming up with these unimpressive futures had begun to open up a more complete understanding of "the forces behind the system." When Wack returned to his spiritual adviser, Svamiji, for advice, the Indian mystic said this assignment was his "yoga: It will be the test that will allow you to verify whether you see things as they are, establish interrelations, see through and be one with it."[29] Why had the natural gas business evolved this way? How were French attitudes about heating fuel changing? These questions needed serious investigation. "Forget about this year's work," he told André Bénard, the chief executive of Shell Française. "Let me start again next year, and we'll do it correctly."

But Bénard was promoted the next year, in 1970, to become the Royal Dutch/Shell coordinator for Europe (roughly equivalent to an executive vice president for the region). The following year, he moved up again, to become a managing director for the worldwide Group.[30] Even before leaving France, Bénard had already begun to tell people in Shell Centre of this man at Shell Française with the gift of sparking people's imaginations, of making them see the world as he had seen it. Thus, for at least a year, Jimmy Davidson avidly courted Pierre Wack to join Group Planning. But Wack refused Davidson's first offers to move. He enjoyed his position in France, and he did not want to subject his dog to England's mandatory six-month quarantine for immigrant pets. When his dog died early in 1970, he agreed to take the job. But first, he said, Bénard had once promised him a year's sabbatical in Japan, and he wanted to take it now: "It will be the reverse of the trip the Japanese make when they come to the West to learn from us."

———————— o ————————

Pierre Wack spent much of 1970 in Japan. This was a rare opportunity for a Westerner. Knowing that the hardest task would be gaining entrée to Japanese companies, he acquired a series of letters of introduction to the *keidanren* (the Japanese Federation of Economic Organizations), the most powerful association of manufacturers from that country. A vice president of the keidanren agreed to act as Wack's "godfather," and Wack was granted time with senior executives at such companies as Sony, Matsushita, Nippon Steel, and Honda. Even then, he didn't approach them directly. In many cases, he wrote out thirty or more questions, submitted them in a respectful letter, and returned two months later to discuss the answers.

Wack later said that he found Japanese firms surprisingly vulnerable to external shocks and surprisingly unconcerned with predicting future events. "We do not share your enthusiasm in the West for planning," a Sony executive told him, smiling with satisfaction. "We merely have a clear vision of what company we want to be." All the companies he visited had decided which strengths they wanted their company to have in the future ("strengths they would rely on as an animal relies on its claws, its beak, or its capacity to hide," Wack later said) and had set out to build that strength in themselves. Sony's leaders, for instance, had chosen to become *ichiban* (excellent) in three technologies: color video, solid-state electronics, and magnetic tape recording. "Other companies may be better in one of those three," the executive told Wack, "but no one will be as good in all of them together." Indeed, Sony held on to this long-range goal for more than a decade—until it had achieved and outgrown it.

When Pierre returned to Shell Centre in early 1971, the rest of the scenario planning team began to work out a strategy for using their method to inform decision makers. Jimmy Davidson devoted himself to creating an atmosphere not only in which people like Pierre and Ted could thrive, but from which they could be heard. He knew how to soothe ruffled feathers, mediate when tempers flared, and maintain good relations with people throughout the Shell system.[31]

Newland, meanwhile, formed a bond with Wack. Their talents were intensely complementary. "I think I was much stronger in intuition," Newland would say. "He was much stronger in intellect." Newland would later compare the two of them to Tweedledum and Tweedledee; Wack saw them as two pieces of jade that, by rubbing against each other, became polished. Pierre reminded some Shell people of Agatha Christie's detective Hercule Poirot, methodically deducing the psychological and social factors that had produced a seemingly impossible set of events. Then he would describe them in metaphors and parables, which he delivered with the other-worldly mien of a stage magician. Ted was more like Sherlock Holmes. As he mulled over the facts, he would mumble darkly, lost in his thoughts. Then suddenly he would leap to an insight, and his voice would grow more and more emphatic, until (as one Shell planner put it), "you couldn't help but feel that his warnings were terribly important."

Both Newland and Wack believed that Kahn's scenario methods needed a full overhaul, but they did not quite know how to invent one. In 1971, they developed four new exploratory scenarios—images of the world as it might look in 1976—using a Kahn-style matrix to generate them. There was a "surprise-free" world, for instance, in which the shocks that everyone dreaded simply never came to pass. There was a "high-take" scenario, in which the Arab countries demanded more money and received it from a desperate world starving for oil, and a "low-demand" scenario, in which economic depression deflated the need for oil. Finally, there was a scenario in which the energy picture switched from oil to nuclear, coal, and other alternative sources.

As with the scenarios that Wack had done for Shell Française, these were lavishly fleshed out with numerical forecasts. Worldwide oil demand would rise by the mid-1970s, they said, to somewhere between 56 and 62 million barrels per day. But the planning staffers understood that the scenarios had little value except for their own education. Wack said as much privately to André Bénard: "Look, this is not the real stuff yet," he said. "These are just our own learning tools, which we are using to leap into the jungles."

The directors were suitably unimpressed. Frank McFadzean, who had once been responsible for planning (and a partisan of the UPM), grumbled that he could have done as well on the back of an envelope. Newland assumed this was their last chance. He was relieved when he and Wack learned that their job was still on. Both men knew that they could do much better next time.

———— o ————

It might seem surprising that the task was so difficult. By now, in mid-1972, everyone at Shell and the other oil companies knew that the old oil game was falling apart. The OPEC governments, in the gentle voice of their new spokesman (the Cheshire Cat–like Saudi oil minister, Sheikh Ahmed Zhaki Yamani), were asking for "participation." They were no longer content to rent their land to oil companies; they wanted stock in the companies that drilled the wells. The major oil companies thus found themselves threatened with the possibility that they might lose their holdings. To the oil executives (and to most American citizens), it was as if a gang of belligerent street thugs had suddenly gained the power to dominate the world. (Of course, the Arabs, seeing the West through the light of their Islamic faith, felt the same way, except that in *their* view, the thugs had been in charge since the end of the Ottoman empire.)[32]

The managing directors at Shell recognized the danger. If industrial growth depended on oil, then an oil crisis could soon lead to global shortages and even economic collapse. The chairman of the CMD, Sir David Barran, an erudite Cambridge alumnus who wore a monocle in public, began to say in speeches that the industrial world was "peering down the muzzle of a gun." André Bénard later recalled visiting his European contacts, including Henri Simonet, the Common Market energy commissioner in Brussels. He warned of the impending crisis and explained some possible remedies, including setting up an oil reserves storage system for Europe or encouraging exploration. Simonet was a socialist, suspicious of multinational corporations in general and Shell in particular. "I'll be damned," he responded, "if I understand why a representative of one of the most capitalistic companies in the world should come and explain this to me."

"Listen, it's very simple," Bénard replied. "Until now, I had this on my conscience. Now *you* have it."

Yet Shell's own policies had not changed. The organization, from managing directors on down, was still buying the same types of drilling equipment, refineries, and tankers and making the same trading arrangements, as if nothing was going to happen. It's not that the managing directors lacked capability. In fact, they were among the most sophisticated people alive, particularly in dealing with uncertainty. They had worked in the oil industry all their lives. They had an innate sense, a tangible sense of judgment, for the geological realities and the markets of the oil business. They could easily handle a question of whether to invest $200 million in Greenland looking for oil or to drill offshore Brazil instead.

But when told, by these first scenarios, about a future potential oil market that might be either 56 or 87 million barrels per day, the managing directors seemed to become paralyzed. They lacked the necessary gut feel for the new world that Wack and Newland were trying to describe. They did not clearly see its geopolitics, changing markets, and inconstant cultures. And without that gut feel, they could not act. If the planners wanted the company to succeed, then they would have to make this new world tangible somehow. That, in turn, would mean reaching the part of the managers' minds that harbored their perceptions. In late 1971, after Wack was ensconced in London, he, Newland, and the team of planners began to figure out how to design scenarios to accomplish this goal.

○

The planners first focused on what Wack called "breathing in"—gathering intelligence from the outside world. With his background in magazine publishing, Wack knew the first rule of information gathering: you cannot take in without giving something back. Most corporations, including Shell, conducted their research in strict secrecy, which meant they could not share information. They had to buy it from consultants like Herman Kahn and McKinsey. But Wack hated to spend money on information. Moreover, the most successful oil industry consultants were constrained by conventional views. Instead, Wack and the planners cultivated their own network of "remarkable people." Wherever Wack traveled, making presentations to Shell offices, he sought out people, inside and outside the company, who seemed to have some depth of understanding. As others followed his example, the phrase "remarkable people" gradually became a recurring idiom at Shell. When asked how to recognize remarkable people, he would say, "You know very well who they are when you meet them." Sometimes a remarkable person from outside Shell might stumble into a scenario presentation, as an Iranian physician did in the early 1970s, looking for stimulating conversation ("You know," Wack recalled, "it's rather boring to be in a Middle Eastern country"). The two men became close friends. Each year Pierre would visit and ask how his perception had changed.

Wack's reliance on "remarkable people" was not universally palatable at Shell. Some reasoned that if they weren't chosen as "remarkable," that must make them *un*remarkable. More significant, the idea contradicted an unwritten axiom of postwar management: that any manager would be "remarkable" enough to step into any role. Wack therefore played down his research methods at Shell Centre, where he focused on the other half of the task. For following "breathing in," an organism must "breathe out."

The twenty-odd members of the scenario team spent much of 1972 plotting out the elements of six stories about the future, weighing them according to what would "really make a difference." They overlaid these scenarios with a triangle, as they called it, of the most significant energy actors: the oil-producing countries of the Middle East, the oil-consuming countries of the West, and the oil companies. They picked the most promising combinations and then they role-played them—taking the part of every significant player on the scene. What would the shah of Iran do? How would Richard Nixon react? How about Gadhafi? And Exxon? As they played out the results, sometimes shouting at each other in character across the conference room table, they listened for contradictions.

For their first great exhalation, scheduled for September 1972, Wack asked for an unprecedented half-day to talk before the managing directors. "They can leave if they are not interested," he said. "But if they *are* interested, they must be able to stay the whole morning." He had spoken to some of the managing directors ahead of time, dropping hints about what he would say. He knew that they would stay.

———————— o ————————

Twenty years later, after they had retired, at least three of the managing directors would vividly remember the way Wack talked to them that September.[33] With the directors seated at a semicircular table before him and a screen for slides behind him, he began with a quiet, but still heretical, statement about forecasts. Trying to predict the future was not just impossible, he said, but dangerous. The most perilous forecasts to listen to are those, like the UPM, that have recently been correct, "because probably they have been right for the wrong reasons, and you are tempted to believe them. Sooner or later their forecasts will fail, when you need them most."[34]

However, in some cases, he said, the forces that create the future have already shown themselves. He asked them to consider the Ganges River, which he knew well because his Indian teacher lived near its source. "From spring to mouth," he said, "it is an extraordinary river, some fifteen hundred miles long. If you notice extraordinarily heavy monsoon rains at the upper part of the basin, you can anticipate *with certainty* that within two days something extraordinary is going to happen at Rishikesh, at the foothills of the Himalayas." Three days later, there would be a flood at Allahabad, which is southeast of Delhi, and five days later in Benares. "Now the people down here in Benares don't know that this flood is on its way," he said, "but I do. Because I've been at the spring where it comes from. I've seen it! This is not fortune telling. This is not crystal-ball gazing. This is merely describing future implications of something that has already happened."

What predetermined events, then, were rolling down like monsoon water to flood the world? To start with, Wack said, Westerners had always thought of Arab countries as a common bloc. Shell, for example, had an expert whose function was to analyze the Organization of Petroleum Exporting Countries (OPEC), but his analyses always lumped all of the Arab countries together. Henceforth, he would need to look at each of the Arab nations separately. For example, the shah of Iran had been the West's most eager and compliant oil supplier, but Iran had only fifteen or twenty years' worth of oil reserves left, and it desperately needed revenues. Its impoverished population was continuing to grow—a seedbed, though most of the world didn't know it yet, of the most virulent Islamic fundamentalism. The Shell planners had role-played the shah of Iran in a variety of situations. He was like a chess player with only one feasible move left on the board: no matter how he felt personally, he would push for higher oil prices and cut supplies. "If we were Iran, we would do the same," Wack said.

Saudi Arabia was so sparsely populated and rich in oil that the ruling Saudi family members had more money than they could invest. They could open up more reserves, but that excess oil was worth more to them under the ground, without the expense of pulling it out. (Saudi officials had been saying as much for months.[35]) If you looked at pressures like these, you could see that after twenty years of enmity, the oil-producing countries would now find it irresistible to act in concert. They would unite against their former Western allies. If any oil-producing country had had large oil reserves and the need for more investment capital, OPEC would have collapsed immediately. But there was no such country.

That was why, Wack said, the fears of the managing directors were correct. Instead of OPEC, the governing structure of international oil production would collapse. This would inevitably change the underlying balance of power in the industrial world. It would begin with an "energy crisis," the break in the apparent availability of oil—certainly in the short-term availability of oil. This would probably happen before 1975, when the existing Teheran Agreement between OPEC and the oil companies was set to expire. The exact moment of collapse was unpredictable, but the collapse itself was unavoidable—and imminent.

So was another apparently "predetermined element": the expanding need for oil in the West. At that time, energy demand in the United States was accelerating. People were driving more, air-conditioning their homes, embracing air travel. Europe and Japan were rapidly building roads and electrifying, which would drive up fuel costs generally, and the nations of the developing world, the independent former colonies of the Far East, South America, and Africa, were all hungry for fuel. Oil exports would probably grow at a rate between 3.5 and 4.0 million barrels a day per year—four times the annual increase of the 1950s. Thus, a shortage seemed unavoidable. What he did not know, Wack said, was how each of these governments would react to the pressure of a shortage. The Americans would be angry, the Japanese anxious—but would they panic? Would they muddle their way into a depression? Was it possible to tell?

At this point, if not sooner, members of the CMD interrupted with questions. Wack handled them as he always would: "I'm coming to that!" he said, and then hurried on ("very politely," Gerrit Wagner remembered). He now projected a chart on the screen behind him. The planning people who had prepared it called it the delta chart, because it looked like a river delta, with the flow of time split into six forks, each one a different scenario describing an alternative future (Figure 5.2). In the bottom three tributaries, the crisis was averted somehow, and oil remained

Figure 5.2. Wack's Delta Chart

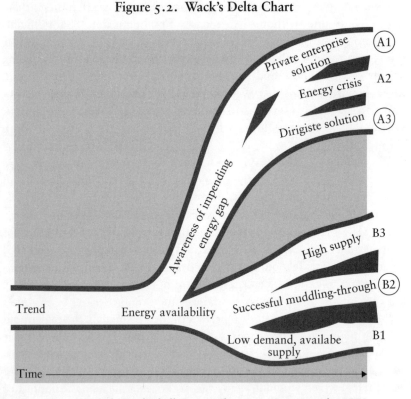

Source: *Royal Dutch/Shell Group Planning, "Scenarios for 1973 Planning Cycle" (1973).*

plentiful throughout the world. In the top three, an oil shortage took place but with different types of political response.

Only one of the forks, A2, led to crisis. The other five represented the hidden hopes of the people in the room. Thus, there was a moment of relief until Wack began to describe each of the alternatives and the CMD members could hear how absurd they sounded.

The *private enterprise solution* (A1) suggested that free market forces would solve the problem in the form of higher prices charged by oil companies. This future, however, depended on governments' recognizing the crisis before it happened—in time to undo their price controls on oil. Shell's managers knew they could not count on this future.

In the *dirigiste* scenario (A3), the industrial governments would take the role of strategists. They would act together ahead of time: collaborating on policies to control prices, allocating the flow of oil among themselves, and negotiating as a bloc with the Arab world. This future, to anyone who knew the governments, was even more unlikely.

The *successful muddling-through* scenario (B2) was Wack's response to one of his British colleagues in the planning department. "Look, you are French," the planner had said. "You guillotine your kings. But here in England, we tend to muddle through these crises, and come out the other end. Why couldn't that happen with the oil crisis?" A muddling-through scenario was reasonable, Wack said, "as long as we do not probe too deeply into current forces." In order to muddle through successfully, the West would have to encourage energy saving ahead of time (reducing the demand for oil) and find some leverage with which to get the OPEC countries to back down. (In some respects, the events Wack described for this scenario did take place—but it would take another fifteen years, and the success would be short-lived.)

A *low-demand* scenario (B1) posited that new countercultural values (or, as the planning people called them, "the change in social attitudes toward work and achievement"[36]) would abort the rat race of industrial expansion. People would voluntarily consume less, corporations would produce less, governments would promote energy efficiency, and the need for oil would decrease. The idea had seemed plausible during the European recession of 1971, but the recession had ended. The stoutly successful businessmen of the CMD had little trouble dismissing this scenario.

Finally, that left what Wack called the "three miracles" scenario—the image of the future that some of the CMD men still held dear. On the chart, it was labeled *high supply* (B3): it said that through the heroic efforts of oil companies, the West would develop enough new oil to keep on top of the world's demand. Mild shortages might take place temporarily, but they would simply reinforce the instincts of most oil executives: to explore, drill, refine, ship, and market oil even more aggressively than they had in the past. In this scenario, the crisis would be merely an opportunity to show what they could do.[37]

"But let us see," Wack said dryly, "what would have to come to pass." This future would require three simultaneous miraculous events. First, oil companies would have to find and retrieve new reserves incredibly quickly—including 13 million barrels from Africa, and 6 million from Alaska and Canada.[38] These regions were all unprepared for new drilling, and, in some cases, closed to it. Second, the OPEC countries would have to undergo a change of heart and become willing to sell as much oil as they could produce, happier with massive amounts of money in the bank ("exposed to erosion by inflation") than with oil in the ground. And, finally, there would have to be no extra strain on oil production capabilities— no wars, no extra-cold winters or sudden demand for off-road vehicles, and no natural disasters. Most daunting of all, there could be no more oil spills or refinery fires that would waste oil. "Any single small accident could upset the whole system. Again," continued Wack, brandishing a pointer at the screen, "nothing short of miraculous."

Most of the managing directors could see that now, and the mood of the room rapidly deflated. They already knew that the easy years were over, that they could no longer count on the financial cushion of a steady, unwavering stream of oil supply money. ("We sensed it more than we knew it," Gerrit Wagner would later recall.[39]) They could no longer build unneeded refineries just to preempt a competitor in some region; they could no longer buy unneeded tankers. For the first time, they had a visceral sense of what type of age was coming. It was represented by the only scenario left on the chart: the energy crisis (A2). The price of oil might jump fivefold within a few years: from $1.90 per barrel, where it was now, to $10.00.[40] Shell would now have to work much harder at weighing its investments, and every other major oil company would be in the same position.

Toward the end of the session, one of the managing directors asked Pierre Wack a question that scenario presenters are always asked. Which scenario was most probable? Which should they choose to prepare for? Wack refused to answer directly. "Look," he said. "Each of these scenarios is serious. You should weigh the probability against the seriousness of the consequence—if it happens and you are not prepared for it." Probabilities, he said, were subjective. People tended, despite themselves, to assume that the scenario that felt most familiar was the most probable. "These scenarios," he said, "help you not to prepare for the last war.

Sometimes you have to prepare for a nuclear war and a guerrilla war, two wars that are completely different, and you have to do it at the same time because both may come."

At this point, we may imagine, he clicked off the projector and stood impassively for a moment. And then discussion began.

○

When Pierre Wack and Jimmy Davidson walked out of the room a couple of hours later, they had two new assignments. First, they must present the scenarios to Shell managers around the world; henceforth, Shell managers would have to justify their decisions in the light of the scenarios. Second, Shell would make a concerted effort to describe the forthcoming world to government officials and try to persuade them to act. There was one sticking point: even the worst energy crisis scenario, said the managing directors, should predict a crude oil price of only six dollars per barrel, in constant dollars. Ten dollars was too outrageous; no one would accept it.[41] (Within a year, the price would rise above thirteen dollars. In later years, of course, it would oscillate even more dramatically, up to forty dollars, back down to seven dollars, and ultimately over a hundred dollars.[42])

A sense of urgency overtook the scenario team. Late in 1972, they produced a small white book with their estimates of every Middle Eastern country's oil reserves. In January, the "eggshell-blue" book appeared. This one, for Shell eyes only, laid out the six scenarios that Pierre Wack had shown the managing directors three months before. Meanwhile, Wack and Newland found themselves on tour. Wack made more than fifty presentations that year. First, he laid out the scenarios before the coordinators of functions and regions. They were a blunter, more skeptical group than the managing directors, and they had walked into the room without preparation, expecting a barrage of standard UPM-style projections and figures. When Wack finished, they applauded him—a gesture they had never made for any speaker before.

The operating company managers were far less receptive—but, of course, the message for them was more difficult. In Shell, as in nearly all other major oil companies, there are two separate cultures: upstream (exploration and production) and downstream (refining and marketing). To upstream managers, Wack and Newland offered a new unthinkable to think about: "You are going to lose your mining rents." In the oil industry, "mining rents"—an economic term for the revenues from low-cost oil fields— represented the most lucrative aspect of the upstream business. Now Wack said, "They're finished. You had better find new sources of profitability."[43]

To the downstream people, there was the equally frightening warning that they would now become a low-growth company. "No longer," Wack told them, "will the normal growth of the market make [a poor investment] all better in a year or two. You're going to have to be fully responsible for what you do. You cannot trust your normal reflexes."

Many Shell managers walked away from the presentations angry. "Just give me a number," they pleaded. Capital-intensive businesses like Shell Marine, with its need to plan for buying tanker ships, could not move forward without a number to plug into their calculations. But the scenarios offered no single number, so the managers chose one. Many of them took the projections from the "three miracles" future, which felt the most reasonable, and plugged that into their formulas. Never mind that the results were a recommendation to buy more tankers than a crisis would support.

"We were in a new dimension," one of the staff members, Napier Collyns, would later recall. "We were imagining things which were unimaginable—chief among them this impending shortage. And I think we all knew that it would be rejected by the rest of the Group. Ted and Pierre weren't too involved with our colleagues in operations, but I was much closer to some of them; I counted them among my close friends. And now I had to put up with them regarding our ideas as mad. I was reminded of the myth of Cassandra—you tell the truth about the future but no one believes you—over and over and over and over again."

Government officials were even less receptive. Wack flew around Europe and North America, handing out what the scenario planners called the "pink book"—the scenarios edited for non-Shell eyes. Like many other documents that must reveal closely held insights but not competitive secrets, it was extraordinarily difficult to produce, and even Frank McFadzean, the UPM promoter, praised it as one of Shell's most effective publications. But most government officials gave them only perfunctory attention. The Americans refused to make time for Wack, whom they perceived as a middle-level Shell planner—a particular disappointment because the United States was the world's greatest waster of energy and could have done the most to avert the crisis in advance. At that time, the Americans were doing exactly the opposite of what was prudent: depleting their reserves of oil instead of building them up. There was no political support for petroleum taxes or even for encouraging energy efficiency. The U.S. government was like a man who, hearing a warning that he may lose his job, goes on a spending spree, and the American oil companies were like an investment counselor who advises him to do exactly that.[44]

"We thought naively at the time," Wack recalled, "that governments would be wise enough to see what we told them and act immediately on it. Instead everybody thought we exaggerated. There was the same first reaction everywhere: 'Why does Shell tell us these horrible stories?' They tried to find out what interest we had. And obviously we had no interest; after all, we were predicting that our property would be nationalized. Secondly, they said: 'Oh, you exaggerate. It will not come in 1975. It may come in 1980.' Finally, the government officials would ask: 'How can I take advantage of this?'" One high-level politician from Alaska, for instance, wondered out loud whether an impending oil crisis meant they would be in a much better bargaining position for putting through the Alaska pipeline. No one ever seemed to hear Wack's main point: that by acting wisely and in concert, the developed nations could anticipate the crisis and stop it.

———————— o ————————

As bleak as things seemed, change did begin at the Royal Dutch/Shell Group—lurchingly, arbitrarily, and almost unconsciously. In some operating companies, managers began to alter their land purchases; parcels slated for refineries were also designed to be suitable for chemical plants in case the refineries became impractical. A few Shell engineers began designing refineries that could switch from Kuwait crude to Saudi or Iranian (they had different technical requirements), depending on what was available. In refining, they increasingly used a technique called cracking to upgrade more of the less valuable heavy oil and convert it into lighter, more valuable gasoline. The worldwide manufacturing coordinator, Jan Choufoer, had proposed these improvements in the past, but they had been considered too expensive under the old planning requirements. Now the scenarios gave them a broader base of support, and Shell moved, in oil company parlance, to the "highest-technology barrel." (Later Choufoer would advance to managing director.)

Bit by bit, Shell executives began to put in place many of the commonsense, mundane frugalities that had been lost amid the frenetic growth of the 1950s and 1960s but that all oil companies would have to learn to practice during the following years. The managers who made these decisions were, in effect, trapped by the scenarios; if they continued the profligate policies and the crisis indeed came to pass, they would not be able to claim now that they hadn't seen it coming.

"We had too long acted," Gerrit Wagner later wrote to Wack, "on the implicit assumption that the energy world revolved around Shell together with some other companies, without realizing that we were approaching the end of the oil era. We now had to observe a much larger scene and also consider a wider time horizon."[45]

By the following summer, Group Planning had begun to prepare the final version of a new, crisper set of three scenarios, designed to give managers a more intuitive, almost visceral understanding of their choices in the new world. These were scheduled to be presented to Wack's most cherished audience, the CMD, in October 1973. But there was never a chance to learn what the new approach might achieve. By the date of the presentation, the crisis had arrived, three years ahead of schedule, with its own existential imperative.

———— o ————

First, in September, OPEC brandished the "oil weapon" against the United States and the United Kingdom, trying to pressure them and other countries into cutting off aid to Israel.[46] Emulating America's own use of economic sanctions, the OPEC ministers told the oil companies that their current contracts, which were supposedly valid for another three years, were no good. They agreed to meet in Vienna on October 6 to negotiate new contracts. This happened to be set on Yom Kippur, the Jewish Day of Atonement, as well as during the Muslim feast of Ramadan.

The night before the Vienna conference was to begin, war broke out between Israel and an Egyptian-Syrian alliance. Over the next six days, the advantage shifted from the Arabs to the Israelis. Meanwhile the Vienna talks reached an impasse: OPEC and the oil companies could not agree on a price.[47]

On the evening of October 12, Gerrit Wagner was having dinner with his daughter, a college student who lived in a houseboat on a canal in The Hague. Midway through the meal, the phone rang; when his daughter handed him the receiver, he heard André Bénard's voice. Bénard was the Shell representative on the oil industry's negotiating team. "These guys are crazy," he said. The OPEC leaders were demanding a doubling in the price of oil—to the outlandish sum of five dollars per barrel.

Wagner told him what all the oilmen already knew: the stakes were too great for the companies to negotiate on their own. They would have to check with the governments of Western nations, which would take at least two weeks. But Sheikh Yamani, the Saudi oil minister and OPEC spokesman, said there was no time. If they didn't set a new price immediately, the Arab leaders, enraged by the war, would break the deals entirely. They might even cut off all shipments to America.

Yamani himself did not want this to happen. He believed that the retaliatory climate from the West would be awful for his country, which depended on U.S. military protection. He wanted the Arabs to raise the price incrementally. That night, after midnight, he received Bénard in his suite, along with George Piercy from Exxon and two other oilmen, in one last-ditch effort to avoid a cutoff. Insisting that a deal was necessary that night, he tried a variety of tactics to get them to agree before leaving the room. He offered them soft drinks, and when Piercy accepted a Coke, Yamani cut open a lime to squeeze into it and passed around a plate of dates. "I always bring my own dates from Saudi Arabia," he said. "They're the best in the world." As evidence of good faith, he called another negotiator at the hotel, a delegate from Kuwait, who arrived in his pajamas. He called Baghdad, talking vigorously in Arabic, and when he got off the phone, he told the oilmen, "They're mad at you." He scrambled around looking for airline timetables, hoping to find the oilmen later flights. But in the very early morning, he let them leave with no deal struck. "If you want to know what happens next," Yamani said, "Listen to the radio."[48]

During the next few days, government officials crowded into the offices of oil company officials. Everyone wanted to make sure their country would not be shortchanged in relation to the others. Each country put pressure where it could; while the British enlisted Lord Rothschild to lobby Royal Dutch/Shell, the French threatened to tax or seize Shell's assets in France. "All right," said Wagner to each of them. "We'll do as you wish, provided you go and explain why they will get so much less oil in Bonn or Zurich or Barcelona." In the end, he felt that none of the countries had been prepared. "Nobody was ready. The whole thing was put back into our lap and we had to just make the best of it"—in other words, to meet the Arabs' terms.

Meanwhile, Israel pressed its military advantage against Syria and Egypt. The United States sent contradictory signals about whether it would join in. Arab leaders teetered between their fear of U.S. reprisal and their fear of Islamic popular rage. Then, on October 16, they struck with the oil weapon full force. Hereafter, they announced, they would set the price of crude oil themselves. The oil companies could take the arrangement or leave it, and the Arabs would find other commercial partners. At this moment, the oil companies finally lost their domination over the international labyrinth of pipes and pumps, or so it seemed. Lack of control would make them richer at times, but also more insecure.

A second blow to the West came on October 20, when the Arab oil ministers announced that they would punish "Western supporters of Israel" with an embargo. Only a limited number of barrels would flow to consuming countries. They would deal particularly harshly with the United States. The embargo decision and the price decision had been made independently, by two separate bodies of OPEC ministers. Together the two had the kind of devastating impact that still shapes political attitudes today, a generation later. Royal Dutch/Shell, as it happened, was the only major oil company that had taken measures to become more resilient before the shock. It would never again be thought of as the "ugly sister"; indeed, it would become Exxon's greatest rival. That was far in the future, but even in the short run, the October War and its catastrophic aftermath provided an enormous boost to the morale of scenario planners. "Having told everybody that the unthinkable would happen," Napier Collyns later remembered, "and then having it confirmed so incredibly quickly, gave us unbelievable self-confidence." Hard-boiled managers from Shell U.K. or Shell Malaysia could actually be observed wandering the corridors at Shell Centre, saying, "Perhaps we should have listened to these guys."

Within ten days after the war started, the planners had put out a written scenario package that explained what was happening. Their speed was particularly impressive because they were also busy making presentations. Managers from most of the 270 operating companies were called in to hear Pierre Wack and Ted Newland. Then, while the planners took notes, each of the major operating companies—Shell Japan, Shell Oil/ U.S., Shell Française, Deutsche Shell, and others—described how the supply system looked from their end. This meeting was a crucial strategic move, because Shell, like all the other oil companies, was about to be placed in the uncomfortable position of allocating oil among all of its consumer countries, and at times there would not be enough to go around. Having talked together about the problem, the executives were at least reasonably well prepared to weather the crisis.

Nonetheless, the morale boost at Group Planning was short-lived. The operating companies and the departments of Shell Centre were still too slow to change their behavior.

Despite all their unheeded warnings to public officials, the Shell managers still had their own "microcosms"—Wack's term for the inner views of the world that, contrary to whatever they espoused, would govern their actions. As long as they felt in their hearts, for instance, that the best policies were to "explore and drill, build refineries, order tankers, and expand markets," then they could not help perceiving evidence in support of these policies wherever they looked. More than one planning staffer, for instance, vividly remembers his visits with Pierre Wack to Shell Marine, the international company that bought and managed Shell oil tankers and sea transport. Wack would conclude his presentation by saying, "Look, under every scenario we will need fewer tankers." He would ask them to reconsider their current purchasing plans. In return, some Marine people would tell him to come back in three months: "The boss is away in Japan, ordering ships, and the number two man is ordering some ships in Finland." Others would burst out in frustration: "I don't know whether to hire or build more tankers or get rid of the whole fleet! I thought your job as planners was to tell me what the future would be." And yet others would say, "Well, we've looked at all these scenarios, and even if we believe them, we have such marvelous advantages with our superior ship designs that we don't need to stop ordering." Wack began to grumble that the scenarios had been like water on a stone, dissipating without leaving a single trace; other staffers recalled him saying that nothing was more difficult than changing the mind of a Dutch engineer.

Wack began to think of his scenario method as a loud and ineffective machine, like a vacuum cleaner—wasting 40 percent of its energy in producing heat and noise. What was missing, he would later say, was "existential effectiveness," which he defined by quoting the Japanese proverb: "When there is no break, not even the thickness of a hair, between a man's vision and his action." To affect behavior in a useful way, he decided, the task was not just to argue with managers or to lay out facts before them but to influence their "mental maps": to enlighten them, broaden their perceptions, and thus help them change the underlying assumptions they held about the way the world worked.

In the meantime, the scenario writers had to start thinking about what to say next. The oil price crisis, they suspected, would open the world up to far more turbulent changes. Companies like Shell would have to pay attention to many things that had never concerned them before. There were obvious concerns, like environmentalism—which one of the planners, a Dutch enthusiast named Hans DuMoulin, had suggested looking into—or energy efficiency, which another planner named Gareth Price was beginning to champion. And there were less obvious concerns, like the legal and public relations barriers that would keep Shell (and other companies) from being trusted in the future. Shell's policy in South Africa, for instance, would become a source of great controversy a decade later.

The planners didn't know most of the details yet, but they knew (along with a growing number of people) that relationships among corporations, governments, and the rest of society were about to change fundamentally. A time of shaking up was coming, a bottleneck of trends in which all assumptions would be up for grabs. This period would last for years before things settled into a new equilibrium. Gareth Price had given the period to come a name, "The Rapids," and Pierre Wack began incorporating the image in his talks. The Royal Dutch/Shell group of companies, and industrial society as a whole, were like whitewater rafters who hear the sound of the rapids they are approaching just around the bend. Two prodigies meet. Amory Lovins and Herman Kahn in the offices of California Governor Edmund G. Brown, December 1, 1976. Left to right: Lovins, Kahn (back to camera), press secretary Elizabeth Coleman, Jim Harding (assistant to the State Energy Commission), Jerry Brown, and chief-of-staff Gray Davis (later governor himself). (Photograph by Stewart Brand, first published in *CoEvolution Quarterly* in 1977, then in Brand and Kleiner, News That Stayed News, 1986, Berkeley, CA: North Point Press) Willis Harman in the 1990s. (Courtesy of Institute of Noetic Sciences) Jay Forrester at MIT during the early 1960s, around the vtime he developed Industrial Dynamics. (Courtesy of the MIT Museum)

Social psychologist Kurt Lewin, participant Frank Simpson, and an unidentified man at the 1946 "Connecticut Workshop." This workshop successfully blurred the boundaries between "social science experts" and ordinary participants so that they could learn together about the dynamics of their group experience. (Courtesy of David Bradford)

The staff of the first workshop at National Training Laboratories in Bethel, Maine, Summer 1947: The first designated "T-Group." From left to right, the staff members are Glenn Kendall, Alvin Zander, Paul Sheats, Robert Polson (of Cornell University), Ronald Lippitt, Leland Bradford, and Kenneth Benne. Lippitt, Bradford, and Benne formed the triumvirate of NTL's early leadership. (Courtesy of David Bradford)

A typical T-Group session in the early years of NTL (in this case, Summer 1950). Lee Bradford is sixth from the left in the back row, in a dark shirt. In the back corner, in a striped shirt, is Dick Beckhard, who would later become a key figure in the evolution of organization development. Note the use of blackboards and butcher paper. (Courtesy of David Bradford)

Afternoon sessions at NTL were devoted to talk about theory and practice. Here is one such session, held in the Gould Academy (note the old school desks). From left to right, this photo shows Lee Bradford, Ken Benne, Alvin Zander, and Ron Lippitt, all listening. (Courtesy of David Bradford)

The National Training Labs Summer staff at Bethel, 1953. Some key figures include Dick Beckhard (at far left in back row, seated next to the dog on the parapet); Robert Blake (fourth from the right in back row); Ken Benne (second from the right in back row); Lee Bradford (third from left in third row, in front of Robert Blake and to his right); and Fritz Roethlesberger, who was not an NTL'er, but who was a Harvard Business School professor and a developer of the Hawthorne experiments that had established the field of human relations. (Courtesy of David Bradford)

The three founders of NTL, in 1968, toward the end of their era. Left to right are Ken Benne, Lee Bradford, and Ron Lippitt. The occasion is the incorporation of NTL as a separate entity, outside the National Education Association. (Courtesy of David Bradford)

Douglas McGregor, progenitor of Theory X and Theory Y, photographed in 1952, towards the end of his tenure as Antioch College president. (Courtesy of Antiochiana, photographed by Halberstadt Photographs, Boston, Massachusetts)

Jane Mouton, co-developer of the "Management Grid" system, editing a manuscript between workshop sessions in the early 1960s. (Photo courtesy of Jacqueline Mouton)

Jane Mouton at a flip chart at a conference in the 1960s; probably one of the earliest uses of flip charts. (Photo courtesy of Jacqueline Mouton)

Robert Blake delivers his part of the "Grid" training workshop, early 1960s. Workshops like these represented a deliberate effort to move from T-Groups to large-scale corporate change systems.

A scene from the Gaines Dog Food plant in Topeka, Kansas, around 1972. Gravy Train is packaged near the base of the processing tower. Everyone on a team took turns as a "humper," piling those fifty-pound bags of Gravy Train onto wooden pallets. From a promotional brochure published by General Foods. (Courtesy of Ed Dulworth)

If it's a fish-eye lens photograph, this must be the early 1970s. This shot shows the central console in the process control room at Topeka, in which team members, as part of their assembly line tasks, monitored production operations. From a promotional brochure published by General Foods. (Courtesy of Ed Dulworth)

One hundred sixty-eight feet of vertical factory, rising from the Kansas prairie: The Gaines Dog Food plant in Topeka, circa 1972. Grain and by-products entered at the top of the tower, gradually becoming Gravy Train by the time they reached the bottom. (Courtesy of Ed Dulworth)

Inside the main corridor of the Topeka plant, around 1972. Within the glass-walled office, at his desk, is plant manager Ed Dulworth.
(Courtesy of Ed Dulworth)

Lyman Ketchum, during
the 1990s. (Courtesy of
Lyman Ketchum)

The "flowering organization." This diagram of an "open systems"
organization chart was painted by a technician at the Procter & Gamble
Ivorydale plant, in response to Charles Krone's point that an
organization should be an open system. (Courtesy of Ken Wessel)

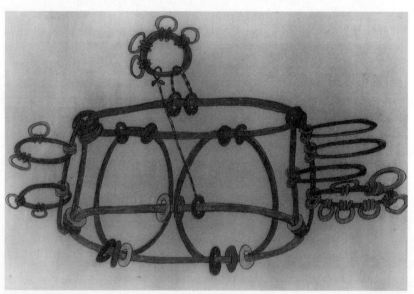

Herman Kahn, scenario innovator, in a pensive moment at the Hudson Institute during the mid 1970s. (Courtesy of Hudson Institute)

André Bénard in the 1990s, when he was co-chairman of the Channel Tunnel Project. In the 1960s, as president of Shell Française, he had been Pierre Wack's mentor; later, in the 1970s, as a managing director of Royal Dutch/ Shell, he had championed the evolution of Shell's internal commodities exchange, the "Shell International Trading Company," a model for how decentralization could work within large corporations. (Courtesy of André Bénard)

André Bénard during his tenure as managing director at Royal Dutch/Shell, with the Sultan of Oman. (Courtesy of André Bénard)

Pierre Wack, head of scenario planning at Royal Dutch/Shell, and James C. (Jimmy) Davidson, the coordinator of Group Planning, in the early 1970s. (Courtesy of Pierre Wack)

Hendrik Gideonse in 1972. This photograph was taken shortly after the young education visionary left the U.S. Office of Education (where he had been a client for Herman Kahn, Willis Harman, and other futurists), and became dean of education at the University of Cincinnati. (Courtesy of Archives and Rare Books Department, University of Cincinnati)

A 1950 photograph posed on behalf of Antioch College community government, and retouched for publication: Douglas McGregor, Edith Whitfield, and two other students on the college lawn. (Courtesy of Antiochiana, photograph by Tom Owen)

Edie Whitfield (later Edie Seashore) as a college senior in 1950. This was taken on the occasion of her election to the post of community manager (equivalent to student body president, but with more responsibility and a $60,000 budget) at Antioch College. Seated next to her in one photo is another student, her assistant, Louis King. A year later, she became a regular at Bethel's summer sessions. (Courtesy of Antiochiana)

Chris Argyris, developer of "Theories In Use," in the 1990s. (Courtesy of Chris Argyris)

Warren Bennis at one of his lowest moments at the University of Cincinnati: Signing a collective bargaining agreement with the faculty union, the American Association of University Professors. When the faculty organized a union during his watch, Bennis, the "management expert," lost the confidence of the Cincinnati business community. From left to right, the signers are James M. Hall, AAUP chapter president; Bennis; George Engberg, chairman of the faculty bargaining council; and Jane Earley, chairman of the UC Board of Trustees. (Courtesy of Archives and Rare Books Department, University of Cincinnati)

Warren Bennis at a high point: Primary night on June 8, 1976, in the alumni lounge of the University of Cincinnati, as the voters of Cincinnati ratify a vote to approve the takeover of the University by the State of Ohio. This change, which probably would never have happened without Bennis' energetic campaign, guaranteed the University's survival. (Courtesy of Archives and Rare Books Department, University of Cincinnati)

"Open Hours" in Warren Bennis' office, as President of the University of Cincinnati. This must have been one of the last "Open Hours" sessions, in which Bennis served as an informal ombudsman to the entire campus. It took place on February 10, 1976. Bennis is seated at left, in an armchair, addressing the crowd with a microphone. (Courtesy Archives and Rare Books Department, University of Cincinnati)

Warren Bennis, returning from vacation back to the University of Cincinnati. This photo foreshadows his transition from University president to writer and lecturer. (Courtesy of Archives and Rare Books Department, University of Cincinnati)

Warren Bennis, champion of students, sits in on an impromptu
gathering of undergraduates—probably a protest. (Courtesy of Archives
and Rare Books Department, University of Cincinnati)

Amory Lovins in the early
1970s, shortly before he
sketched out the "Soft
Energy Path" on a Royal
Dutch/Shell blackboard.
(Courtesy of the Rocky
Mountain Institute)

Two prodigies meet. Amory Lovins and Herman Kahn in the offices of California Governor Edmund G. Brown, December 1, 1976. Left to right: Lovins, Kahn (back to camera), press secretary Elizabeth Coleman, Jim Harding (assistant to the State Energy Commission), Jerry Brown, and chief-of-staff Gray Davis (later governor himself). (Photograph by Stewart Brand, first published in *CoEvolution Quarterly* in 1977, then in Brand and Kleiner, *News That Stayed News*, 1986, Berkeley, CA: North Point Press)

Willis Harman in the 1990s. (Courtesy of Institute of Noetic Sciences)

Jay Forrester at MIT during the early 1960s, around the time he developed Industrial Dynamics. (Courtesy of the MIT Museum)

6

LOVERS OF FAITH
AND REASON

HERETICAL ENGINEERS AT STANFORD RESEARCH
INSTITUTE AND MIT, 1955–1971

Heresy: A mechanistic way of thinking cannot sustain itself.

The great professor and lover Peter Abélard was thirty-seven when he fell in love with a Parisian schoolgirl named Héloïse. He schemed to become her tutor, she gave her heart to him, and they married secretly. At that moment, early in the twelfth century, they became one of the first medieval couples (that we know of) to break the precedent of prearranged marriage in the name of romantic passion. Because professors at the University of Paris lost their privileges when they married, Abélard hid Héloïse in a convent after she became pregnant. Her uncle, after this insult, hired men to assault and castrate Abélard. For the rest of their lives, he and Héloïse lived married but apart. As a nun, she mourned for the passion they once felt, for the object of his adoration had shifted from her back to theology.[1]

A passionate lover seeks to know everything that can be learned about the beloved. Abélard, caught up in the love of his church, used his classrooms and colloquiums to peer deeply into the motives and habits of Christian faith. He held the doctrines of the Church up to examine them in the light of dialectic inquiry. Which, he asked his students, was more fundamental: the universality of God or the Trinity of the Church? He invited his students to express their doubts and reasoning, quoting from the sayings of Jesus Sirach: "He who believes quickly is frivolous." In an age when miracles were no longer commonplace, what other buttress could exist for faith except the understanding that comes from open reasoning and logical debate?

This passion became his crime. His teachings and writings became evidence of heresy. Abélard was forced to recant and was imprisoned, and his books were burned. His sentence was pronounced by a group of drunken bishops at a bacchanalian feast. They fell asleep, one by one, below the table while Abélard wept, hearing his work read aloud and condemned.

When Abélard died of a skin disease six months into his imprisonment, Héloïse requested his body. It was sent to her convent for burial. She lived for another twenty years and then was buried with her husband. Eventually Abélard's students and other people trained in logical discourse developed much of Europe's scientific tradition. Abélard may not have inspired or trained all of them (though he had many students), but he exemplified their sense of purpose. Through their faith, they discovered the gripping joy of reason.

○

NINE HUNDRED YEARS LATER, IN THE 1960S, there was a man in California who lived his life as a sort of Abélard in reverse: through reason, he discovered the compelling force of faith. His official profession was futurist, an occupation that had not existed a few years before. His background included teaching circuitry design and philosophy to engineering students at Stanford University, a key role in an alternative religious movement, and another leading role in psychedelic drug and parapsychology research. The same drive that had led him into engineering, the drive to take apart and understand the world, had pushed him into mysticism.

This man was known in some business circles for his gift of engaging people in casual but deep conversation. An executive would stumble across his path, perhaps after a speech or in an airport bar between planes. Half an hour later, everything in the executive's life would be changed. Goals would shift. Possibilities would feel more open. The petty rules and formal procedures that seemed so confining before now seemed irrelevant. Spiritual growth was no longer something to be sneered at. It was a tool to be used, a part of daily life inside and outside the organization. It could be pursued without having to give up a job selling Coca-Cola or designing plastic components. Eventually dozens of people in corporations throughout the world would carry fond memories of their brief but pivotal chat with this fellow from Stanford named Bill Harman.

Willis Harman was a part of a small but long-standing tradition of visionary engineers. This is the tradition of Nikola Tesla and Alexander Graham Bell, of Claude Shannon and Buckminster Fuller, of Igor Sikorsky and Charles Kettering, of Gordon Moore and Douglas Engelbart. They all built and crafted machines, often making fortunes by doing so, but in the process of building and designing they found themselves facing broader, more complex questions than they had ever imagined when they began their careers. They devoted their lives to a rational way of thinking and suddenly came up against problems that could not be explained rationally: human emotion, aspiration, and ineffable purpose. Willis Harman, when that happened to him, embraced the extrarational qualities of life with an Abélard's devotion. He spent his life trying to understand them— so wholeheartedly that he renounced the value of rationality. In the process, he engineered the beginning of the new age movement.

Another visionary engineer, Jay W. Forrester, a very different man, demonstrated that the causes of behavior of any system can be translated into mathematical formulas that will then reveal truths that most of us would find counterintuitive. His models were deeply rational, but they led their users through rationality into an experience of faith. The most famous of the models, known as limits to growth, diagnosed a potential for global calamity, inherent in the rationalistic mind-set of the industrial age. To produce a worthwhile future, policymakers would have to develop a less mechanistic way of thinking about population, economic growth, technology, and human aspiration. These were all related; they could not be considered apart from each other. Faith and reason were part of one system, and somehow they would have to be reconciled.

○

It's worth noting the intellectual background against which Willis Harman and Jay Forrester worked. World War II had been an extraordinary catalyst for the study of complex systems. Just as the war had mingled social scientists in unprecedented numbers, leading to the invention of the T-Group, it had also assembled physicists, mathematicians, logicians, game theorists, and physiologists to work together on logistics and coordination problems using sophisticated math. Known as operations research, this new field helped wartime military leaders set up complex radar mechanisms, calculate how the fewest boats could patrol the most water, and predict the casualties from bombing raids.

After the war, similar game theory and decision analysis techniques were adopted in business, generating mathematical models of advertising campaigns, factory openings, or procurement efforts.[2] Meanwhile, in technical research centers like Bell Laboratories, a separate field called systems engineering emerged, inspired by information theory and telephone network design. Although these methodologies came from separate sources, they had one critical element in common: both discarded the Cartesian approach of traditional engineering—breaking problems into manageable parts, dealing with the pieces individually, and then reassembling them—and instead looked at complex challenges as system problems demanding holistic solutions. Building an automated refinery or installing a complex grid of traffic lights in an urban downtown required new types of analysis, blending computer science, engineering, mathematics, and even the social sciences.[3] With these disciplines as a starting point, Harman and Forrester were the first to go one step further: to use the insights of engineering to try to understand the world in a way that transcended mechanics itself.

————————— o —————————

Despite the esoteric travels that consumed most of his adult life, there was always something a bit rumpled and down-to-earth, a bit prosaic, about Willis W. Harman. He had unusually penetrating eyes, set in a face like that of a middle-aged policeman: bushy eyebrows, a thick nose and jowls, and a quick, uneven smile. He talked a little out of the side of his mouth, like Buddy Hackett. His voice was sonorous and soothing; his words tended to be matter-of-fact. The most important thing about him, perhaps, was the way he pursued his philosophical quest with an engineer's deliberation.

Harman had grown up in a rural town in Washington State during the Depression. After World War II, he moved to California and became a professor of electrical engineering. "I was minding my own business, with no thought of changing anything," he would later say. But in 1954, while teaching at Stanford University, his life changed when a Stanford business law professor named Harry Rathbun, a man Willis knew casually and liked, invited him to an informal off-campus seminar. The subject of the seminar was values.

Willis expected an intellectual discussion group. Instead, he found himself in a sort of secular church. Its members studied scripture and spoke of Jesus Christ as a teacher, but they also studied Jungian psychology and mysticism. They sat in circles and described their own feelings and what they wanted most deeply for their lives. They meditated as a group to music; they painted with their left hands, trying to release locked-up creativity.[4] Willis signed up for a two-week program that Rathbun called a "Sequoia Seminar," held at a modest lodge in the hills above San Jose.

"The seminar was an upending experience for me," he would say years later. "It hit below the belt. I was aware of thinking about value issues and so on, but on the last day I started to report to the group what I felt I had learned and I burst into tears. I wasn't sad. They might have been tears of joy, except that I didn't know what I was joyful about either. I had no intellectual comprehension."

Richard Rathbun was the group's spiritual leader. He had been an electrical engineer (like Harman) before going to law school. He was one of the most popular professors on campus, but he had never risen far in Stanford's academic circles. Instead he spent most of his time, together with his wife, Emilia, producing their Sequoia Seminars, named after the nearby redwoods, in which people studied the life of the historical Jesus Christ as a model for how to live.[5] Like T-Groups or Saul Alinsky's community organizing groups, the Sequoia Seminars gave people a chance to delve below surface conversation. Members stood up and talked, often for the first time in public, about the unseen patterns in their lives, their fears and angers, and how they perceived each other. Repressed, hidden rage would burst forth, to be replaced by cathartic sobbing or fierce, unexplainable joy. In California in 1954, there were not many opportunities for this, especially if you wanted to keep your job as an electrical engineering professor.

Like many other engineers, Willis had held an image of himself as a supremely rational person, a person who kept his emotions sternly in control. But in the seminars, he saw the extent to which emotions often governed him: fear of other people, eagerness for approval, bottled-up rage—and genuine love of life. Years later, remembering his sobbing, he decided that those had been tears of gratitude: "At last I had gotten off dead center and was starting on some sort of path. But at that time it didn't mean anything to me, except that I was impelled to go and look into areas I had never looked into before—comparative religion, parapsychology, mysticism, the whole works."

Harman was a dogged researcher, and Stanford had an excellent library on mysticism and religion. For two years, he spent every on-campus moment in the stacks, ducking out just long enough to teach his engineering classes. At night, after his wife and three children had gone to bed, he would hit the books. He continued taking seminars and gradually became part of the group's inner circle. Things might have ended there, except that in 1956, the group introduced him to another type of catalytic agent.

―――――――― o ――――――――

The Rathbuns knew a British-born philosopher and mystic named Gerald Heard, who lived in a Los Angeles canyon and whose worries about atomic war had influenced them. Heard was also a close friend of Aldous Huxley, the British author who had written *Brave New World* and, more recently, *The Doors of Perception,* a book about his experiences with psychedelic drugs.[6] When, thanks to the Sequoia Seminars connection, Heard came up from his Los Angeles home to give a lecture at Stanford, someone in the audience asked him about his experiences with mescaline and lysergic acid diethylamide (LSD). Heard gave a ten-minute reply, describing what it felt like to take a mind-altering drug. Listening, Harman suddenly felt that this kind of consciousness-raising experience was what he had been searching for.

Today, in a time when the word *psychedelics* conjures sensationalistic images of ruined lives or spent morals, it is difficult to convey—especially to businesspeople—the great value that people once found in the drug LSD-25. In the early years of its existence, many psychologists hoped that LSD would become part of their everyday tool kit. Some clinical psychologists claimed to have used it successfully to treat psychotics, alcoholics, and other psychiatric patients (although their findings were contested by others in the field), and some research psychologists, in those years before MRI and CAT scan machines, saw it as a way to learn more about the workings and potential of the human brain. In the early 1960s, when the Food and Drug Administration banned the drug's casual use and strictly limited its use in research, a significant number of experimental psychologists felt deflated.

Thereafter, LSD's supporters tended to keep a low profile. For every Timothy Leary, thrown out of Harvard, discredited, and arrested, there was at least one Willis Harman, who spoke of the drug openly throughout his career but never as a missionary. He never proselytized or insisted. He never even lost a job over it.

When in 1957 he asked Gerald Heard for more information about the psychedelics, Heard referred him to Captain Alfred M. Hubbard, a man who would eventually be known as the Johnny Appleseed of LSD. A boisterous, coarse, crafty man who loved uniforms, drank rum, and took long meditation trips out in the desert, "Cappy" Hubbard was one of the first people to conceive of using LSD as therapy. He said, for instance, that at three Canadian hospitals, he had used it to help alcoholics make the first step in an Alcoholics Anonymous program.

But when Cappy Hubbard talked about his past, his friends never quite knew what to believe. He said he was a World War II veteran of the Office of Strategic Services (which had become the Central Intelligence Agency) and that the CIA still owed him back pay. He had designed and built a nuclear-powered motorboat, which he piloted around Lake Union in Seattle. (According to Harman, he disassembled his motor and buried the pieces on an island in the Vancouver Gulf to prevent any government from misusing it.) After the war, he had become a millionaire by running a small northwest airline—and then had walked away from his business (he said) after having a mystical experience in a forest. An angel appeared before him and told him that he could play a role in the birth of something very important to humankind. Shortly after, he heard of a psychologist at the University of British Columbia who was experimenting with rats and LSD. Hubbard wandered in, introduced himself, took the drug, and thereafter devoted the rest of his life to it.

American LSD research was closely linked with the CIA's "truth serum" experiments of the early 1950s. CIA agents not only took LSD themselves but doped their unsuspecting peers and monitored the results.[7] Hubbard, however, hated the CIA, not just because of the way he claimed they'd mistreated him but also because he disapproved of their purpose. LSD was for enhancing awareness, not for manipulation. Hubbard felt closer to other branches of the federal government, particularly the Treasury Department. He claimed that he and J. Edgar Hoover were friends and that Hoover was one of the few political figures he hadn't been able to turn on.

Meanwhile, however, the gentle people of 1950s suburbia "didn't have the vaguest idea of what's going on out there," he'd say. "Most people are walking in their sleep," he told Willis Harman. A dose of LSD would wake them up. If enough people took the drug (Hubbard felt), it would free the world.[8]

With Hubbard visiting increasingly often, the inner circle of the Sequoia movement began to experiment with LSD—generally at their retreat, with one member taking the drug and the rest watching. LSD was still legal at that time (the late 1950s), but it was hard to obtain and was never taken casually. Fearful, intrepid, like a traveler pushing aside branches in an unexplored forest, the user in the center would call out every sensation so the others could monitor his (or her) progress. Having taken the drug, there was no going back: it took an hour or two before the effects took hold, and they lasted eight hours or more. Always, an experienced veteran sat nearby, ready to calm the tripper in case of panic (Captain Hubbard took this role whenever he visited), but the Sequoia trippers rarely panicked, no more than a trained sky diver would panic, during a normal jump, halfway to the ground.

Harman took his first "trip" at a Sequoia member's home, with a half-dozen members in a circle around him. Before long, he began to feel as if he had a jug inside himself, into which he had spent his life stuffing emotions. Now someone had pulled the plug. He saw the emotions, beaming glorious light, spill out and cascade around him. Then he grew light-bodied and floated above the rest of them, looking down. He tried to test his perceptions, seeing how many different corners he could look down from, and trying to remember, so he could describe it later, how his inert body looked when seen from above. He could also see, he discovered, through the wall into the next room. Then he was overtaken with the sensation that he didn't belong up there. "And right on the heels of *that,* was the reaction that I was not my body. I was not the gray stuff inside my cranium. I was something else that's not in the world of space and time. Finally, I understood why people spend their time praying."

After an hour or two, he fell back into his body, moved his limbs, and, still under the drug's influence, began to describe what had happened. The others had, of course, seen only his physical form lying in front of them, and they had never heard anything like what he described. Driving home with him that night, his wife said, "If you keep getting mixed up with this sort of thing, we're going to have to get divorced, because it's all too frightening." But within a couple of months, she had taken the drug too and forgotten her qualms.

Harman later recalled the following year as his introduction, through regular LSD use, to a new way of looking at the world. It was thrilling to see the form of a face or a house or a tree shift, turning into a creature of imagination that also somehow revealed its essential self. He peeled away layer after layer of his own temperament, drawing continually closer to the primal heartbeat that he shared with every vertebrate on the planet. Sometimes he saw links between himself and other people, hanging like sparkling circuitry patterns in the air. Later, when he came down, he could remember those patterns and theorize about them. Did they exist only in his mind, or were they always present but the LSD made them visible? The drug started Harman into his lifelong fascination with the nonrational—an engineer's fascination, driven by the need to pin down the essence of the nonrational, name its parts, and try to spell out how it worked. He felt he had a special role to play because he still had credibility in the world of technology. Somebody needed to introduce the two worlds to each other.

○

There were already a few sympathetic people with experience in both worlds. One of the first was Myron Stolaroff, an executive with the Ampex Corporation, the foremost manufacturer of magnetic tape recording equipment. Ampex was also a military contractor, specializing in telemetry and monitoring equipment. In 1958, when Stolaroff was in his late thirties, he began to explore the use of LSD as a management tool. Like Willis Harman, he was both an engineer by training and a long-standing member of the Sequoia Seminars. He was good friends with both Gerald Heard and Al Hubbard, and his job—assistant to Ampex's president, with particular responsibilities for long-range planning—included the task of keeping track of new esoteric fields.

In using the drug, he had come to states where the mind was unusually clear and new perspectives and ideas could burst through. "Such heightened perceptions," he argued to the management committee, "could be valuable in improving business operations," and he urged them to sponsor a series of experiments with the drug. However, the management committee of the company vetoed the idea, and he acted alone instead. He brought a group of friends, all engineers, to a cabin in the Sierra Nevada, with Captain Al administering the drug. He found the results fruitful enough to keep conducting experiments and recruiting more engineers, until finally, in 1961, he resigned from Ampex and founded his own nonprofit corporation for psychedelics research, which he called the Institute for Advanced Study (IAS).

From the beginning, Harman was an enthusiastic volunteer consultant and a board member. So was Captain Hubbard, who arranged to have the LSD shipped from Canada and also apparently leaned on some of his Washington connections to protect the institute from the increasingly strict LSD research bans.[9] Hubbard had also made an arrangement (with some of the National Park Service rangers, he claimed) to conduct LSD trips at Death Valley National Monument. He called the monument his "laboratory," and he regularly drove friends down there for weekend sessions. Meanwhile, at the Menlo Park offices of the institute with a clinical psychiatrist on hand, Hubbard, Harman, and Stolaroff conducted trips for executives from firms like Ampex and Teledyne, a Los Angeles–based defense conglomerate.

"We were meticulous in *not* suggesting the kind of experience a person should have," Harman later recalled. "We put them in a room with light pop music in the beginning, which would shift after two or three hours to some deeply spiritual classical music, perhaps Bach. In the room there would be a red rose and other objects with spiritual significance. A mirror was always very important. One person, who was fairly controlled and obsessive, looked in the mirror and saw his face made of stone, with faint cracks. He was profoundly moved. You can call it a hallucination, but it was very creative, and it was what we were looking for—the psychedelic experience as a new concept in psychotherapy. Instead of going back and examining all your past traumas, you could have a conscious experience which set you off on a different course in your life."

Engineers, it turned out, were particularly good candidates for LSD research. They were often emotionally sensitive men with painful early lives. "This [had] resulted," Stolaroff later wrote, "in the choice of a vocation that dealt with inanimate objects, sparing further emotional pain. LSD was a marvelous tool for discovering and releasing buried feelings."[10]

There was a wide range of responses, ranging from the mundane to the mystical. Some alcoholics stopped drinking; some engineers found themselves capable of solving technical problems that had bedeviled them. There were measurable improvements in scores related to rigidity and neurosis on personality inventories. Managers became more poised; they handled disputes among people more effectively. Under the direction of some LSD experimenters high in the company, Teledyne began to treat its largely Mexican workforce with more respect and to invest more in educating and paying them. Stolaroff himself found that his ability to play the piano remarkably improved.

And there were uncanny cases, like that of a Teledyne engineer who later became one of the company's most senior officers. He took a walk in the desert on LSD with Captain Hubbard and Hubbard's pomeranian puppy. Along the way, the engineer conceived the notion that he and the dog had a mental link, that they could sense each other's "higher mind." All through the car trip home, the engineer kept trying to think up an experiment that could prove or disprove whether the mind link actually existed. Then, at a restaurant where he and Hubbard stopped for coffee, he looked up and said, "Al, we'd better check on the dog. He's in pain." He persuaded Hubbard to step out to the car. From the outside, the dog looked fine, but when they opened the car door, they could see the puppy had jammed its paw between the seats and broken its leg.

Cases like that showed why LSD research met up with such resistance. How could you talk about paranormal phenomena in any rational way among a community of engineers without triggering distaste? And yet those were the experiences that kept people returning to the drug.

How could you *keep* from talking about them? There was also resistance from people who worried that "nonrational" experiences were evidence of insanity. Finally, although LSD was still legal, being a psychedelics enthusiast was not a terrific career enhancer, particularly for anyone who worked for a defense contractor that had to put its people through security clearance checks. For all these reasons, the experimenters who visited the IAS tended to keep their enthusiasm to themselves.

One other factor made it difficult to talk openly about the LSD use: it tended to destroy the faith that the engineers had in technology itself as a panacea for social problems. After a week with Hubbard in the desert, one middle-aged Teledyne engineer described to Willis Harman a vision he had seen of the industrialized future. The world was like a train, barreling down a technological track, but the tracks were about to bend sharply. The engineer didn't know where the new direction would lead and could not tell whether the train would go off the tracks entirely. If they took their visions seriously, then men like this engineer—and men like Hubbard—would have to think seriously about how to keep civilization from derailing. After all, they had laid the track.

———————— ○ ————————

In the early 1960s, the Rathbuns shrank back from using LSD in the Sequoia Seminars, and Harman drifted away from the seminars.[11] Stanford was spinning off a new systems engineering department, a potentially congenial place for him. No one would look too askance at him if he began to raise general philosophical issues, or even spirituality, as part of his courses. Soon he was teaching a course on the human potentiality, funded by a Ford Foundation grant for interdisciplinary studies. Because he was an engineering professor, Stanford's administrators assumed that his course wouldn't be too flaky. It would have practical relevance. But Harman focused it on Eastern religious traditions, "which we Westerners have neglected through the supreme arrogance of our belief system." He used material on indigenous North Americans, some Greek philosophy and European poetry, encounter group sessions modeled after the Sequoia Seminars (but without psychedelics), and books by the two psychologists who had been so important to National Training Laboratories: Carl Rogers and Abraham Maslow. They were now becoming known as the founders of humanistic psychology.

The students in the course were young business majors, educators, and social scientists. Some were there on the earliest Vietnam War draft deferments for graduate students. Others had wives and young children. Most of them had never been asked to reveal their thoughts in a classroom before. But Harman was skilled enough to create a welcoming, nonthreatening atmosphere in his class. One of his 1963 students, a young man named Oliver "Mark" Markley, recalled Willis handing out a one-page poem by W. H. Auden, about an archetypal man ("Anthropos apteros," Auden called him, meaning "wingless man"), lost in a British garden maze:

> No question can be asked unless
> It has an answer, so I can
> Assume this maze has got a plan.[12]

Each of the stanzas that followed was like a rung on a theological ladder. A plan implied that God designed the maze. That, in turn, implied that a path existed out of it. But how could Anthropos find the path? Through his senses? Through logic? Through the dictates of feeling or some form of spiritual renunciation? Then Auden parodied the idea that we create our own fate:

> I'm only lost until I see
> I'm lost because I want to be.

Auden had set the last stanza of the poem in italics:

> *Anthropos apteros, perplexed*
> *To know which turning to take next,*
> *Looked up and wished he were the bird*
> *To whom such doubts must seem absurd.*

"What do you make of this?" Harman asked in class when they began to discuss the poem. Nobody replied. Eventually Markley inched up his hand. He was in his mid-twenties, a gangly sandy-haired youth raised in Kansas by fundamentalist Christian parents. He had come to Stanford for a bachelor's degree in engineering on a fellowship designed for people with strict religious values. The course had been a disturbing initiation into esoteric mysticism for him. "I think it has to do with something transcendental," he said.

Harman smiled. "What do you mean by that, Mark?"

"I haven't the vaguest idea in hell," Markley blurted out. Harman smiled and moved on to the next student.

Markley felt his own mind racing; Harman had not answered him but accepted him. That was typical of Harman. Male students from repressive backgrounds in particular tended to come away from his classes understanding that Harman accepted them with all their blocks and stiffnesses intact. "You didn't have to go all the way," another of his students would remember. "He didn't make judgments about you being good or bad, and, as a result, he was very supportive."

○

Late in the course each semester, Harman described his LSD research and then told the mesmerized class that there was still a little research going on in a private center in Menlo Park, where he was a volunteer consultant. Any student with five hundred dollars could buy his or her way into the research project. That would pay for the rigorous testing and counseling that led up to the trip and for a male and female sitter who would accompany the initiate through an all-day experience.

Markley lost no time signing up. For his first trip, Willis was the male sitter, and Markley's hallucinations foreshadowed the career both men would soon share. He saw the stream of history flowing as if it were a river between two banks: one side of fear and one of love. The two banks existed in perpetual balance: when torture, tyranny, and cruelty had risen in the Middle Ages, Markley saw them being balanced by the prayers of the Cathars and other heretical monastic orders. ("I could taste the personality venues of the different medieval orders, and say to myself, 'Oh, and here's what *they* contributed.' It was all visible in a synthesizic realm.") When he came down, he and Willis both agreed that they had heard something calling them. "It seems like there's something new that's wanting to emerge," Willis said. "Various of us can take part in helping the birth if we choose—or not if we choose."

Markley instantly changed the direction of his life. He had been pursuing a graduate degree in design engineering, but now he switched to social psychology, the field of Kurt Lewin. He didn't want to be a psychologist. He dreamed of being a "social engineer." He wanted to be the bird flying over the hedge in Auden's poem. He wanted to see, and then help shape, the pattern of the labyrinth.

○

Markley spent another year in graduate school, now in psychology, before returning to the IAS. This time he joined Harman (and some other Stanford instructors) for a one-day experiment with mescaline: Would the drug make people do better, or worse, on some standardized educational tests of creativity? After scoring high on the creativity tests, the men spent the rest of the day experimenting with extrasensory perception, in which Harman's interest was increasing. He also knew that it had been a hot topic at the CIA during the 1950s. The spies had seriously tried to view faraway missile bases through some form of drug-enhanced imagination.[13]

During the next couple of years, Markley sought out, and began to study with, the psychologists whose work had been so pivotal to Willis's class: Abraham Maslow and Carl Rogers. By mid-1967, he had a post-doctorate fellowship at the Western Behavioral Sciences Institute in La Jolla, near San Diego—the institute that Carl Rogers had cofounded, whose leaders aspired to build it into a West Coast counterpart of NTL. Meanwhile, Willis had been invited to leave Stanford University and join a group of technological researchers assembling at the Stanford Research Institute, the commercial research firm associated with the university. There was a growing trend in social science research: under the label of "technological forecasting," engineers and technologists were increasingly being asked to identify the social and political implications of the tools they built. Policymakers wanted to know, for instance, how they should plan in advance for the advent of communication satellites or new types of rail links.

For Willis, the timing couldn't have been better. The FDA was about to ban LSD research entirely. Here was an opportunity not just to conduct research on broad social and philosophical issues but to be influential.

They even had a potentially permanent client with deep pockets: the U.S. Office of Education, part of the Department of Health, Education, and Welfare. As part of the Great Society agenda of the 1960s, the education bureaucrats wanted someone to study how to design schools with an eye toward the future. What sorts of people would be needed in the year 2000, and how could they be educated now to meet those needs? This was a chance to look at the culture of the United States in the year 2000, to express what they thought it should become, and to suggest how the U.S. educational system could help it get there. Was Markley interested in signing on?

o

The Stanford Research Institute (SRI), where Oliver Markley joined Willis Harman in mid-1968, was a hybrid institution: part commercial and part academic, part liberal and part deeply conservative. Its founding fathers included President Herbert Hoover. An ardent alumnus of Stanford University (the Hoover Institute at Stanford is named for him), Hoover had pressed the university for years to create a research institute.[14] Ohio's industrial corridor had Battelle; the East had Arthur D. Little in Cambridge, Massachusetts; Bell Labs in New Jersey; and General Electric's "Works" in Schenectady, New York. But there was no place where industrialists on the West Coast could hire academic scientists on a contract basis.

Many Stanford professors loved the idea; they taught on the quarter system, which gave them several months of free time each year. But they had no venue through which to peddle themselves.

The Depression and World War II delayed the birth of SRI. It opened in 1947, just in time to take advantage of the great postwar economic boom. SRI's bread-and-butter work in the early years came from oil companies. But thanks in part to persistent lobbying from Hoover,[15] it also became one of the two primary outside research groups advising the U.S. military. (The other was the RAND corporation, where Herman Kahn was involved in developing the scenario method.) SRI's first military projects included a navy-funded search for a domestically grown rubber tree and a study for the air force: With the war over, could that branch of the military switch to handling domestic emergencies? Perhaps because of projects like these, SRI became the first university-related think tank to include long-range planning for business, incorporating operations research, economics, and political strategy, alongside its hard-science and military consulting.[16]

Around 1967, as the Vietnam War drained military budgets, government support for technology, hard science, and military research dwindled. (Herman Kahn had felt the same pinch.) At SRI, the futures research and other "soft" social science programs (which charged clients as much as 110 percent overhead, compared with the 50 to 80 percent a university might charge) picked up the slack.[17] Hence, the SRI administrators welcomed projects like Willis Harman's, which must first have seemed as if it would be confined to the innocuous domain of education research. Few people knew that Harman and Markley—and their client, a thirty-two-year-old U.S. Office of Education researcher named Hendrik Gideonse—were already talking about reshaping society.

Gideonse was lanky, abrupt, idealistic, and a bit self-conscious. His small planning office had a budget of about $1 million per year, and he was encouraged to use it in a visionary fashion. Studies showed that it took fifty years for new education ideas to percolate into actual schools, and Gideonse thought ("with the hubris of youth," he later remarked) that this time could be halved to twenty-five years. To shape the schools now, the federal agencies needed to know everything they could about the social context of year 2000. One of their first contacts was Herman Kahn, who was then enmeshed in work on his book *The Year 2000*. To Gideonse's surprise, Kahn spent hours tutoring them—not just on the future of the culture, but on how to write a grant proposal and how to structure a research project so it had a better chance of snaking through the bureaucracy.

Kahn even visited Gideonse at his apartment in Arlington, Virginia; Gideonse watched nervously as the three-hundred-pound futurist gestured animatedly, shifting his weight on Gideonse's modest sofa bed.

Gideonse funded five ongoing projects in 1967 on the future of education. Herman Kahn's organization, the Hudson Institute, was hired to oversee and advise all five.[18] Harman and Markley won a contract for SRI because of the way they proposed to combine hardheaded engineering approaches with the softer, values-oriented concerns of humanistic psychology. In early 1968, the SRI futures group (as Harman and Markley called it) began its research. The group members spun themselves through a variety of future-gazing methods, from straight-line numerical forecasts to literature searches on utopias and dystopias from science fiction. They pored through forecasts, coded trends onto punch cards, fed them into an SRI mainframe, and sorted through the resulting printouts of hundreds of alternative futures.[19] For the education project, Harman and his group chose two key dimensions of uncertainty. One was the degree of "Faustianness"—how inept or adept society as a whole would be at controlling its destiny. The other dimension was "openness"—whether society would be flexible, open, tolerant, and civil or authoritarian, violent, and efficient. They ended up with a tree of destinies that split into five main trunks, each representing a path that America might travel.

The SRI planners dramatized the full range of possible futures by walking into Hendrik Gideonse's office with a miniature tree that they had commissioned a sculptor to produce from clear Lucite. There were five main trunks on the tree, each representing a different future scenario. These futures ranged from bureaucratic stultification and a raging recession ("Imprudent Optimism") to an apocalyptic future of pandemic violence and brutal police crackdowns in response ("Violence Escalated").[20] Schools would become armed camps taken over by street gangs. Terrorism, in the United States and abroad, would increase, and armies would mobilize against it. It seemed all too plausible in 1969, only a year or two after the U.S. Civil Rights Commission had implied that nothing could be done to avoid urban violence. Some of the details that Harman spelled out, in story form, to the Education Office bureaucrats were startlingly similar to the way that the Symbionese Liberation Army/Patty Hearst saga would unfold five years later.

One scenario, "Status Quo Extended," portrayed the optimistic official future of prevailing conventional wisdom. Such problems as population growth, dissent, race relations, ecological destruction, and urban problems would simply take care of themselves. This was Herman Kahn's projected future, but neither Harman nor Markley nor any of the other

SRI staffers believed it could happen. Wealth was concentrated too much in the hands of the wealthy; the American middle class, the path of social mobility, was shrinking.[21]

The SRI researchers found only one path through which a desirable future could unfold. They called this the "New Society," notable for its high levels of both openness and adeptness. But realistically, this couldn't happen under prevailing government policies and the prevailing corporate structure. In fact, it couldn't happen unless the cultural values of industrialization shifted. People would have to learn to stop keeping up with the Joneses, or buying a new car each year, or filling their lives with junk. Government would have to learn to adopt an ecological ethic.

In 1971, Willis Harman took that message to Hendrik Gideonse and Gideonse's bosses, the directors of the U.S. Education Office. As officials of the U.S. government, he said, they had an important mission before them. Never mind that the scenarios had been commissioned as guides for school planning, not as a blueprint for large-scale social change. As the developers of educational policy for the next twenty-five years, said Harman, the bureaucrats of the U.S. Education Office would be the perfect people to lead a transformation into a postindustrial way of thinking.

Sure they would.

---

o

Gideonse's superiors at the Education Office listened blandly to Harman, Markley, and the other SRI staffers talk of terrorists and ecological values, and then said that there was nothing to fear. The government was conducting raids on the New Left and expected to collect all its weaponry and explosives before long. The economy was in stable condition. All this talk of paradigm shifts seemed "so far out and touchy-feely and irrelevant," as Gideonse would later recall, "that they felt public money shouldn't support it."

Another factor made it inevitable that the project would peter out. Even before SRI's researchers had finished their first report or commissioned their Lucite sculpture, the Great Society had begun to grind to a halt. Around 1970, the Office of Education's budget and horizons shrank to simple projects—curriculum guidelines and school construction support programs. Like many other idealists in government agencies during those years, Gideonse felt deeply betrayed by the way that events in Washington undermined the sense of possibility for long-term social change. He left in 1971. Meanwhile, Harman's group began looking for new clients: corporations and private foundations. Willis didn't mourn. Education, as these bureaucrats saw it, bored him. "The really exciting stuff," he would later say, "was going on outside the educational system. And still is."

This was the period when extrasensory perception experiments swung into high gear at SRI. First the National Aeronautics and Space Administration (NASA) and then the military began funding a small group of SRI researchers to experiment with remote viewing: spying on faraway sites using psychic means. Even within the institute, there was disagreement about whether remote viewing worked, and if so, whether it was ethically justifiable. But in those years, the futures group members were both enthusiastic supporters and occasional research subjects.

To Harman, the extrasensory perception (ESP) work was significant because it demonstrated a giant flaw in the existing rationalist mind-set. He did not see it as a renunciation of science; indeed, he had arrived at ESP through science. He was trying to portray the ineffable as a tangible thing, a component of the world that science and engineering must describe. It was difficult because ESP work, no matter how vivid, confounded all attempts to measure or replicate it. Yet some experiences (they felt) couldn't be dismissed. In one SRI-sponsored session in group self-hypnosis, the researchers mentally followed the *Apollo 13* moon flight and (as Markley later wrote) got a distinct impression that something spherical was leaking. The next morning's news was filled with the emergency caused by leakage of the *Apollo 13* tanks.[22]

Admittedly there wasn't much that Harman and Markley could do with experiences like this. They couldn't write about it in SRI reports or sell it in consultation. Nonetheless, the implications of the psychic work saturated their thoughts. If other people at SRI felt skepticism, well, that was just more evidence of the old materialistic, Western mind-set embedded within people's tacit points of view. As that mind-set fell away, as people left the attitudes of industrialized society behind, they would become more aware of the most exciting prospect of their time: designing a postindustrial, participative society no longer hamstrung by the tired political debates or the fixation on economic growth of the industrial era. Even representative democracy was outmoded. Like Alvin and Heidi Toffler, whose book *Future Shock* was published in 1970 (and whom he knew), Harman saw a different kind of interconnectedness as plausible, where individuals could gain their own power over the future by bringing into action the ideas of an emerging new age.

—————— o ——————

Around that same time, as it happened, the values of the industrial era were questioned, loudly and publicly, through the computer modeling work of another engineer: Jay W. Forrester, a fifty-two-year-old professor at Massachusetts Institute of Technology. While people like Harman might be ignored, Forrester could not because he was one of the most accomplished engineers alive. He had invented the addressing system for digital computer memory.

Forrester grew up on a cattle ranch in the Sand Hills region of northwestern Nebraska.[23] His aptitude for engineering appeared early; while a senior in high school in the 1930s, he built a wind-driven power generator for the ranch, using cast-off automobile parts.[24] After getting a graduate degree in electrical engineering at MIT, he designed servomechanisms (mechanical control devices), radar controls, and flight-training computers for the U.S. Navy. That led him, during the early 1950s, to a job managing Project Whirlwind, a team at MIT that built one of the first digital computers.[25] At Whirlwind, he figured out a way to organize into a grid the magnetic cores that stored information so that the contents of their memory could be retrieved.[26] This became one of the foundational technologies of the modern computer. "It took us about seven years to convince the industry that random-access magnetic-core memory was the solution to a missing link in computer technology," Forrester later said. "Then we spent the following seven years in the patent courts convincing them that they had not all thought of it first."

In 1956, still in his thirties, Forrester walked away from computer design, feeling that the exciting pioneering days were over. He joined the School of Management at MIT, which had just welcomed back Douglas McGregor, looking for a way to use his intellect in the study of real-world problems. At first Forrester planned to work in operations research, but he grew impatient with a methodology aimed, as he perceived it, at finding "little efficiencies in the corners." He wanted to work on "issues that made the difference between corporate success and failure."[27]

Soon after he arrived, a few managers from General Electric's household appliance division found their way to his office with a problem endemic to any manufacturing business, which no one had been able to solve.[28] Some months the factories had so many orders they couldn't keep up, even with massive amounts of overtime. Other months they wanted to lay off half their people. Why couldn't they develop a steady production flow? Why did orders rise and fall?

Traditionally managers blamed these types of fluctuations on business cycles. Sometimes consumers bought more, sometimes bought less, and there was nothing anyone could do about it. But that explanation didn't sit right with Forrester. The dynamics reminded him too much of servomechanism controllers, the automatic control devices that inspired the field of cybernetics in the mid-twentieth century, which he had spent years designing for the U.S. Navy. All machines can be used as analogues of deeper processes; Sigmund Freud had based his depth-plumbing psychology on an analogy to the hydraulic pump. Forrester built a modeling language on the servomechanisms he knew from his navy days. A servomechanism is a mechanical device hooked to a sensor, like a thermostat on a building's automated heating unit. The first signals to come in from temperature sensors often report that the building is still too cold. Thus, the thermostat may continue dispensing heat, and the building becomes too hot. So then the thermostat signals for cooling, but once again, it takes time to change the temperature, and the building becomes too cold. The fluctuation has to do not with the actual outside temperatures but with the synchronization (or lack of it) between the heating and measuring devices.

It seemed to Forrester that the General Electric managers were faced with a similar problem—and, if so, they could fix it. He computed manually how production, employment, inventories, and backlogs would behave when controlled by the management policies then in use at General Electric. He showed that even with constant demand from consumers, those policies were themselves able to produce the instability of production that had been observed. He tested his diagnosis by tracing back a series of horrible fluctuations at the factory to the original orders that came in from retail stores, plotting the inventory levels and the number of goods on order, week by week, at every point in the distribution chain. Then he entered all the numbers into a computer model he had developed, translating the manufacturer's policies into algorithms that demonstrated their effects over time.

Unlike most other computer models of its time, Forrester's incorporated the principle of feedback: the way that a circuit, an ecological niche, a human body, an organization, a culture, or any other system will regulate itself, growing or seeking stability. In any system involving feedback (which includes all of nature and human activity), influence is cyclical. There is no single cause-and-effect; the effect always influences the cause. You turn a faucet to produce a stream of water and fill a glass, but the volume of water in the glass is also controlling your hand by influencing it to stop when the glass gets full. Feedback relationships could interact for years, with various management policies pushing each other in intricate patterns, producing complex results that would seem thoroughly mysterious unless you understood the dynamics of their interrelationships over time.[29]

In the first quarter of GE's data that Forrester studied, for instance, retail appliance sales increased by 10 percent.[30] Retailers then ordered more appliances to refill their inventories. But it took weeks for orders to work their way through the wholesaling channels and for the GE factories to ship their products. While they waited, retailers tended to panic—and to pile on more orders than they needed. This in turn caused distributors and wholesalers to pile on their orders, and that added pressure at the factory, where orders jumped by 51 percent.

After six months, when all the orders had finally arrived, there was a glut at appliance stores, so they cut orders and returned their extra stock to the warehouses. Distributors sent them back to GE. Factory production eventually dropped to 3 percent below where it had started—a disaster. The result was a series of curves that rose and crashed in succession (Figure 6.1).[31]

That tiny 10 percent jump in sales had been amplified again and again as it worked its way back and forth along the distribution chain, until it resulted in hundreds of thousands of dollars' worth of excess toasters on warehouse skids. It was all exacerbated by the managers' reactions to what they perceived as outside problems, like seasonal demand or competitors' actions, because they had no understanding, Forrester said, of how the system worked. If they really wanted to smooth out the fluctuation, he suggested, they could eliminate a level of distributors or react more slowly to surges in orders. That's where the leverage existed.

Figure 6.1. Fluctuations in a Production-Distribution Cycle

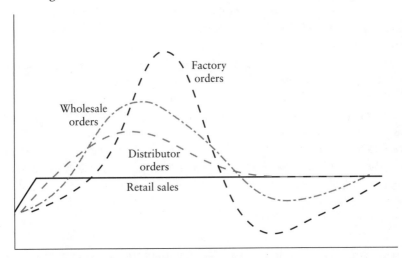

Source: *Adapted from J. Forrester,* Industrial Dynamics *(Cambridge, Mass.: MIT Press, 1968).*

Soon Forrester developed a computer model of GE's supply chain, which some of his MIT students turned into a board game for team play in the early 1960s. As college students, they found beer more appealing than toasters, and they called it the "MIT Beer Game." It is still played frequently in corporate training programs.[32] But there was a lot more to Forrester's method than streamlining the production-distribution cycle. Concepts from engineering, such as noise (irrelevant signals) and the use of nonlinear equations, all had implications for organizational leaders. And at least one of those implications was very hard to accept: most problems that corporate leaders (or leaders of any other system) face aren't caused by outside forces: competitors, market trends, or regulation. Problems tend to derive from the unintended consequences of the leaders' own ideas and efforts.

"That's a very treacherous situation," Forrester later told writer Larry Fisher, "because if you believe [your] policies solve a problem, and you do not see that they are causing the problem, you keep repeating more of the very policies that create the problems in the first place. This can produce a downward spiral toward failure."[33]

During the next few years, Forrester refined his appliance model into a more general-purpose computer modeling language called DYNAMO. It represented managers' decisions in terms of the vessels and pipeline valves ("stocks" and "flows") of fluid dynamics. The resulting simulations were particularly good at explaining the gradual accumulations and accelerations of the kinds of forces that creep up slowly and unnoticed, until one day the entire system shifts. (Malcolm Gladwell would later popularize this concept in his book *The Tipping Point*.) Modeling this kind of growth and resistance requires nonlinear calculus, a form of math so intricate that even the most gifted and highly trained mathematicians are incapable of solving nonlinear equations in their heads.[34]

Over the next decade, Forrester consulted in arenas as diverse as manufacturing, city government, and medical research. In one celebrated case, he advised the Digital Equipment Corporation (whose founder and CEO, Ken Olsen, had been his student and a collaborator on Project Whirlwind), to expand production, while the company was still small, into the full floor of the former woolen mill where DEC had started in Maynard, Massachusetts. "A lot of companies think they expand as a consequence of orders," he told the other members of the Digital board of directors. But orders, he argued, actually come in as a consequence of expansion. They held their next meeting in the new space, an empty floor as big as two football fields. Standing in the middle of the room, they could barely see the windows at the opposite end. Nine months later, the floor was completely full of machines and people, returning a net profit of 15 percent of after-tax revenues. Digital continued to buy buildings and land in the area anticipating when they would be needed. Forrester's suggestion contributed to the development of the Route 128 industrial corridor outside Boston.

But Forrester was also disillusioned with the response he got from many corporate leaders: they often lost interest when his models suggested fundamental change was needed. Clients would thank him politely and then ignore his suggestions. He began meeting regularly with Douglas McGregor, in part to talk about this curiously resistant aspect of corporate nature. One result was a paper Forrester wrote suggesting that American management was hamstrung by the same "authoritarian, socialist" bureaucratic style that business leaders strongly criticized in socialist governments.[35] Like Pierre Wack, he felt that mental models were so deeply embedded in managers' images of themselves that they could not appreciate alternatives.

Part of the problem was his own personality. Jay Forrester had a superciliousness to match his brilliance. He was known for being a tough student adviser and stubborn in his arguments; his stiff demeanor (he looked a little like the farmer in Grant Wood's *American Gothic* painting) conveyed the impression, whether he intended it or not, that nobody understood the truth about a system as well as he did. Indeed, as the years went by, Forrester and his students were occasionally heard to say that nobody should make policy decisions unless they understood the counterintuitive math of nonlinear equations; otherwise they would never understand how systems, influenced by those dynamics, interacted in the real world. And it might take a few generations of computer education to spread that understanding; seventy-five years or more might pass before the awareness of society's leaders caught up with the complexity of the problems they faced.

———————— o ————————

When Forrester's first book on corporate systemic patterns, *Industrial Dynamics,* came out in 1961, it was compared with the work of Galileo, Malthus, Rousseau, and John Stuart Mill.[36] And like all other efforts to delineate the behavior of systems, the same techniques could be applied to a wide variety of endeavors. In 1968, for instance, Forrester began working with John Collins, a former mayor of Boston, on a theory about urban growth and poverty. Using his dynamics modeling language, he was one of the first analysts to recognize how postwar measures such as urban renewal created more of the poverty that they were designed to eliminate. That led to a second book, *Urban Dynamics,* as dense and provocative as the first. A story circulated among his students at MIT that on a visit to Johns Hopkins University, Forrester had heard a group of cancer researchers describing some tests and said, "Excuse me. Here's what I think will happen to your treatment if you continue." They turned and stared at him; obviously he had no medical background. "The structure of the progression of this disease," he continued, "is the same structure I see in urban decay."

In 1970, a small but influential group of business leaders, government ministers, and academics invited Forrester to use his system dynamics approach on an unprecedented scale. The invitation came from the Club of Rome, an informal society deliberately designed to be international, entered through invitation only, and limited in its by-laws to one hundred people. They had organized themselves in 1968 to investigate what they called the world's *problematique humaine:* their feeling that world population, pollution, poverty levels, natural resource depletion, crime, international terrorism, and youth rebellion were all bound inexorably for crisis and were also somehow interrelated. Could any of these problems be addressed in the long run without addressing the others?

Aurelio Peccei, the founder, didn't think so. The prime mover behind the club, he was a sixty-two-year-old former Fiat executive, a long-time member of the Olivetti board, a former World War II anti-Fascist resistance leader, and the founder of ItalConsult, Italy's most prominent economic consulting firm.[37] Peccei had intended the club to be a carefully selected group of people who could investigate the *problematique* and present the public with an approach to solving it. There was always a long waiting list to get into the club, for the members included a variety of eminences and thinkers: Hassan Ozbekan, a Wharton professor who had prodded Peccei to start the club; Eduard Pestel, president of the University of Hanover in Germany; Saburo Okita, head of the Economic Research Center, a private institute in Tokyo; and Carroll Wilson, one of the first people appointed to the U.S. Atomic Energy Commission and now one of the most respected and beloved members of MIT's faculty—a physicist who had spent the past few years researching the longtime effects of pollution.

Wilson introduced Jay Forrester as a new member at a club meeting in Bern, Switzerland, in June 1970. The club had been promised a $400,000 grant from the Volkswagen Foundation if they could propose a viable research project. Hassan Ozbekan, the Wharton professor, had written a preliminary proposal, but the foundation had rejected it; they had sent $40,000 instead, to finance another proposal. Now the sixty-odd members of the club couldn't agree on how to proceed. As a result, the whole project was floundering. Forrester sat through the first day without saying anything, feeling self-conscious about being an "ugly American" in this international gathering. Then, at 6:00 P.M., someone mentioned that Volkswagen would cancel the grant unless the club could show they had a satisfactory methodology.

"Excuse me," Forrester said, "I think I have the methodology you are looking for." He explained briefly and invited them to visit MIT and see for themselves. Nobody seemed to hear him. He settled back in his seat until another lull in the conversation, when someone remembered him and asked him to elaborate. "This isn't something I can cover briefly," Forrester said, and once again invited them to visit—but either for two full weeks, he added, or not at all, because it would take that long to understand.

They agreed to come three weeks hence. Suddenly Forrester had only days to organize a massive conference. On the flight home, he began to muse about what he would show them. He began scribbling out a design for a model of the *problematique;* before long, his diagrams occupied nine empty coach seats. On the following Saturday, the Fourth of July, Forrester worked until eleven at night, converting his equations into a computer model (which he named "World").[38] By the time the Club of Rome members arrived in mid-July, his model was virtually complete. Forrester's graduate students quickly painted it onto a white bedsheet, which covered one wall of the MIT classroom where the group met.

Like all of Forrester's other models, World was a computerized network of interrelated policies, all affecting each other over time, as the model evolved. When "population" rose, for example, that caused "demand for goods and services" (such as schools and medical care) to rise, which increased "employment" and "capital investment," which allowed "population" to rise still further. A cycle was in place, pushing "population" continually higher unless other forces intervened. There were many such interrelated cycles in the model, and they all came alive when researchers ran the simulation. A researcher could enter a scenario of zero population growth, or of rapid population growth, along with various policies for economic development and agricultural production. Then the model would churn out its calculations and simulate the fate of the world over the course of two hundred years. The model was not intended to be accurate in local detail, but the plausibility of its relationships was confirmed later by research that the club funded.

As soon as the club members saw the model at MIT, there was flak, especially from Ozbekan, the project's own director. He resigned in protest after a stormy confrontation in Forrester's office. "You're selling out!" he said, meaning that he did not trust a technique based on a computer simulation. Then the Volkswagen Foundation trustees, apparently unwilling to send $400,000 to the United States, reduced the size of the grant to $240,000. The Club of Rome wanted Forrester to drop all his other work and devote the next year to refining, testing, and reporting on the model, but he refused: instead, he delegated the job to a team of MIT-based researchers.

The team was led by two young postgraduates, around thirty years old, who were married to each other and had just finished a year-long trip around Asia together. Their names were Dennis and Donella (Dana) Meadows. Dennis was lanky, long-faced, long-sideburned, slow-speaking, and cerebral; his previous system dynamics work had focused on the fluctuations of pork bellies in commodities markets.[39] Dana was talkative, a bit elfin in her features, and an avid writer. Her background was in biophysics and ecology: "I saw the world through the second law of thermodynamics," she later said.

They had stepped forward as volunteers to claim the project, and Forrester did not object. He completed his model, now called World2, and produced his third book, *World Dynamics*. "It had everything necessary to guarantee there would be no public notice," he later said. It had forty pages of equations and dealt with issues decades in the future. He doubted it would get reviewed, but it garnered notices in the *London Observer*, the *Christian Science Monitor*, the *Wall Street Journal*, and *Fortune*. The notices were generally receptive; they focused on the message that the model seemed to substantiate, based primarily on the interrelationships of economic growth, pollution, and the consumption of resources. If unchecked and unmodified, industrial civilization would overshoot its ecological and population limits—and painfully collapse.

That was the nature of exponential growth—growth that builds on itself, faster and faster. It can lead to deep trouble that isn't seen as deep trouble until it's too late. In their model (now named World3), the MIT researchers tracked five key variables: population, food production, industrial production, pollution, and the consumption of natural resources. If you looked at each of these growth patterns separately, they all seemed relatively easy to cope with, and some seemed like cause for celebration: the changes in industrial output suggested that the world's overall living standard would double by 1984.

But growth in each of the five key variables seemed to accelerate the growth of the others, and to a dangerous degree. The modelers entered various proposed "fixes," such as technological investment, higher-yield agriculture, and higher prices," into the program. In every case, unless industrial growth in its current form leveled off somehow, the model led to calamitous decreases in population, and finally in pollution, as industrial civilization faltered. Even without a decline in natural resources (for instance, if low-cost nuclear energy replaced oil), industrial growth would still be stopped by the accelerated rise of toxic pollution.[40]

Dana Meadows didn't fully see the implications until a meeting at a resort outside Ottawa early in 1971 where the MIT team made a presentation to the Club of Rome. The Meadowses struggled for a while as they tried to explain the notion of exponential growth and the finite limits of the world, without getting through to the club members. Then Forrester stood up. "This growth and these limits are structural," he said. "It's built into the system." He had seen growth overshoot itself before, at Digital and Cummins Engine. When they introduced a new product, they often expected sales to continue growing indefinitely and were unprepared for the time when sales leveled off. It wasn't much of a leap to observe the same pending dynamic in the statistics on global population and resources.

Listening to Forrester, Dana had a vision of the Asian countries she'd visited the year before. She'd seen places where local economies collapsed after the villagers burned up their forests for fuel. The same thing could happen to the world as a whole, she thought. With half an ear, she heard the Club of Rome members argue back. Poverty was the key problem, one member said, so we needed to focus on economic growth in developing countries. No, another member said; pollution was fundamental, and we need economic growth to develop technological solutions. No, said yet another; the problem was energy. "We have to find more oil and build nuclear power plants."

They were trying to solve every problem with economic growth. As she listened, it seemed to her that this fixation on growth—this "mental model," as Forrester called it—was a boastful, bullying living thing, with its own malignant needs. It seemed to believe that although the world's resources and pollution capacities were infinite, the wherewithal for a decent life was scarce. The only effective way to live well was to grasp and hoard. What civilization really needed, she thought, was the reverse: an attitude where the Earth was seen as finite and sharing was appropriate. If people managed their own endeavors more efficiently, there would be enough for everybody's physical and emotional needs. Businesses would have to find ways to be innovative without the emphasis on growing—by providing better services and better goods. We'd need to start asking ourselves, she decided, What we are growing *for*? For whom? For how long? And at what cost?

Questions like these were gaining urgency. Not long before, in January 1969, five thousand barrels of oil had burst through undersea fissures beneath a Union Oil Company drilling platform a few miles offshore, near the Santa Barbara coastline. It later came out that the U.S. Geological Survey had granted Union Oil an exemption to drilling regulations, allowing the company's technical crews to install a shorter-than-standard casing inside the well's hole. Moreover, the company's geologists had known in advance that the channel's frequent earthquakes made it vulnerable to seepage. Nevertheless, they cut corners and discovered only after the fact that they couldn't contain the damage. The eruption left behind an oil slick that extended over eight hundred square miles, thirty miles of sludgy beaches, some memorable photographs of oil-slicked gulls, two years of lawsuits and investigations, and a permanently foul reputation for offshore drilling.[41]

Previous conservation movements had been created by a love for natural environments. But the environmentalist new wave was motivated by a keen sense of loss. People felt personally bereaved. They had seen forests lost to development, streams lost to pollution, rivers to dams, and beaches to oil spills. They blamed corporations; they blamed government. They did not want it to happen again, but they lacked any sense of how to prevent it.

At that meeting, Dana volunteered for the job of preparing a ten-page summary of the results of World3. Instead of 10 pages, she turned in 20, which (after comments and questions from various Club members) expanded to 110. Aurelio Peccei, who of the leading Club of Rome members was probably the most impressed with the project's results, finally took the Meadowses aside. "The technical report is fine, but what we really need is Dana's little memo as a book." It was published as *The Limits to Growth* early in 1972 and rapidly became a best-seller.

o

The first major negative review appeared in the *New York Times* in April, written by Harvard economist Peter Passell and two Columbia University economists, Marc Roberts and Leonard Ross. *The Limits to Growth,* they said, was "empty and misleading": it was based on an "intellectual Rube Goldberg device," full of "arbitrary conclusions that have the ring of science," but were really "less than pseudoscience."[42] *Nature* and the

Economic Journal were harsher still. Economists and economic writers turned on *The Limits to Growth* throughout America and Europe, setting off a firestorm that would inflame the debate about economic growth for another twenty years.

The popularity of the small book made it an easy target. But even if it had been nothing but technical documentation, *The Limits to Growth* would probably have been attacked. To leftist economists, it was a slap in the face to developing nations that were trying to improve their standards of living. To rightist economists, the *Limits* argument was an argument for global-scale planning, the kind of planning that would pave the way for a domineering world government. Forrester (in his earlier book *World Dynamics*) had suggested that governments should restrict the supply of available money for investment as a curb on industrial growth and to cut back on the green revolution—deliberately producing less food to discourage population growth.

The model treated the entire world as one place, said critics, ignoring the divisions between the industrialized North and the developing countries of Asia, Latin America, and Africa. (This charge was true.) The model didn't seem to recognize that when timber fuel ran out, it would be replaced by coal fuel; when copper ran out, it would be replaced by fiber optics. (This was false; the World model builders did recognize substitution and built some into their calculations. But they also felt that there are limits to substitution.) Some space enthusiasts, like science-fiction writer Jerry Pournelle, criticized the model for leaving out the resources that would come from colonizing other planets.[43]

Most damning of all to the critics was the lack of a pricing mechanism. The last drop of oil would cost the same as the first drop to come out of the ground. If true, it would have made the model patently ridiculous. This charge, however, was false. The price variable was present, but it was aggregated into other factors and covered so obscurely in the text that most readers overlooked it. It was just one more example of how a central factor to economists could seem trivial to engineers, and vice versa, in a way that made conversation about the issues very difficult.

Finally, critics charged that the model left no choice but zero growth. This, too, was wrong. The Meadowses, Forrester, and Aurelio Peccei found themselves insisting, time and time again, that they wanted to change the nature of growth to make it more responsive and intelligent. Moreover, like all other scenario builders, they were not predicting the future. They wanted to open up debate. In the tradition of system dynamics modeling, producing a model was only the first stage. Then you brought the model into the open for critique and refinement. Instead, debate polarized: either the *Limits* argument was sacrosanct, or it was demonic. Growth was either the culprit, or it should not be questioned at all.

○

A few corporate managers refused to ignore the questions raised by *The Limits to Growth*. Robert Rodale of the Rodale Press, Ted Turner of the then-fledgling Turner Cable Network, and Robert Anderson, the CEO of Arco Oil, made public statements supporting discussion of the nature of throughput and the future of economic growth. Anderson might have gone further—he had even written his own report on the subject—but the vice presidents at Arco banded together and asked him not to publish it. This was one of several incidents that led Forrester to decide that the *Limits to Growth* theory was far more threatening to people inside organizational hierarchies than to those who had already risen to the top.

Dana Meadows saw the same thing when she spoke at business gatherings, as she did dozens of times during 1972 and 1973. In her memory, all the conversations blended into one recurring exchange: "You're telling me my company can't grow?" "Well, you could always deliver higher quality or concentrate on improving services." Then she would look slyly up at them and ask, "And why does your business have to grow, anyway?"

Later, in her memory, the answers all blended together. Why did they need to grow? Because that was how they measured success. The more their company grew, the more profits they could claim they created and the more opportunities they would be given to increase their bailiwick. It was like asking why they needed to breathe oxygen.

○

Willis Harman began to quote from *The Limits to Growth* soon after it came out. Its conclusions meshed perfectly with his renunciation of rationality. The industrial world, built by engineers, was enmeshed in a reductionist way of thinking. People, *without even realizing it,* had fragmented their lives. They separated their work life from their home life, as if they were two different people. They solved their family and personal problems by tearing them into pieces. They shrank back when conversations led to areas that might cross cherished boundaries.

This sudden awareness of fragmentation was a compelling insight for engineers, social scientists, and managers who all their lives had been taught to compartmentalize. Even at the most operational level, there were dramatic implications for designing work flow. You could not look at one division or department or function without considering the ramifications of your work for everyone else in the company. Marketing and finance, operations and research, were all part of one huge system, and an effective chief executive had to look out for all of them instead of boosting one at the expense of another.

Fortunately, you didn't have to see all the pieces completely or understand them in a mechanistic way to be able to act effectively. You could develop a good enough understanding of the relationships among the pieces that you could act compassionately and elegantly for the benefit of the whole. That was powerful—and novel in corporate circles. It explained why even as Willis Harman and Oliver Markley, the SRI engineers, grew increasingly extreme, they continued to find young engineers and managers willing to follow their lead. They had seen the sheer, pragmatic, exalting usefulness of system-centered, holistic faith.

7

PARZIVAL'S DILEMMA

EDIE SEASHORE, CHRIS ARGYRIS, AND
WARREN BENNIS, 1959–1979

Heresy: To change an organization, you must know—and change—yourself.

The stories of the Knights of the Round Table, hybrids of Christian and Celtic tradition, incorporated heretical influences as well.[1] Perhaps some of the influences trained back, through the chains of song and sermon, to Pelagius himself. Pelagius had said that salvation depends on people's own faith and deeds, and his followers, through the centuries, faced an eternal dilemma. If we are damned for our actions but don't know our actions' results, then how dare we act? And yet when our help is called for, how dare we refrain?

Parzival, a young knight of the Round Table, faced this dilemma at the turning point of his life. His story, written in verse by a twelfth-century German knight named Wolfram von Eschenbach, is perhaps the most gripping of all the courtly tales. Eschenbach may have been a heretic himself; some sources link him with the Cathars, the most durable of the forbidden sects.

Parzival is a bumptious, unschooled youth whose mother deliberately tries to keep him from becoming a knight for fear that he will be killed. Nonetheless, he finds his way to Arthur's court and the most solemn quest imaginable: the quest for the Holy Grail. At the pivotal moment in his travels, Parzival visits the castle of Anfortas the Fisher King, the keeper of the Grail. The king is borne on a pallet into the great banquet hall. He has been wounded by a spear in his genitals and cannot stand or sit. He can barely lie still. The room glistens with luxury and expectation. It has been foretold that the spontaneous act of a knight's noble heart can cure the king. For his part, when he sees the prone figure surrounded by weeping attendants, Parzival feels drawn to rise to his feet and ask: "What afflicts thee, Uncle?"[2]

But Parzival holds his tongue. He has been taught that a knight refrains from asking too many questions.[3] It would be dishonorable and improper. The festivities continue, albeit with a melancholy air, for by keeping still, Parzival has missed his chance to heal the king. Behind his politeness was the universal fearful desire, spawned in all of us by institutional life and manners: the desire to figure out the rules and be safe, to know ahead of time whether our action will lead to success or failure.

Parzival awakes alone the next morning; all the residents of the castle have vanished. He spends the next five years lost and ashamed. Eventually he finds his way back to the castle and heals the king, which, as Joseph Campbell pointed out, represented a dramatic shift for medieval mythmaking: at last, salvation could take place not just by being chosen but by persevering in our muddled way toward the aspirations we know are right. Every act is Pelagian in its intent, full of grace, and yet every well-intentioned act produces bitter consequences, just as the Augustinians warn. Given that harsh reality, Wolfram counseled his readers, there is only one course to follow: lean toward the good. Turn your mind to humility. Deepen your own understanding, so that when called on to say, "What afflicts thee, Uncle?" you can confidently rise to the occasion.[4]

---

o

IN THE 1960S, AS ORGANIZATION DEVELOPMENT (OD) burst from its birthplace at the National Training Laboratories out into large mainstream companies, its practitioners faced their own version of Parzival's dilemma: How did they know when their actions would do more harm than good? This had never been a problem in the past. The founders of National Training Laboratories, as purveyors of a vehicle of uncommon power (the T-Group), had always kept that power under strict control. The elaborate gauntlet of mentors that researchers had to pass to become fellows at NTL made the group dynamics community as fiercely protective of its secrets as a medieval guild. But then Douglas McGregor had published *The Human Side of Enterprise* and made the secrets visible. Robert Blake and Jane Mouton had commercialized them with the grid system. Other NTL regulars had set up their own consulting operations, so that by the early 1960s, a nascent profession of OD specialists and human potential advocates already existed. They sold T-Groups and other forms of group dynamics as a set of methods to help develop and nurture the human resources of the firm. After all, weren't the employees assets just as much as the capital investments, equipment, and receivables that showed up on the balance sheets?

If you were an OD practitioner during those years (or, in the language of the profession, a "process consultant"[5] or an expert on "team building"), you would become a coach to a team, sitting in on their meetings as they deliberated investment decisions or customer problems. You would help them talk safely about dangerous subjects, encourage them to build up enough trust, and bring to their attention their own behavior as a clue to their deeper personal attitudes, the culture of their company, and how the two fit together.[6]

You might film the team's sessions, just as the T-Groups had been recorded, or let half the team watch the other half discuss its work in a simulated "fishbowl." You might conduct surveys: On a scale of 1 to 5, were the team members clear or uncertain about the team's purpose? Did they feel free to speak, or were they cautious and guarded? Then you would feed back the anonymous results, in a package, to the team. In short, you would explicitly engineer all the types of conversation that in preindustrial vernacular village life had flowed naturally through the well-worn channels of custom. But in the formal ambiance of corporate culture, those channels did not seem to exist and managers could not manage their relationships on their own.[7]

As an OD consultant, Parzival's dilemma was built into the nature of your job. Your most fundamental premise came from Kurt Lewin: to understand a system, you must try to change it. You had to intervene. You had to stand up and ask, "What afflicts you, Uncle?" Yet your paycheck or consultant's fee came from the old established system that you were trying to change. And your entire discipline of T-Group practice was only twenty years old. T-Groups seemed to work fine in the rarefied hotels where executives went for off-sites. But inside the organization's own walls, who knew how easily they might backfire?

There are hundreds of people whose stories could be told here as part of the continuing story of NTL, but three people in particular stand out. Among them, they encapsulated the influence that NTL would have on the rest of the culture. Each started out to change the world, and each ran up against Parzival's dilemma. Each had to find a way to act, balancing a new understanding against the old orthodoxy, while the potential for mistakes grew ever higher. Each found a different resolution—a different way of muddling through.

All three of them would eventually become famous, at least in organizational circles. Edie Seashore would be known as the matriarch of the OD field, the NTL president-cum-house-mother who lived next door to the Bethel Campus and the codesigner of the most innovative effort to achieve organizational diversity in management history. Chris Argyris would be known as the theorist who found a way for managers to reconcile their imperfect behavior with their professed ideals. And then there was Warren Bennis—lecturer, professor, essayist, university president, author of prominent books on leadership, dreamer of grand visions, and the only NTLer to take the helm of a large organization and try to reshape it from the top.

―――――― o ――――――

There was a lot of joy in OD work. If you were good at it, you could both earn a living and design a life for yourself with far more verve and flexibility than the humdrum work lives of most of your clients. You could help heal organizations—and, better still, you wouldn't have to work in one.

Consider the life of Edith Whitfield Seashore. She was, by many accounts (including her own), the most popular trainer in NTL's history. She was a vivacious, fast-talking, auburn-haired Jewish woman from a New York City suburb who had gone to Antioch College, participated in student politics, met college president Douglas McGregor, and turned her life around to follow his example. McGregor had recommended her to NTL in 1950 just as she was leaving her senior year at Antioch College. That summer, in exchange for T-Group training, she bartered her time, putting together course materials and running contests on the golf course. She was not only the youngest person on the NTL grounds in Bethel but one of only two women staff members. And yet among all those pompously earnest middle-aged men, she naturally fit in. She had the NTL gift for speaking plainly without offending, and she had an uncanny ability to attract friendship. When she got home in the fall, as she later recalled, Edie Whitfield was surprised to receive a call from Lee Bradford himself, the director. He had barely spoken to her during the summer. "We'd like to have you back next year," he said.

"That's wonderful," she replied. "I loved it up there."

"It's obvious you did." He mentioned a survey they had conducted that year asking everyone at Bethel to name the people with whom they felt simpatico. "You were the star," Bradford said, "the one person whom everyone related to most."

For the next nine summers, she cultivated that role. She cotrained with nearly every established group leader on the premises, while men moved on to lead T-Groups after a year or two of cotraining. She also led the "spouse's group," the only women's group at NTL during those years. "The participants said, 'So this is group work? We can do this!'" Edie later recalled to writer Sally Helgesen. "They ended up entering the field, teaching NTL sessions, getting PhDs, divorcing their husbands, completely changing their lives."[8] Finally, one of her cotrainers, a psychologist and writer named Jack Glidewell, admonished her not to come back "until they can accept you as a trainer. You're too good to keep apprenticing."

By that time, she was based in New York, working as a consultant with RB Associates, a newly formed management consultancy. The proprietor was Richard (Dick) Beckhard, a long-standing friend and associate of Douglas McGregor and one of the founders of OD. He was an unusual man at both NTL and MIT, where he had a permanent part-time professorship, because he had no academic background. He had been an actor (the voice of radio's Henry Aldrich), then a stage director, then a meeting and workshop planner, and finally an expert on training. While Robert Blake was inaugurating his grid system at Esso, Beckhard had conducted his own team consultations at General Mills, the TRW aerospace company, and the Tennessee Valley Authority. He was one of the first to recognize how fast the field would grow and how important it would be to train competent practitioners. So he and some colleagues created a four-week training sequence at Bethel, which became the model for how universities teach the field of OD to this day.

Edie was now in her late twenties, and Beckhard delegated much of his consulting work to her. He concentrated on CEOs and finance officers, while she specialized in the areas that seemed appropriate for women: nonprofits, religious groups, and the wives of CEOs. With each new client, like the handful of other consulting women in business in the early 1960s, she fought a constant subliminal battle to be accepted as a professional. Each time she discovered how the NTL training gave her a Houdini-like ability to find her own way out of the trickiest situations.

Once, assigned to meet with the Hebrew Congregations of New York, she found herself at the head of a table of twenty viciously funny rabbis, all from different congregations and levels of orthodoxy, all arrogant as only successful religious leaders can be—bickering over the design of their next conference, except when they were making jokes about this woman who was supposedly going to help *them* talk together. The chief rabbi leaned over and whispered to her: "If you can pull this off, I'm taking you to lunch. And if you don't pull it off, then Beckhard doesn't have a client any more." She sat, daunted, watching the conversation flow around the table in Yiddish, English, and occasionally in Hebrew, awash in the abstruse complexities of metropolitan rabbinical politics. *There's only one edge I've got here,* she told herself. *I can see their process, and they can't.*

"Listen," she finally said. "You're not doing anything but putting each other down. Does that happen just because I'm around, or does it happen all the time?"

"Well, it happens all the time," one of the rabbis said.

"Does it get you where you want to go?"

The rabbis looked at each other. This kind of feedback was the simplest technique a consultant had. But it worked. They stopped bickering and started designing the session. The chief rabbi took Edie to lunch and became a good friend of hers. When she married, the rabbis of New York chipped in and planted a tree in Israel in her honor.

Through dozens of such encounters, bit by bit, she built up a following of loyal clients. She discovered what a generation of women consultants was likely to discover a decade later: there was a natural advantage to being a woman in that role. It required visible compassion, which many men at that time in the American mainstream business culture found hard to demonstrate. But clients naturally assumed that Edie was compassionate, even when she merely felt callous and sardonic. And having the independent role of a consultant blunted any implicit sexual harassment. Her clients knew that she could always resign, and then they would have to explain to their bosses and colleagues why they had alienated Edie Whitfield, the great consultant.

Being a woman at NTL was more difficult to deal with. She was never voted in as an NTL fellow despite years of close involvement with the labs. Lee Bradford continually seemed to assume that her gender made her automatically savvy about domestic things. When NTL bought its house in Bethel, he insisted on hiring her to furnish it, even though she had never furnished anything, not even her own apartment. She stumbled around its nineteenth-century rooms with a tape measure, not quite sure how to use it. In 1959, when Bradford finally offered her a full-time job, it wasn't to lead T-Groups but to be the office manager at NTL's Washington headquarters. Her consulting practice was just then taking off. "Lee, it's too late," she replied. "You trained me too well. I'm more trained than anyone else NTL has ever sent out into the world."

She got married in 1961 to another NTLer, one year younger than herself, named Charlie Seashore. Charlie's grandfather and father were both influential psychologists; his grandfather had helped bring Kurt Lewin to the University of Iowa. Charlie wasn't taken as seriously as he might have been because he perpetually clowned around—indeed, he occasionally performed professionally as a unicyclist or juggler. He was tall, rangy, and known for his tolerant cheer; he wore western-style clothing and a constant grin. He was the kind of man who could tell a girlfriend named Sandra that she should marry him, because then her name would be Sandy Seashore. When Sandra turned him down, he began seeing more of Edie, and he proposed to her, more or less, by accident. Other boyfriends had hinted, or demanded, that she should put them through graduate school and then stop working. Charlie, on an early date, raised a wine glass and said, "If you were to marry me, you could work and travel as much as you please."

"I accept," Edie said.

"Wait a minute," he said. "That was only a hypothetical statement."

"Yes," she said, "but it's too late. I've already accepted."

In 1963, Edie was finally voted in as an NTL fellow. Bradford called her to give the news himself. Several board members had resisted to the end, he said, because she was a woman and had no Ph.D. (She found graduate school too boring to get one.) "We didn't get through with that board meeting until three in the morning," he told her. "Finally we decided that it wasn't our choice anyway. You were a symbolic figure of where NTL was going to go." Now, he said, he was calling because she was the first candidate this year "to be unanimously approved by your colleagues."

Seashore was laughing. "It doesn't surprise me," she told Bradford. "They all trained me. They'd *better* come through. Otherwise, they'd have to ask themselves what *they* did wrong!"

And Edie was, just as Bradford said, a forerunner of NTL's destiny. Organization development was increasingly to be a woman's game—not just because human resources and facilitator positions were lower-status slots (which they were) but also because women seemed to have a knack for keeping a conversation going well. (This stereotype would eventually dwindle, but not for another thirty years.) In the meantime, Edie benefited: her consulting business took off during the 1960s. Years later, she credited part of her success to Douglas McGregor, who advised her to "listen, listen, listen," and then give the client just one good idea that would justify the money they paid her.[9] Even having two daughters didn't deter her; she applied her relentless drive to the tough task of coordinating nurses, babysitters, clients, and colleagues. She gave a dinner party the night before one of her children was born; when sudden trips called her to California or Europe, she paid her babysitters to come along. "I really was out to show that you could have it all," she recalled later, and she was, in fact, setting a pattern. It was frenetic, but a consultant mother's life was easier than the lives of women struggling to rise within corporations. It was a charmed life, and it looked as though it might go on forever. And yet it went on within the context of a professional umbrella—the NTL community—that was beginning to fall apart.

○

As early as 1957, the center began to unravel at NTL.[10] Every year more of the trainers slipped out for visits or sabbaticals to the new, looser, encounter group centers in California such as Esalen or the Western Behavioral Sciences Institute in San Diego, where personal growth was expected to be part of the purpose of the T-Group, body work was an integral part of therapy, and understanding group power dynamics was less and less important. More and more, the western influence trickled back to Bethel and the other NTL gatherings. It became normal to touch, and then to hug, the other people in your T-Group. The oak tables gave way to chairs without tables, then to cushions on the floor. On the West Coast, they were taking off their clothes and taking psychedelics; in the East, they never went that far, but they did invite business executives to crawl around on the floor, in the dark, bumping into each other in an effort to experience each other in a fresh way.[11]

NTL trainers also began to employ the techniques of self-hypnosis. Instead of merely talking about their "preferred vision," stolid corporate engineers or school administrators were now encouraged to visualize every aspect of it, as if it hung in the air before them. If they couldn't master visualization, they could attend training sessions where the leader handed them a lemon and told them to acquaint themselves with every minuscule detail of the pitted, sour fruit. Then they'd throw their lemons into a big pile in the center of the room. "Go get your lemon," the trainer would say. Each participant's citrus stood out from its fellows as clearly as a lover's face.

Dick Beckhard, conducting this exercise with a group of rear admirals of the U.S. Navy, daydreamed about snapping a photograph of them crawling on the floor, in uniform, grabbing their lemons from the pile. He could send it with a note to the secretary of defense: "Dear Mr. Secretary. We are learning. Love, your boys." And there was, in fact, a valuable lesson here: if you could learn to recognize your lemon in a crowd by moving past your ordinary preconceptions, then consider how much you could see in the people around you, or in your own aspirations, if you gave yourself the time to really look.[12]

"I can remember working with a group in the Connecticut mountains," an organizational development pioneer named Kathy Dannemiller recalled years later. "We were rocking this man. He was about fifty or sixty years old and I was holding his head. He was bald. When we rocked someone, at some point we'd say, 'Let go. You can let go now'—meaning that they could let themselves move into heavy-duty emotional release. At that moment, I leaned down and kissed him, and I suddenly saw two tears come out of his eyes, which were closed. He opened them and looked up at me and said, 'Was that you that kissed me?' I said yes. He said, 'I think that was the first kiss I ever felt.' That was the kind of experience we had with T-Groups, and why we kept coming back to them— because we had buried our emotions and perceptions so deeply as children of the Depression and the war."

But the looser the T-Groups grew and the more they were oriented to "therapy for normals," the harder it was for the core academics of NTL to keep track of, let alone control, what the sessions contained. Standards at Bethel remained relatively strict, but other T-Groups, held around the country under a variety of auspices, far outnumbered the offerings from Bethel. Even if Lee Bradford, NTL's director, had had the funds and staff to enforce strict standards (which he didn't), he didn't have the heart. After all, this *was* the 1960s; the world seemed to need to loosen up. And the old dream of the NTL triumvirate, to build a cadre of change agents who would reform organizations everywhere from the inside, now looked as if it would finally come true.

○

The downside of the NTL dream first came to public light around 1963. That year Cornell University brought Chris Argyris together with George Odiorne for a debate on the value of T-Groups. Odiorne was the popularizer of management by objectives (MBO), a system originally proposed by the management writer Peter Drucker as a way of fostering account-ability. In the early 1950s, Drucker had become friendly with McGregor and learned about Ron Lippitt's "preferred future" exercises, but envisioning a desirable long-term future was, in Drucker's view, too far removed from day-to-day business goals, so he developed the MBO concept as a more tangible cousin.[13] Under the MBO system as Drucker conceived it, managers would choose a few numerical goals and meet them; this would help them remain attuned to the organization's overall needs.[14] For instance, Crown Zellerbach's senior managers decided on an objective of providing the pulp and paper needs of the next fifty years. As a result, they became more avid forest managers, planting thousands of trees in 1950 that were not due to be harvested until the year 2000.[15]

But at most companies, the practice of MBO soon devolved to a "hard bargain," as Odiorne later put it, approvingly. Once a manager agreed to a measurement and ratified it by signing the appropriate appraisal form, he had to live up to it. If he failed, that would affect his salary or bonus.[16] At some companies, the MBO package was called a "do-it-yourself hangman's kit." The name of the MBO game rapidly became setting expectations—designing the objectives so that you would look good on the report forms, no matter how successful your performance in reality. If anyone had seriously wanted to make a system like MBO work, they would have had to combine it with honest conversation about *why* these particular numbers and what unspoken demands were operating behind the scenes.[17] But Odiorne had no faith in any soft training method like T-Groups that purported to "make people talk honestly." From the Cornell stage, Odiorne said that "sensitivity training," as the new group dynamics workshops had begun to be called, should be legally banned, "like amateur surgery." He scoffed at group dynamics in business as a hypocritical, unprovable, self-indulgent, and downright dangerous "con game" whose purpose was to rake in corporate fees.[18]

To the *Business Week* writer who covered the event, the testimonials of managers in the audience made the strongest impression. One by one, they stood up to talk about how they had been pressed to reveal secrets or humiliatingly identified as an SOB. The flood of complaints abated only when one of the speakers mused, "You know, whenever you say anything negative about [T-Groups], you're just proving to your bosses that you're sick." Suddenly the realization dawned across the face of everyone who had spoken: Who might have heard them?[19]

Argyris, in the meantime, was cast as NTL's defender. It was not a role he preferred; he had doubts about T-Groups himself. He deplored the way that they seemed to make people dependent on the trainers.[20] He had come to the debate with no advance warning that Odiorne was planning to attack T-Groups; he had hoped that Odiorne and he could mutually inquire about the T-Group's viability. Instead he felt forced into the role of advocate for NTL's case—forced to argue that T-Group trainers were not sleazy con-men. He later remembered a particularly revealing moment at the end when Odiorne pulled him aside. "Chris," he said, "you give me the word, and we'll take this act throughout the United States. We'll make a pile of money."[21]

Argyris didn't join Odiorne on the road, but the meeting, and other encounters like it, raised questions that would be central to his career, and ultimately to our understanding of how corporations change. Then thirty-nine years old, Argyris was a Yale professor of administrative science. Like Edie Seashore, he had grown up in a suburb of New York City. He had also spent several years as a child with his grandparents in Greece. He was bespectacled, dark-complexioned, and slender, with a narrow face that tended, almost despite himself, to break into a delighted grin when arguments grew hot, as if he was overjoyed at the chance to test himself. His voice was distinctively mild-mannered and reedy, with a slight European accent. His style of debate was analytical—indeed, his approach to life was passionately devoted to inquiry, reasoning, and theory. But he was drawn to the kinds of problems that most analytical people eschew: the riddles of human nature. In particular, why did people not live up to their own professed ideals? Why was so much human behavior so self-frustrating, particularly in organizations?[22]

In 1957, Argyris had published *Personality and Organization,* a book in which he had demonstrated, with full academic rigor, that corporations inevitably turned their employees into infantile people. No matter how much the company's managers espoused self-reliance and resourcefulness, the mere presence of mature, independent-minded people felt threatening to the senior leaders of the enterprise. It was not that senior managers were vile individuals; most were reasonably decent people. But an authoritarian chain of command, by its nature, placed managers into a double bind. If they spoke up, they automatically fell into the role of challenging their superiors, which meant they couldn't play the political games that led to success. Or they could remain obeisant and give up their maturity, ultimately passing on their babyishness to the next generation (if only by running their families in an authoritarian manner). Thus, the immaturity of organizations, Argyris posited, would endure into eternity.[23]

This was the value to Argyris of a T-Group in business. The group confronted people with the direct record—Argyris called this the "data"—of their own conversations, so they could see how they had been locked into destructive ways of thinking and relating. Nobody could confront a group with its "data" the way Argyris could. He was fearless in the facilitator's role; he seemed oblivious to whether people might be offended or have their feelings hurt as long as they were learning. Listening to the conversation, his eyes would brighten and intensify until he became like a bird of prey, perching at the edge of the table, alert to the nuance in every phrase. Then suddenly he would pounce.

"From your last remark," he would say to a CEO, surrounded by his loyal lieutenants, "it sounds to me like you don't trust this group." Then he would turn to the other managers: "Is that true? Does it sound like he doesn't trust you?"

If they insisted that he did trust them, Argyris would ask them exactly which part of the CEO's remark implied trust.

"Well, it wasn't that remark," they would say. And Argyris would ask them to nail down some remark until they were forced to admit there was no trust there.[24] Around and around they would go, peeling off one layer after another of the appearance of trust while Argyris sat watching, stoking the conversation like a fire, never raising his voice, never losing his bemused smile, and never letting go. "Five minutes into a conversation," a close colleague of his later recalled, "he'd have anyone that he was talking to back up against the wall and fighting for their life with the kind of accusation about how they contradicted themselves a moment ago. He was always right. But he never backed off."

The healthier that corporate people claimed their company to be, the more effective Argyris seemed to be in bringing their deep, intractable problems to the surface. He regularly offered to pay all his own consulting fees and expenses in a corporate study if the company turned out to be healthy; a Yale alumnus had set up an endowment to underwrite the offer. No company ever took up the challenge. He also insisted on a rule that allowed either himself or his clients to cancel the consulting contract with only fifty seconds' notice; but by the same rule, the other party could demand four hours to have the decision explained. Nobody ever cancelled a contract with Argyris, no matter how angry he made them. No doubt the thought of those four hours, satisfying Argyris's relentless pursuit of the data, was too excruciating.

○

And yet Argyris had to admit that many T-Group projects were ending badly. He had become entangled himself in 1964 with NTL's most visible failure, a highly public project with the U.S. State Department. The oldest federal agency, State was known around Washington as the Fudge Factory. Foreign service officers spent most of their time infighting or holding each other to the letter of the abstruse mass of State Department regulations. In 1963, as part of a reorganization effort that would require these foreign service officers to manage their embassies competently, the new deputy under secretary for administration, William Crockett, decided to bring in a team of OD specialists from NTL. The United States was sending rockets into space; why couldn't it make the State Department work right?[25]

At first there were terrific results. The young foreign officers who had signed up during the Kennedy presidency and seriously believed in "asking what they could do for their country" were wildly enthusiastic. T-Groups seemed like the answer to the hidebound bureaucracy in which they found themselves snared. The sessions brought deeply hidden problems, like the misunderstandings between ambassadorial diplomats and civil service administrators, to the surface—first in argument, then in a kind of thoughtful, creative conversation between the two groups. "If we could bring this technique to Israel or Russia," mused the enthusiasts at State, "just think what we could accomplish!"

But that was before the power structure fought back. By 1965 the T-Group effort and its champions found themselves sabotaged from within. Foreign service officers began to spread rumors that Crockett was resigning; his superiors, including Secretary of State Dean Rusk, started to worry out loud that he was "out of control." Otherwise why would he want to delegate authority? Staffers threatened to leak their stories of shattered morale to the press. Finally, Crockett accepted a job offer from IBM in early 1967. His replacement cancelled all the NTL-related contracts.

But it was too late to stop Argyris, who was halfway through writing up the report on the project, which he had agreed to write as part of the deal.[26] It no longer mattered that the contract had exploded or that the clients no longer wanted a report. An agreement was an agreement. When the report came out describing the personnel policies that inhibited effectiveness at State, it was guarded more carefully than some top secret documents. Representative John Rooney, chairman of the House Appropriations Subcommittee, obtained a copy and held a hearing to denounce it. ("Who is this fellow Argyris?" he asked. "Has he ever worked for the State Department?")[27]

○

By the mid-1960s, such denouements were becoming sadly typical in NTL-inspired projects. First, there would be stellar success. In some companies, a meeting wasn't considered important unless it had its own process consultant sitting in, offering expert guidance on the flow, interjecting comments about honesty and fulfillment, and taking notes on big sheets of paper on the wall. But then the effects would wear off. Bullying managers who had learned to listen openheartedly began bullying again. Managers who had finally learned how to speak up at meetings, and to care about their company's future as a whole, reverted back to being passive-aggressive bureaucrats. OD consultants themselves sometimes assumed the burden of making everything better, which often took the form of becoming internal advocates for the lower-level managers. They took it on themselves, as Ed Schein later recalled, to "seduce or cajole bosses into new ways of behaving while continuing their team-building activities down below." Among themselves, the OD people would tend to talk about how to reform or change top management, which of course had the effect of reinforcing senior executives' desire to have nothing to do with them.

Sometimes things got worse after an NTL effort. This particularly seemed to happen when a company began to use OD on a large scale and the T-Groups were no longer held on a cultural island. At Bethel, trainers needed years of apprenticeship under their belt before they could lead a group. But in companies, the eager audience was so large, particularly when the CEO endorsed a T-Group program, that some OD people were impressed into leading groups after having been to only one or two themselves. Relatively inexperienced and caught in the company's internal politics, they tended to prod and poke at any disputes that came up as if they were itchy lesions. And all too often, the wounds broke open.

It might take weeks of group sessions, for instance, before a manager was ready to describe how he hated his boss's micromanagement. But the facilitator, tensely aware of the boss's presence in the room, might interrupt the manager midsentence and turn to the boss: "Ralph, how do Sam's remarks make you feel?"

"Well, it makes me feel like I haven't been much of a friend," Ralph the boss might say, in the nurturing spirit of the session. And all eyes would turn back to Sam.

"Are you ready," the facilitator would inquire, "to ask Ralph if you can trust him as a friend?"

Sam would look dumbfounded at the consultant. In truth, the answer was no. Ralph *wasn't* his friend. Sam *didn't* trust him. But he could not say, "No, I'm not ready," while other managers were listening. The remark, and its implied insult of Ralph, would be remembered for years.

Nor could he assent. The words would stick in his throat. And if he got them out, he would never be able to protest again, for fear of hearing Ralph say, "But you *said* I was your friend." All the old abuses would continue, covered over by his acquiescence.

If he had any savvy at all, Sam would find a way out of the jam—probably by swallowing his pride and making a halfhearted show of friendship—but he'd never speak openly in that organization again. If he had no savvy, he might choose to speak honestly—and feel reprisals. The following Tuesday, Ralph might drop by his office. "I understand you don't have much faith in me. In that light, I guess we don't need you on my project." And if Sam displayed emotion anytime in a T-Group—if, for example, he burst into anger or tears when someone tore his personality to shreds—the notoriety would haunt him years later: "Can we trust this allocation to Sam when we've seen how unstable he is?"

Nor could Sam escape by avoiding taking part in T-Groups at all, for then he would become known as "someone who couldn't communicate." Thus, in many companies, one of the key skills (along with finessing the performance appraisals, and the MBO meetings) was finessing the T-Group. Sam had to learn to act willing to expose his deepest feelings at any moment and be searingly honest—but without actually saying anything to incriminate himself.[28]

In 1967 and 1968, as if in unplanned choreography, corporate people began to drop out of the NTL networks. Businesses everywhere stopped signing up for T-Groups; too many people within the companies had begun to complain about the abuses. At General Foods, one manager of a testing laboratory committed suicide after a T-Group session with engineers who worked with him. "Anyone who runs a testing laboratory is a bastard," they told him, "and you always have been."[29] He had been unstable before, but the episode demonstrated how incomplete the T-Group method was for its use in business settings and how unprepared NTL was—in the sense that it had no malpractice insurance. The manager's family sued both the labs and the company and settled out of court.

Everyone at NTL saw this case as a wake-up call. To some, like Argyris and Ed Schein, it provided one more reason for reevaluating their practice. Others saw the solution as obvious: they weren't thinking big enough. To make an impact, NTL itself would have to change.

At age sixty-four, NTL president Leland Bradford was ready to quit. There were plenty of reasons to feel tired. Critics like Odiorne continued to appear.[30] Income was high, but expenses continued to rise, in part because the increased enrollments had prompted $250,000 worth of renovations to the old Victorian house up in Bethel.[31] Tensions from the outside world were seeping in. In the summer of 1968, NTL had its first racial confrontation when a group of black leaders, in Bethel for a T-Group workshop, revolted against the staff and delivered a list of non-negotiable demands to Bradford: set up a program to hire black trainers and include more people of color in NTL's governance. Bradford refused but agreed, in time-honored NTL fashion, to talk through their concerns, which took the next three days. When the dust cleared, Bradford had agreed to design a program to train black facilitators, set a goal for 15 to 20 percent black representation in most NTL programs, and set up a community center in an urban setting. Going over these demands must have seemed deeply ironic to him; after all, NTL had been born at a race relations conference. Saul Alinsky had known enough to step out of the way in Rochester and let black leaders like Franklin Florence emerge, but the NTLers had never recognized the need to do the same.

Most pressing of all, Bradford was beset by medical problems, including a serious infection in his retina. He recognized that it was time to step down. At his suggestion, the NTL board sent everyone in the NTL community a ballot with three candidates for the position as his successor. Nearly all the votes came in for Warren Bennis, the third of the central figures of this chapter. Bennis was more than a candidate. In that bleak year, he was the great hope of NTL—the pioneering leader who could finally push the labs to the lofty social role that its members still felt it deserved.

Bennis was forty-four. In a sense, he had been groomed for the NTL presidency all his life. He was one of the most prominent experts on social change in the world and one of the leading academic figures of his generation. He had a Ph.D. in economics from MIT's Sloan School, where he had been a professor of industrial management in Douglas McGregor's department. (Like Edie Seashore, he was an Antioch alumnus and had been a McGregor protégé since college.) While at MIT, he had coedited *The Planning of Change,* a book of readings that had codified Kurt Lewin's insights and made the idea of professional change agents respectable in academic circles. He had participated in several key organizational development consultancies, including the State Department project. In his current day job, Bennis was a college administrator: vice president for academic affairs at the State University of Buffalo. He also had a wide reputation as a pathfinding commentator—one of the few social psychologists who could write engagingly for the general public. His essays rang with references to Kafka, Thoreau, Japanese folk wisdom, and his own feelings, even as he dissected the theories of his fellow social scientists.

Warren was a compact man, handsome and energetic, with a resonant tenor voice, blue eyes, a mouth that might have been painted into a portrait of Cupid, and thick brown hair that was rapidly turning white. He was effortlessly charming in person; among his friends he counted the psychologists Carl Rogers, Abraham Maslow, and Erik Erikson; the management writers Peter Drucker and Douglas McGregor; the composer Leonard Bernstein; and the columnist Eppie Lederer (better known as Ann Landers)—to list only a few whose names appeared in his essays during the 1960s. He and his wife at the time, Clurie, had been gently lampooned by a Buffalo newspaper for the massive dinner parties they gave. When McGregor and Maslow died, Warren gave the eulogies at their funerals.

He seemed capable of anything. But he also had the plaintive air of an outsider. He had grown up lonely and withdrawn in the 1930s, a shy Jewish kid in the WASPish suburb of Westwood, New Jersey. In his early twenties, after serving in Europe during World War II, he had deliberately reconstructed himself into a sophisticated, soulful adult. (He titled his most autobiographical essay, written in the 1990s, "An Invented Life."[32]) He cheerfully described himself as the sort of person (like Leonard Bernstein) who aspired to be not just liked but loved by every human being he met. Many of his friends knew that he also aspired to a greater role in the public sphere. He didn't want elected office. He wanted to set in motion a chain of events that would reshape the nature of political governance in America.

In collaboration with a sociologist from Brandeis University named Philip Slater, Bennis had published an audacious article in 1964 in the *Harvard Business Review*.[33] Like Herman Kahn, they foresaw the Soviet Union collapsing—along with all other totalitarian regimes—even if the United States did nothing to defeat it. Democracy, meanwhile, would undergo a full-scale cultural change, a movement beyond government by political parties and interest groups. It would be a society of people engaging in "full and free communication, regardless of rank and power," relieving conflicts through consensus instead of power bloc voting, expressing themselves through self-actualization, not just through accumulating wealth or brokering status. While this sort of democracy was inevitable, it was a little slow in arriving, and the two authors urged their readers to find ways "to give a little push here and there."

Now, with this job offer, Bennis had an opportunity to give a little push of his own. There was only one problem: for an institution of such potential influence, the NTL was an unprepossessing enterprise. It gave courses around the world, but it had only two headquarters—the remote cul-de-sac in Maine and the dingy administrative office in Washington, D.C. It would be hard to change the world from either place. If Warren left Buffalo to take this job, NTL would have to expand—not just to match his stature, but its own long-awaited destiny.

He laid out his idea before the executive committee, the twelve-man group in charge of NTL's affairs, on March 16, 1969. NTL, he proposed, should become an "international university for social change," with a new campus to be built somewhere near Washington. There would be a conference center where business managers would learn more effective teamwork, community developers would compare methods, and journalists would learn to cover the deep forces behind the everyday news. "I think we could really reach into government," he told the board. There would be a center for conflict resolution, sending crack teams of negotiators to tense locales like Yugoslavia and the Middle East. (A few years later, law professor Roger Fisher and some colleagues would develop a center much like that, the Harvard Negotiation Project at Harvard University.) And finally, there would be a "small elite program" for advanced graduate work in social sciences, blending humanistic psychology with philosophy and law, "to work on utopias and how you build new communities."[34]

The university would be designed to give people the intellectual tools they needed to accomplish the tasks that the times seemed to be crying for: Ending the war in Vietnam and all other wars. Stopping pollution and expanding the general level of quality of life. Banishing racism and sexism. And showing the managers of large bureaucracies—the giant mainstream corporations and government agencies that dominated society—how they too could contribute to making a better world. The NTL board members, listening to Bennis speak, could close their eyes and imagine cadres of sophisticated young peace soldiers fanning out into society—a living counterpoint to the American troops ravaging Vietnam and to the insular, arrogant technocrats of the military-industrial complex. *These* soldiers would have skilled conversation, empathy, and small-group workshops as weapons—the same weapons that Mahatma Gandhi and other peacemakers had used so eloquently. The culture of America was crying out for those weapons to emerge on a large scale.[35]

But they could not think small, Bennis insisted. Building the university would require between $5 and $15 million. A million dollars must be raised right away, earmarked for an endowment. Years later, he marveled at his own naiveté. He imagined that on the first day he showed up for work, there would a bank account with a million dollars in it, which the new school could immediately cash in.

One of the first things they would do with that money would be to establish part-time endowed chairs for faculty members—and Bennis announced, with evident pleasure, that Chris Argyris was eager to join in. The NTLers knew Argyris as an uncompromising promoter of scholastic rigor. If *he* was enthusiastic, that was a major selling point. "Chris said to me," Bennis reported, "and I think he really believes it," that an endowed chair could pull him away from his Ivy League post. Yale wasn't moving quickly enough in group dynamics research for Argyris, Bennis said. "Chris has already committed himself to six months in 1971."

The executive committee immediately agreed to the plan. To show Bennis that the million dollars could be raised, they began recruiting financial pledges within a few days.[36] The fundraising chore fell, as it happened, to Edie Seashore. She had never raised funds before, but she was doughty and irrepressible, and she had a hidden asset. As a woman, she had had to lead many workshops, over the years, with the wives of CEOs. Now she got on the phone to the husbands of her old trainees. "We're creating an institution," she told them, "where you could send people for the rest of your life."

Bennis, meanwhile, came through with a land grant from the father of one of his students at Buffalo. The father, a prominent Washington real estate broker, agreed to donate 175 acres near Dulles Airport, in the Virginia countryside. He offered another 250 acres for a bargain-basement forty thousand dollars, which the board also agreed to buy. To sketch out a campus, Bennis recruited the innovative architect Jim Rouse, who had designed the planned city of Columbia, Maryland. Construction would begin as early as January. Bennis and his wife flew to Washington to look for a house.

---------- o ----------

But at the same time, Warren was privately developing doubts. The previous year, in July 1968, he had dined with Michael Murphy, the founder of the Esalen Institute on the West Coast. Murphy was upset that night. *Life* magazine had just sent him an advance copy of the July 12 issue with a big feature story on Esalen. Called "Inhibitions Thrown to the Gentle Winds," it included sniggering, thinly veiled references to free love and photographs of nude workshop visitors slipping in and out of the institute's cliffside baths. "On the cover of the same issue," Bennis later recalled, "was another nude group—Biafran children who were dying of famine. It struck me that I didn't want to spend my life dealing with nude bathing."[37] Bennis agreed with Murphy that the article treated Esalen unfairly. But thoughts of irrelevance and self-indulgence continued to haunt him. NTL was much more conservative, academically grounded, and cautious than Esalen, but in the end wasn't it also guilty of the same self-centered irrelevance?

"I felt that NTL and T-groups were never going to really make a difference," he said, years later. "I didn't know quite why. Why weren't we having the impact of *The Organization Man,* or Rachel Carson's *Silent Spring?*" The problem, he felt, was in the group process itself, which operated on such a tiny scale—ten or twelve people at a time—that it would never have much impact on large-scale problems like Biafra. It was a sobering thought for a dedicated idealist who had spent his life working with small groups and was deeply interested in getting the most leverage from his talents.

Then there was the problem of money. Only $250,000 of Bennis's million dollars had been raised,[38] and very little of that arrived in Bennis's cherished bank account. There wasn't even money to buy the land near Dulles airport, whose owner was clamoring to close the deal.

And that $1 million had been intended as only a starting point. Moreover, NTL's efforts in the past to raise funds didn't inspire much confidence; its fundraisers had always cost more in expenses than their efforts brought in. For its operating expenses, the institute depended on the money from training seminars, which had unexpectedly plummeted. The organization had to take out loans to pay its staff salaries that fall.[39]

Privately staff members and trainers complained that the organization was sliding downhill fast. Then the same people stood up in board meetings and said, "The organization is in great shape." This was a terrible warning sign, because people came to T-Groups to cure exactly that sort of duplicity. Many of the staff members seemed unenthusiastic or simply burned out. Many of the trainers seemed to assume that a prestigious faculty post was theirs for the asking or that Warren would take their side in the inevitable turf wars. On the surface, Bennis remained as enthusiastic as ever. But every week, it became clearer to him how he could become mired in a self-defeating position, without enough money or power to act, without the ability to attract sharp people, and without a critical level of faculty support. He would become the visible symbol of a struggling enterprise, doomed to spending all his time begging, dealing with finances, negotiating between fractious factions that were fighting each other for scarce resources, and keeping the dream afloat. After taking part in a two-day meeting at Bethel, where they could see both the attitudes of NTL's existing staff and Warren's own ambivalence, Chris Argyris and Don Michael advised him to decline the job. "Don't take the job if you're ambivalent," Argyris said. "The last thing in the world NTL needs is ambivalence."

On November 14, Bennis betrayed no ambivalence at all in a speech to the NTL board. "The mere fact," he told them, "that a place exists that is coinhabited by executives and revolutionaries, young and old, parents and their children, will be mindblowing. . . . No one is going to be excited about the fact that master's degrees are given there. They are going to be excited because this is the place where people who are concerned about social change are coming and meeting and learning and teaching. I know dozens of professionals who would drop out of good universities, temporarily or permanently, to come to such a place, were it implemented in an uncompromising way."[40]

The board eagerly agreed to move forward. They spent the lion's share of the meeting deliberating over the name, torn between "The NTL University for Applied Behavioral Science" and "The University for Man." They leaned toward the latter, with its echoes of humanism, but they worried timidly, in those early days of feminism, how women might feel about it.[41] Lee Bradford, the departing president, felt "entranced" (his own word) by Warren's performance and by the knowledge that his little institute would evolve into a well-endowed, world-renowned institution.[42]

The trance continued for two more weeks. Then, on November 24, a terse one-page telegram from Warren Bennis arrived on Lee Bradford's desk. It said simply that he was turning down the job for "personal reasons." At the NTL offices, the people who received it were so angry that they remembered it years later as an endless document, rambling on about the lack of support and the need to raise money in a lost cause. Edie Seashore later claimed that people at the NTL offices were so angry that no one could finish reading it. "Somebody handed it to me and said, 'Here—you see if you can make any sense out of it.'"

Plain and simply, Bennis had finally recognized that the task was beyond him, perhaps beyond anyone, to pull off. "I handled what I did very badly," Bennis would say in an interview in the 1990s, "but I was absolutely correct in what I did." A decade after that, he would voice ambivalence in an e-mail: "If I have any regret in my life, the only one would have been not pioneering with a University of Applied Behavioral Sciences. Through the shining ether of time, I do think it could have worked and what a need for that today." But it would have taken dedication on a demonic scale to bring that dream to life.

That was the end of the NTL university. No one else appeared to lead it into being. Years later there are still members of the organization who have never forgiven Bennis. They hear his story told around the old Victorian house in Bethel—the man who let the dream die. And in the wake of his departure, even the old NTL fell into jeopardy. Lee Bradford, despite his health problems, had to postpone retirement. Corporate enrollments stagnated. The black caucus continued to raise objections and press for training. Bills piled up from renovations and other half-hearted projects begun in preparation for the renaissance that had been aborted.

And if the NTL university could somehow have come to pass, how might that have affected the world? At best, it might have served as a galvanizing point, a place from which reform of the culture would have rippled out, like circles in a turbulent pool. Yet in the end, something similar happened—but without the university and without anybody noticing: members of the NTL community went underground. They fanned out into a thousand organizations and locales. By the mid-1980s, many of them had positions of minor influence. By the mid-1990s, they were entrenched in senior echelons of major institutions. This ultimately was Lee Bradford's legacy: a widespread influence more subtly powerful than any university could have been.

And yet there was no getting around the fact that Bennis had let the NTL dream crash. Like Parzival the first time around, he had kept himself from looking up and saying, "What afflicts you, Uncle?" The 1960s were showing him, and perhaps millions of other people, that you cannot hold a grand dream unless you are willing to sacrifice everything for it—especially your ideas about what would be prudent. That's why no one who identifies with the 1960s can ever agree on the single moment when it ended. For each individual, the 1960s ended at the moment when they realized they could no longer give over their private lives in the service of a grand dream. Once that moment has come and gone, your dreams never completely fade away. They linger, reproachfully reminding you of the betrayals you felt forced to make. You may wander for years, as Parzival did, waiting for another chance.

———— o ————

Through the early 1970s, NTL struggled along, barely paying bills but still conducting T-Groups. Lee Bradford resigned in 1971. The presidency passed to a relative outsider, a family therapist from St. Louis named Vladimir Dupre. Other associates, coveting the job, tried to undermine or resist him. Some kept envisioning NTL as a membership organization that would run occasional programs for its members, while others (including Dupre) saw it as a consulting firm that could focus on getting billings and clients. While they bickered, many of the OD jobs that had once naturally gone to NTL moved to outside consultants, including many of the former regulars. Each year NTL's offerings shrank a little bit more and its debts mounted. In the awful summer of 1972, advance fees from the August sessions were used to pay the salaries in April. Then trainer salaries ceased entirely. Within a year or two, the institute had five dollars in outstanding debt for every dollar in assets. Where once they had looked forward to the inventiveness of their colloquy at Bethel, now trainers jetted in as closely as possible to the start of a T-Group and left as quickly as they could when it was over. There were still participants walking around Bethel in the summer heat, sitting under trees with their arms around each other, still living those magical experiences. But as a center, the place was rapidly withering away.

The only people who acted as if it were still vibrant were Edie and Charlie Seashore, who retained roles as trainer and administrator, respectively. As the official leadership of NTL fragmented, they increasingly took on the unofficial roles of leaders of the institute. It was ironic for Edie, because at the same time she was engaged in a revolt—a woman's revolt from within.

After all these years, there were now almost five hundred members of the inner circle of NTL trainers—the fellows elected by their peers—but only a handful of them were women. In the early 1970s, during the era of consciousness raising, a few women in the inner NTL circle began to compare notes. Edie Seashore, Barbara Bunker, Billie Alban, and Jane Moosbrucker were all prominent NTL trainers and renowned organizational consultants with expanding networks of colleagues around the world. And they had all, it turned out, experienced the same dynamics. Privately Edie, Barbara, Billie, or Jane would make a suggestion to a member of the NTL nominating committee: "There are a lot of competent women out there. We ought to name more of them as fellows."

"Gee, that's terrific," the committee member would say. "Send us a list."

The list would be dispatched. Then a few weeks later, the same committee member would say in a meeting, "It's too bad there are no competent women around to nominate."

And Edie, Barbara, Billie, or Jane would exclaim: "What about the lists we sent you?"

"What lists?"

By the time the women compared notes, they could count several sets of lists that had mysteriously disappeared. It wasn't conscious sabotage, they concluded, but it might as well have been. In some cases, they realized, they had colluded too, if only because it was nice to be labeled one of the few token "acceptable" women who had made it past the barrier.

They also realized, comparing notes, that being insiders did not prevent them from being demeaned. During a planning meeting before a T-Group session, one of the women would make a suggestion. No one would reply, but a few minutes later, a man would make the same suggestion. Another man would chime in, "That's a great idea, Bill."

The woman who spoke would spend the rest of the meeting castigating herself ("Maybe I said it wrong") or wondering if the men were deliberately trying to ignore her. But *these* men, dedicated to improving communication and understanding, couldn't be trying to undermine their peers deliberately, could they? Was NTL really a sexist male club that needed to be changed?

In 1973, a women's caucus emerged at NTL. At the same time, Edie Seashore and some of the other NTL regulars began to find themselves increasingly called on to handle gender and racial issues at companies. The first affirmative action programs, started in the mid-1960s as part of the short-lived corporate social responsibility movement, had indeed produced results: Ford, AT&T, Procter & Gamble, Polaroid, and a number of insurance companies, as a result of their efforts, found themselves with growing numbers of black and women managers. Now a host of new problems erupted, problems that only techniques like group dynamics, with the ability to bring hidden feelings to the surface, could handle effectively.

In the back of their minds, the managers who hired these people no doubt expected them to be grateful—for these *were* groundbreaking efforts. Like immigrants, the new black and women staff were expected to dig in, work hard, find ways to assimilate, and gradually melt into the existing ambience of the company. In other words, as all immigrants find wherever they settle, the game was rigged against them. They were supposed to adapt as best they could, keep their noses clean and their bosses satisfied at all costs, and wait until the second or third generation to achieve equality.

Except that (even if you accepted this depressing premise about how the world ought to work) most of these people weren't immigrants. They had been around all along in the United States. They were merely moving into new roles. Moreover, a corporation wasn't like a vernacular community, where you could settle into an enclave of fellow immigrants who watched out for each other. Frequently the person of color, or the woman, would be the only such person on their team. They were often expected to fail, but they could master the work easily enough. The hard part was learning to assimilate the constant belittling of their identity: "Stop moving your hands that way. Stop making those kinds of jokes. Dress like the CEO dresses. Act like the finance manager acts."

When everyone comes from a similar culture, these restraints are learned from childhood, but for women and members of ethnic minorities (Edie Seashore and others began to realize), corporate culture was thoroughly alien. (In a few years, a book called *Games Mother Never Taught You* would appear, explaining to women how corporate life was based on conforming to attitudes that stemmed from the team sports that boys played.)[43] The pressure was immense. Black managers or women in line positions would get ulcers. Their hair would fall out. People from ethnic backgrounds would rage internally at the fact that they couldn't include their old Chicano or Japanese or Jewish or African heritage in their proposals or presentations. The newcomers would wonder: Will I ever find a place that's right for me? They would become aware, as only an outsider would become aware, of every slight detail of the prevailing ambiance of the white male organizational culture. At least, they thought of it as white and male. In reality, it was primarily the numbers culture of corporate power—flavored most of all not by race or gender but by the bouquet of industrial finance.

Because it was new to them, the newcomers could see, more clearly than anyone else, how the prevailing ambiance undermined the company's performance. Fred Miller, for instance, was a young black manager at the Connecticut General Life Insurance Company in Hartford in those years. (That company is now called CIGNA.) He had gotten his job through the company's desire to integrate its management, and he would eventually go on to become one of Edie Seashore's consulting colleagues, an NTL board member, and president and CEO of the Kaleel Jamison consulting group.[44] At Connecticut, he worked under a supervisor with a law degree, handling policies for inner-city gas station owners. When someone didn't pay the bill, Miller's supervisor would send a long legalistic dunning letter. The gas station owners couldn't understand the letters ("In fact," Miller recalled, "neither did I half the time"), so they ignored them and became credit risks. Every once in a while, when he couldn't stand it anymore, Miller would surreptitiously call the gas station owners to find out why they hadn't paid their bill and clean up the case. It was his way of asking Parzival's question: "What afflicts you?" But when Miller's bosses found out, he was reprimanded. Insurance managers were not supposed to call up customers directly. That wasn't culturally acceptable.

A man like Miller was trapped in the role of heretic, in a way that Ed Dulworth of General Foods, John Mulder of Kodak, and Warren Bennis of the University of Cincinnati were not. They could choose whether to speak out. But people like Fred Miller and Edie Seashore felt they had no choice. "As a white man looking for upward mobility," Miller later recalled, "my supervisor knew that if he played by the rules he would be rewarded and be taken care of. I knew that I couldn't win by those rules. I could never live up to the company's image of what you had to be to be a manager. Even if I did everything right I would still be black. So to be successful, I had to break the rules. Fortunately, I was in a company where I *could* break a lot of rules. I was ordered to be fired twice while I was there. Both times, the president of the company rescued me because he saw that some rule-breaking was necessary for the organization's success, and he saw me as one of the few people who could do it effectively."

There are hundreds of stories from those years of people caught in similar double binds. Edie Seashore heard many of them in 1973, when AT&T hired her in the aftermath of a class action suit before the Equal Employment Opportunity Commission. Twenty-six thousand women and minority managers who had been routinely shortchanged in pay and benefits compared to white men were awarded pay increases collectively worth $51 million the first year. Part of the deal included an agreement for training—originally, training for women and minority managers in the skills they needed to advance. But as Edie Seashore and the other trainers from NTL soon recognized, the white men needed the most help. They might talk about tolerance and ethnic diversity, but if you looked at their actions, it was obvious: they viewed these new people as competitors who, like all other competitors, must be blocked. The results were expensive. Corporations spent millions to recruit top-notch women and people of color, and then the new recruits left in frustration after a couple of years.

The new groups that Seashore and other NTLers established became known as diversity training, focusing on the advantages that the company as a whole had to gain from admitting other points of view.[45] Companies would be much better equipped, for instance, for approaching global markets. They would be more resilient, less bound by foolish strictures (like the custom of not phoning customers). Managers would be honed and sharpened by the need to make themselves understood across lines of race, class, ethnic group, and gender. But all of these advantages were unproven. There was no organization to point to that had been founded on principles of diversity, to show what could be possible. And it didn't seem likely that any such organization could exist, not in the near future.

○

In 1975 the National Training Laboratories finally went bankrupt. Creditors stopped underwriting loans. The NTL board, which consisted largely of executives from companies that still booked training programs, insisted that they sell off their assets and pay the debts. A "For Sale" sign was posted in front of the old Victorian house in Bethel. The board began to debate how they might avoid a lawsuit brought by their creditors. In desperation, Vlad Dupre, the president, looked for someone to rescue the labs. At least one of the people he contacted declined, but he found four volunteers: Edie Seashore, Barbara Bunker (one of the other NTL inner circle women), Hal Kellner (one of Seashore's partners in the AT&T awareness sessions), and Peter Vaill, a business professor at George Washington University who had recently become an NTL trainer. Together they resolved to reshape NTL into a model of a diverse, integrated organization. Since it was about to go under, they had nothing to lose. They called themselves "the four horsepersons."

"We had the best time!" said Edie Seashore years later. "We usually had our meetings over a weekend, or from eleven at night until 2:00 A.M. on the telephone. We were all juggling full practices." They knew that rebuilding NTL with diversity as the first principle would force them to experience the ups and downs of cross-cultural exchange for themselves, and they could draw on that experience in their client work. If (as Lewin had said) you couldn't understand a system without trying to change it, then the growing business of diversity consulting—probably NTL's best hope for steady work—depended on their ability to change NTL itself.

First, the four horsepersons needed to convince the NTL board. They had a sure-fire argument: reforming the company would free the board members from their liability. They could resign without feeling that they had abandoned the enterprise. To show that the business acumen of these new horsepersons could be trusted, Edie Seashore and Peter Vaill flew out from Washington, D.C., to meet a key group of Houston-based board members for lunch. That in itself showed they weren't stuffy academics. They made a simple proposal: the four horsepersons would line up seventy-five former NTL members as volunteers. Collectively they would donate $200,000 worth of time to the enterprise without pay. That, plus the facilities NTL owned, was enough to offer a year's worth of courses, which would generate enough cash to begin paying off debts and bring some life back into the system.

"We let them think that they had a choice," Edie Seashore remembered. "We pretended that they could decide whether to reorganize or dissolve NTL. Which was ridiculous, because either way we could still rebuild the organization." Nonetheless, it would be much easier to have continuity, and the four horsepersons were relieved when the board accepted their idea—and, as their first act under the new regime, collectively resigned.

Then the four horsepersons gathered in a hotel for an extended week-end. Their first task was to select which seventy-five people to invite to form the new organization. They decided that the group should be divided, more or less equally, among all four of the diversity "quadrants": white males, nonwhite males, white females, and nonwhite females. They went down the list of candidates in rapid-fire succession. Any one of the horsepersons had veto power. They were merely following the old NTL precedent of selecting new members through a vote of their peers, but they had turned the process upside down, and in a way that brought the arbitrariness of NTL membership into sharp relief.

"We made a lot of people very angry," recalled Seashore. "The new members had to be people we thought would be committed to a new type of institution based on social justice. A lot of former NTL big shots were rejected. We crossed people off without even talking about it, as long as any one of us was willing to reject them. One of the people we rejected was a very close friend of mine. I told her that I didn't even remember who had vetoed her, because it all went by so fast. 'Who did you think you were—God?' she asked. And I said, 'That's exactly right.' We acted like God. It was a terrible experience at one level, because we had people's lives in our hands."

The following month, in November 1975, the sixty-five new members (ten of the invitees had declined) gathered at the same hotel to elect a board. This time they set up the quadrant system as a strict rule. One-fourth of the board members would be white men, one-fourth white women. Another fourth would be "men of color" (a category that included Asians, Native Americans, and Latin Americans), and another fourth would be "women of color." Balloting was secret, or sort of secret: members covered their eyes as they raised their hands to vote.

Edie was elected to the board, and then the board members elected her as president. In her youth, she had been the organization's token woman, its unofficial cheerleader; now she was leading a transition to a system where there would be no tokens. She agreed to the job as long as she could work part time. A trainer named Elsie Cross, a black woman, was elected as NTL's chair of the board—another part-time position.

Within a year or two, NTL had recovered from its financial crisis. Some problems persisted, though, concerning qualifications. At NTL, new members were admitted only under a cohort system. For every white male trainer admitted, there had to be one white female, one male of color, and one female of color. White male trainers with impeccable academic credentials felt shut out; few of the minority and women trainers had Ph.D.s. (Edie Seashore herself did not have one.) Thus, the prevailing

NTL attitude had to change. Theoretical debates about organizational behavior disappeared. Conversations rarely focused on peak experiences either; the day of the human potential movement was over, at least at NTL. Instead trainers talked pragmatically. What techniques had been effective with clients? What were they learning about race and gender in companies? Occasionally they talked about the most worrisome aspect of the cohort system: Was it, in effect, a quota system? Would it lead to selecting less competent trainers over more competent ones?

It was difficult to talk honestly about those sorts of questions, or any other serious issues, in racially mixed groups. It took patience and the willingness to sit in a room where people exploded in anger at each other. In fact, the first retreat for the new NTL board, early in 1976, erupted in dispute—not between the men and women in the room, which Edie had expected, or between the whites and blacks, but between the white and black *women*. They fought over the design of the NTL programs: Should they focus first on sexism or racism? White women didn't see themselves as racist, but suddenly their racism was on the table. It took painful hours to sort out the different ways in which white and black women interpreted the same simple conversations. And if they couldn't overcome their misunderstandings with each other, what hope did they have for helping outsiders?[46]

Although Edie resigned as president in 1979, the Seashores continued as the unofficial house parents at Bethel. They bought the house next door to the NTL's Victorian mansion; all summer long, there was now a continuing, warmhearted party at the Seashores' house. Although the transition was painful, the four horsepersons succeeded in forcing NTL out of its paternalistic, elitist culture. Now it was the kind of democracy that Lee Bradford, Ken Benne, and Ron Lippitt had talked about but never been able to achieve. Standing committees, for the first time in NTL's history, organized their own programs. Their decisions could no longer be vetoed by board fiat.[47] And NTL meetings had people from every conceivable ethnic background, of both genders at every age, in all sexual orientations, wearing a wide variety of garments, and speaking in a broad range of accents and styles. Yet somehow they all seemed to be able to operate in sync. They had faced the tribulations that came from their differences and talked through them enough so that they understood each other. The new NTL approach would be a significant (and controversial) force in the organization change movement of the 1980s and 1990s.

To anyone who knew NTL's past, there was something bittersweet about the change. NTL had been born amid the Pelagian attitudes of people like Kurt Lewin, Douglas McGregor, and Lee Bradford. Human beings are innately good: racism and sexism somehow stem from social institutions. There must be a way to restructure society that could bring racism and sexism to the surface and wipe them away.

The new NTL approach seemed at least partially Augustinian: grounded in the belief that people at heart are inherently racist and sexist. Oppression is built into human nature. Organizations must be designed to contain, regulate, and manage the racist and sexist impulses of their members.[48] Many of the NTLers found ways to synthesize the Augustinian critique of oppression with the Pelagian spirit of T-Groups; they taught communication techniques that drew forth the basic goodwill and appreciation of diversity that existed in the hearts of most of their clients. Nonetheless, increasingly during the 1980s, some of the diversity management pioneers would be accused of using the encounter group to instill their own points of view in people—abandoning the attitude of inquiry that made the T-Group worthwhile in the first place.

———————— o ————————

After the plans for an NTL university collapsed, Chris Argyris resolved to investigate NTL's own lack of learning head-on. He was embarking on his own, equivalent perhaps to the years that Parzival spent wandering, wrapped up in questions about his own capabilities and motives. Argyris, however, took on that burden not just for himself but for all his colleagues and peers.

His investigations into the effects of the T-Groups had led him there. He would watch an authoritarian executive change, heart and soul. The executive would return to his ordinary life with a new, more open way of speaking, a taste for hearing what others had to say, and even a warmer relationship with his family. It would last for six months or even a year. But then the company would hit a period of stress: a cutback in orders, a tricky labor negotiation, or some other crisis. And the executive would revert back to being a snapping, subordinate-blasting, self-righteous SOB, as if the T-Group had never happened. There was no theory to explain this reversion. "How come the good stuff doesn't last," Argyris asked himself, "and the lousy stuff seems to persevere?"

In 1971, after moving to Harvard University, he took part in a Ford Foundation–funded project on school leadership, and there he began to work regularly with an MIT urban studies and education professor named Donald Schön (pronounced to rhyme with "churn"). Schön had been trained in philosophy; although he had grown up in New York, he had, as one colleague put it, "an elegant Oxford Don temperament." He had been puzzled by the lack of willingness to learn among professional experts, such as architects, psychiatrists, and educators. Why, when their techniques went awry, did they cling to them? Why did they struggle so hard to justify their own school of thought instead of inquiring into possible solutions offered by their rivals?

It seemed to both Argyris and Schön that they had stumbled onto a fundamental generic principle of human behavior. For the next three years, they met twice a week, usually talking long into the evenings—first to articulate their idea and then to figure out how to test it. Their resulting theory of action has been at the core of organizational learning practice ever since and has also been highly influential in professional education. Without an understanding of this concept, arguably, every attempt to change an organization for the better will fail, foundering on the hubris of both the insiders and the outside consultants. And yet it's very hard to put the theory of action into practice. To do so requires going on an internal Grail quest of your own—stepping back through your own mind's levels of abstraction, becoming increasingly aware of your own stumbling blocks and those of others, and continually building the capacity in yourself to stop the action and say to yourself: "What is keeping me from asking what afflicts the King?"

Argyris and Schön posited that each of us carries two sets of theories in our heads. Closer to the surface lies the espoused theory: the principles and attitudes about the world that we wish to believe that we believe. Thus, an executive going through a T-Group would come out espousing theory Y–style beliefs: that people are intrinsically interested in making a contribution and learning. When that executive returns to his company, he will pay lip-service to those beliefs. He may send other people to training programs so they'll "get it" about theory Y. He may even institute some new policies or take other actions that reflect this espoused theory. But since it remains at the level of espoused theory, it never goes very deep.

Then comes a moment of stress. Suddenly the executive's actions are no longer guided by the espoused theory Y. They are guided by whatever theory-in-use has operated all along, which could be theory X: that people basically will not take any initiative unless prodded by the carrot and stick. Since theories-in-use have taken a lifetime to develop, they usually operate below the surface. A manager may loudly espouse egalitarian treatment of all people, regardless of status—but in the boss's presence, a quavering voice and sweaty palms may reveal a very different theory-in-use about authority. These tacit theories provide the constancy in our perceptions and our identities: in a sense, we *are* our theories-in-use about the world. In other words, not only is there an unconscious force driving our human behavior, but it's possible to understand, map, and maybe even change that unconscious driver—if you know enough about the theories that exist there.

With the concept of theories-in-use, Argyris could explain the frustrations in his earlier consultations. For example, the State Department bureaucrats had held a theory-in-use that revealing their feelings and attitudes made them vulnerable. No T-Group could have overcome that. In some role-playing workshops he had facilitated for IBM's senior leaders in the early 1960s at Yale, he had seen the president, Thomas Watson Jr., repeatedly try to provoke people to tell him critical or bad news. "I'm worried," he would say, "that IBM could become a big, inflexible organization which won't be able to change when the computer business goes through its next shift."

"It'll never happen, Tom," his direct reports would say. "This is a world-class organization, with world-class people." Yet when there was trouble at a factory or in a design lab, at each step up the hierarchy another sliver of bad news would be extracted, until by the time it reached the top, the debacle had gradually become wonderful.[49]

Now, looking back on it, Argyris could see how Watson was trapped by the theories-in-use of his own subordinates ("who were first-rate people," Argyris later recalled). IBM had been built on the unspoken theory that the most important result of a meeting was making sure everyone was pleased, particularly the boss.

If you want to change someone's behavior, Argyris and Schön stated, you cannot simply force them to espouse a different theory. You must change their theory-in-use. To explain this, they borrowed a concept from the epistemologist and anthropologist Gregory Bateson. Most everyday learning (which they called "single loop") merely allowed you to pick up new knowledge or skills. But in the kind of double-loop learning that could overcome defensiveness and mental blinders, you had to examine the "data"—the details of your behavior and thoughts, in the forms of transcripts of your conversations (and your imagined conversations in which you wrote down what you could have said or wanted to say). In the process, you would bring your deeply held theories-in-use to the surface, look closely at them, test them against new experience, and (most difficult of all) practice living as if your theories-in-use were already changing. And then, most difficult of all, you would have to speak openly about your assumptions, attitudes, and reactions with your colleagues at work, until all of you had developed a habitual willingness to talk through the roots of any misunderstanding. Argyris has published numerous books and articles on this subject (first with Schön and then alone after Schön's untimely death in 1997); his most famous article, aptly enough, was titled "Teaching Smart People How to Learn."[50]

○

In the 1970s, Argyris became one of the most controversial faculty members at Harvard. He had taken a twin post, half-time at the business school and half-time at the education school. At the business school, he was dismissed as a Lewin protégé. (Unlike McGregor's group at MIT, most Harvard professors had never embraced Lewin's dictum that you could not understand an organization without trying to change it. After all, the famous case study method pioneered at Harvard was based on describing a company objectively, with no intent of changing it.) Across the Charles River in Cambridge at the education school, he found himself regarded as an apologist for corporations. His students were future therapists, counselors, and educators, earning their "Master's of Saving the World" social work degrees. In one of his earliest classes, Argyris was denounced simply for teaching at the business school. A student stood up and proclaimed, "As long as they're businessmen they're no damn good," and the class erupted in applause.

Argyris was deeply offended. The student might be right; businessmen might indeed be no damn good. But a statement like that should be based on data. So the next week, he opened the class by calling on a black student. "I'd like to ask you," he said, "about the concept of 'nigger.'" There was dead silence. "What is the meaning of that concept? How would you describe it? What are its properties?"

The student replied, "Are you crazy, Professor?"

"This is being taped," Argyris said. (He taped every class.) "You can have the tape. But I want to know the answer." After a half-hour's discussion, he summarized the main points the students had made: "The concept of 'nigger' treats a human being as part of a class stereotype. It shows no respect for what a human being can be. No matter whether you are a good black, a hard-working black, a lazy black—if you're black, according to that concept, you are no damn good. Is that right?"

The class agreed. Argyris pressed the button on the other tape recorder and they heard the voice from the previous week: "As long as they're businessmen they're no damn good!" Then he clicked off the tape and asked, "Ladies and gentlemen, what's the difference?" And this time the class gave *him* a round of applause.

That week the Black Student Caucus met to discuss whether to censure him. Argyris, hearing of the meeting, said he would love to attend, but the caucus refused. Instead, two students came to him afterward to tell him that the group had censured him, but personally they felt he was right: "You have the courage that a lot of other faculty don't seem to have. And we need that."

"Thank you," said Argyris. "Now would you say that in public?"

"No," the students told him. "That would start another war."

That episode set the tone for his years at the school. He often opened classes by saying to his graduate students in counseling or social work, "A lot of what goes by the name of counseling theory, or caring and support, is incompetence covered up by love." When they protested, he offered to prove it from their own counseling cases. His awareness of conversational nuance was razor-sharp—and since it was based on a theoretical framework that he had developed himself, few people could challenge it. In courses filled with self-satisfied Harvard students, he systematically shattered their illusion that they were going to do good simply by following their instincts. In the process, he would work himself up to a fever pitch, dancing at the front of the room, occasionally forgetting where he was, and bumping into the podium—then turning to look at it as if to wonder, What was *that* doing there?

Students tended to remember Argyris's classes for years—some with deep affection, others with the feeling of having been brutalized. Argyris knew, from his work with T-Groups, that an intervention is a kind of drug—an experience based on a dramatically powerful technique for changing relationships, reframing attitudes, and raising new feelings of identity. These interventionists would be going out into the real world. The quality of their reasoning would dominate every encounter. If they were made anxious when examining their own reasoning dispassionately, then they were like surgery students who fainted at the sight of blood. Maybe they should find another job. "We'd better make damn well sure," Argyris told his students, "that we have the highest possible commitment to increasing the knowledge about our impact." And in the process of articulating that impact, Argyris would become a kind of human lightning rod, sparking emotions among his students that ran from adulation to revulsion. Years later some students (and some clients) would find they still kept arguing with Chris Argyris in their minds.

The practice of double-loop learning, as Argyris called it, was aimed at the heart of Parzival's dilemma. You can learn to reduce the unfortunate, unintended consequences of your actions by becoming hyperaware of your own impulses and thoughts, particularly those that drive your behavior toward results you don't intend. Argyris and the few students he trained in depth developed a way of speaking that stepped carefully around emotional land mines. It was almost precious, yet it seemed to get to the heart of the matter: "What is it that leads you to believe this?" Or, "What exactly prevented you from bringing up that difficult issue?" Or, "Have you tested your assumptions about this? What makes you sure they're correct?"[51] The conversations sounded stilted; they had to be in order to slow down thought patterns so participants could see how to redesign their habits.

To have that language gave people a remarkable feeling of power. They were no longer hung up by the strictures of their own misunderstandings. They could challenge their bosses safely; they could lay their assumptions on the table, as if they were tangible, and talk through their differences.[52] People who worked with Argyris, particularly in his business consultations, began to look at the relationship between people's espoused theory and theory-in-use as a finance officer would look at a balance sheet. It was concrete, testable. You could diagram it, and the diagram would match reality. You could never capture all the complexity of human interchange, but neither could a balance sheet. Once people had the skills of double-loop learning, Argyris noticed, they never forgot them. Even if a new boss came in to an organization and told everyone to drop the talk of theories and inferences, the people retained the skills. T-Groups had never been able to accomplish that.

———————— o ————————

By the end of the 1970s, each of the three key NTL figures had come to a kind of resolution. Edie Seashore, with the other three horsepersons, had built an organization that no one had thought was possible, on the foundation of acknowledging the categories in which life had placed people. Chris Argyris had developed a rigorous path for self-understanding, free of mysticism, and replicable even in the most numbers-driven industrial organization. And Warren Bennis took a job as the leader of a large university, which he set out to remake in the image of, if not NTL's dream, then a vision closer to his own. For the first time since his old mentor Douglas McGregor had held the presidency of Antioch College twenty-five years before, someone schooled in group dynamics and change agentry would actually run a mainstream organization: not just as a consultant but as the chief executive. In that sense, this school, the University of Cincinnati, provided the first full-scale opportunity to show what the Pelagians could do.

UC was a commuter university of thirty-five thousand students, standing on a hill half a mile from downtown. Founded in 1819, it was the largest university in one of America's internal border cities; Cincinnati merged the Great Lakes culture of Ohio and the former confederacy culture of Kentucky, just across the Ohio River. By American urban standards, particularly in those years, it was a conservative town. The university's board, under great pressure to conclude its presidency search, had reluctantly hired Bennis; he was the least politically leftist candidate whom the college search committee had found. Nonetheless, he once again proposed a flamboyantly lofty vision for a university's destiny: UC would be "the greatest urban university of the century."[53] Instead of an encumbered bureaucracy, it would be an exemplar of collaborative management. It would not just train social workers and police, but develop ways to revitalize schools and communities in Cincinnati's poor neighborhoods. New interdisciplinary programs would span UC's autonomous colleges, which heretofore had been fierce rivals. Bennis was impatient to galvanize this parochial commuter college into a full-scale educational centerpiece.

His presidency lasted six years. It is considered by many Cincinnatians to be a low point in the university's history, and for almost thirty years he was the only UC president emeritus who was never offered an honorary degree by the university trustees. (He finally received one in 2007.) Yet in retrospect, he had a remarkably successful administration. He ensured the university's survival by moving it from its part-public, part-private status completely into the state university system, and he set in motion a shift toward urban relevance that still serves the university well. He merely failed to accomplish the NTL ideal: leading a new kind of institution that would change society.

Warren was a thoroughly charismatic leader. He was exciting, vibrant, tanned, cosmopolitan, and a bit bohemian (a photograph ran in the local newspaper of his wife, Clurie, wearing sandals, which were still unorthodox in Cincinnati then, at least for the wife of a university president).[54] He seemed to be everywhere; striding into the Student Union with a small entourage straggling after him, charming faculty members in his office, hosting a local TV talk show, or sitting down for lunch on the college lawn with a group of students. Seemingly immune to circadian rhythms, he would hold all-night staff meetings at his house or wake faculty members in the wee hours, phoning about an idea he had. He sent key staffers off to National Training Labs seminars. He brought old NTL friends like Chris Argyris and Edie Seashore to lecture on campus. He hired well-known figures like Neil Armstrong, the first man to step on the moon, to teach on campus. He and his staffers drew map after map for reconceiving the flow of work in the university, sometimes commissioning plywood sculptures of the results if they were too complex for two dimensions.

Perhaps the most successful of his many innovations was the open door policy.[55] Universities are profoundly authoritarian institutions; there is frequently no recourse against a recalcitrant bureaucrat, an inaccessible dean, or an exploitative and malevolent Ph.D. adviser. Now students (and junior faculty members) could turn directly to the president during specified hours. "My office looked like an old-fashioned Middle Eastern court for a while," Bennis recalled years later. "I would get heartsick at every session, at the real problems students were having." Some people just showed up to observe; one woman, who always brought her knitting, told Bennis that it was the most interesting show on campus. Bennis made no decisions on the spot but always appointed a staff member to investigate and carry the message to the appropriate dean. Occasionally the complaints were made public. "That's why it was threatening to the deans and vice presidents. I undercut their authority."

The first serious sign of trouble for Bennis came in 1973, when his new dean of the education school, Hendrik Gideonse, began taking care of his newborn son at work two days a week.[56] He simply didn't want to be an absentee father. (This was the same Gideonse who had been Willis Harman's client at the U.S. Education Office.) Almost immediately a secretary's mother phoned Bennis's office to complain. "Why doesn't he get a baby-sitter like everyone else?" she asked. "Why isn't he taking care of his duties?" A staff member forwarded the complaint on to Bennis, who taped it to a box of Pampers and sent it to Gideonse. But the *Cincinnati Enquirer* got wind of the story and sent a photographer to Gideonse's office. Suddenly there was the baby in his bassinet in the morning paper, surrounded by Gideonse's shelves of books. United Press International, and then worldwide TV, picked up the story: a father who loved his child so much that he took the baby to work.

In Cincinnati, however, men were not supposed to take care of children. "My in basket," wrote Bennis, "has been flowing . . . with letters that urge his arrest or merely his immediate dismissal. My only public comment has been that . . . if Hendrik can engage in this form of applied humanism and still accomplish the things we both want done in education, then, like Lincoln with Grant's whiskey, I'd gladly send him several new babies for adoption. Nevertheless, Hendrik's baby is eating up quite a bit of my time."

This was just one of the irritations that seemed to bedevil Bennis. A professor complained the building temperature was sixty-five degrees. ("I suppose he expects me to grab a wrench and fix it," Bennis groused.) A group of students complained that two beloved trees had been cut down to make room for a sign with a benefactor's name on it. (Bennis, despite his authority, couldn't find out who had authorized the trees cut. No one seemed to know.)[57] As he dealt with crisis after crisis, he felt his time and aspirations for the school drip away bit by bit. "Routine work drives out all nonroutine work," he opined—thanks to an "unconscious conspiracy" that sent all problems up to his desk and made sure that nothing substantive actually happened.[58] No matter how hard he tried to be a leader, he couldn't lead. He was too busy managing.

And yet anyone who watched Bennis noticed that he encouraged all communications to flow directly through his office. When his attention wandered away from a project, other people felt it had become a low priority; they waited for him to prod them again before resuming. Anyone could say anything to him without fear of reprisal and watch him agree, but more often than not, people walked out of his office thinking they hadn't made a difference. He would just change his mind again when the next person walked in. It was as if Warren himself was the chief unconscious conspirator.

In 1974 the school was overwhelmed by a severe budget crunch.[59] Bennis embarked on a passionate lobbying campaign to merge the school into the Ohio state university system. This meant selling the idea to the legislators and winning a Cincinnati city referendum. He forced himself into the role of politician, making speeches and canvassing for the support he would need to lobby the state legislature—and the deal went through. Five years before, he had refused the presidency of the NTL university because he didn't want to deal with financial scarcity. But at Cincinnati, the crunch became an opportunity for his greatest triumph.

Meanwhile, human relations, his area of expertise, was the source of his worst disaster. Torn between his desire to promote participative management and his need to be an authority figure, Bennis asked all the department heads to work out a budget plan together for the common good of the school. But consensus management was a pipe dream when people had to divide an ever-shrinking budgetary pie. The department heads and college deans all fought each other bitterly. They were especially outraged when Bennis cut special deals for some faculty members he considered particularly worthy. He organized faculty T-Groups, which might have helped, but they dissipated into apathy when people realized that some participants were acting as moles, going back to Warren and telling him what everyone had said.

Finally the faculty voted to join a union and institute collective bargaining. Warren was stunned. "Why do you suppose they did that?" he asked one of his faculty supporters.

"They figured, in the final analysis," came the reply, "that was the only way they could get a fair share, because all the other claimants for money were closer to the front of the line."

Bennis had nothing against unions, but to the board of directors—with its roots in the established Cincinnati business community—there was no surer signal that he was out of control.

In 1977, just after the State of Ohio finally accepted the University of Cincinnati as a fully funded state school, Bennis abruptly resigned. On one level, the deal meant that he could finally achieve his transformative ideas without the constant chokehold of austerity budgets. But he had had enough. His resignation was accepted quickly by the governor, who apparently leaked it to the press without telling Bennis he would do so; and Bennis left with equal haste—so much so that the university had to clean out his books and papers from his offices. Most of them are still in the school's library. It was widely assumed that he had been forced out of his job.

But he had resigned on his own, for a variety of reasons. It was a good time to leave, since the merger with the state system had just been completed. He had learned something about running a large institution, something he wanted to think about. The new governor of Ohio, James Rhodes, was a Republican who would be appointing new members to the university board soon. They were certain to disagree with Bennis's aspirations for the school. He had, in one of his vice presidents, a reliable successor whom he could recommend. Most of all, he was tired. He didn't want the responsibility any longer. His life, which had been so public for so many years, became private. His marriage broke apart. He lived quietly, particularly after a heart attack in 1979. Then in the early 1980s, he broke into the public eye again as a management author with a series of popular books on leadership.

He had written about leadership throughout his career, starting in the early 1960s, but his interest accelerated after his Cincinnati experience. Managers were people who do things right, he said, while leaders do the right thing. He now believed, as Buckminster Fuller did, that organizations needed people not just with "know-how" but also with "know-why." To articulate this concept more clearly, he began interviewing leaders of other institutions—first universities, then corporations and government agencies. He interviewed dozens during the late 1970s and early 1980s, and this led directly to his first best-selling book on leadership, *Leaders: The Strategies for Taking Charge* (coauthored with Bert Nanus and published in 1985).[60] Thereafter, he became a college professor and writer—a better-known individual than he had ever been before and arguably the most widely read writer on leadership in the world. But he would never again lead a large institution himself.

Certainly Bennis deserved more credit than he ever got—from either the Cincinnati business community or the NTL community—for running an institution. He had invigorated the university and saved it from almost certain dissolution. No one else at NTL ever took the same level of risk. But his strength was the reason for his failure: he was too preoccupied with his own learning. The result was an enterprise that couldn't help but be centered on Bennis himself, as if the university were an extension of the man. Nonetheless, in the end, taking the presidency of the university had been a thoroughly heroic action. Bennis had met Parzival's dilemma by choosing to act, and anyone who paid attention could know henceforth that the knowledge of change-agentry theory, in itself, was necessary, but not sufficient, for changing the world.

Bennis's last commencement speech to the students, in 1977, summed up the force that had propelled him into an active role again and again, despite all of his mistakes. He quoted a long letter to the daughter of a friend. She had written him to ask for advice on what to do with the rest of her life. Should she stay in the small Colorado town where she lived? If she moved to a city, wouldn't she get trapped in a dehumanizing workplace? Bennis scolded her (and, by extension, the students sitting before him). He knew her as a bold and gutsy young woman, yet every career she conceived for herself sounded dull, dreary, unimaginative.

What made her think, Bennis asked, that she could abandon work just because workplaces were dehumanizing? Did she think that one ordered one's workplace from a Sears catalogue? One built one's workplace, attitude by attitude, conversation by conversation. One built one's life by making a commitment to it and being willing to be broken by that commitment:

> For many years [Bennis quoted from his letter to her], I believed in predestination. I believed that people were born, doll-like, wound up by the Master Toymaker, to "run down" over a period of time along a given course. Life, in that view, is a kind of maze. Not frightening exactly if you watch closely for the clues and have faith, but risky, thanks to "free will" (an extra little gear invented by the Toymaker to keep from getting bored).
>
> I can't remember when or why I stopped believing in predestination. . . . I seem to have spent a good deal of my life trying to understand from failure and always believing that that's what we are really here for: to learn from ourselves and others, and some anticipation of failure has to be a part of that. But can you see the paradox? If learning is the centerpiece of living, as I think it to be, how can we ever *really* fail unless we decide: "Choice is too dangerous, failure is something we cannot handle or tolerate, and learning is only peripheral to living?" If we come to that, then our shutters close off life.[61]

8

MILLENARIANS

EREWHON, THE SRI FUTURES GROUP,

HERMAN KAHN, ROYAL DUTCH/SHELL,

AND AMORY LOVINS,

1968–1979

---

*Heresy: That corporations might play a role in shifting the world
to a more ecologically responsible, humanist age.*

In the last years of the twelfth century, in the mountains of northern
Italy and southern France, disaffected preachers talked quietly of a
golden era about to come, glistening with inevitability, in which the
rich would share their wealth with the poor. Earth would return to
the natural harmony of Eden. Most important of all, the ordinary
people—not the established Church—would make this happen
themselves.

The Church was disorganized in those years, and alternative congregations gathered in the streets. Millenarian preachers spoke from
pulpits throughout Europe. If you were sympathetic in Moravia, you
might be led by the hand, on foot, to a commune of like-minded
people in Cologne. There you might take part in shared trances,
imagining the world to come. You might take a vow of voluntary
poverty and become a deliberately homeless pilgrim, living on alms,

engaging wherever you went in a rootless, endless conversation about the values of the world.

The millenarians of that time were known as the "brethren of the free spirit" or (since many of their leaders were women) as the "beguines." They came from well-to-do backgrounds; they were widows and spinsters from merchant families, rebellious artisans, younger scions of aristocrats, and youthful members of the clergy. They were articulate; as fast as their writings could be suppressed and burned, they turned out new tracts. They preached in common languages, not in Latin. Many of them felt that they should be exempt from the strictures of ordinary morality. For was not the Church, the sovereign institution of ordinary morality, inherently corrupt? And would it not be swept away as the world changed?

Much of what the millenarians had to say has been distorted and lost, and they are known, largely through their critics' accusations, as dissolute, orgying, syphilitic thieves. Their influence could not have been all dreadful, however, for it endured four hundred years. There was a sweetness to their preachings and a sense of self-renunciation. They were a lot like some of the people you might meet in, say, university towns in the early to mid-1970s. You wouldn't know whether to marvel at their naiveté or admire their prescience.[1]

○

IN THE EARLY 1960S, IF YOU WERE A COLLEGE STUDENT positioned among the best and brightest of your peers, you might have wanted to become an engineer or physicist and contribute to America's landing on the moon. In the early 1980s, you would set your sights on becoming an investment banker or corporate magnate, and a millionaire by forty. In the early 1990s, you would be preparing yourself for a career launching some new Internet-driven entrepreneurial enterprise. But in the early 1970s, there were only two appropriate choices: to be an artist or to save the world. In both cases, like the genteel aristocrats of the British Empire, you weren't really supposed to think about money, overt status, or even achievement. Instead, as the mythologist Joseph Campbell began to tell his students at lectures, you were supposed to "follow your bliss"— follow the goals you felt called on to pursue.

In that self-indulgent, idealistic era, even those who went into creative businesses—for instance, those who went to work making movies in Hollywood or recording rock music—were considered sell-outs, even by themselves. Joni Mitchell's evocative song "For Free," released in 1970, described a saxophone player on a street corner, with no apparent income; she wistfully admires the quality of his craft while being hustled off to her next million-dollar gig.[2]

For a few years, the bottom dropped out of the primary emotional currency of business: pecuniary ambition. Millions of young people supported themselves on odd jobs and allowances from their parents. They lived three, four, or six to an apartment, choosing poverty; they weren't trapped in it and felt no loss of dignity. Indeed, if you were bright (and had no children), poverty was exalting. It meant (though nobody used this language) that you had found a way to reembrace the vernacular spirit that society had tried to discard. You could live in a utopian sphere where everyone was an aristocrat. You did not commute, learn to balance a checkbook, or buy a business suit. You experienced life at each moment and felt no need to poison the quality of the moment by preparing for the future.

Counterculture people could afford to take their stance precisely because living was easy. Rents were cheap; the parks, the streets, and the love of fellow members of the tribe were all available for nothing. As Herman Kahn noted, it cost as little as five hundred dollars a year to live as a hippie in the late 1960s and early 1970s, which meant that twelve young people could share a large house, each working one month a year in the post office and taking eleven off.[3] (Nobody actually did this, but it gave Kahn a mythically apt image to use in speeches.) The idea prevailed that sharing with each other, even with strangers, was the most natural thing in the world. "Free" stores and clinics opened in neighborhoods like the Haight-Ashbury of San Francisco and in Cambridge, Massachusetts: distributing food, used clothing, emergency medical care, and dense mimeographed broadsides about the coming apocalypse.

By contrast, a corporate career was a life in prison: a life of making choices based on what someone else would tell you to do, gradually internalizing that tyrannical authority in your own mind. The young actor Dustin Hoffman famously captured the horror in his deadpan expression as an uncle leered over him with advice in *The Graduate*: "I'm going to say one word to you. Plastics!"

Indeed, that would have been much-appreciated advice a decade later. Plastics was not only a growth field, but it was relatively free-wheeling. At General Electric, the people in the plastics operation in western Massachusetts were the rebels of the company, unwilling to kowtow to the corporate bureaucracy. The flamboyant president of the group, a young executive named Jack Welch, had already gained a reputation for ignoring, or pushing back against, the bureaucratic strictures of his parent corporation. Yet even GE Plastics had trouble recruiting the brightest young people in the early 1970s.[4]

So did fields like advertising, an industry enthralled at that time by the "creative revolution," the most rebellious, artistically rewarding period in its history. For the first time, ad men were rewarded for intimating the truth: that life might not be perfect. Jerry Della Femina broke into big time advertising by asking the question for a woman's foot care product: "What's the ugliest part of your body?"[5] There were dozens of guys like Della Femina on Madison Avenue: in their late thirties or early forties, they had grown up in the back alleys of Brooklyn, Pittsburgh, or Baltimore, and now felt that they'd landed in the big time. But very few twenty-one- and twenty-three-year-old applicants wanted to step in as first-year copy-writers or art directors. "We lost a lot of people to the war in Vietnam," Della Femina would say, years later, "not because they were drafted, but because they walked away from business." The war in Vietnam may have been a triggering factor, but the counterculture's revulsion against business continued after the draft ended in the United States. A large number of young people had become aware of the bitterness and malaise of the industrial world.

A few who dropped out never returned. But most of the members of the counterculture discovered that they could not simply renounce an old establishment. They had to create a new one. In the process, they gave birth to the notion of a secular millennium: a postindustrial, countercultural, ecologically aware attitude shift affecting every aspect of society.

This idea was grounded in talk. The counterculture was rife with groups, clubs, cells, meeting grounds, and mutual enterprises in which people talked constantly. Living in some counterculture neighborhoods was like living in a community-wide T-Group. Nothing was decided except through drawn-out dialogues and consensus sessions. The hippies were as intensely Pelagian as the academics of the National Training Laboratories, but their Pelagianism came straight from the heart. They didn't have to take people away to a cultural island like Bethel; they lived and breathed it right where they were.

They were so keenly aware of the benefits of their life, and the poisonous qualities of the life they had rejected, that they assumed everyone else would soon want to live the same way. Nothing less than a mass delusion existed in, for instance, Berkeley and Cambridge, that society-wide revolution was imminent. "The people's consciousness is shifting," young radical hippies would say to each other. "Look at the signs. It will be another two or three years, and then the structure of the establishment will come tumbling down." After all, there was so much less waste in their lives; they did not drown themselves in unnecessary, addictive consumer products. They did not pollute or try to control each other (at least they thought they didn't). Everything was shared; people operated for the good of the entire clan. Wasn't that how Native Americans had lived? Admittedly those who had money and success sometimes felt as if they were carrying the burden of the tribe. Rock musicians with record contracts were under constant pressure to distribute their largesse. The music was an expression of the crowd flowing through them, so didn't the rewards from that music belong to everyone? The San Francisco concert promoter Bill Graham often found himself in shouting matches with young would-be concert-goers who wanted him to stop charging money for music. "What does your father do? Is he a plumber? Well, I want my pipes fixed for free! Is he a baker? Well, I want my bread for free!"[6]

In retrospect, the startling thing about the counterculture was the disconnect between production and consumption. How could so many smart people fail to see a link between the work people did, the investments they made, and the rewards they gained? Though counterculture people grew up with an enormously sophisticated understanding of media—the web of moving images on media and how those affected (and were affected by) public attitudes—they had little visceral understanding of the structures of material life. A Berkeley student of that era, who later became a management consultant, recalled being approached to join a radical group. "Don't talk to me," she told them, "until you have some indication of how you're going to get the fruits, nuts and vegetables from California and Florida up to New York and Chicago. Until then, I haven't got time to listen. Don't tell me what you're going to blow up; this country works on distribution systems and networks."[7] But the radicals she spoke to didn't know what she was talking about.

Many young people had this blind spot, perhaps because they had lived their entire lives in a world dominated by the giant, all-nurturing postwar corporations—institutions that separated work and sustenance. Daddy produced; Mommy consumed. Children never went to the office, for there was nothing resembling day care there, even in offices with women managers. ("Someday," the writer Betty Harragan would later point out, "reactionary management may understand that the poor 'image' of business in the public opinion polls will never be successfully counteracted as long as children in their most impressionable, formative years grow up with the idea that a business work site is an unfriendly, repelling, and sinister place which refuses to accept them until they are over twenty years old.")[8] Instead of going to work, children of the 1950s and 1960s went to school, where they learned that the rewards for their labor and achievement were never tangible. The reward was an empty grade, a classification of a rank in relation to your peers. What was the point of living a life measured by that?

———————— o ————————

Because the trappings of capitalism were so dismal—the ambition and competitiveness of their parents—some tried to do without capitalism entirely and produce everything they needed themselves. Self-sufficiency was an organizing principle in many of the communes of the late 1960s and early 1970s. But as historian Fernand Braudel has pointed out, existence without a market is "the lowest plane of human existence, where each man must himself produce almost all he needs."[9] Only a few communards who tried that game, the purest mystics and ideologues, managed to sustain themselves. The rest turned their communes into businesses (the Farm, in Summertown, Tennessee, earned its income by publishing books about midwifery, ham radios, and their own experience). Or else they came running back to the city, creating enterprises of their own.

The first urban countercultural businesses emerged in the early- to mid-1960s. These included whimsical, flamboyant restaurants serving cheap, whole-grain food to people in ragged clothes, and boutiques selling artifacts brought back from Kathmandu or Machu Picchu by young travelers. The proprietors of these businesses had often learned the rudimentary skills of marketing and management by dealing such drugs as marijuana and LSD.[10] Like the bootleggers of the 1920s, they had had to learn the intricacies of bookkeeping, or else they would get swindled by their suppliers or hurt by their customers. They had also learned some time-honored sales promotion techniques, like giving away free joints to attract new customers. Around 1969, organized crime had moved into the lucrative narcotics trade of neighborhoods like San Francisco's Haight-Ashbury and New York's East Village. The hippies had stepped away from selling dope; they parlayed their account-keeping and budgeting knowledge into new lines of work, unabashedly aiming their goods and services at the members of the "tribe."

By the early 1970s, most mainstream services had counterculture equivalents. There were clothing stores that sold new and used merchandise, stores specializing in bootleg records and rock concert posters, food co-ops with organic grains that customers scooped into their own jars from large wooden barrels, and transient hotels, like the Head Inn in New Orleans. For one dollar a night you could sleep in a sleeping bag on a rickety iron-grille balcony overlooking a French Quarter alleyway.[11] There were hippie bus lines, on which for thirty dollars (after waiting a day or two for the bus driver to be ready), you could ride in the back of a gaily painted van—drinking beer and making out with your fellow passengers all the way from San Francisco to New York. There were wild-eyed experiments with electronic gear, solar panels, and Buckminster Fuller-inspired domes, experiments that begat sophisticated small manufacturing companies. And there were publishers of magazines and books rooted in rock and roll, which the mainstream publishers didn't imagine would sell.

At first, these new forms of commerce lacked infrastructure. Counterculture businesspeople hardly ever knew about each other; they rarely knew how to keep going. The large-scale information in conventional business publications—the *Wall Street Journal* and *Fortune*—was worse than useless to them. So the counterculture began to invent its own infrastructure and its own information sources. Instead of slipping through the cracks in the mainstream, they widened the cracks. Gradually this alternative infrastructure and information network (which, after all, used the same postal, shipping, and telecommunications systems that the mainstream used) infiltrated and assimilated its way into American business culture.

Consider, for instance, the history of the Erewhon Trading Company, which for a time was the largest natural foods distributorship in the United States. It began when two Japanese-born teachers of macrobiotics, Michio and Aveline Kushi, began to sell food and books out of their home in Cambridge, Massachusetts. The Kushis had been countercultural even back in Japan in the 1950s. They had met at Maison Ignoramus, a macrobiotic institute based outside Tokyo that had been founded by a Japanese writer, former expatriate (he had lived in Paris), and Zen scholar named George Ohsawa. Ohsawa, who claimed to have cured himself of tuberculosis through a diet of brown rice, miso soup, cooked vegetables, beans, and seaweed, argued that improper diets (and other personal imbalances) caused not just health problems and depression but social ills as well. Ohsawa also believed in world government and recruited the Kushis (among others) to travel abroad to promote the idea. In the United States, they fell in love and eventually established a teaching practice in Cambridge. They had hoped for serious students, but they seemed to attract hippies, who puzzled the Kushis by saying things like, "Brown rice makes you high."

Yet although they were tempted to write off their counterculture students as disorderly, the restrained and disciplined Kushis admired their creativity and adventurousness, as well as their rebellious stance against the sicknesses (as they saw them) of industrial culture. "We felt it was our responsibility to guide them," Aveline Kushi later wrote, "and help them recover their health and dream in life." And the Kushis adopted the countercultural ethic of self-sufficiency themselves—so much so that when they were prosecuted for practicing acupuncture without a medical license, Michio resisted hiring a lawyer because he did not believe in the legal system on principle.[12]

Macrobiotic diets involved staples that were hard to come by in a typical East Coast supermarket: brown rice, miso, tamari, and whole-grain barley. To help students procure the grains, the Kushis opened a small store, and one of their students, Paul Hawken, took over as the clerk. Hawken, only eighteen, was a lean, handsome young man from California with a raspy voice; he had suffered all his life from asthma, turned to macrobiotics for relief, and then discovered how difficult it was to find the food. In the mid-1960s, health food stores were still predominantly antiseptic places, tinged with the medicinal odor of vitamins and staffed by women wearing white uniforms and hosiery, like nurses on night duty. They rarely carried organic rice or beans, and their staffers had no knowledge of the sources of their foods: What types of farms were they grown on? Did those farms use pesticides or other agricultural chemicals? These concerns, irrelevant by most standards, were of crucial importance in a discipline like macrobiotics, where every bite is designed as a component of the whole of one's life.

Although Hawken had no business background—his ambition had always been to be a writer—the Kushis accepted him as a partner. They renamed the business the Erewhon Trading Company—after Samuel Butler's classic utopia story, a favorite of their Japanese mentor George Ohsawa. Soon Erewhon was grossing more than three hundred dollars per day (up from its original twenty-five dollars), and Hawken discovered that the natural foods business had a supply crisis.

One day a student came into the store and said, "How do you know this oil from Hain is cold-pressed?" Hain was a family-owned concern, based in Los Angeles, that supplied many new stores like Erewhon with canned and bottled groceries. Hawken defended his supplier, but his curiosity was piqued, so he wrote to the manufacturer. They wrote back saying that "cold-pressed" simply meant that the oil was processed at very low temperatures so that fatty chemicals, such as steareates, would be drawn off. Hawken knew that wasn't correct, and he was heartsick; he had unwittingly betrayed his customers' trust. He began investigating his other suppliers and discovered that many of the packaged products they sold had labels that were (unconsciously or deliberately) deceptive.

Angry at what he saw as the lies of intermediaries, Hawken began to visit family farms himself. He traveled throughout the country, persuading them to adopt organic farming methods by promising to provide a market for their grains. But in order to guarantee a large enough market, he also had to line up other natural food stores to carry the grain. He did the same with small family-owned manufacturing firms, such as those that made soy sauce in wooden casks. Since he didn't know the rules of wholesaling, he naively experimented in ways that later turned out to shape the natural foods business. Erewhon always labeled its bags of grain with the farmer's name, location, and growing practices. "We made it entirely transparent," he later said. Because they eliminated the middleman, they could keep the prices down. Now Erewhon really took off, and suddenly Hawken was the president of a burgeoning international natural foods wholesaling firm, with its own chain of retail stores around New England.

One of the first things he realized, as early as 1967, was the paucity of useful business information available to him. The *Wall Street Journal, Fortune,* and the Harvard Business School classes he sneaked into all confused him. They seemed to relate to some official world of business that had nothing to do with the enterprise he had founded. Hawken— and most of his counterculture business colleagues—had to invent the rules all over again. They redesigned food labels using calligraphy or simple handwriting to give products an informal feel; they priced goods clearly ($5.00 instead of $4.99) so the prices would be easy to add up. And they dealt with questions of ethical loyalty that an ordinary grocery owner wouldn't have thought about twice. For instance, the Kushis' macrobiotic regime was limited to a narrow channel: no cheese, few sweeteners, no salty prepared foods, and most cooking in the Japanese idiom. But customers came into Erewhon's store off fashionable Newbury Street in Boston looking for natural ice cream or organic honey. Should or should not Erewhon stock nonmacrobiotic foods? Eventually the store did, in part when Hawken's own eating habits broadened. By 1970, the business's purpose was itself; it no longer existed merely to serve the Kushis' macrobiotic community, except perhaps through its profits.

There was also the question of keeping employees involved. Most of them were students of the Kushis. Often they were former hippies who wanted to kick drugs, straighten out their relationships with their parents, and find meaningful work. There was always an implicit assumption that a job at Erewhon was not just a job; like the food you ate, it was integrated into your identity and life. Few businesses could live up to that ideal, in part because there was no good information around about how to design a business on that model. McGregor's *The Human Side of Enterprise* might have provided a first step, but it was focused almost exclusively on very large corporations. Businesses like Erewhon were a completely different type of creature.

Most counterculture businesses held, for example, that "process is our most important product." How they made a decision, and how they felt afterward, was—in the long run—as important as the content of the actual decision itself. Thus, at Erewhon, Hawken continually struggled between two imperatives. On one hand, he needed to make decisions fast, and often he felt that only he had the experience to make them. Only he had been to Japan; only he had built up the business from the beginning; and he really had confidence only in himself to sustain the business, particularly in a long-hair milieu where people talked regularly about dropping out. On the other hand, he believed strongly in the principle of consensus. "Decisions at Erewhon," he would later proclaim, "are almost always the consensus, if not the unanimous wish, of those people who have been there for a while."[13]

Erewhon was one of hundreds of distribution, information, or financial networks created during those years. There were even networks of networks, such as *The Whole Earth Catalog,* the National Book Award–winning million-dollar publication that began as a "truck store," carrying books and other essential goods to communes in the remote Southwest. Alternative publishing enterprises, like Whole Earth, begat alternative philanthropic foundations; alternative distribution networks begat alternative financial enterprises. All of them maintained, in one way or another, the idea that business should be personal.

As they cast about for ways to govern themselves without rigid hierarchies, many of them turned to group dynamics, or to the consensus management that some of them knew from left-wing organizing. By mainstream business standards, these operations tended to have endless meetings, but a few countercultural businesses learned, through trial and error, to make those consensus meetings work more effectively. They learned to hustle when they needed to—to say, "I can feel that there's ten minutes of steam left in us. If we're gonna get to the last two items on the agenda here, that's how much time we've got." They learned, in short, to put the purpose of the enterprise before their own immediate needs. The alternative, as in all other enterprises, was to stagnate.

○

When a counterculture is forced to create its own infrastructure, sooner or later the mainstream culture catches on. When it happened to medieval millenarian preachers, they were turned over to the Inquisition. When it happened to Erewhon, the reaction was more subtle. One day in 1972, Paul Hawken walked into Erewhon's original store on Newbury Street in Boston and found four executives from a supermarket chain measuring the floor space and tallying register totals. "They were trying to figure out our sales per square foot, which were phenomenally high for the food industry," he later wrote. "Hi, guys."[14]

Hawken and several of his fellow managers saw that they had reached the point where the business would move beyond its origins; it would no longer be the Kushis' business but an entity with its own identity. They also had an opportunity to try to build a big business with counterculture values—an intriguing challenge because it had never been attempted. With all of this in mind, they arranged for private financing, more than a million dollars' worth, from sympathetic sources. (One source was George Alpert, the railroad president and lawyer whose son was Ram Dass, the Harvard professor turned spiritual leader who wrote the hippie classic *Be Here Now.*)[15]

While waiting for the contracts to be signed, Hawken arranged a bridge loan from a bank to finance the expansion they were planning. But then (as Hawken later told the story) the Kushis rejected the deal. They apparently realized that a transition into the mainstream world would remove their control over the business. But to Hawken, Erewhon's growth made that mainstream transition inevitable. He felt betrayed. More urgent, the company now owed more than $1 million, five times the company's net worth, and the bank began calling back its notes in 1972. At first, he paid the loan bills instead of meeting his payroll or paying his suppliers. But after a few agonizing weeks, he realized he had the upper hand. He called his banker to tell him to back off, and the banker invited him up to the top of the Prudential Tower for lunch. It was Hawken's first exposure to business hardball. Because Erewhon's assets were all tied up, the bankers didn't have much leverage; they had as much to lose as Hawken did if Erewhon defaulted. "In their eyes," he later wrote, "I became a 'good' customer once I'd become a bad one."[16]

Having mollified the bank, Hawken still had to make severe cutbacks in the business. At the same time, he began to push for an employee-owned structure to give some of the managers a stake in the company. Hawken was one of the first counterculture entrepreneurs to notice that his employees were growing up. They were getting married, and some were expecting children; most had no equity. If Erewhon persisted in its state of constant austerity, they would never be able to build a sustainable livelihood there. In short, the counterculture had reached a point where it needed the magic of mainstream business—particularly the ability to build for a future, inherent in an understanding of the numbers. But once again the Kushis blocked him, backing out of the stock-sharing arrangement. Hawken resigned, and a year later, he sold his interest. The Kushis hired new presidents, and Erewhon kept growing. But now there was competition from new natural food stores and distribution networks. Austerity measures became commonplace. In 1977, the Erewhon workers voted to join a union—an almost unimaginable step from the viewpoint of the days when Kushi was strictly a teacher and the workers were all his grateful students. In 1984, Erewhon went into Chapter 11 bankruptcy and was sold.

———————o———————

Other types of alternative enterprises floundered in other ways. Let one company's story stand in for the hundreds that might be told. This was an alternative consulting firm, formed by some young former National Training Laboratories members. Called Development Research Associates, its principals conducted leadership development workshops with Sun Oil and the U.S. Navy.

Government contracts required that contractors allocate a large percentage for overhead costs. But Development Research Associates had no employees or office. They ended their first year, in the early 1970s, with a huge surplus of cash. They spent much of that bonus on a Christmas trip for the entire group to an island in the Caribbean. One evening on the island, all seven of the principals of the firm gathered in a single hotel room. One of the founders, Dave Berlew, later recalled placing $100,000 in bills in the middle of the floor. Then he laid out the rules of the game:

> Based on our individual contributions to this organization this year, you can:
>
> 1. Take out any amount of money and put it in front of yourself;
> 2. Take any amount of money and put it in front of someone else;
> 3. Take any amount of money from any pile and move it to another pile.
>
> But you have to tell the rest of us why you've made that move. Finally, we'll know we're finished when nobody has made a move for half an hour or more.

It took them until two in the morning to shuffle the bills around. One guy had brought in the lucrative Navy contract, so he got more. A European associate, who did less work, saw his pile dwindle. Another associate argued for a hefty share because he had written a best-selling book that helped bring in business. "That's fine," someone else said, "but you get the royalties and it makes you less committed here. As far as I'm concerned, it's not worth a thing."

That night, all seven of them dreamed about the exchange. They all showed up spontaneously, back in the room the next morning; all of them felt there was unfinished business. But after an hour back in a circle, no more money had moved. In theory, peer feedback and peer review could solve any situation. They had handled the problem in a warm-hearted, truthful, and open-minded way. And yet somehow there was still unfinished business.

"We never did that again," Dave Berlew later recalled. "And I think it was the beginning of the end of our little company. Nobody said so at the time, but the results somehow clashed with our images of ourselves as people. We were friends as well as partners. People felt rejected at a level that had nothing to do with simply their contribution to the business. It's as if we went right up to a peak and looked over the edge and then decided to turn back."

———————— ○ ————————

It had been the vibrancy of the emerging counterculture, in part, that had convinced the scenario planners of Stanford Research Institute (SRI) that the basic attitudes of industrial society would have to be reshaped. Otherwise the Western world would drift into a chaotic, highly stressed, over-policed environment.[17] Willis Harman and Oliver Markley also concluded, partly from their experience with the U.S. Department of Education and partly from work they'd done with the Environmental Protection Agency, that government would not lead the way. Every time they described a plausible future that contradicted the official plans of the government, their clients would shut down and say, "That can't happen."

But SRI's corporate clients were much easier to talk to. Businesspeople tended to be direct and blunt; they had no interest in wasting time. Willis Harman in particular became convinced that large multinational corporations—as the dominant institution in our society, the modern equivalent to the Holy Roman Empire, as he put it—would be profoundly important in the coming quarter-century. If mainstream corporations learned to cope with the postindustrial imperative, so would the rest of the world. "It's very important for all the rest of us," he told his staff, "that business should know what it's doing when it goes through that change, so that it doesn't make wrong decisions and make it a much more traumatic thing."

To articulate this message, the SRI researchers borrowed the notion of a paradigm shift from Thomas Kuhn, the Princeton-based historian of science who had written *The Structure of Scientific Revolutions*. They were the first to adapt this term to mean a general shift of attitude—bowdlerizing the idea to such an extent that Kuhn himself, a stickler for precision, would eventually, and quietly, renounce his own use of it.[18] Kuhn had used the term to mean the process by which a scientific community changes its ideas about the acceptable boundaries of experimentation. In the context of science, a paradigm shift was a broad change in the shared set of agreements about what types of examples and scientific puzzles are acceptable and credible. But it was not nearly as broad as the concept that Harman and the SRI team was looking for: a broad-based shift in the prevailing ideas of a culture or mind-set. Before they were introduced to Kuhn's book, Harman and Markley had been toying unhappily with terms like *Zeitgeist change.* The word *paradigm,* with its vague connotations of learning and colloquy, conveyed the idea much better. The SRI futures group thus found itself leading the new age movement, and later such pundits of corporate change as Joel Barker, in using this new term.

Undoubtedly this bowdlerization was inevitable, if not by SRI then by someone else, because some new word was needed to describe the millenarian shifts of attitude that were evident in many places. In 1972, the SRI futures group won a massive assignment to develop a full-scale report about them, assessing their potential impact on the culture, politics, and economy of the United States. The assignment came from the Kettering Foundation, based in Dayton, Ohio—an educational foundation started by Charles Kettering, the mercurial engineer who had invented the cash register, the electric automobile starter, and Freon. The foundation had recently been endowed with $6 million per year to look at the long-range future of education. Since Kettering's president, Robert Chollar, knew SRI's president Charles Anderson, a day-long private bazaar was established for this project. One by one, various SRI subgroups and bailiwicks paraded before the Kettering staffers, presenting esoteric forms of systems analysis or forecasting techniques.

Willis Harman was the only one who showed up without a flashy slide show or presentation. "We don't quite know *what* methods we're going to use," he said quietly. "But I know what question you're trying to answer, and it has to do with holism and learning to change people's belief systems." As he had done with Gideonse several years before, he got the client's attention. Soon after, Harmon's team was asked to prepare a small presentation, which they delivered in a southern Ohio motel. In that confined room, with traffic whizzing past on the highway outside, they told the Kettering staff that in the next few years, the Western image of the purpose of humankind was about to change.

The resulting study, titled *Changing Images of Man,* was delivered to Kettering in 1974. It was not released publicly for eight more years (in 1982, Pergamon Press published an edition), but it enjoyed a wide pass-along photocopy circulation that continues today in PDF form. As part of the research process, the SRI team held a series of conferences at which researchers, anthropologists, social scientists, and artists locked horns over fundamental social concerns, and many of their comments were incorporated into the paper's footnotes. The resulting effect is like being at a seminar where Margaret Mead, René Dubos, Elise Boulding, and Geoffrey Vickers whisper back and forth around you, taking issue with the basic message and with each other. (The discussion of Thomas Kuhn "is very bad," says Mead. "It is an undiscriminating use of material." Then right below it, Boulding says, "The basic concept that we need a new knowledge paradigm, and the use of Kuhn, are excellent."[19])

As its title suggests, the report missed one key influence: the changing role of women and the effects of that change on the culture. This was a grave lapse, for this was already 1973; the feminist movement was having an effect on the workplace, and many of the key contributors to *Changing Images of Man* were women. (All of the staff members who prepared the report, however, were men.) The absence of any feminist spirit, plus the academic tone of the prose, showed that the report itself was not a creation out of the new paradigm it hoped to foster. It was like a screed by monks, remaining in their old world but looking ahead with longing to the moment of the flaming chariot that they knew would arrive.

The report asks us to consider what Chris Argyris might have called the theories-in-use of industrial culture: not the espoused value but the values that could be inferred from observing social behavior. For instance, people in industrial society saw themselves as separate, conscious, fundamentally rational beings. The goal of life was material fulfillment—certainly much more than mental or spiritual fulfillment. Rational materialism was paramount: mystic experiences (including the SRI work with extrasensory perception or Harman's LSD-based mysticism) were automatically suspect.

But this dominant image of economic man, said the report, "no longer fits the physical reality."[20] Adam Smith's doctrine of the invisible hand—in which individual decisions, made for self-interest, add up to the common good—wasn't working; such decisions had produced a 4 percent annual growth rate in energy use, a dramatic rate of environmental degradation, and an overall decline in civilization.

What should replace the invisible hand? Not representative government, but a new image of humankind. The new paradigm would be influenced by Jay Forrester's systems modeling, LSD and parapsychology research, and corporate social responsibility. But the heart of the change was a shift (said the report) in how people see themselves. Cultures that see people as "animated machines of physical parts" tend to ignore religious growth and learning (said the report), but cultures that see people as primarily spiritual tend to neglect the human needs for health, employment, and housing—while both of those cultures, if they see humans as detached from nature, tend to foster an exploitative ethic.[21] The increasingly dense, increasingly dangerous world of the next century would need to counteract all of these tendencies and undo the reductionist mind-set of the industrial era.[22]

Harman and Markley wrote of trying to "'love our neighbor as ourself,' not because it is what we have been taught is proper but because we hold the underlying image and perception that our neighbor is in a real sense ourself." Such an ethic might make it feasible "to arrive at meaningful social goals that can be satisfied within ecological constraints." And if people didn't go along with those goals, there might be "regulation and restraint of behavior," at least in the short run—a worrisome note, because *Changing Images of Man* didn't really say who would have power when disputes raged in this postindustrial world. Disputes were an old-paradigm condition; in the new world, people would simply come to understand each other.[23] (Indeed, this distaste for the messy questions about authority and control has been criticized over the years; like Robert Blake's critiques of NTL, it has been said that the blithe lack of concern about power and authority tends to open the door to totalitarianism.)

To set a context for its message of fundamental change, Harman sought out Joseph Campbell, the charismatic Sarah Lawrence mythology teacher who had written *The Hero with a Thousand Faces* and, just recently, *The Masks of God*. Campbell had devoted his life to myth in order to understand, as he put it, "the rapture of being alive"—which meant, at least in part, devoting oneself as part of something greater than oneself. Unlike the rest of the project staffers, Harman and Campbell considered themselves conservatives. They believed that the individualism and rootlessness of the counterculture—the ethic of "do your own thing"—was dangerous. Campbell saw the desire for a "world without money" as just another form of materialism—a different set of empty totems to collect. Certainly Campbell was known for telling people to "follow their bliss,"[24] but what he meant by that was the opposite of "doing your own thing." He meant finding the thing that compelled you, that required a lifelong sacrificial commitment, like the commitment to a marriage.

Campbell made several trips to SRI to help put together the lengthy mythological history that opened *Changing Images of Man*, and his visits always seemed to end in heated political arguments. In the midst of composing a passage about communal renunciation during the Bronze Age, he would start arguing about antiwar demonstrators and how the counterculture was wrecking civilization. A young staffer would counterattack: "No, Joe, the counterculture is exactly the people who have a strong sense of community values. It's the politicians who won't get us out of Vietnam, who are wrecking civilization." It reminded some onlookers of the battles in *All in the Family*—except the words had twice as many syllables.

For Harman, like everything else, this battle ultimately came down to a matter of personal preference: "Some people really drop out and totally change the outward form of their lives. I eventually concluded that right living, for me, means being *in* the establishment, being more or less acceptable to it. But by no means would I be *of* it. My destiny seems to be to help it to change."

Not long after the study was finished, in 1975, Oliver Markley wrote an op-ed piece for the *New York Times* about it.[25] One of the SRI board members, an officer of the Searle pharmaceutical company, was incensed enough to call the SRI president. "If I understand what this guy is saying," said the board member, "he's calling for the end of the industrial era! Is that how you let your people talk? What's going on over there?" A new policy statement followed a few weeks later: SRI employees could say anything they wanted to the media as long as they made it clear they were not speaking for the institute. "Please keep in mind," the statement concluded, "that we cannot exist if we infuriate our clients."

───────── ○ ─────────

And perhaps that warning was appropriate, for now the SRI millenarian idea evolved into perhaps the most unlikely form imaginable: a marketing strategy. This probably would not have happened if Willis Harman had stayed. He had no objection to marketing strategies; he assumed that they were a useful way of transmitting the millenarian paradigm into mainstream culture, where it belonged. But they did not interest him, and he had no flair for them. After 1974, he spent less and less of his time with the futures group. Meetings went by without him; project leaders found their own clients and assembled their own staffs. He even avoided eating lunch with the staff. As often as not, he was gone from the offices, in a meditation session out in the desert with Captain Al Hubbard, the Johnny Appleseed of LSD.

Al Hubbard was now in his late sixties, and Willis had gotten him a job as special investigator at SRI. He was there, Harman said privately, to offer SRI's bright young people a kind of psychedelic commando training that they would find nowhere else. Unfortunately Hubbard seemed burned out. He wore a uniform to work composed of bits and pieces from the various services. He packed a gun, and his closest friends weren't the young researchers but the security guards. His real job, so far as the lower-echelon staffers could tell, was to bundle off Harman and friends in his big Lincoln for psychedelics and meditation. Most of the staffers' wives had been brushed off or put off by Hubbard; he would taunt them, make sexual or crude remarks about them in their hearing, or suggest that they didn't have what it took to go down and become enlightened with the boys in the desert.

Meanwhile, Harman was becoming a counterculture figure. He was increasingly off lecturing at conferences about religion and spirituality. When he did show up at SRI, he seemed authoritarian, snobbish, and a bit vague about details. He announced a "plagiaristic ethos" for the futures group: people would no longer get individual credit for their ideas and writing. "The overmind," he said, "provides these ideas to be used by everyone." Since he was the most public figure, that meant it would all appear under his name. Some of his colleagues protested; Don Michael later recalled saying, "Willis, as long as we are recognized for our own work on *this* plane, then I want to be credited!" But increasingly they ignored him.

The oversight role shifted to the assistant director of the group, a writer and analyst named Arnold Mitchell. Mitchell was an old-timer at SRI; he held ID badge number 22, which he would jokingly brandish to demonstrate his seniority. (Badges, numbered sequentially from the earliest days, had gotten up to 11,000 by then.) He had struggled all his life to resolve ideas about integrity, materialism, and privilege. He was tall, slim, handsome, shy, slightly hard of hearing, and genuinely devoted to the people he worked with. Friendship and collegiality were paramount values for him. His father was the economist Wesley Clare Mitchell, a founder of the New School for Social Research, chairman of the first President's Council of Economic Advisors, and a creator of the theory of business cycles. His mother was Lucy Sprague Mitchell, the founder of the Bank Street College of Education; a dormitory at the University of California at Berkeley had been named for her. She had also written an autobiography of her married life, in which she devoted exactly one sentence to her only child. It was a childhood that might have been designed to produce someone determined to find an independent path.

Unlike his parents, Arnold Mitchell had no advanced degrees beyond a B.A. in English. In his youth, he had been a small-press poet, and he had stumbled into the nascent SRI at the moment it needed an editor to produce its first reports (in the late 1940s). Within the futures group, he had tackled the question of social indicators. If they really wanted society to change, how could they measure their success? How would they know they were making a difference? He wrote prolifically, always in pencil, and he took over Willis's role as mentor to the young, poetic policy analysts and scenario crafters of the futures group.

On Friday afternoons, whoever was in town from the futures group would meet at Arnold Mitchell's large house in Atherton. Being careful not to drink alcohol (because it dulled the visioning capacity), they would talk about their projects and the questions they needed to answer. After they agreed on a topic, Oliver Markley would bring them down to trance level and guide them through an off-the-cuff narration. One week, for research on the future of air pollution over the Los Angeles basin, they visualized an eyeball fifteen feet in diameter. Markley guided them inside it, and the eyeball flew off to an altitude of ten thousand feet. It sped ahead to the year 2000, then to the year 2025, and each member of the group saw in his mind the air lighten and clear. Clean air legislation might indeed be successful. The futurists did not have to worry about whether they were "really" seeing the air pollution of the year 2025. They merely needed to see what was plausible, what might spark their client, the Department of Transportation, toward more realistic decisions. None of the clients, of course, ever learned that their $100,000 reports had been partly researched through psychic visualization.

As meditation practice sometimes does, Markley's experiments took on their own momentum. Years later, he recalled that when bicycling home one afternoon, he heard a voice inside his head: "Hello. I am Henri. I have something I'd like to show. Would you come with me?"

Still pedaling, Markley found himself taken (in a corner of his mind) to a wonderful jewel-like city hanging in the middle of space. He entered a building that looked like the Hollywood Palladium, where a swarm of sentient creatures who looked like little white lights, separate yet united in a single conscious entity, greeted him telepathically from inside a coat-check window. When Markley asked where he was, the entity replied, "*You* would use a name like the 'Omniverse Center for Cultural Development.'" The Omniverse, Markley gathered, was the collection of all possible universes at all possible times. He could explore any he chose. He asked, "What is the ratio of war to peace here?" He saw a panel of red and white lights, representing war and peace respectively. About 30 percent of the lights were red. Always the futurist, Markley asked: "But what are the trends?"

After a long silence, a new voice, slow and almost mournful, replied from above his head, "We judge that your mind is not sufficiently developed to understand a valid answer to that question. But if you insist we'll find a way to answer it."

"I'm a guest here," Markley said. "Far be it from me to press."

By now he had almost finished his bicycle ride home, and he was reluctant to continue; thanks in part to Captain Hubbard's bullying, his wife was uncomfortable with anything that smacked of psychic research or psychedelics, so Markley, in his mind, floated out of the Omniverse Center, pausing to say good-bye to Henri. "Can I come back?" he asked. Certainly, said his guide. In any moment of need, the center would be there.

A few days later, the group at Arnold Mitchell's included three staffers working on a scenario they called "The Man on a White Horse," in which technological crises and a charismatic new Hitler brought the Western world back to the Dark Ages. This future might offer some valuable lessons for their client, the Department of Transportation, but they couldn't make it hang together plausibly. Markley felt drawn to guide his colleagues to the Omniverse Center. He didn't dare second-guess his intuition; he put on a cassette of his most powerful telepathy-enhancing background music: Bartok's "Night Music for Strings, Celesta and Percussion."

Together, with Markley's smooth voice guiding them, they entered the city-sphere in the sky. They spent about a half-hour there. When they opened their eyes back in Arnold's living room, the three people closest to the "White Horse" study were too emotionally moved to speak right away. All three had seen different versions of the same message: charismatic villains could never be persuasive again. Because Hitler, Stalin, and Mao had provided such unavoidable lessons of the pitfalls of ideological totalitarianism, their examples could not be repeated on any multinational scale.

The staffers used that vision to rework their story line. Instead of a "Man on a White Horse," they suggested that a Gandhi-like figure might emerge, a religious leader speaking out against dissension. This became known at SRI as the "Apocalyptic Transformation" scenario. It eventually found its way into *Seven Tomorrows,* a book of scenarios published in 1980.[26] One of the authors of that book was a staffer at SRI, Peter Schwartz, who a few years later would be invited to be Pierre Wack's replacement at Royal Dutch/Shell. The second was philosopher Jay Ogilvy, who was leaving academia to come to work at SRI. The third was Paul Hawken, formerly of Erewhon and now living in the Menlo Park area. The three of them would become influential carriers of the millenarian idea into the global business community of the 1980s.[27]

○

But first, in 1976 and 1977, the SRI futures group members began to apply their new paradigm as a prescription for businesses. They had found an article by a mystic-ascetic writer named Richard Gregg, a Harvard-educated American who had studied and lived with Mahatma Gandhi. Gregg, writing in 1936, had borrowed the idea of voluntary poverty from the medieval millenarians and rechristened it as "voluntary simplicity." He advocated the ascetic life not because it was spiritually more meaningful (although it was) but because it made life more effective. Voluntary simplicity meant "singleness of purpose, sincerity and honesty within, as well as avoidance of exterior clutter, of many possessions irrelevant to the chief purpose of life."[28]

The futures group members found they could translate this into the terms they could sell to their clients. By now it was 1976, the era of limits. Oil prices had tripled from their previous levels and stayed high. Inflation was raging. It made sense for a shopper to consume with voluntary simplicity—to bring awareness and intelligence to every purchase. It would mean buying no junk, making each piece of property last, and cultivating natural elegance. Voluntary simplicity, as they saw it, was no longer something that only an ascetic might aspire to. It was a lifestyle choice. Businesses would have to learn to adjust because voluntary simplicity represented the core of where the market was going.

One of the first expressions of the voluntary simplicity idea (though they didn't yet use the name) occurred in 1975 when SRI began to examine the future of cars for the Ford Motor Company. Peter Schwartz, Arnold Mitchell, and another researcher, Duane Elgin (the men who had unearthed the Richard Gregg article), soon began to look at the effect that rising oil prices might have on the choices made by car buyers. They predicted a slow but steady growth of a "frugal society"—a society compelled by ecological concerns and mobility of mind and spirit instead of fettered by the complexities of material possessions.[29] People would trade in their cars every five or ten years rather than every two. Ford's profit margins per car would be smaller because smaller cars had smaller margins. Auto dealers would shift from selling new cars to providing expert repair, service, and even upgrading. Certainly Japanese manufacturers would be a threat, although they didn't put this part of the prediction into writing.[30]

None of the SRI staffers knew that Henry Ford II had already heard this message from Ford's internal planners. He had come to SRI for a second (and, he hoped, a dissenting) opinion. His battles with his own charismatic "man on a white horse" lieutenant, Ford president Lee Iacocca, were moving into full swing. Iacocca argued that the company should produce more small, well-built cars to provide better gas mileage during the crisis.[31] As long as he was fighting Iacocca, Henry Ford had to defend large cars (which even Iacocca had to admit provided the company with better margins). That forced Ford into a stance against more energy-efficient automobiles.

"What with the environmentalists crapping all over any suggestion before it's even tried," he had told a table-full of *Fortune* editors in April 1973,[32] "I don't see the power system of this country meeting the needs." He proposed that the United States should develop vast new oil fields and many new nuclear plants. All that held them back was environmental restrictions. "I hope to hell," he said, "New York goes dark for a week." That would show 'em.[33]

With attitudes like that, "Hank the Deuce" had no chance of reacting favorably to the futures group's ideas, and the SRI directors knew it. When they read Elgin's preliminary draft,[34] they cut the group's budget and nearly dropped the project. Peter Schwartz was allowed to make a brief presentation to "Mr. Ford" and his entourage. Ford listened stolidly, with the same bored, semicontemptuous expression that he had shown during thousands of presentations in his lifetime. When it was over, Ford turned and spoke to his assistant.

"No," he said. "The Arabs are gonna go away. They'll be gone in a few years. And Americans ain't ever gonna want Jap cars." Then he turned and looked at Schwartz with his piercing blue eyes. "If they wanted 'em, we would do 'em, but Americans don't want 'em."

In meetings like that, you do not argue. You take it, with military bearing if possible. Never mind that, a year or two later, Ford would experience devastating losses, precisely because they couldn't compete with Japanese cars. Never mind that customers were ready—as SRI's research showed—for durability, energy efficiency, and quality in their cars. Never mind that the "Arabs" would preoccupy both government and energy planners for the next three decades. The futures group still didn't know how to get their message across.

○

Duane Elgin and Arnold Mitchell kept trying. They took the voluntary simplicity message on the road in 1977. They were joined by another young SRI recruit, a graduate from the Harvard Business School named Marie Spengler.

Spengler, a fast-talking, bright, and attractive woman, presented quite a contrast to the burly and hirsute Elgin. Elgin was the most countercultural member of SRI; Spengler, the group's first feminist, believed in synthesizing the countercultural stance with the attitudes of conventional business. She had grown up in Berkeley, been the first in her family to go to college, and taken a job in the 1960s as a systems engineer for IBM. But then she began to feel that she couldn't subscribe to the company's values. She couldn't devote her life to making money. Finally, in 1969, after a divorce, she took a negotiated settlement, left the company, and fled to Paris. After a stint in marketing there, she went to Harvard for an M.B.A., where she became increasingly disenchanted as well.

Marie later recalled going in 1976 to hear Dana Meadows speak about *Limits to Growth* for the Century Club, an elite group of Harvard Business School students. Listening to her, Marie had an epiphany: she had seen how pathetic conventional business practices were, but she hadn't known why. Afterward she went up to Meadows and said she now understood her career path: to help "make business become a humanistic place, a place where people can bring their values to work." After Meadows told her about a Willis Harman paper on humanistic capitalism, Marie wangled a plane fare to San Francisco (ostensibly for an interview at McKinsey). Then she drove down to see Harman. He offered her far less than McKinsey had, but Spengler said, "I don't care about the money. I want to do this work. Not only that, but you *need* me. You're talking about transforming business culture, but you don't know how to talk to business."

She arrived just in time for Duane Elgin's report on voluntary simplicity to be produced. The report struck a nerve; it was the most popular report that SRI had ever produced. There were five hundred or more requests for extra copies—a number so unprecedented that the marketing department at SRI decided to follow it up with a speaking tour. Suddenly Marie Spengler, Duane Elgin, and Arnold Mitchell found themselves on a six-city tour. Their audience, primarily composed of businessmen and other SRI clients, would pay five hundred dollars or more per person per day to sit in an energy-wasting hotel, eating overpriced, cosmetically elegant food, and hear about the value of simple living. Elgin and Spengler would both remember those days clearly in future years, because they fell zealously into a love affair. Since it couldn't be revealed back at the office, only Arnold knew, and the three of them developed the close friendship that occurs among fellow conspirators.

Each had a role to play. Arnold was the "brawn" (although *brahmin* might have been a better term). The father figure of the group, he presented a dignified overview and carried the imprimatur of Stanford Research Institute. Marie was the "beauty": she came on like a sharp, well-dressed Harvard M.B.A., as if delivering a McKinsey marketing presentation. And then came Duane, the "beard" (years later, he remembered himself as the "beast"). He was the radical from Idaho, coming onto the stage in cowboy boots, without a necktie, in a sports jacket that he'd found in a thrift shop. He was the living example of voluntary simplicity, and while Arnold gave it respectability and Marie made it seem profitable, he had come to advocate it for the sake of the listeners' souls.

They would speak for half a day, talking about the evolution of vernacular values and the demographic changes they implied. There were 5 million people practicing some form of industrial renunciation, but 75 million with "simple" sympathies. That represented about half the U.S. population, and by 1987, ten years hence, they imagined it could be two-thirds of the country. To give these businesspeople a sense for the attitude, the program segued into a 35 mm slide show, accompanied by a recording of the Quaker spiritual, "'Tis a Gift to Be Simple." Aerial views of tract homes dissolved into slides of farm communities; consumer goods, from high-tech kitchen equipment to cheap toys, were shown as addictive nemeses. These corny images came through, somehow, as a heartfelt repudiation of the growth that people in the room had devoted their lives to. At the show's end, they sat silently, as if bewildered.

Then, after a coffee break, Marie and Arnold came back with the marketing implications. First-class durable products would sell; shoddy, cheap stuff would not. Sturdy, natural fiber clothing would overwhelm synthetics. Do-it-yourself stores would proliferate. Appliances and automobiles would have to become easy to repair; planned obsolescence would no longer sell. And leisure activities would be geared to country living. Tied up with this would be more of a market for services, far more money spent on travel and other experiences instead of possessions, and an increasing willingness to pay for health prevention instead of expensive cures. Consumption with a voluntary simplicity orientation hovered around $35 billion per year, they said, but by 1985, it could reach $140 billion and $300 billion in the year 2000.[35]

At lunch, the three speakers always sat at different tables. Depending on where you sat, you could congratulate Arnold, get marketing details from Marie, or snap back at Duane. In his cheap jacket, he seemed to be a magnet for resentful comments: All this talk of "sharing" was communist. He was betraying the American dream. Health and simplicity were considered "hippie values"; it might take twenty years or more for them to become mainstream. (For example, around this same time, in a national meeting of McDonald's franchisees, the owner of a Boston store had suggested that the company offer salads and other less salt-laden foods. According to one observer, the executive presiding over the meeting snapped, "Lettuce is for flower children." He was a fast-tracking, charismatic, somewhat brash man named Edward Rensi who later became company president during the era when McDonald's introduced salads as a universal entrée.)[36]

But even if McDonald's embraced salad, that wouldn't come close to the changes that Duane Elgin wanted to see, and he grew increasingly cynical about the value of their efforts. He had hoped that this series on voluntary simplicity would help businesspeople realize that the world's ecological survival depended on people changing their fundamental habits. Instead, the SRI message somehow had devolved into a seminar to help companies market products to "simple-living people." He decided to change his own career. Henceforth, he would write directly for ordinary people, to help them unshackle themselves from the tyranny of the consumer culture. He would start, he decided, by writing a book based on his report on voluntary simplicity. But his bosses at SRI refused to let him publish it; the high-priced report was a major cash cow for them. So Elgin resigned. He had had enough of preaching voluntary simplicity; he wanted to practice it.[37]

Marie and Arnold retained their close friendship with Duane, but they stayed at Stanford Research Institute. In 1978, they unveiled a new marketing consultation service called "Values and Lifestyles": a division of the American consumer population into nine different categories based on the way they chose to live. Only one of those reflected full-scale voluntary simplicity; the rest were loosely based on the hierarchy of needs developed by Abraham Maslow, a friend of Arnold Mitchell. Soon this type of lifestyle segmentation would become a mainstay of marketing practice.[38] But Duane Elgin's hopes would not come to pass. Voluntary simplicity would never overwhelm the culture. The SRI researchers had misinterpreted survival strategies—people cutting back their purchases in the era of inflation—as lifestyle choices.

—————— o ——————

The most significant resistance to the millenarian idea came from Herman Kahn. Kahn and his colleagues (most notably Tony Weiner and Barry Bruce-Briggs, two writers who had worked with him since the mid-1960s) had been brooding about *Limits to Growth* for years. They resented the prominence that the Club of Rome-sponsored report had gained. It was more famous than any other future study, almost a household word— and, as Kahn and his cohorts saw it, a dangerous and offensive one.[39] In their view, Jay Forrester, the Meadowses, and the other authors had deliberately tried to lead society astray—if not maliciously, then at least recklessly. By basing a "crash-and-burn" future on a computer model of economic growth, the MIT modelers were encouraging people to short-change their own collective aspirations.

Most important, Kahn said, the MIT modelers hadn't taken into account the natural way that postindustrial society would have to evolve. All of the problems that *Limits to Growth* foresaw—and *Changing Images of Man* spelled out—merely represented growing pains in a transition to a golden age of increased human capability.[40] This would require no massive cultural change or paradigm shift; it would happen automatically as a result of technological innovation and the accelerating growth of the middle class around the world as globalization increased. (Kahn was once again among the first to see the trend of corporate trade leading to worldwide interconnection and expanding wealth, or, as he called it, "gross world product.") Having once explicitly described the "unthinkable" prospects of nuclear war, Kahn now offered a new "unthinkable" heresy: the prospect of an optimistic future.

To understand Kahn's reasoning, you must go back one hundred years before, to when industrial society kicked into high gear and the twin scourges of *Limits to Growth*, population and consumption of materials, began to increase. For one hundred years, Kahn said, these had risen exponentially. Not only had their growth increased, but their rate of growth had also increased. But mathematical forces prevent a rate of growth from increasing forever, and in the 1970s, there was already evidence (in analysis of population and pollution rates) that the acceleration was decreasing. By 1976, the growth of both population and gross world product—the growth of industrial "throughput"—would hit a point of inflection, after which it would start to decrease. (Kahn selected 1976, the American bicentennial, as the probable point of inflection; it turned out, when the statistics came in, that he'd been late by a few years. "And there was no celebration," he told audiences. "Raise your hand if you attended the celebration. You know, this culture doesn't celebrate.")[41]

There might still be a long period of malaise, particularly if the anti-growth millenarians prevailed. But Kahn predicted that a new "belle epoque" would follow. The original belle epoque had lasted fifteen years: idyllic years of peace, rapid economic growth, free trade, and hedonism in Europe just before World War I. The second belle epoque, according to Kahn, would not end in war.[42] Instead, the world would evolve into a permanently prosperous postindustrial society. "Two hundred years ago," he said, "mankind was everywhere poor, everywhere scarce, everywhere powerless before the forces of nature. Two hundred years from now, barring bad luck and bad management, mankind should be almost everywhere numerous, almost everywhere wealthy, almost everywhere in control of the forces of nature."[43]

The world, in Kahn's view, would be not like a global village but a global metropolis—the sort of place where people carved out intricate webs of relationships with others around the planet, living increasingly cosmopolitan and pluralistic lives, with the balance of power split not between the United States and the Soviet Union but among five or six nations. The rise of multinational corporations would be a driving force in all this, "playing the central role," as Kahn put it, "in the development of an interdependent world economy." Despite multinational corporations' increasing power, Kahn pooh-poohed the fears that they would dominate the world; they would still have no sovereign authority or armed forces. "No one will kill or die for General Motors," he wrote.[44] But corporations would be intensive laboratories for productivity, because (thanks to global competition), the bureaucratic mind-set of current management would burn itself away.

Yes, Kahn agreed, the pollution issue was a harbinger of a potentially serious technological crisis; the way it was handled would have a tremendous effect on society's evolution.[45] Yes, environmentalists were correct to mistrust the leaders of corporations and government; these institutions had been untrustworthy. And yes, the human race had indeed made a Faustian bargain with technology. But according to the Faust story, he reminded people, Goethe's hero "bought magical knowledge and powers that he was compelled to use, and then perforce he had to proceed to the next experience, the next project—or be forever damned."[46] Having started down the road of industrialization, humanity had doomed itself to finishing the course. Only technological progress could solve the problems that technological progress had created. To shrink back, for fear of "limits to growth," would make *Limits* a self-fulfilling prophecy.

Kahn's ideas (and the Hudson Institute, which moved to Indianapolis after his death in 1983) would ultimately be associated with conservative politics, but he himself was neither conservative nor liberal; like Walt Whitman, he contained multitudes. On the liberal side, he agreed that *Limits to Growth* itself was a valuable cultural argument that needed to be made, for growth would have to slow down—but not so quickly, please. He wanted the rest of the world to catch up with America first.[47] On the conservative side, he used Irving Kristol's label of the "New Class" for liberal intellectuals and environmentalists, along with highly educated members of the media, law, management, and government professions, as effete, out of touch, dangerously self-serving people.[48]

The counterculturalists of the New Class were obsessed with environmental issues and other out-of-touch concerns, Kahn argued, because they were trying to protect their own privileged position in society, under the guise of helping society as a whole move forward. He specifically attacked their Pelagian strain. "Have you ever noticed a baby?" he would say to groups. "They're not known for tolerance, moderation. Babies will destroy the universe if they're empowered."[49] If the New Class was the class of heretics and reformers, then the Augustinians of the Silent Majority represented (in Kahn's words) a counterreformation. They included the growing number of people who belonged to fundamentalist and orthodox religions, but their bedrock concern was the defense of American square culture: Preserving marriage. Avoiding displays of public immorality. Keeping streets safe.

Middle America was a hunting culture, a culture to which members of the New Class were oblivious. Kahn himself had been oblivious to this culture until he had learned about it from the workers in the Hudson Institute print shop. In speeches to Harvard students during the early 1970s, Kahn would ask, "How many of you have three guns at home?" About one-third of the class would raise their hands. He'd ask the others, "Why do they have three guns?" There would be silence, and then wild guesses: To shoot blacks? To protect themselves against the government? Then he would turn back to the 30 percent who had three guns and draw the story out of them: At age twelve, they had all been given .22 rifles— weapons powerful enough to kill a person. They had been trained, during the next two years, to use the gun, to make and break a camp, and to act responsibly around firearms. At age fourteen, they'd been given shotguns. At age sixteen, they'd been given .30-caliber rifles. By the time they were old enough to vote, they would have shown they had been responsible adults for several years. The guns were used for teaching.

While Kahn admired the counterreformationists, he argued that history was on the side of the New Class. For in a postindustrial society, everyone would have a chance to be educated. Meanwhile, the Silent Majority members would be the most impassioned American political force of the near future because they felt themselves the most misunderstood. The New Class didn't see them clearly. No matter how obnoxious the dialogue Norman Lear wrote for his bigoted television bully, Archie Bunker, the character always tested as lovable. The Silent Majority recognized him as one of their own.

If it seemed improbable that the millenarian idea about paradigm shift and voluntary simplicity could evolve into a marketing strategy, there was an even more improbable leap taking place across the Atlantic, at the headquarters of Royal Dutch/Shell. Gerrit Wagner, now the chairman of the Committee of Managing Directors, instigated it in 1974. Wagner was still avuncular and still a bit rumpled, but he now had an international reputation. His intrepid diplomacy during the oil crisis had made him a well-known business figure in Europe.

Wagner had also been involved for five years in a series of international meetings and hearings, held by various United Nations-sponsored and other global commissions, aimed at defining a code of multinational corporate conduct. In these meetings, Wagner heard charge after charge about how multinational corporations had taken on the imperialistic role of colonial powers. They built factories where labor was cheap and regulations were few; they extracted natural resources without putting enough capital into the countries to spur growth; they used cartel tactics to boost prices of precious commodities like quinine;[50] and they propped up corrupt regimes with bribes.[51]

With the stubborn inquisitiveness of a Shell man, Wagner began to consider whether the critics were correct. The more he thought about it, the more convinced he became that companies like Shell had a social responsibility that went deeper than speeches and publicity efforts. Shell couldn't simply acquiesce to the demands of (for example) environmentalist groups who protested oil spills and offshore drilling. That would mean abdicating control of the company's destiny; he and the other managing directors would be thrown out by shareholders if they did. But there was a strategic imperative hidden, as if in code, within the environmentalists' messages. Shell's canny managers would have to learn to decode those messages. Moreover, if Herman Kahn was right—if multinational corporations would be the primary drivers of affluence and social values during the next two hundred years—then businesspeople would have to take seriously their role in developing the future. Otherwise they wouldn't prosper; they'd be overtaken by those competitors that managed the social role most effectively.

But how could you translate that sentiment into day-to-day policies? Wagner was a slow-speaking, thoughtful man, and he mistrusted glib ebullience. If he had learned anything from Shell's scenario triumph, Wagner mused, it was the need to paint a future image in specific detail, so that you could truly understand (in this case) the forces that had put Shell under such fierce political and social pressure. Thus, he set out to write a Shell code of ethical conduct—one of the first of the ethical codes that many companies would adopt during the 1970s and 1980s.

Shell would feel "an interdependent responsibility," wrote Wagner (and his coauthor, a Shell staff writer). The company would be responsible for keeping shareholder returns acceptable, the quality of products high, working conditions safe, wages fair, and environmental standards maintained. On the controversial issues of the 1970s, such as political payments to government officials, the code hedged a bit. Offering, paying, or taking bribes was "unacceptable," and there were always strong arguments against political payments, but Shell had to recognize that some cultures (such as Arab cultures) had enshrined them as regular practice.[52]

Now, when a Shell man felt pressure to step beyond the boundaries of his own ethics, he could refer back to the code. "I'd like to go along with this, but I can't, because I'm going to have to sign a statement at the end of the year that I have not cheated on my books."

At the same time, Wagner asked the Group Planning scenario people to study the future of social values. In any other year, the planners might have shrunk from such an audacious assignment. But this was 1974, and they were in the first flush of their success. They knew about *Changing Images of Man;* Pierre Wack had begun to make regular visits out to SRI's headquarters. But they were interested in producing something more practical, more incisive. If there was indeed a new paradigm ready to shape the world, then oil company executives needed to see it clearly. And the scenario planners, said Wack, would be like the eyes of the wolf at the head of the pack.[53]

○

Shell Française owned an old cloister on a mountaintop a hundred miles north of Marseille, in the town of Lurs. The windows looked out from a thousand-foot-high cliff onto the desolate, parched region of the Durance. The light was clear, like the light in Greece; the hillsides were barren below the tree line; and there was only one restaurant nearby. The next village was an hour's drive away, on winding, mountainous roads. Shell Française supposedly used it for executive seminars, but the seminars must have been unusually austere. The rooms were the size of railway compartments, and there were no phones and few hot showers.

Retreats were common at Shell Française, but the Anglo-Dutch cultures of London and the Hague disapproved of them. So when eight planners rode down to Lurs in a minibus in May 1974, they traveled with the vague sense that they were doing something illicit. At the same time, they needed a period of collaborative "intense suffering," as Ted Newland called it, particularly because people tended not to congregate in groups in the warren-like offices of Shell Centre.[54] With their 1973 scenarios, the planners had produced a seminal work together, but they still didn't really understand how each other thought and felt.

After their trip to Lurs, they did. For a week, from nine in the morning until eleven at night, they met at the big round table in the Lurs priory dining hall. Each of them had come with a subject to introduce: the world economy, the Arab nations, the Cold War, the unpopularity of multinationals. Hans DuMoulin, a young Dutch engineer with a schoolmasterish temperament, had been trying to introduce the idea of environmental responsibility at Shell for several years. Nuclear power, he argued, would become socially unacceptable. Concern over acid rain would provoke laws forcing industries to reduce the sulfur emitted from their smokestacks. Gareth Price, a convivial man of Welsh descent, challenged the then-sacrosanct view that oil demand would keep growing. If the price of oil stayed high, that would force a slow shift to conservation measures and alternative fuels. Gradually demand for oil could level off or even drop.

But would the price of oil stay high? Already the conventional experts of the industry were saying that the price would soon collapse. OPEC, after all, was just a cartel, and cartels cannot sustain themselves. Herman Kahn had predicted a fall in the price of oil as part of his belle epoque economic expansion scenario.[55] Managers in other industries, such as auto and electric companies, had come to believe that the energy crisis wasn't real. It was just the invention of wicked oilmen. Things would soon be back to normal.

But Pierre Wack and Ted Newland believed that the oil price would not drop, not right away. The price was like a soccer ball held in the air by jets of pressure. At that moment, all the significant pressure was coming from one direction: from OPEC, pushing the ball higher. No single oil-producing country had good reason to defy OPEC—not yet, anyway. As the planners shouted and wrestled in their monastic isolation, breaking out into at least one fistfight, they came to the conclusion that they could not present any credible scenario in which the price of oil fell soon.

———————— o ————————

Instead, they developed two geopolitical scenarios for a world of continuing rapids. They named their first scenario "Belle Epoque" after Herman Kahn's utopian future. Kahn had suggested that the belle epoque would come about naturally, but the Shell planners were not that optimistic. Their millennial future was a hybrid of those from Kahn and *Changing Images of Man*: to bring about a belle epoque, everyone—governments and business—would have to take a "high road," acting beyond their selfish interests. There would be "effective political leadership," as DuMoulin later wrote, "in which governments understand and foster the process of wealth creation; the profit motive is recognized as natural and desirable, provided it is exercised responsibly."[56]

The Shell planners were short on details about how the high road might evolve, or precisely what policy changes would be required, but they knew that high economic growth was a key component. If it was high enough to create a middle class in developing countries, then it would drive other reforms, including environmental reforms. If not, then the result would be a "World of Internal Contradictions"—a phrase they also borrowed from Kahn, who had borrowed it from Karl Marx. Politicians and business leaders would continue to hunker inward, pursuing their own gains. In this world, wrote DuMoulin, "The work ethic is not that of 'makers and doers' but more that of 'takers and escapists'; the interest is in dividing the national cake rather than adding to it; increasing unemployment is absorbed in sinecure jobs; egalitarianism figures prominently . . . as a result, one finds that investment is sluggish, industrial performance very disappointing and the world's economic motor is really not functioning on all of its cylinders."[57] The world would set off on a "low road" of self-interest, not much different from the crisis that SRI's planners had warned about.

All the planners felt an overwhelming sense of exhilaration at having wrestled these issues into something comprehensible. On the way back, they began to talk excitedly about going into business on their own, freelancing scenarios to businesses. When the idea emerged, Napier Collyns, who was driving the minibus around a mountainous curve, could not resist turning back to his colleagues to exclaim his approval. "At that moment," Gareth Price later remarked, "we might have lost the whole study." Later when they stopped for a drink to calm their nerves, the place they found happened to be named the Café Belle Epoque.

---------- o ----------

Back home the scenarios from Lurs raised more questions than they answered. Most people at Shell, including most of the planners, believed that events had already taken them into the "World of Internal Contradictions"—and for a few years, that phrase served as common parlance at Shell for describing the turbulent economics of the 1970s. The idea of a stable, long-lasting belle epoque suddenly seemed so ludicrous that the planners quickly changed the name.[58] Unfortunately they had already prepared slides showing a "BE" scenario; to avoid having to redo them (this was still years before personal computer presentation software like PowerPoint would be invented), they settled on "Business Expands."

Many Shell managers, including Pierre Wack at first, saw these scenarios as a degeneration—a move to the murky arena of social change, away from strictly defined views of the oil industry. But for Ted Newland, the "Belle Epoque" and "World of Internal Contradictions" scenarios represented the beginning of a lifelong preoccupation. He saw that he could make a contribution to the world by defining a high road path that would genuinely lead to a prosperous world, as opposed to a low road of political strife. Once again he was following Herman Kahn's example, but this time, he could be more influential. He and several other Shell planners intuitively felt that there was some kind of policy choice, which both governments and corporations could set in place, which might lead them to the high road.

Fortuitously the planners were about to meet a man who would help define that policy choice—and reintroduce, in the process, the millenarian idea. They met him through Dennis Gabor, a Hungarian physicist, who had just won the Nobel Prize for inventing the hologram and written a book called *Inventing the Future*. They sought out Gabor as an expert on energy efficiency; the physicist said he was too old to help, "but I've met this young man who knows the answers to all of your questions."

Amory Lovins was a staff member of the international environmental organization Friends of the Earth. He was twenty-seven years old, a third-generation American, the grandson of Ukrainian immigrants, and a lifelong prodigy. As a baby, he had been completely silent; then at the age of twenty months, he had begun speaking in complete, grammatically correct sentences. "I didn't need to talk," he had explained to his parents. "Everybody did everything for me." He had pushed himself out of a sickly youth by joining (and then leading) mountaineering treks. He received his first patent, on nuclear magnetic resonance technology, at age seventeen, and in 1968, at age twenty-one, he became one of the first scientists to publish a paper about global climate change.

Around the same time, Lovins had dropped out of a physics program at Harvard after fighting with his professors (he wanted a more interdisciplinary curriculum). Applying to Oxford University at age twenty-one for a student position, he had been appointed to the research faculty instead.[59] While there, in his spare time, he had put together a book of photographs and essays about a Welsh national park, Snowdonia, chosen because he had learned that Kennecott, the world's largest copper mining company, wanted to dig there. David Brower, who had founded Friends of the Earth a few years before, published them as a book titled *Eryri*. Then Brower had prodded Lovins to begin his investigations into energy policy for Friends of the Earth. It was a natural convergence of the young researcher's interest in resources, climatology, culture, and economics. He seemed to regard this last discipline as the fascinating, intricate, and confounding diversions of some kind of alien species.

The planners at Shell—indeed, everyone he met—found Lovins to be a captivating man. Slight and lean, he had the jerky, unworldly motions of a social misfit, along with black horn-rims, and a thick shock of dark hair. His voice was oddly deep, and he spoke quickly. Like Herman Kahn (whose iconoclastic, polyintellectual background resembled his own), he was one of the few people who could reel off complex scientific theory and literary quotations with equal facility. He couldn't make small talk; his favorite epithet for himself was "techno-twit." But he was empathic. He knew how to listen closely to people and resonate emotionally with them, while his posture remained stiff and his face never lost its bemused, distant smile. All of this gave him an endearing, Chaplinesque air, which he used to full advantage. Lovins was also a missionary, a devotee to a cause. After a couple of years of energy studies, he now believed that the world was embarking on an economic and ecological disaster.

The disaster had to do with scale. At that time, the conventional wisdom of the electric power and oil industries followed the logic of the old horse's tail diagram that Shell planners had discarded. Demand for power would continue to burgeon, as it had since the 1950s, with the increasing use of air conditioners and other appliances. The industry's answer was massive construction: coal and nuclear plants. Dams. Heavy-duty transmission grids. And offshore drilling platforms. In fact, Shell was building a city-sized platform in the North Sea off the coast of Scotland, named, like all Shell's other North Sea oil fields, after a local bird—in this case, the Brent goose.

Lovins insisted that the "hard path" (continued reliance on massive sources of energy supply) would self-destruct—not just because of the inherent ecological impact or the threat of terrorism and nuclear theft (although, he said, those problems were grave), but because of the immense amount of capital investment that the hard path required. Large companies had to plan for nuclear plants or drilling platforms years in advance, basing their loan agreements on assumptions about future energy demand. (Hence the cry that the planners at Royal Dutch/Shell always heard: "Just give me a number!") As energy sources became more capital intensive, Lovins argued, prices would keep rising to pay the capital costs. Demand would falter as prices rose, with the result that the income would not exist to pay back the investments. A scenario built around rising energy demand was actually a recipe for bankruptcy.

There were other reasons, too, that the hard path would fail. It was horribly inefficient. A white-hot nuclear reactor emitted immense amounts of wasted heat to produce a current of electricity that, in the end, heated a home to seventy degrees. This was, to Lovins, inexcusably crude—"Like cutting butter with a chainsaw."[60] And every step along the way, more energy was squandered as it was converted from one power system to another. The world already had more energy than it needed, Lovins said. It simply had to stop squandering fuel in cars "that inefficiently convert oil into smog" and houses "that space-heat the outdoors." He compared the untapped potential of motor vehicle fuel efficiency to a 5-million-barrel-a-day oil field lying underneath Detroit.

As an alternative, he proposed an industrialized "soft path"—a redesign of the infrastructure of energy use with efficiency as an inherent quality instead of tacked on as an afterthought. Factories might "cogenerate" their own electricity as a by-product of the steam they already produced. Buildings everywhere would have solar panels and intensive insulation. Cars would be redesigned with lightweight materials and more efficient engines, perhaps getting a hundred miles to a gallon, and cities would be built and designed so routine trips required no car at all. The power grid itself might be decentralized so that electricity might be produced in a small-scale neighborhood power plant or wind farm rather than a massive nuclear plant six hundred miles away. Instead of producing economic pressures and energy crises, this soft path would lead to decentralized businesses, increased renewable energy use, and independence from Arab or other foreign oil sources.

Though he knew nothing of Shell's scenario thinking, Lovins had hit on his own version of Ted Newland's low road and high road. If the country was serious about renewable energy and efficiency, it would have to turn away from the low road: the official future of expanding nuclear, oil, and coal use. Investing in large-scale capital projects would consume the money, skills, attention, and time needed for the high road: decentralized, distributed, small-scale systems. To be sure, one could build a windmill in the shadow of a nuclear reactor, but in the real world of capital investment, the two approaches could not coexist, any more than "high economic growth" could coexist with "no economic growth."

At first, Ted Newland himself didn't recognize the parallels between his ideas and Lovins's thesis. Immersed in Herman Kahn's theory and his Royal Dutch/Shell experience, he (like most of the other planners) viewed Lovins's ideas as extremist. Wack and Newland were both strong supporters of nuclear power, which they saw as a necessary component of international development. They regarded the antinuclear movement as an American indulgence, stemming from a nation that could afford to cut back one of its major sources of energy. Most other nations could not make that sacrifice.

But the planners also recognized the plausibility of energy efficiency as a force acting on the world. Japan had already begun an intensive energy-efficiency program based on a fervent desire to escape OPEC's stranglehold. If the rest of the industrial world followed suit, overcoming the inertia of its existing energy-wasting practices, the possibilities for decreasing energy demand were enormous. But if energy demand continued to build steadily (as it had since World War II), then no supply could keep up. There simply wasn't enough money extant to buy the extra energy supplies—not when that money would also be required for the new buildings, vehicles, and factories that were supposed to use all that energy worldwide. Something would have to give.

———— o ————

In 1975 the Shell planners invited Lovins to visit their offices and spell out all of the calculations implicit in the soft path. He was delighted. He had never worked with a large corporation, but he was shifting away from the adversarial attitude that had fueled his fight with Kennecott. To his compatriots at British Friends of the Earth, who said organizations like Shell were inherently evil and one shouldn't talk to them, Lovins replied, "On that basis one would hardly wish to talk to one's own government. Or anyone else's." Any major corporation, he believed, was an important reservoir of skills and resources, and progress toward the soft path would inevitably move faster through the "well-organized, profit-motivated, goal-oriented" private sector, especially as companies picked up experience.

Lovins was particularly pleased because Shell's planners were sophisticated, far more than most of the government people he had met. They were always looking for pragmatic measures that Shell could implement quickly, and they were bright, curious, and intellectually tough. They taught Lovins their methods for whole-system costing—calculating how the projected cost of a barrel of oil included everything from the wellhead to the gas pump. This was valuable for Lovins because it gave him a way to calculate the real costs, including all the hidden costs that power companies ignored, of electricity and heating. Even more useful to Lovins was the prodding he received from the Shell planners: to translate his tables of numbers into graphs that people could understand. He drew on Gareth Price's blackboard the line of energy demand under the millenarian soft path: instead of continually rising, it would taper off as countries around the world adopted not just the efficiencies that Lovins knew about, but other efficiencies to come.[61] By 2025, the American power supply could come almost entirely from renewable sources such as wind, passive solar, photovoltaics, biofuels, and hydropower. In addition, the carbon dioxide and other greenhouse gases that he already saw threatening the biosphere would no longer be produced.

It was an audacious scenario for the mid-1970s, but it was analytically based and internally consistent. And some of the Shell planners found themselves agreeing with it. Gareth Price, for instance, had studied electrification in developing countries and come to the conclusion that no country outside the Persian Gulf could afford large-scale power plants.

They would achieve their goals much more effectively with a grid of small-scale, decentralized power generation systems.

○

During his visits to Shell Centre, Amory Lovins never met Pierre Wack. He would always regret that, because he recognized Wack's scenario method as a powerful method of storytelling, a way of changing people's viewpoints. The following year, he put that method to the test when his paper "Energy Strategy: The Road Not Taken?" was published (after fourteen revisions) in the eminent journal *Foreign Affairs*.[62] It was largely a scenario-style presentation of the hard and soft futures, with all of Lovins's formidable statistics mustered to show the dangers of the hard path. To defend the values inherent in the soft path, he quoted Willis Harman.

Lovins had been introduced to *Foreign Affairs* by Carroll Wilson, the MIT professor who had introduced Jay Forrester to the Club of Rome, and the reaction to Lovins's paper echoed the storm of protests that Forrester and his students had provoked with *Limits to Growth*. This time the most virulent attacks came from the electric power and nuclear construction industries. They accepted his recommendations for energy efficiency and solar power, but they would not accept his argument that society had to choose between the soft path and the hard path.

Lovins battled with them in Senate hearings (2,854 transcript pages' worth), in letters to the editor (Lovins wrote several every week), and ultimately in scores of panel discussions and industry debates.[63] In person, Lovins was diffident and self-effacing, but he developed a rapid-fire stage style. He would take down his opponents' statistics and cost figures as they were speaking, whip them through his pocket calculator while listening, and then use them during his rebuttal to prove his own case.

For the moment, he won few converts in industry; oil companies were generally more sympathetic than electric utilities. He might have persuaded more people with another phrase than "soft path," with its connotations of mushy humanism. "I have nowhere said that a soft path is *easy*," Lovins said. "I have simply said that the problems are easier than if you don't take it."[64] And also at stake, of course, were twenty years of investment, by government, industry, and big customers, in large-scale nuclear power plants.

His industrial critics (and some of his supporters) painted him as a seductive self-aggrandizer, manipulating utopian fantasies.[65] To achieve the gains he predicted, they charged, people would have to change their lifestyles to adapt the kind of voluntary simplicity that Duane Elgin wanted— except that this would be involuntary. "It's true that much energy would be saved by ordering Detroit to manufacture only Volkswagens," snapped Ralph Lapp, an energy/nuclear consultant. "But the politics and socioeconomics of this conversion are formidable challenges to any society. Would Mr. Lovins practice what he preaches? Or would he continue to live a high-energy lifestyle with globe-circling jet plane travel?"

Lovins did in fact try to live a minimal lifestyle; he had never owned a car, and he took trains or turned down speaking invitations to cut back air travel. But as he retorted, "I have nowhere proposed the sort of ham-fisted direction of industry that Dr. Lapp tries to put into my mouth, and think it would be a bad idea. . . . Being a pluralist, I happen to think that people who want to drive big gas-guzzling cars should be free to do so—provided they pay the full social costs."[66]

Lapp missed an important distinction. Lovins *was* pushing voluntary simplicity—not for consumers, but for producers. Corporate managers would have to reconsider their own purpose. They would have to realize that their organizations existed for the sake of producing what people wanted: not oil by the barrel or electricity by the amp, but "warm houses and cold beer." They needed to change the tendency toward centralized control: the habit of investing in large-scale plants and factories, all owned and vertically integrated by a single megacorporation. Soft energy production would occur on a decentralized grid.[67] Twenty years hence, there would be a useful model in the decentralized Internet, where hundreds of companies fit their equipment and services into a dynamic, ever-changing technological grid that no one company could control. But that model did not exist yet. Nonetheless, there was a model extant, and it happened to exist within Royal Dutch/Shell itself.

———————— o ————————

Back in the 1960s, Shell's senior managers had prided themselves on their global, decentralized structure, with hundreds of operating countries around the world controlling their hiring and operations. But the traders at headquarters still directed the allocations of oil among companies. The decision to send barrels from Venezuela to Argentina, for instance, had to pass for approval through an office in Shell Centre in London.

In 1971 André Bénard (who had just become managing director) proposed making the operating companies into truly independent entities. The group had just been through the worst quarter in its history, the third quarter of that year. "We are excavating our own graves," he argued. The prices they charged operating companies for oil were often undermined by open market prices, over which they had no control, and which looked as if they would fluctuate increasingly erratically. Instead of trying to keep up by frantically dictating prices and allocations from the central office, Bénard proposed letting the operating companies buy and sell oil freely from each other and from other oil companies, as if they had no common owners. Let them gain the flexibility that comes when every trading decision is separate, when no authority is in charge. Let the market be the authority. To coordinate the logistics, the managing directors set up a new trading firm, the Shell International Trading Company (SITC), as a kind of shared in-house commodities exchange.

Even as early as 1976, it was obvious that this experiment was wildly successful. In the turbulent years after the energy crisis, Shell's resilience was perhaps the most critical factor in its success. It was especially apparent during the boycott, when other oil companies were hamstrung by their ties to the United States, but Shell France or Shell Italy could benefit from the agreements that their countries had made with OPEC. The SITC existed as a harbinger of new corporate forms: a self-organizing system that managed, without top-down controls, to flexibly and profitably respond to the turbulence of the new oil environment.

———————— o ————————

The legacy of Shell's scenario planning team is by now well known. In the early 1980s, Pierre Wack and Jimmy Davidson would both retire. Davidson would be replaced as planning coordinator by Arie de Geus, a Dutch accountant with a strong interest in psychology. Both Wack and de Geus would go on to write seminal articles in the *Harvard Business Review*. Wack's started as a presentation at Harvard Business School in December 1984, entitled "Scenarios: The Gentle Art of Reperceiving." It retold the story of the oil price scenarios as a case study in changing the mental maps of decision makers.[68] De Geus's article, "Planning as Learning," argued that a company that continually expanded its capabilities would always remain one step ahead of its competitors. No matter how fast they stole the learning company's ideas, it would leap ahead to another innovation. In the latter part of the 1980s, de Geus had begun to meet regularly with a young MIT lecturer (and Jay Forrester protégé) named Peter Senge. Together, regular meetings among a broad group composed of Senge, de Geus, Chris Argyris, Edgar Schein, a family systems psychologist named David Kantor, a student of physicist David Bohm named Bill Isaacs, and others would spark the learning organization concept that would take hold with Senge's 1990 book *The Fifth Discipline*.[69]

Meanwhile, Wack's successor was Peter Schwartz from SRI; Schwartz would then cofound a small scenario-planning–oriented firm, Global Business Network; his cofounders would include his SRI colleague

Jay Ogilvy (a philosopher who had inherited the Values and Lifestyles practice from Arnold Mitchell), *Whole Earth Catalog* founder and editor Stewart Brand, and Shell group planning alumnus Napier Collyns (who had taken to heart the idea of remarkable people and spent the rest of his career as a celebrated finder, cultivator, and convener of remarkable people everywhere).[70] Ted Newland would stay at Shell until the early 1980s; long after his retirement, he would be remembered for one of the last speeches he delivered to the managing directors, in the early 1980s, foreseeing the 1986 oil price drop, and intoning the nursery rhyme "Humpty Dumpty" in stentorian tones to make it clear how abrupt and disorienting this price drop would be.[71] Meanwhile, he never lost sight of the high road idea, and his writing in the 1990s, arguing that only 10 percent economic growth rates could bring emerging nations out of poverty, would presciently foreshadow the actual growth rates of the countries that are emerging in the twenty-first century.

But perhaps the most remarkable legacy—in the sense of both being noteworthy and encouraging better vision and foresight—was the contribution that scenario planners made to political transition in South Africa. In 1982, Wack retired from Royal Dutch/Shell and began consulting for Anglo American, the South African mining corporation, on its efforts to become a multinational corporation. These were perhaps the harshest years of the South African government's apartheid policies, which for forty years had institutionalized racial separation and inferior education, job opportunities, and political status for nonwhites, enforced by draconian police measures. In response to this "crime against humanity" (as the United Nations General Assembly formally called it in 1973), economic sanctions were put in place in the early 1960s, starting with arms sale embargoes. But the impact of economic isolation didn't become intolerable for the country until the 1980s, when trade boycotts, sports boycotts, and divestiture initiatives (like those put forth by the Reverend Leon Sullivan) effectively cut South Africa, and its businesses, off from much of the rest of the world.

Anglo American's chairman, Gavin Relly, had heard Wack make presentations at Shell, and he asked Wack to work with them. Wack's futures at first concerned Anglo American's efforts to do business outside South Africa and the demand for gold (which was slated to increase substantially in both China and India). But in talking about the price of gold, he also felt compelled to describe the effect of apartheid.

"South Africans live with the feeling that they are blessed with a geological miracle: their gold and diamond deposits," said Wack. "But it is actually a human miracle: People work in horrible conditions for very low wages because they have to." He told the South Africans to be careful. "You are going to be the highest-cost producer, because this human miracle is not going to last."

To Anglo American executives, Wack seemed to be predicting the end of apartheid, and they wanted to hear more. They were not apartheid supporters; indeed, the Anglo American founder, James Oppenheimer, was a long-standing and outspoken apartheid opponent, and Relly would later become known for leading a business delegation, in defiance of the government, to meet the exiled African National Congress in 1985. The wives of the executives also wanted to hear more—specifically, was there a future for their children in South Africa? Or should they emigrate now, before the country erupted into race war?

Among the executives who worked closest with Wack was Clem Sunter, the financial director of the gold division: an English-born man married to a South African woman. He picked up the challenge of tackling this question, and over the next two years, he and Wack (along with a team of other senior executives and some outsiders, including Ted Newland) developed a set of scenarios for the future of the company, drawing on Shell's corporate economics departments in South Africa and London.

They started with the premise that the National Party could not keep apartheid going much longer, no matter how much its leaders wanted to. They could not hold out against the demographic reality of an immense nonwhite majority, and they could not maintain either their isolation from the global economy or the heavy costs of maintaining a police state. Nor would they necessarily want to. As Shell planner Graham Galer later wrote in a research paper on the impact of the scenarios, "It began to be recognized that . . . apartheid was not working. A new Afrikaner intellectual elite, more travelled and sophisticated than its elders, was growing up which increasingly recognized these problems."[72] They particularly resonated with Sunter's statement that "apartheid will have to go, because it is being overtaken by the demands of an increasingly integrated and complex economy."[73]

But how would the transition out of apartheid take place? The scenarios painted two alternative paths, in a sort of variation of the "Belle Epoque" and "World of Internal Contradictions" scenarios that the Shell planners had worked out in Lurs several years before. The white South Africans could take the low road: they could "coopt a few tame black and colored representatives," as Sunter put it, and relinquish power slowly and half-heartedly, "in which case sanctions would remain and the masses would revolt." The result would be civil war and wasteland. Or they could take the high road of "negotiation leading to a political settlement,"[74] accepting the inevitability of a multiracial society and opening their institutions up.

That might allow the kind of widespread economic growth that would be needed for the country to thrive, in part by bringing South African business back into the flow of the international economy. It would be an almost unimaginably difficult task, but the Anglo American scenarios made it clear that, for all but the most adamant supporters of apartheid, the low-road alternative would be worse.

With the blessing of the company's leaders, Sunter and his colleagues began presenting them to more extensive audiences through the country, including government officials and nonwhite groups as well, starting with business leaders from the black townships. His first presentation to an African National Congress audience was to Nelson Mandela, while the future president of the country was still incarcerated on Robben Island. "I thought that Mandela might be hostile," Sunter later recalled, "but he was utterly gracious; he asked very specific questions about the world economy and the kinds of ideologies which made economies successful." As the presentations grew increasingly popular (ultimately, about one hundred thousand people heard them), Clem Sunter began writing them up as a book. It was published in 1987. Despite its prosaic title (*The World and South Africa in the 1990s*), this became an immediate bestseller in South Africa. Its sales of seventy-three thousand copies set a record for nonfiction surpassed only by Nelson Mandela's autobiography, *Long Walk to Freedom*.

The peaceful transition of South Africa from a racist regime to a multiracial, multilanguage democracy happened in the space of a few years. During the transition, it was never certain that it would sustain itself; the country often seemed poised to collapse under the weight of international sanctions, crime, AIDS, the lack of education among the black majority, and the difficulty of reaching closure (the task of South Africa's famous "truth and reconciliation" commission).

The Anglo American scenarios did not take place in a vacuum; they were one of a number of forms of dialogue emerging at this time, including unprecedented meetings between Afrikaner business people and ANC leaders, many of which represented a reaction against the increased violence of the 1980s. But the scenarios helped lay the groundwork for at least some of this success; they are credited not so much with influencing the elites at the head of the government but with influencing a broad number of white citizens to see the inevitability of change.[75] (They also partially inspired other scenario sessions, such as the Montfleur scenarios of 1991, which helped the new leaders of the postapartheid country chart a course toward a sustainable government.)[76]

o

South Africa's story ultimately provided an example for millenarians and utopians everywhere. A peaceful transition was possible. South Africa's future would be troubled by violence and its extensive AIDS epidemic, but its survival as a democracy and a free economy was clearly established. For those paying attention inside corporations, the South Africa story also showed that they could play a clear role in making society more congenial, for themselves and for others at the same time. But first they would have to put their own houses in order. For it was only in the mid to late 1980s that the awareness of their own managerial shortcomings—one of the essential messages of corporate heretics for the previous forty years—finally reached the attention of those in the executive suite.

THE RAPIDS

HAYES AND ABERNATHY, TOM PETERS,
W. EDWARDS DEMING, THE CREATORS OF
GE WORK-OUT, AND OTHER SYNTHESIZERS OF
MANAGEMENT CHANGE, 1974–1982

Heresy: The purpose of a corporation is to change the world.

The chattering crowd outside Notre Dame Cathedral heard a man pronounce from a burning pyre a curse on the pope, the king of France, and all of their fourteenth-century world. The man at the stake, whose name was Jacques de Molay, was the fierce, elderly Grand Master of the sacred order of the Templars. His knights had been elite champions of the Church all through the Crusades and its first line against the forces of Islam. But now the prevailing currents had turned against the Templars. They were accused of sorcery and devil worship; their property was confiscated. Despite his age, de Molay had been tortured and starved until he had confessed to desecrating sacred relics. Then, after recovering his senses, he had recanted his confession. And that, in turn, had led to his immolation. Burning at the stake was deemed appropriate for heretics only *after* they recanted.[1]

Perhaps the authorities should have found a way to keep de Molay from pronouncing his curse. Within a year, the king and pope both died. First their houses, then their countries fell rapidly into disarray. Noble families sank into debt, unable to command (or reward) the loyalty of peasants who had tilled their lands. Famine struck; shortages, unknown in earlier years, became commonplace. An epidemic of bubonic plague spread through France. In former times, the plague would have sent people back to the stability and comfort of the Church, but they could no longer trust it. This was the age in which indulgences were offered for sale, Church endowments were lent out at interest, and money stacked high in the countinghouses of monasteries. Two popes existed, one in Rome and one in Avignon, scheming against each other, until the rivalries between the kings who supported them erupted into outright war.

As the bedrock assumptions of society shimmered and collapsed, memory itself seemed unreliable. When had things turned sour? No one quite knew. When had the estates collapsed? Where had the wealth gone? No one could say. People felt themselves carried forward at accelerated speeds toward unknown calamity, with no way to halt or go back.

In a time like that, who dares to hope for something better out of life? And yet who can avoid being drawn by the magnetic pull of unfulfilled possibility?[2]

○

QUITE A FEW CORPORATE HERETICS, in one way or another, foresaw that the stability of postwar business would give way to perpetual change. Eric Trist, with his collaborator Fred Emery, had predicted this back in 1967: they called it the "salience of a turbulent environment." Herman Kahn had made it part of his "next 200 years" time line. Alvin Toffler's book *Future Shock* had become a best-seller with the basic message that continual change would be a new kind of equilibrium. NTL "horseperson" Peter Vaill would begin publishing articles on "permanent white water" during the 1980s.[3] The planners of Royal Dutch/Shell referred to it as "the rapids" in print as early as May 1975. In the report from their deliberations at Lurs, they described a medium-term future in which two seemingly contradictory economic trends—inflation and deflation—were both predetermined. Prices would rise, but demand would fall. Several scenarios were possible with these forces extant, but all of them carried one basic message. The managers at Shell, they said, would never be able to return to a life where they could follow the easy answers of straight line predictions like the Unified Planning Machinery.[4]

Most businesspeople in the United States and Europe could see this state of affairs themselves. There were several obvious indicators. One was the rise of global competitors, first in automobiles and steel, first from Japan and Korea; competitors from Brazil, China, India, and other emerging nations were still below the horizon. Another signal was rising oil prices and the stagflation—simultaneous rises in prices and unemployment—that it seemed to engender. A third signal was a loss of legitimacy for business leaders themselves, at least in the public eye. They had been criticized from the left, sure, but they had always been respectable in the mainstream. They had, after all, defined the mainstream.

Early in 1974, Senator Henry Jackson subpoenaed the chief executives of America's leading oil companies to testify, in televised hearings, before the special investigations subcommittee of the Senate.[5] The executives spent the sessions staring stoically at Jackson, stiffly enduring his charges of "obscene profits"—for they had nearly all posted record-level net earnings in the last quarter of 1973—and offering only hazy answers to his questions. The only candid executive at the hearings was Harold Bridges, the president of Shell Oil—Royal Dutch/Shell's isolated American subsidiary. Bridges wryly pointed out that he and the others would be much more cogent and forthcoming if the senators interviewed them separately instead of in a lineup with their chief competitors. The public might think of them lumped together as a conspiring cartel. ("They're like Siamese twins," Ralph Nader said about them in December, having turned his accusatory attention from the auto industry to big oil. "They don't have to meet furtively. They know exactly what they are doing without meeting.")[6] But the executives themselves were all excruciatingly aware of their long-standing rivalries and differences, as well as the antitrust laws that kept them from communicating freely.[7]

Other industries faced calumny too. It came to the light that food-packing companies sold cyclamate-laden fruit abroad, after the Food and Drug Administration banned it in the United States.[8] It was discovered that McDonnell Douglas managers suppressed their own engineers' warnings of cargo door defects and (in the public interpretation) thus murdered 346 people in a plane crash in Paris.[9] In early 1975, a fifty-three-year-old man named Eli Black smashed his office window with an attaché case and leaped forty-four floors to his death on a Manhattan street. He was the president of the United Fruit Company. Within a few days came the revelation of a $2.5 million bribe that United Fruit executives had given the government of Honduras. The bribe was particularly damaging because the managers had listed it as a business expense on United Fruit's tax forms.[10]

"Nobody gives a damn about us," said a CEO at the Conference Board meetings. "Not the government, not the consumers, not our workers."[11] Executives, used to the adulation of people who worked for them, couldn't understand what people saw who looked at corporations from the outside: the trappings of hierarchy and stiff competition for perks, the fear that pervaded every conversation (even senior executives were terrified of cutting loose with what they really thought), and the results: shoddy products, pollution, and planned obsolescence. Instead of looking more closely at their own practices, they sought outsiders to blame: the professors, journalists, activists, and regulators, for instance, who had never had to meet a payroll. They particularly blamed the so-called public interest lawyers (like Ralph Nader) who proclaimed ideal-istic aspirations; after all, they knew firsthand about the idealistic aspirations of their own lawyers. (At one meeting, the CEOs considered a suggestion to recoup their lost honor by writing up a code of ethics for themselves. "You mean," snapped a voice across the room, "one that would work as well as the Bar Association's?"[12]) And they blamed the environmental movement and the sinister influence of books like *Limits to Growth*.

When our intuitions fail, we yearn for strategy. Thus, in the mid-1970s, the idea of building a corporate strategic plan, with its echoes of Napoleon, Clausewitz, and Sun Tzu, evolved into an irresistible management fashion. This often took the form of financial portfolio management: companies analyzed their divisions according to market share and growth rates and assigned each a status accordingly. "Stars," with high growth and market share, should be fostered. "Question marks," with high growth but low market share, should be investigated. "Cash cows," with high market share but low growth, should be milked because they did not need their cash for growth any more. And the woebegone "dogs," with low growth and low market position, were cash traps. They should be shut down or sold. This growth-share matrix, first put forward by Boston Consulting Group founder Bruce Henderson, represented the first in a new set of refinements to financial magic, refinements that would continue to develop through the 1980s.[13]

Henderson had begun his career as a heretic himself; as a young engi-neer in the mid-1960s, he had recognized when nobody else did the value of learning to a company's bottom line. He unearthed a discovery called the "learning curve." It dated back to Curtiss Aircraft in the 1920s: a factory manager had discovered that when a work team stayed on the line long enough to double their experience, costs dropped by 20 percent. During the final three years of World War II, Curtiss used the learning curve to design a remarkably effective and inexpensive production schedule.[14] Once the war's production demands had ended, though, the learning curve fell out of fashion.

Then Henderson had resuscitated it. In the mid-1960s, he had helped Texas Instruments (TI) use it to repeatedly cut the price of its semiconductor chips and electronic calculators. As prices fell, more people bought the devices, which pushed production levels up, which meant that TI learned more about production, which meant that costs fell still further. To emphasize that this wasn't just a shop-floor phenomenon (it also worked on advertising budgets and billing procedures), Henderson renamed it the "experience curve." He claimed it was as real as the law of gravity, and he set out to prove it by plotting the curve in client after client, showing that the more a company learned about production, the more its costs fell.

He also discovered that the experience curve and market share fed each other. When a company dominated its competitors, it produced more products, which sent it faster along the experience curve. The rich really did get richer in Henderson's world. In theory at least, Coke learned better than Pepsi; GM more effectively than Ford; and Texas Instruments, then the leader in calculators, had an advantage over its then-upstart competitor Hewlett-Packard.

When Union Carbide asked Henderson to help them judge where they could compete against their two big rivals, DuPont and Dow, the analysis was startling. All three chemical companies, plus Monsanto, had lost money by giving in to the irresistible temptation of undermining their best-performing "star" divisions while overfeeding their "dogs." They seemed unable to distinguish high-potential from low-potential product lines, so they bled away their profits on lost causes.

The growth-share matrix was meant to fix all that. To use it, a manager need only think of the business as a portfolio of product lines. Decision making became a matter of controlled ruthlessness. It was worth borrowing money to keep a star shining because a star might end up dominating its market niche. As for the dogs, Henderson said, discard them quickly and unsentimentally.[15]

Boston Consulting Group built its business on the matrix's sudden popularity, but its true legacy was an attitude that persists in business to this day. Even in expanding markets, the focus on market share made managers act as if they were in a zero-sum game. Every automaker tried to be General Motors; every consumer products company sought to be Procter & Gamble; everyone assumed that only the leaders in a particular market segment could survive. The purpose of a business, if you believed in market share, was not providing a service, making a good product, or even generating profits but dominating a niche. Years later, the Internet bubble would rise rapidly as investors flooded cash into companies that were trying hard to build their market share at the expense of common sense.

Madison Avenue loved the growth-share matrix. Since market share depended on the largest mass audiences possible, the matrix engendered a kind of war for customers en masse, in which broadcast television was the weapon of choice. In 1976, American television advertising expenditures hit an all-time high: $25 billion.[16] Nearly all of that money went to the big three—NBC, CBS, and ABC—or their affiliates. It was seen at the time as an indication that the industrial world was pulling out of its slump. Prosperity might be coming back.

But the eerie bicentennial boom of 1976 didn't last long. All it really meant was that the finance way of thinking had overtaken all decision-making functions of American enterprises. As financial management took up more and more of the attention of the executive suite, CEOs increasingly delegated operational decisions and capacity building to lower-echelon manufacturing leaders.[17] Meanwhile, this greater financial sophistication took place at the end of the 1970s, side-by-side in many companies with the most severe recession since World War II. The auto industry, building and construction, and iron and steel—the industries paying the highest wages—suffered the most intense shortfalls.[18] Managers ran through every trick they knew, every conventional device for controlling purchasing, operations, or marketing, and every approach that made sense, and yet the balance sheet projections refused to play along. In 1978, Chrysler lost $205 million. This was enough, after a decade of ups and downs, to prompt the car company to apply for its famous bailout.[19] The following year, managers at the Ford Motor Company—in the midst of a crisis over who would succeed Henry Ford II after Lee Iacocca left for Chrysler—saw their projected $600 million profit turn into a $500 million loss.[20] Then General Motors experienced a calendar-year loss of $763 million, its first loss in sixty years.[21] Kodak, Xerox, General Foods, and many other companies all saw their market share drop.[22]

As the business world spun further out of control, the fascination with control in conventional management circles intensified. The more turbulent things became, the more ardently managers sought quick solutions: anything to get back fast to a relatively predictable, relatively manageable status quo. It was still possible to believe that the turbulence was temporary; those who made it through would return to business as usual, and once again experience the joy of being successful at their work. From the bottom of their hearts, the managers of the early 1980s did not want to hear that the rapids were here to stay.

———— o ————

The heretics of the business world at this stage were a glum group. Their strategies for boosting performance had failed or were ignored. Only a few companies, such as Procter & Gamble, continued to move forward. (P&G by now was implementing its technician system, still ruthlessly kept secret, in plants throughout Europe and South America.) Before anything more could be done to improve corporations, the message of the heretics had to be heard in the central bastions of the numbers—in places like the Harvard Business School and the McKinsey Consulting Group.

In 1979, two members of the operations management department at Harvard Business School—a section of the school that had been gradually losing status through the 1960s and 1970s to the finance-oriented departments—found themselves thrown together in Vevey, Switzerland, for the summer. They were William Abernathy, the HBS resident expert on auto manufacturing, and Bob Hayes, known for applying operations research to the assembly line. Both men were in their late forties; both had backgrounds in industry (Abernathy at DuPont and General Dynamics and Hayes at IBM) before coming to Harvard. Both were considered conventional, easygoing men; neither would have been considered a heretic (although Abernathy was known for his rapid-fire, stream-of-consciousness, wide-ranging conversation).

Hayes had just spent two years researching the differences in management styles between European and American multinationals. He had the idea that since Europeans tended to speak more languages, they should have an easier time with cultural diversity; Americans should clearly have the technological edge. But they didn't. Hayes visited a tiny machine tool manufacturer in southern Germany, a company of thirty or forty people. Sophisticated Americans barely understood computer-aided manufacturing software, but this firm was using it on a daily basis and getting remarkably resilient at quickly producing custom-made tools. It wasn't just Germany; he began to see signs of sophisticated machine tools coming from Czechoslovakia, Switzerland, Hungary, and Japan. By comparison, American-made machine tools, even from the leaders in the field, looked huge and clunky, as if they had been designed in the 1950s. The more he looked, the lower his morale fell. At a ball-bearing plant in

Germany, a subsidiary of the American Timken Company, he heard the plant manager laugh about the ridiculous suggestions brought in by the Timken executives—until they saw the German plant producing parts at tolerances that the Americans couldn't hope to match. Japanese and French managers started telling him about the American subsidiaries that had been forced to leave their countries because they couldn't compete. They had diversified into areas where they had no expertise. Or they focused on drawing quick profits instead of investing in building up their factories and technologies. Or they hadn't developed any long-term relationships with suppliers.

Finally, while Hayes was teaching a class to European businessmen, someone asked him why American productivity had declined so completely during the past ten years. He hauled out the standard answers: organized labor, government regulations, the oil crisis, and the attitudes of the baby boom. His students looked at him with polite amusement. "We have all those factors here," one of them said, "and *our* productivity is increasing."[23]

Confused and shaken, Hayes began taking regular hikes with Abernathy, who had just arrived in Vevey. Abernathy was going through a similar set of shocks. He had come to compare the European auto industry with the Detroit big three. Seeing the same stagnation, they began comparing notes and eventually settled on the only explanation that made sense to them: the core of the business magic, the reliance on numbers that had made American business so powerful, was now a barrier to success.

Consider, for instance, what happens when a manager becomes dependent on return on investment (ROI), the fundamental calculation that Donaldson Brown had developed during the 1910s and 1920s. Managers who used it as their primary yardstick would always give a higher ranking to the projects that got good ROI figures. Those projects would get the bulk of investment. In theory, that meant the company would prosper—fewer "dogs" and more "stars" would be supported. (Hayes and Abernathy singled out the growth-share matrix, and its emphasis on short-term results, as a particularly pernicious influence.) In practice, a dependence on ROI meant that risky initiatives, long-term projects, and anything driven by a manager's personal aspiration or care would be shoved into the background. These projects might be started, but the managers faced an irresistible temptation to shut them down if they didn't yield quick results. To Hayes and Abernathy, many companies that had followed this approach had already lost ground; as their goals shrank to pursuing ROI to shareholders, at the expense of all other purposes or objectives, they lost their special competence and capability. Their products and services became commoditized; customers and investors rushed to any company that could do the same things more cheaply, and the entire American economy was suffering as a result.

Not daring to believe their ideas, Hayes and Abernathy tested them on some of the American managers in their European program—and received the worst sort of confirmation. Managers agreed and shrugged their shoulders. "It's much more difficult to come up with a synthetic meat product than a lemon-lime cake mix," a senior vice president of research told Hayes. "But you work on the lemon-lime cake mix because you know exactly what that return is going to be. A synthetic steak is going to take a lot longer, require a much bigger investment, and the risk of failure will be greater." Given that kind of logic, Hayes and Abernathy asked themselves, why would any individual manager want to shoulder the risks of making a better product? Or innovating a new type of product? Or going out on any type of limb anywhere? Why take the chance?

That October Hayes wrote up their ideas in a lead article for the *Harvard Business Review* titled "Managing Our Way to Economic Decline." It was published in October 1980, one full year later. Most of the delay was due to a controversy among the members of the review board about whether to print it. And it was easy to understand why: among other things, it indicted both business leaders and academia with "a preoccupation with a false and shallow concept of the professional manager, a 'pseudo professional' really—an individual having no special expertise in any particular industry or technology who nevertheless can step into an unfamiliar company and run it successfully through strict application of financial controls, portfolio concepts, and a market-driven strategy."[24] The reaction was correspondingly intense. For at least fifteen years, it ranked as the most requested *Harvard Business Review* reprint in absolute numbers, and it divided the business school and the business world. There was vitriolic criticism from economists who claimed there was no productivity decline, no loss of American competitiveness, no American malaise. And there was a great sigh of relief from a surprisingly wide group of managers who said that, yes, somebody finally had articulated what they had felt for the past few years but hadn't been willing to say out loud.

Hayes and Abernathy had tapped into a growing feeling of shame, in fact, among business school academics, who felt they had to take some of the blame for the virulent wave of hostile mergers that was beginning at that time. "My own problem," Hayes later said, "was really with my colleagues. One could read into the article that I was being critical of finance.

I was being critical of control measurement systems, and of strategy. And a lot of my good friends on the faculty were teaching those things. I hoped they wouldn't see it as a personal attack on them. That didn't happen. A number of them came to me and said, 'Gee, you've verbalized some things that I've been worried about.'" No doubt the authors could have taken their protests further, but Hayes and Abernathy were more concerned about validity and research than about making a public splash. The next popularizer to pick up their ideas didn't have that inhibition.

———————— o ————————

Tom Peters has always been an excitable man. His speeches, as many observers have noted, are like a stump preacher's rants. He works himself up until his voice rises and falls, his arms wave, and his eyebrows waggle with the force of moral invocation. In ordinary conversation, he is much calmer and more mannered, but there is always the fidgety sense of constant churning within him. His weight fluctuates too; when he is thin he resembles the actor Harrison Ford. To some extent, Peters cultivates the image of himself as an excitable man; he has been known to introduce himself to other managerial authors by writing, "I just read some of your work, and I *went berserk!*"[25] In a world of staid management consultants and academics, including most of his former colleagues at the McKinsey management consultancy, this has given him an edge.

If they had known what they were getting, it's doubtful that McKinsey, with its clipped, sharp, staid young overachievers, would ever have hired him. In fact, they never had a chance to test him as they would an ordinary associate. He lasted only eighteen months, paying his dues, before being swept up into the project that would make him one of McKinsey's most famous alumni.

He joined McKinsey in 1974 as a thirty-two-year-old Stanford business school graduate. He had chosen business school as an escape from the dreary career that he had fallen into—a scientific computer programmer, modeling simulations of oil fields for Getty and Skelly. Unlike Harvard, Stanford Business School in the early 1970s was full of professors who, as Peters later wrote, had "thumbed their noses at conventional thinking for decades."[26] David Bradford, the son of NTL founder Lee Bradford (and a regular at Bethel since his childhood), had just joined the Stanford faculty. So had William Ouchi, the expert on Japanese management. Tom Peters knew most of the business heretics (one of them, Gene Webb, was his mentor), but his interests lay elsewhere. He was so eager to work in the federal policy arena that other students called him "Mr. Big Government." Instead of finishing his dissertation, he took a job in Washington for a new agency devoted to international narcotics control—"looking at opium poppies in Turkey," he later called it. For a year or two, he was happy there; as Hendrik Gideonse had been, he was thoroughly convinced that he was doing something to make a better world.

Then his leave of absence in the government ended. Not anxious to return to school, he looked for a job in San Francisco and found McKinsey. He went through the motions as an ordinary McKinsey associate, still not completely convinced of the value of business in society, and then he fell ill with a congenital kidney problem. While recuperating from surgery, he resolved to finish his Ph.D., which meant another leave of absence, this time back at Stanford. When he finally returned to McKinsey, his superiors tapped him for a special assignment instead of moving him back on the ordinary track.

McKinsey, for the first time in its history, was irritated by a competitor. Its traditional role as the slavishly devoted, impeccably sophisticated clinical psychologists of the consulting world had been preempted by the Boston Consulting Group (BCG). Clients who switched because of Bruce Henderson's growth-share matrix were defecting, essentially, because they thought BCG was smarter—an insult that could not be ignored. Thus, in 1977, McKinsey's managing director initiated two new research projects. The first was an effort to come up with principles for strategic management and beat BCG at its own game.

The other project was a minor spin-off: an effort to find out what was going on in the practice of management worldwide. Peters, perhaps because of his Stanford M.B.A., perhaps because he wasn't urgently needed for any billable assignment or, more likely, because he was based in San Francisco, was tapped for the project. "Wouldn't it be nice," mused a senior McKinsey partner named Warren Cannon, "if when people talk about organizational management they actually quoted us as knowing something?" He told Peters, in effect, to go out and find something quotable.

Although he was an extremely junior consultant from a small, eccentric office, Peters had virtually a free hand at first. He had an unlimited travel budget and (as he saw it) an unparalleled chance to talk firsthand with people whom he had read about at Stanford, people "McKinsey couldn't have found with a Hubble telescope on their own." He went first to Scandinavia, one of the hotbeds of the sociotechnical movement. In the United States, the quality of working life movement was no longer influential. But in Norway and Sweden whole industries were being revamped around the principles of self-governing work teams. Peters interviewed Einar Thorsrud, Eric Trist's old friend and a former Nazi resistance leader, who was applying the principles of self-government to work teams on Norwegian oil tankers. He visited the shop floor at Volvo, where teams of technicians were taking over the work flow. He talked to fifty or sixty people in Scandinavia and Britain. And instead of falling into despair, like Hayes and Abernathy, he fell in love (his own phrase) with the ideas.

It was not easy to communicate that infatuation to his bosses back at McKinsey. Peters's initial reports were rebuked as irrelevant. Worse still, he seemed unable to stop making snide remarks about strategic planning, which was regarded, at McKinsey now, as their primary weapon against BCG. Fortunately for Peters, there was a sympathetic soul in the San Francisco office: Robert Waterman Jr., a McKinsey consultant since 1963 who had spent the past few years successfully turning around a disastrously performing McKinsey office in Australia. Waterman was a natural foil for Peters; he had a gift for speaking plainly in a subdued and reasonable way that raised controversies without raising hackles. And he was close to the renowned Harvard business professor Anthony Athos, consistently rated as one of the country's best college teachers.

Athos had operated for years on McKinsey's fringes as a kind of consultant to the consultants, and he happened to be taking a year's leave in San Francisco. He also knew Richard Pascale, a Stanford professor who had just spent a year studying management in Japan. In 1978 Waterman convened the four of them together to spend a week developing some training materials out of Tom Peters's discovery. On Monday morning, Athos and Pascale met for breakfast and then walked together through the Financial District to McKinsey's offices.

"You know," one of them said to the other, "We're facing a whole week in a small room with Tom Peters."

They mulled over the prospect—already he had his excitable reputation—and Athos finally said, "We need an agenda to keep him from running scattershot all over the place." Pascale agreed. "Why don't we start with strategy?" Athos continued. "McKinsey has a lot to say about that. We'll spend Monday on it." Then they decided to devote Tuesday to structure ("They love to reorganize companies over there") and Wednesday on systems. For Thursday, Athos proposed "shared values." By the time they reached the office, they had six out of the seven topics in what eventually became known, around McKinsey, as the Seven S framework. The first three elements were conventional issues: structure, strategy, and systems; the other four represented the soft management concerns that McKinsey (and most other management consultancies) habitually ignored: skills, style, staff, and shared values.[27]

Consultants always appreciated a framework that showed how everything fit together. The Seven S model was meant to be a sort of road map, like a compass. If, as a management team, you were thinking about only one direction of activity (say, upward toward the McKinsey traditional approach or downward toward the arenas of T-Groups), then you were missing something important. With this model, a consultant could talk about any subject that came to mind, even something related to nurturing people or building teams, and it would still manage to "look McKinsey."

At this time, as Bob Waterman later recalled, a quiet network of sympathetic "excellence" people was emerging within the firm. By any outside criteria they were hardly countercultural; they wore the standard black suits with white shirts, and if they held unusual political opinions, they were careful not to espouse them. But they all had worries about the quantitative strategic approach. They had heard McKinsey consultants tell clients, "It's very important *not* to understand too well the products you make, because you can't allow yourself any kind of passionate attachment to them." They had seen declining performance (much as Hayes and Abernathy had) in the companies that took strategy to heart. As they compared notes and then talked quietly about their hidden fears and hopes, the same question continued to arise again and again. If it wasn't the strategy, then what was it that made some McKinsey clients continually succeed while others continually failed?

The "excellence" name emerged when the managing director of the San Francisco office, who was emphatically skeptical of this "Seven S stuff," nonetheless asked Tom Peters to fill in on a client presentation (to Dart Industries in Los Angeles) when their original material died in a computer crash. "Excellence is something everyone likes," the managing director said. "Why don't you do something on that?" Peters wrote it up as a small paper based on his research and gave a wildly successful speech. Suddenly his report began circulating around McKinsey. Hearing of it, Royal Dutch/ Shell, Siemens, and PepsiCo all asked for presentations—which bombed. Each, however, funded a bit of the ensuing "excellence" research, and today each of the three companies has managers who take credit for "starting Tom Peters on the path to *In Search of Excellence.*"

Years later Peters credited the PepsiCo presentation in particular for forcing him to boil down his seven-hundred-slide presentation to a simple set of eight precepts, including "stick to your knitting" and "have a bias for action."[28] But if any single company could take most of the credit, it would be Hewlett-Packard. To prepare for their Shell speech, Peters and Waterman went to interview John Young, the CEO there.

They asked a question that McKinsey had never asked before: "What do you do to promote excellence at your company?" Startlingly enough, Young told them, and he introduced them (as he had once introduced Michael Maccoby) to other managers for further interviews. Then Peters and a research associate went to 3M, IBM, P&G, Frito-Lay, and a dozen other firms, collecting stories from vice presidents, plant managers, and team leaders. They learned about the way various managers kept memos to one page, set up ad hoc projects, cultivated suggestions from their customers, or pursued hundreds of other innovations.[29] They rarely looked in depth; at Procter & Gamble, for instance, they never learned about the radical plant designs of Lima and Augusta. (Years later Waterman would finally learn about these P&G plants and devote much of a book to them.)[30] Nonetheless, their frenetic interviewing represented a radical departure from conventional McKinsey research, which ordinarily involved interviewing the CEO alone. "We were not talking to the people in the front line, as I had done at the Volvo factory," Peters later recalled, "but by McKinsey standards, we were talking to real people."

While Waterman accentuated the positive, Peters took his drive from the negative. Another McKinsey consultant, Alan Kennedy, invited him to meet a group of renegade executives at Xerox. This was before Xerox's celebrated turnaround in the early 1980s, but the ground was already fertile for change. Peters would sit with the engineers and managers over beers in Rochester, talking about how to change their management methods. As he wrote up his results, he targeted every word, in his mind, to "those idiots who run Xerox."

In 1980, still feeling competitive with BCG, McKinsey hired its first-ever public relations officer, who arranged a *Business Week* article with Peters's byline. Suddenly Peters was a celebrity, deluged with requests for speeches, flying off the handle chaotically on stage, delighting crowds, making his McKinsey colleagues suspicious and resentful—and getting a book contract with Harper & Row. The advance was for five thousand dollars, a respectable sum, considering that the subject was management.

Originally Peters and Waterman each intended to do a book. They were already underway with one, *The Art of Japanese Management*, based in part on the Seven S framework. Neither Peters nor Waterman found it easy to get started until Peters was involved in a car accident in 1981. Confined to his home, he finally began drafting. With the seven "S's" taken, he refined as chapter headings the eight precepts that he had developed, on the fly, for his presentation to PepsiCo. Back at the firm's offices, he felt more and more isolated, and acted more and more obstreperous, until several months before the book's final deadline, Waterman asked him to quit McKinsey, if only for his own good. To help make the exit smooth, Waterman negotiated a deal in which Peters would get to keep his royalties. Nobody thought they would amount to much; the first printing was slated for only ten thousand copies. The book appeared in October 1982, hit the best-seller list in April 1983, and went on to sell five million copies.

In Search of Excellence was, on the surface, a validation of American management ("It all but had the frigging flag on the cover of the damn thing," Peters later said), but at its heart it was a powerful indictment. Everything the book lauded and praised was a departure from the corporate norm. It was a paean to the ideas of the heretics. (Chris Argyris, Warren Bennis, Abernathy and Hayes, and Peter Vaill were cited). More important, it took its insights from the people on the job who were struggling to implement them. It quoted Sam Walton saying that his best ideas came not from highly paid staff or consultants but from his clerks and stockboys. It recognized upstart companies like Apple (then only three years old) and quoted Steve Jobs describing how he succeeded by "hiring great people" and creating an environment where they could "make mistakes and grow."[31] And it reminded readers of Thomas Watson's "respect for the individual" at IBM.

Certainly Peters was already turning his act into shtick, and during the years to come, managers would see exactly how difficult it was to follow his precepts. Certainly Peters and Waterman were Manichaean—every story in their book represents a purported struggle between corporate good and pure evil, with little in between. Within just a couple of years, there would be a backlash, when some of the praised companies, such as Atari, Revlon, and General Foods, were scorned as poor performers or takeover targets.[32] Later still, academic researchers would isolate the mistakes in research that Peters and Waterman had made; for example, management scientist Philip Rosenzweig would eventually dub their error "the delusion of connecting the winning dots": identifying characteristics of winning companies as the sources of those companies' success, without having the evidence to do so and/or any solid reason to believe that these factors would help any company.[33]

Nonetheless, to reread *In Search of Excellence* now, twenty-six years after its publication, is to be impressed by its cheerful candor and roar of genuine feeling, the blending of hard and soft approaches, and the usefulness of its ideas—especially considering the tepid, overblown business books that would follow through the 1980s.

Right at the beginning of the book, Peters and Waterman invoked the magic paradigm shift that Willis Harman had championed ten years earlier. They declared "disturbers of the peace" and "fanatical champions" to be the most vital people in the enterprise, and they attacked the fundamental tacit principle of scientific management: "If you can read the financial statement, you can manage anything." They also attacked the continual drive to growth at all costs.

Unlike Willis Harman, Peters and Waterman were insiders, and, more important, the world was ready to hear them. The Age of Heretics as outside gadflies or covert double agents was over. Henceforth, the heretics would move out into the open.

———————————— o ————————————

Around this time, something else happened, something fundamental, something that made the rapids even more turbulent: the speed of transactions accelerated once again. In the 1400s, families had dominated business simply because trade and enterprise had moved too slowly for individuals to oversee within the space of a single lifetime. By the early twentieth century, because of transportation and communications advances, the speed of commerce had accelerated enough that individuals could create their own large-scale enterprises, throwing away the vernacular ties of family and community. Now, in the 1980s, the Internet and personal computer brought higher-speed telecommunications and computing to a broad population, in particular to the population of businesspeople. Now it might take only a few seconds to find a product or fulfill an order, to send an e-mail or accept a proposal. And if it took more than a few weeks to perform any of those tasks, that was a sign that something was wrong.

The business world was not prepared for the ways in which this speedup would allow the vernacular spirit, the spirit of the counterculture, back inside the belly of the industrial beast. It's no coincidence that the field of management literature grew rapidly during this time. Management had dramatically changed, and people knew that the management techniques of the past—the magic of the numbers—would no longer work. But they did not quite know how.

For answers, businesspeople turned to business schools, where most of them in this era had received their own M.B.A. Here, established academics were questioning the established wisdom of their fields and reaping rewards in the process. Consider, for example, the heretical insight of two accounting professors—one at Carnegie-Mellon University and one at Portland State University in Oregon.

In 1983, Robert S. Kaplan was the dean of the Graduate School of Industrial Administration at Carnegie-Mellon University in Pittsburgh. An affable, outgoing man, his field was managerial accounting, but he felt a sense of disquiet about the companies whose accounting systems he knew. They had far more computer power at their disposal than ever before, and yet they were tracking and reporting the same costs, with the same systems, that they had used for decades. To be sure, the systems were computerized, but most of them (he later wrote) dated back to the moment, perhaps twenty years ago in a given company, when "a computer type first wandered into the factory . . . to automate, with few changes, the manual or electro-mechanical cost system they found there."[34] Because those old accounting approaches had lumped together costs in broad categories like "material," "labor," and "overhead," it was impossible to use that cost information to inform better judgment: to understand which business expenses could be trimmed or eliminated without crippling the capability of the enterprise. The system was relatively simple to learn and use, and it generated the necessary tax information, but for managers, Kaplan suspected, it was "at best useless and more likely misleading."[35]

A Westinghouse Electric Company executive named Thomas J. Murrin (who later became the dean of Duquesne University's business school) pointed Kaplan to the Abernathy and Hayes article, "Managing Our Way to Economic Decline." It said that American companies that lived by the numbers were dying by the numbers; they were shutting down profitable product lines because they looked costly on paper and were making themselves unnecessarily vulnerable to competition from Japan.

Kaplan found the argument convincing and began to talk about it in public. When he was invited to make it the subject of his talk at a major accounting conference, he looked for a business historian to help him trace the roots of the problem. A mutual friend recommended H. Thomas Johnson, a professor at Portland State. A former certified public accountant with Arthur Andersen, Johnson had left that firm for an academic career in economic history; he had then studied with the country's most eminent management historian, Alfred Chandler of Harvard. Kaplan (who had just moved to become a professor at Harvard) and Johnson recognized their symbiotic interests immediately; they went on to collaborate on a book, *Relevance Lost: The Rise and Fall of Management Accounting.*

Published in 1987, the book was a scholarly tour de force and has never gone out of print. The historical chapters (written mostly by

Johnson) showed how management accounting wasn't just a feature of the newly emerging large corporations of the nineteenth century; it probably made them possible. Andrew Carnegie's watchword, for instance, was, "Watch the costs, and the profits will take care of themselves." But cost accounting per se would no longer be adequate (argued Kaplan and Johnson) in a world of global competition, demanding consumers, and fierce uncertainty. Indeed, like many remedies that are overused, cost accounting had become poisonously destructive to its hosts.

The authors asked rhetorically why it had taken so long for the toxicity of calculations like return on investment to become apparent. They answered that originally, managers had compensated for the limits of the numbers by exercising their personal judgment. But when short-term pressures increased and managers had less time to observe day-to-day affairs, their capacity for judgment was diminished. The net effect was to make managers more dependent on the numbers. As Clayton Christensen and Paul Carlile later wrote, "Johnson and Kaplan saw that nested beneath each of [the numbers printed in a financial statement] was a labyrinth of political, negotiated, judgmental processes that could systematically yield inaccurate numbers."[36] In other words, even when forecasts and estimates were valid on the surface—even when they checked out—they were still unreliable.

To Professor Kaplan fell the task of writing most of the material about current management practice, including two chapters describing potential solutions. Since accountants had created this mess, how could they help clean it up? He had recently begun to work with Robin Cooper, another Harvard faculty member whose research focused on innovative cost-management practices and who was writing a case study of Schrader Bellows, a North Carolina hydraulics components company. The company had connected its factory floor computer systems (which ran a kind of operations software known as material requirements planning) directly to its accounting computers. Cooper and Kaplan codified and refined this practice further and gave it a name: activity-based costing (soon known as ABC). Taking advantage of computers to gather information directly from assembly-line measurements and employee surveys, ABC brought into the executive suites a new awareness of the kinds of hidden costs that had traditionally been evident only on the factory floor: errors in a production process as it snowballs out of control, wasted effort in cumbersome part-ordering processes, or time spent traveling from one building to another. Then it divided these costs among particular projects, processes, and products, making cost cutting far more accurate than it had been before.

The term *activity-based costing* was not mentioned directly in *Relevance Lost,* but the prototype ABC practices featured in the book soon became its primary deliverable, and thus the core of Kaplan's and Johnson's speaking and consulting engagements. "We didn't argue," Johnson later recalled. "It was obviously going to be a wave to ride. So we rode it."

Then it was his turn to be approached by a manufacturing guy. Richard Schonberger, an industrial engineering professor from the University of Nebraska, pulled him aside after a talk in 1988 to say, "This is really good stuff. You've told the accountants what we industrial engineers have been trying to tell them for decades. But you don't go far enough. If you could organize the work differently, overhead costs wouldn't be there in the first place. And then why would you need any cost accounting at all?"[37]

That conversation set Professor Johnson off on his own quest. He began to study Japanese and American quality methods, trying to learn if there were companies that didn't use conventional cost accounting procedures to control their factories. And he found one. Its methods were to conventional cost-tracking what Pierre Wack's scenario method was to conventional forecasting: a system based on making use of human awareness and insight. The company was one of the fastest-growing manufacturers in the world and probably the most idiosyncratic. Its success was inspiring a wave of doubt, inquiry, and exploration among many of its competitors. It was at the forefront of a new type of management, often labeled Japanese management because this company was Japanese. But this type of management wasn't really Japanese; relatively few other Japanese companies understood it. Nor was it really new. It was idiosyncratic, and there were few places to learn it. This company welcomed outsiders, because its leaders knew it had taken them sixty years or more to learn it themselves, and they were refining and developing it all the time. This company's name was Toyota.

—————— o ——————

So much has been written about Japanese management, about Toyota, about leading quality movement figures like W. Edwards Deming and Joseph Juran, and about the schools of practice that have emerged as a result, such as lean manufacturing, that it is tempting to assume the reader already knows all about it and just to skip on. But one aspect, perhaps, has never been fully explored: the way that the quality movement and lean production concept both depended on, and reinforced, the heretics within Western companies.

Much of this effect, in the mid to late 1980s and early 1990s, seemed to stem from the personal impact of Deming himself. And that, in turn, had a great deal to do with the mythical legend of his biography: a visionary ignored in his own country until the final fifteen years of a very long life. He was born in 1900 in a western farming community in Wyoming. Like Jay Forrester, he had moved East to study—in Deming's case, mathematical physics and statistics. Starting at Bell Laboratories in the 1920s, working with industrial statistics pioneer Walter Shewhart, and then working for the U.S. Census Bureau as a statistician, he refined a set of methods (statistical process control) for distinguishing the ordinary ebb and flow of day-to-day results (which he called "common causes") versus fundamental problems (which he called "special causes") in a work system. Managers and operations staff who could distinguish the two could learn, as Deming later told writer Mary Walton, "when to act and when to leave a process alone."[38] Over time, they could keep making their operations, products, and services more effective; less prone to unwanted variation; and closer to meeting customers' genuine needs, a process that came to be known as "continuous improvement."

American businesses showed little interest in these ideas. Deming took them to Japan after World War II, originally at the invitation of Douglas MacArthur, who first brought him there to teach methods for statistical surveys of housing, agriculture, and unemployment.[39] Other Americans on MacArthur's team were teaching statistical process control, but unlike most of the Americans, who kept themselves apart from the local culture, Deming was gracious and curious; he immersed himself in Noh plays and complimented his hosts for their mathematical skills. This in turn attracted leading executives in the *keidanren,* the same organization that would later open doors in Japan for Pierre Wack. A leader of that organization, Ichiro Ishikawa, invited Deming to lecture twenty-one leading executives about strategies for building international markets for their products. They knew this would be critical for their small nation's economic recovery.

At this meeting and in others that followed, Deming talked about the emerging global economic environment. He spelled out the "virtuous circle" between quality and cost—the higher the quality, the less need for rework, the greater customer satisfaction, and the lower eventual costs. This in turn provides more money for investing in higher quality. It was much like Henry Ford's 1916 message to his shareholders: "If you give all that, the money will fall into your hands." In postwar Japan, desperate not to remain impoverished, many corporate leaders listened as almost no one had ever listened in America.

Then Deming sketched on the blackboard his own version of an organization chart: a circle of suppliers, designers, assemblers, inspectors, distributors, and customers, through which a product cycled, getting not just more salable, but better with each iteration. He knew from his work as a statistician that even nonmathematically trained workers could perform sophisticated analyses on the fly; he had seen it at the Census Bureau.[40] If they could train everyone to steadily improve the quality of their processes, making the work flow more effectively and less wastefully every day, then it would naturally lead to dramatic improvements in products and considerable cost reductions. Within five years, he told his hosts, other nations' industrialists would beg for trade protection. Looking back years later, he said it had taken four years. As his associate John Dowd later recalled, he also introduced the concept of market research as part of the same cycle of improvement: "Quality begins with the customer."

Other American statisticians and quality experts had influence in Japan as well during those years; Joseph Juran was widely renowned there. And they too were largely ignored in booming postwar America. But Deming was uniquely charismatic and uniquely beloved. In 1951 the Japanese named their prestigious national award for industrial quality, the Deming Prize, after him. And at Toyota, then just beginning its rise to preeminence as an automaker, he was particularly influential. "Every day I think about what he meant to us," said Shoichiro Toyoda, the chairman, at the Deming Prize ceremony in 1991. "Deming is the core of our management."[41]

At the time they first met Deming, Toyota's leaders were just beginning their company's trajectory to become one of the world's most productive and unusual manufacturers—unusual even for Japan. It had begun as a family business, a loom company founded in 1926 by Sakichi Toyoda, a loom inventor (and Shoichiro's grandfather). Many of the celebrated elements of the Toyota method, such as the "five whys" method of asking repeated questions to get to root causes, and the "andon cord," in which anyone who sees a problem can stop the production machine, date back to these earliest days. The deeper quality of continuous craftlike awareness dates back to those days as well. For example, to a casual observer, the presence of an andon cord on an automobile production line would be treated as a symbol that workers were empowered and trusted to stop the line if necessary. But the cord was also a symbol of the maturity of the working arrangement. If anyone slacked off and let a defect go by, it would be discovered at the next station. The only way to thrive in such a system is with calm, confident, steady absorption in the task at hand rather than the scattershot carelessness associated with a more typical command-and-control ethic.

When the Toyota family branched into automobile making in the 1930s, they were particularly influenced by Henry Ford's continuous-flow operations at the Ford assembly plants. Then, within a year or two of Deming's first visit to Japan, Taichi Ohno, Toyota's chief engineer, made the trip in reverse; he went to Dearborn, Michigan, to observe Henry Ford's operations firsthand.[42] But now, in the postwar years of the "whiz kids," Henry Ford II had embraced management by the numbers. Ohno returned home more impressed by the shelf-stocking systems of the local Piggly Wiggly supermarket.

Ohno and others at Toyota began in the 1950s to implement the various methods that have become known as the Toyota Production System. As Eric Trist and Charlie Krone had preached but few companies had ever practiced, they entrusted teams at each station to control their local operations—governed not by metrics but by relationship and continuous observation. Ohno trained engineers by methods that would have seemed brutal to outsiders (forcing them to stand in a chalk circle for hours at a time, looking for problems in the assembly system around them), but that had the effect of harmonizing them with the operation as a whole. Many people in a Toyota factory learned what Pierre Wack would have called "seeing." Or perhaps *sensing* would have been a more apt word because the workflow of a Toyota factory regulated itself through "takt time," an expression that Toyota borrowed from German musicians: a metronome-like beat that was paced to match the daily demand for the factory's products.

This type of sensitized awareness suffused the Toyota system. The company didn't ask dealers to guess what the most popular packages of options and styles would be and produce its wares accordingly. Instead, it assembled each car to match an individual customer's specification in real time. There were no quality inspectors; workers verified each part's reliability before it left the station. There were few, if any, storehouses; Toyota had invented the just-in-time delivery system to ensure that its suppliers delivered parts as soon as they were required, directly to the places that needed them. And there were no labor problems. Toyota had worked out a groundbreaking agreement in 1946, exchanging lifetime employment for flexibility: like the "technicians" of P&G's Lima plant, workers could be redeployed or retrained at any time.

Toyota's customer-based concept of value ("only assets that attract customers are considered valuable") turned many conventional practices upside down. For example, the automaker saw typical adversarial supply chain relationships as intrinsically wasteful and expensive. Instead of playing suppliers off against each other in an effort to squeeze costs as

low as possible, Toyota's purchasers would pick two or three suppliers
for every component and guarantee each a percentage of the business.
Together they would develop work practices on the shop floor that would
reduce waste, cut costs, build supplier profits, and enable further joint
creativity and innovation. This was possible only because the participants
trusted each other. And it's arguable that American companies would
never even have realized the extent to which mistrust was built into their
mind-set if Toyota (and a few other Japanese companies influenced by
Deming) had not suddenly cut into their business.

―――――――― o ――――――――

In 1980 a video documentary producer named Clare Crawford-Mason
stumbled across Deming while researching an NBC-TV news documentary on industrial productivity and the economic decline of America.[43]
Deming was, at that time, making most of his living teaching statistics at
New York University and advising the Interstate Commerce Commission
on how to set trucking rates. She put him onscreen in a segment of the
documentary: an eighty-year-old six-foot-four-inch-tall man murmuring,
"American management thinks that they can just copy from Japan. But
they don't know what to copy." The documentary itself was renamed *If
Japan Can, Why Can't We?* Within a few weeks, Deming had fielded calls
from Ford and General Motors; these were, after all, their worst financial
years since World War II. And within a few years, the basic parameters of
his practice were established: he would visit a company, advise it on its
difficulties, enroll its managers in the four-day seminar he had developed
for Americans on quality, and leave one or two hand-picked protégés in
place to help the company improve.

Deming pushed himself relentlessly, teaching at Columbia and New
York universities on Monday (traveling between them on subway) and
then spending the next four days, most weeks, giving a seminar somewhere around the world. When he wasn't teaching, he consulted; Ford
and General Motors were regular clients in the 1980s. He wrote and
composed choral music on weekends (his wife, whom he married in
1932, had died in 1986).[44] When he was ill (for example, just after having a pacemaker installed), rather than be seen teaching from his wheel-
chair, he insisted on walking out on stage himself, supported by two
canes. He had an uncanny memory for people; while signing books for
attendees at one seminar, he greeted a man whose only previous contact
with him had been asking a question from a crowd of government workers months before. Deming remembered both the man's name (Benjamin
Nelson) and the question he asked (about leveraged buyouts).[45]

A small army of statisticians and quality experts considered it an honor to travel with Deming and help lead his seminars, but he maintained no organization or headquarters—only a secretary who, for thirty-five years, had worked in the basement of his small brick house and who was devoted enough to publish her own biography of him in 1987. He was familiar with manufacturing processes in every industry and locale but knew nothing of popular culture. Crawford-Mason, who by then was producing videotapes based on his ideas, once suggested he use the *Wizard of Oz* as a metaphor for cooperation. "What is Oz?" he asked.

In many settings, and especially in Japan, Deming was revered for his courtesy and humility. But he was also known for bullying Americans, particularly if they were senior corporate leaders. At GM, his name was anathema for several years because he had yelled at the company's president, Jim McDonald, in a national meeting: "Who is responsible for quality problems? *You* are!" He was welcomed more quickly at Ford, especially after a session in 1983 when CEO Donald Petersen invited Deming to talk to the corporate senior staff, directed them to pay close attention, and said he would rejoin them after lunch. As he walked offstage, he felt Deming's presence following close behind him. Petersen turned and asked, "Where are you going?"

"Where are *you* going?" countered Deming. "If this isn't important enough for you, it's not important enough for me." Petersen returned to the stage and canceled his other meetings.[46] He and Deming later became close friends. In 1984, the last official act of chairman Henry Ford II was a presentation of Deming's ideas to a senior management meeting in Boca Raton.

More countercultural than Deming's manner were his ideas, which contradicted some of the most enshrined practices of American management, especially the management of people. Ratings, rankings, incentives, trophies, bonuses, tips, and prizes of any kind were "forces of destruction," he would murmur. They merely set people against each other and destroyed the intrinsic "joy in work" (a phrase he borrowed from Ecclesiastes) that people wanted most from their jobs. Many of his anecdotes depicted the ingrained absurdities of a production system that no one questioned, in which pride of workmanship had been long since pushed aside. "How can a production worker take pride in his work," Deming would say, "when after stopping his machine to adjust it because it was only making defective product, the foreman comes along and orders him in two words, 'Run it'?"[47]

He was particularly fond of a role-play called the bead game in which audience members pretended to be factory workers, sifting red beads from a tray of white beads with a small paddle, while he berated them in the manner of a harsh foreman: "Why did your score drop? Weren't you paying attention?" Or, "Jenny's score improved. Disciplinary action had effect." The game was as frustrating to watch as it was to play, and its lesson was self-evident: the selection of a winner in most work-related contests is arbitrary. Nearly all human errors, even if they seem dramatic at the time, are part of the normal cycle of the system. We do not create our own success. Individual efforts, no matter how valiant, don't improve productivity; only the designer of a system, which in most companies meant senior executives, can shift the results by improving the flow of work.

Other quality experts didn't go as far. Joseph Juran argued that incentives could never be abolished; they fulfilled too primal a need. ("We are still animals, contesting with each other as to who's going to be able to impregnate the females.") And every evening at the seminar workshops, discussion always returned to this point. "Sure, everyone hates being rated by their boss," someone would say. "But how else do you get bright people to achieve? How do you judge people fairly?" Deming's answer essentially was that bosses must be deeply involved in helping every one of their employees improve—a level of human intimacy that (as some attendees grumbled) people went into corporations specifically to escape.

The consequences of ad hoc systems and short-term-oriented management, according to Deming, were evident far beyond the shop floor. Competitive bidding merely ensured that the shoddiest suppliers would get the contracts. Telling workers that quality depended on them was an obvious lie; everyone knew quality depended on top managers because they controlled the system. Quarterly earnings goals and barriers between divisions distracted people from the good of the overall company. And the penalties for retaining all of these forms of conventional American management? They would be apocalyptic; American business would go "down the tubes." When MIT's Center for Advanced Engineering Study (an eminent program for professional training for engineers and managers) published a thick book of his dense, aphoristic writing in 1986, he titled it *Out of the Crisis*.

Perhaps his most controversial point was the simplest: the idea that workplaces should be free of fear and anxiety. Responding to the demand he heard from American managers for precepts for action, Deming included a list of "fourteen points" at the front of his book. Most of them were derived from the talking points in his lectures, and it was easy to imagine them being intoned in his deep, rumbling voice: Cease dependence on inspection to achieve quality. End the practice of awarding business on the basis of price tag. Put everybody in the company to work to accomplish the transformation.

Point number eight said, simply, "Drive out fear, so that everyone may work effectively for the company." Deming was thinking of the smooth operation of a system, which required people to know and trust each other. But Western managers felt, from their bone marrow to the roots of their hair, that without fear, there could be no progress. Fear of competition, of uncertainty, of their own complacency, of their bosses, and of each other was the only thing keeping them from simply sinking back into torpor. Drive out fear? You might just as well paint a "take me over" sign on the headquarters front door.[48]

And yet despite all this (and despite the fear they felt themselves, wondering if the irascible octogenarian would single them out and yell at them in a question-and-answer session), they continued to pile in to his seminars. In his insights, Deming wasn't far off from Douglas McGregor, Abraham Maslow, or any of the Pelagians of NTL, but his style was more assured. It was downright oracular. The Pelagians argued from instinct or experience, while Deming could marshal statistics for support. But all of that didn't explain Deming's appeal, nor did the Japanese connection. It was as if he held some kind of mystical key, a transformation of the mystery of the numbers that would allow you to keep their magic but reclaim the lost spirit of the vernacular. Like an elder from an earlier age rattling his box of beads, he gave the impression that he knew the insomnia, worries, battles, and the late-night nausea of his managerial audiences. He didn't merely understand; he was a walking embodiment of them and of the alternative. They might be bored as he droned on, but they were enraptured all the same. And for a while, it seemed as if everyone, from the bosses on down, was listening.[49]

At its peak, the total quality movement (as it was called) encompassed hundreds of thousands of people. But it always had a countercultural quality. To be seen as a heretic, it wasn't necessary for quality proponents to go to the extreme of banning ratings or rankings. They need only try some of the precepts to see how easy it was for their peers and bosses to misunderstand them.

And yet because the methods worked so well, they spread, and new attitudes spread with them. One typical story occurred at Ford Motor Company, where soon after their first exposure to Deming, some engineers took apart a dozen Japanese transmissions; they were so identical that the inspector thought her measuring instrument was broken. (Reducing unnecessary variation was an important aspect of quality improvement, and one that Western technologists didn't readily appreciate yet.)

Ford quickly hired some young statisticians (the company's first "Deming disciples," as they were soon called) to manage a continuous improvement effort. Suddenly Ford began saving hundreds of thousands of dollars in nitty-gritty shop floor improvements—debunking once and for all the myth that quality is more expensive. They also began to change other management practices; they stopped hiring temporary workers, for example. "If you've been telling your people that motivated, well-trained, concerned workers are essential to quality and success," said the narrator in a Crawford-Mason video about Ford, "how can their work be done by a temporary replacement?"[50]

As the impetus behind the quality movement and Japanese management grew, it also became more prominent in business schools. In 1990, three MIT researchers published a best-seller about the future of the auto industry, informed in particular by studies of Toyota's production system: *The Machine That Changed the World,* a title suggested by the publisher. As one of the authors (James Womack) later pointed out, the production system wasn't a machine, and it never did quite change the world.[51] The authors (Womack, Dan Roos, and Daniel T. Jones) weren't statisticians like Deming; they were management researchers, coming from a business school background, and instead of talking about quality, they used the word *lean* as their generic catchphrase. At first, they had reluctantly used the term *fragile production,* but abandoned it with relief when an MIT researcher named John Krafcik came up with *lean* instead. Krafcik had taken the idea of leanness from Toyota's relentless focus on eliminating waste, which seemed to parallel the ruthless focus on detail needed to remove excess weight and mass from any system. He had come to MIT from the NUMMI (New United Motor Manufacturing Inc.) plant, a well-known joint venture established between Toyota and General Motors in the early 1980s to run a showplace auto plant in Fremont, California. Later Krafcik would go on to a career in strategic planning at Ford and ultimately to Hyundai Motor America.

Because the book's research had been funded by a consortium of auto manufacturers, the authors played down the prominence of Toyota; they described lean production as a generic Japanese approach to automaking that manufacturers worldwide might yet adopt. And indeed, for a few years, it seemed as if the world would adopt lean production, or total quality management, or whatever it was called. Machine or not, this really would change the world.

Deming's and Juran's books, along with *The Machine That Changed the World* and *Quality Is Free,* a book by Philip Crosby, all became best-sellers around then. Crosby, a former quality control manager for the

Pershing missile, was no statistician, but he had understood and popularized the idea that by consistently improving quality, a company would cut its costs. Tom Peters's next major book, on the heels of his first, was equally heretical. It was called *A Passion for Excellence;* then came *Thriving on Chaos.*[52] Being a creative, self-driven manager was fun, and that kind of inner-directed creativity was the only way a company could prosper. He began to champion the next wave of plant managers, like Patricia Carrigan, the first woman plant manager at General Motors, who had a Ph.D. in psychology and a track record of labor-management cooperation and sociotechnical-style improvement—but whose sudden visibility had provoked grumbling among other managers at GM and, arguably, derailed her career.[53] There was also an emerging new group of academics like Rosabeth Moss Kanter, whose dissertation had focused on communes but who was now studying corporations and writing books with titles like *The Change Masters* and *When Giants Learn to Dance.*[54] There was a new quality-oriented practice called six sigma emerging at Motorola, based on reducing defects and errors to as close to zero as possible. At Royal Dutch/Shell's Group Planning department, coordinator Arie de Geus drew on the scenario work there and his own interest in psychology to champion an idea called "planning as learning" in the *Harvard Business Review.*[55] In Springfield, Illinois, at a small industrial company, Springfield Remanufacturing, a former Caterpillar executive named Jack Stack was experimenting with a concept called "open-book management" (later called "financial literacy"), in which people throughout the company, motivated by a broadly based employee stock ownership plan, were taken every week, step by step, through the corporate numbers and systematically trained to track the business impact of their work.[56] All of these threads of insight, and many, many more, seemed to have the same idea in common, at least in principle: if you give people reason to apply their own creativity and capability, with the training, skills, and support needed to rework and improve the processes at work, you can supercharge an enterprise.

Of course, in practice, practices like six sigma or scenario planning could be implemented in just as harsh and top-down a manner as the old scientific management. Even the noblest-seeming efforts had the potential for built-in arrogance or overreach. In 1987, an American equivalent to the Deming Prize was established: the U.S. Department of Commerce's Baldrige Award for quality improvement. Attorney General Edwin Meese had resisted the initiative in the White House, arguing that the government had no business supporting quality. But when Commerce Secretary Malcolm Baldrige, a riding companion of Ronald Reagan, was killed in a rodeo, Congressman Doug Walgren (a friend of a Deming associate and industrial quality expert named Myron Tribus) renamed the award the Baldrige Prize and put it on the president's desk within twenty-four hours. Reagan signed it. Deming's own relationship with the Baldrige award remained uneasy; unlike the Deming Prize, which could be granted to any number of companies, there was a limit of six Baldrige winners every year. And in some cases, it seemed to trigger the opposite impulse of the cooperative, intrinsic "joy in work" that Deming championed. Many companies undertook a crash program to get ready for the award, gathering data, shuffling control charts, and involving people in a never-ending, insecure stress test: Was their job important enough for the quality effort, or would it be cut?

For a while, the quality movement grew far larger, far faster, than sociotechnical or quality of working life had ever grown. Deming in particular found himself called on by dozens of major companies, moving even more rapidly as he aged between seminars and consultations, taking time to push out a simplified book, *The New Economics for Industry, Government, Education,* in 1993.[57] Deming died a few days before Christmas that year; by coincidence, Eric Trist, still alternating between fierce optimism and grim despondency about the future of his ideas, had died the previous June. Then, as if snuffed out by the loss of both leading figures, the prevailing corporate culture seemed to suddenly shift: to lose interest in operational quality, excellence, and developing people. By 1996, many of the quality-oriented projects were evaporating, the managers pushing lean production were taking on other assignments, and demand for $200,000 a year statistical process control experts was waning.

Essentially the numbers culture had reasserted itself.

———————— o ————————

In the early 1990s, Bob Kaplan and Tom Johnson began to feud. It was largely an academic feud, conducted through research papers and book chapters, but while it started as an intellectually driven disagreement, it rapidly escalated into something more personal. Just a few years after their coauthored best-seller appeared, they stopped speaking to each other, and each publicly staked his reputation on the other one being wrong.

In 1992, after his published writing had attracted the interest of several Toyota executives, Tom Johnson was invited to study the company's production system firsthand, spending most of that time in its new plant in Georgetown, Kentucky. The plant was rapidly growing, on track to produce about five hundred thousand cars per year and employing about seventy-five hundred people to do so. As a coauthor of *Relevance Lost,* Johnson was attuned as few other observers would have been to the way Toyota used quantitative indicators of performance. Toyota tracked throughput rates, defect rates, and team leader on-line work rates, but didn't pass them up the line to senior management. Instead, the team members on the shop floor used those numbers themselves as a small part of a much larger, holistic approach to attentiveness. Procedures on the shop floor were defined largely by team members and team leaders; everything around them was designed to improve the alertness, interest, and well-being of people working there. When there was a problem or even an inefficiency, the kind that might show up weeks later as a number on an activity-based costing spreadsheet, people noticed them and dealt with them immediately. He was also impressed by the "andon" cord near each station. When the cord was pulled, people didn't rush around frantically to fix the problem, with supervisors fretting about the thousands of dollars lost during the downtime; instead, only part of the line stopped and support staff members would congregate to think calmly together about the issue. The factory itself was also remarkably clean and quiet, free of the grime and clanging of a more conventional plant. People on the line switched stations every two hours to avoid stress and boredom. A Toyota ergonomics engineer told Johnson that "coming off a shift should feel like finishing a tough but energizing workout."[58]

Johnson also saw that Toyota saved money by giving up the enormous overhead of accounting and control systems. Just as Charlie Krone had found at Lima and Ketchum and Dulworth had found at Topeka, it was much, much cheaper to assume that, given the appropriate training and technological designs, people would manage production more effectively than numbers ever could. "The problem with managing by data," Johnson concluded, "is that it creates a mind-set that leads people to pay less attention to the day-to-day particulars of work."[59]

By September 1992, Tom Johnson had changed his views enough to publish an article in *Management Accounting*: "It's Time to Stop Overselling Activity-Based Concepts." The result of systems like ABC, he wrote, was "unstable processes, unhappy customers, and loss of jobs"; indeed, it contributed "to the modern obsession in business with 'looking good' by the numbers, no matter what damage [that] does to the underlying system of relationships that sustain any human organization." Johnson was ordinarily a reserved, academic person, but he started to come across as a fervent proselytizer. He used words like *crippling* and *lethal* in his subsequent articles; he blamed the troubles that mainstream companies get into—for example, the predicaments of the big three U.S. automakers—on the misuse of measurement. He said that if companies would focus on the means (for instance, designing a production system that makes errors visible and correctable the moment they occur), they wouldn't have to worry about enforcing targets and goals. Error counts would naturally get lower. The ends would take care of themselves.[60]

Kaplan pretended not to be offended personally by all this, but after all, he had invited Johnson into the project that became *Relevance Lost,* had helped him make both a reputation and a potential fortune, and now Johnson was calling their whole approach into question. He published his response in 1994, in the form of a Socratic dialogue. Kaplan's coauthor in this dialogue was Chris Argyris—in a sense, playing the same skeptical role in relation to Johnson that George Odiorne had once played in relation to T-Groups. "Some supporters," Kaplan wrote, obviously meaning his former coauthor, "have developed a mystical faith in the ability of [quality improvement] to solve virtually all managerial and organizational problems." And in Kaplan's defense, the balanced scorecard already involved enough of a cultural change for many companies; it broke down the internal cultural barriers between finance and accounting, on the one hand, and operations-oriented management, on the other, all for the sake of developing strategies for the whole company. Moreover, argued Kaplan, if managers used these tools to cut costs in mechanistic or ineffective ways, then that simply meant they weren't disciplined enough. "A cost is not a natural thing to measure, like revenues," he said. "It's a construct; you have to create it." Without such constructs, he argued, even businesses that emphasized quality could fail financially.[61]

This was about when the two stopped speaking. In books published around this time—*Relevance Regained* in 1992 by Johnson and *Cost and Effect* in 1997 by Kaplan and Cooper—they each devoted a chapter to excoriating the ideas of the other.[62]

Beyond that, Kaplan was moving into a new direction that would give accounting and financial controls even more influence on management practice—and in the process, he believed, finally make all aspects of a company's operations manageable and accountable. Working with Analog Devices, a semiconductor company based in the Boston area, he was developing a system called the balanced scorecard. If ABC helped financial controllers see what operations people saw, then the balanced scorecard would finally help managers naturally incorporate into their decisions the insights of accountants—the best accountants—the ones who know how to draw forth from a mass of numerical data those few statistics and results that genuinely matter.

The original management by objectives (MBO) approach that Peter Drucker and George Odiorne had pioneered in the 1960s had required managers to set financial targets and hold themselves accountable for them. The balanced scorecard expanded this to include not just financial targets but also business process improvement (the sorts of changes that people working in the Toyota Production System naturally made), customer satisfaction goals, and "learning and growth" objectives (for example, "What have you done this quarter to improve the capabilities of people in your department?"). The "balance" in the scorecard was named for the trade-offs among all four of those criteria, thus making it less likely (for instance) that companies would release products that meet bottom-line cost targets but that no one wanted to buy.[63]

"ABC tells you what things cost, but not what they're worth," Kaplan would later say. "The Balanced Scorecard tells you what's creating value. Together, they make the concepts of economics operational for complex organizations."

The balanced scorecard was undeniably successful, at least in terms of uptake. Dozens of companies used it—Exxon Mobil, Fannie Mae, Brown & Root, Cigna, and the city of Charlotte, North Carolina, were all featured in Kaplan's subsequent books—and the idea of using numbers to capture learning filtered out into a variety of other scorecards, dashboards, and other instruments. Some were based on computer data as an input to decision making; others allowed managers to track results themselves. By contrast, almost no companies (except Toyota) were following the kind of approach that Johnson advocated. In many companies, people were deputized to explore the idea of implementing a Toyota-like system and withdrew entirely; it sounded too much like abandoning responsibility for near-term results. Moreover, it took only a year or two to implement a balanced scorecard; it had taken Toyota sixty years to develop its production system, and it wasn't done yet.

But the more popular they became, the more ardently Johnson railed against ABC and the balanced scorecard. Numbers were fine, he would say, as a vehicle for true learning by the people on the line. But as soon as top management began to monitor the measurements, and people felt compelled to make the numbers look good, then learning on the line (and accuracy) inevitably atrophied. Later, he would make the same criticism about lean management: it too depended far too much on financial targets.[64] All too often, these systems became vehicles for control. Indeed, the battle was not over numbers at all; it was really about the question of who was responsible for the work. Did that privilege belong to the boss, who could track the results only with metrics, because nothing else could be compared at a large scale? Or did each of us in a company, in our own way, make a vow of sorts to attend to the value and quality of our work, in collaboration with others, but with accountability for ourselves? Were we adults, or were we children? If you were Pelagian, you'd build a system for adults, as Toyota had; moreover, these were adults in a community who had internalized the need for quality and who didn't want to let down the customers, their colleagues, or their own sense of pride and excellence. If you were Augustinian, you'd want the most full-featured accounting system possible to guide children in making the right decisions, with fear of being punished and hope of being rewarded. Naturally you'd favor the numbers.

○

Not always in the most conscious manner, this tension between the numbers culture and the sensing culture—the tension between counting and seeing, between the balanced scorecard and the Toyota Production System, between forecasts and scenarios, between Augustinianism and Pelagianism—became a recurrent, underlying theme in management circles during the next fifteen years. It had particular resonance for the heretics of high-performance systems, who had learned to train people to be involved and participative at work, watching themselves and the work with the close attentiveness of a master craftsperson. The numbers culture rendered that kind of attentiveness useless, frustrating, and even dangerous. The high-performance approach was so much more ennobling and effective that mainstream management was always drawn to it in theory. But they always found it too discomfiting and difficult to put into practice. This tension could be found within most companies, and on occasion it spilled out into public awareness. For example, in the late 1980s, it struck the group of managers and consultants whom Charlie Krone had assembled around him in Carmel, California.

Having left Procter & Gamble and settled in his rambling house on the ocean, Charlie began a consulting practice with such companies as DuPont, Alcoa, Heinz, Volvo, and Crown Zellerbach. By all accounts, the transformations (as he and colleagues called them) in these companies were remarkably successful. In one DuPont nylon plant in Martinsville, Virginia, for example, there was a dramatic improvement in quality and a decrease in cost. Rather than solely laying off employees as a normal factory restructuring would have done, the company cut management levels from eight to four, and the union agreed to let blue-collar shift operators handle tasks that supervisors had managed in the past. "The operators became innovators," plant manager Ralph Sink later recalled:

> One team designed a US$60,000 spinning unit that solved a technical
> problem that the engineering department had said would cost

$2 million to fix, and another created a sophisticated and efficient sup-
ply chain that delivered the right quantities of fabric at the right times
to a large customer. (This was years before the phrase *just-in-time* had
caught on.) We also kept our part of the bargain; when the operators
saved us millions of dollars a year by managing inventories more precisely, we used that money to seek new business rather than to lay
people off. The shift in responsibility served me well personally,
because it allowed me to focus on developing products and building
customer relationships, which brought me to the attention of other
companies in the region.[65]

   Sink was one of a number of managers who ultimately left their jobs
to work more closely with Krone as a consultant, traveling to Carmel or
attending impromptu sessions elsewhere around the country. (Others
branched out independently; Lou Pritchett, at one point a vice president
of sales at Procter & Gamble and a long-standing devotee of the technician system, went on to Wal-Mart, where he helped develop some of the
retailer's groundbreaking supply chain methods.) Krone continued to
refine and apply his Socratic method: singling out individuals or small
groups of people, giving them the spotlight in front of a larger group, and
asking them one question after another, trying to get them to see the ramifications of the system and help others see it as well. It was the closest he
could get, perhaps, to Taichi Ohno's chalk circle. And it gave people confidence: by the late 1970s, people who worked with Charlie were buoy-
ant, believing that they might well have the answer to the problems of the
industrial future—and the opportunity to put those answers into
practice.
   But there was also a clandestine aspect to Krone's practice. Although
he no longer had to follow P&G's policy of compulsive secrecy, he
worked largely with his own close associates and devotees and created a
nondisclosure agreement that kept tight control over his published work.
Anyone who used his materials, including many of the consultants who
regularly attended his workshops, had to pay a 10 percent commission.
The papers that Krone handed out, with the frameworks photocopied
onto them, were rigorously embargoed from outside eyes. He eschewed
large-scale lectures, delivering keynote addresses at conferences or publishing articles, because that type of mass performance contradicted the
spirit of dialogue. To have a meaningful effect, he said, he had to tailor
the message to each student's ability to accept it. This could be accomplished only in small, face-to-face groups—small enough for him to see
participants and match his message to their eyes.

Despite his Socratic approach, or perhaps because of it, a mysterious, almost cultlike reputation coalesced around Charlie himself. Every once in a while, he tried to dispel it through some more conventional approach to publicity, but that never quite worked out. Once in the late 1980s, for instance, he invited a national business magazine reporter to attend his workshops and interview the participants for an in-depth story, but the reporter eventually called back to say that the story he filed wasn't skeptical enough, and the editor ultimately killed it. They had really wanted a cult exposé. (The *New York Times Magazine* had rejected a profile it had commissioned of W. Edwards Deming around the same time for much the same reason.)

Episodes like this made Charlie all the more determined to keep control over his methods as they went out into the world, to prevent their effectiveness from being diluted. He was well on his way to having a subtle influence—the kind of impact that, years later, would be known as a "viral" influence—on dozens of companies. But then some of his colleagues lost control, in a highly visible way, at California's largest telephone company, and his public image fell apart. In 1987, Pacific Telesis was one of the seven "baby bells," the Regional Bell Operating Companies spun out from the breakup of American Telephone & Telegraph (AT&T). Located far from AT&T's New Jersey headquarters, PacTel had always been considered the least sophisticated and most lackluster of those companies, but its territory (California and Nevada) included some of the most technologically advanced parts of the country. PacTel's subsidiary Pacific Bell provided all the Bell phone service to the state of California. It had just built a massive new headquarters, noteworthy at the time for having the second largest employee cafeteria in the world (the largest was the Pentagon's). The building was located in San Ramon, a southeastern suburb of San Francisco just a few miles away from Silicon Valley. It was thoroughly computer controlled; sensors automatically lowered the blinds and recognized employees' ID cards from their pockets. It was deliberately intended to be a base for rolling out leading-edge technologies, including the then-nascent innovations of cellular telephony and the Internet. A new wave of young executives at PacTel wanted the whole company to shift gears fast and embrace not just new products and services, but new operating models, new technical skills, and new organizational approaches. However, some leaders within the company doubted that its overall culture, rooted in the "Bellhead" bureaucracies of the old AT&T, was ready for this kind of change. The executive vice president in charge of Pacific Bell, a long-standing AT&T veteran named Arthur Latno, could speak eloquently about the need for his company to lead the technological revolution, but when asked in 1986 what kind of computer he used, he said he didn't use one himself. "I facetiously tell my staff that they're my computer."[66]

At the time that interview took place, Latno and his fellow senior executives had a transformation project quietly underway. They had contracted with a consulting firm called Network Associates, run by two of Krone's colleagues (a retired San Jose State business school professor named James V. Clark, who had met Charlie in his previous position at UCLA, and another P&G alumnus named Michael Assum), to run a full-scale transformation project to equip the company to live up to its technological vision. Krone himself wasn't involved, but Clark and Assum used his teaching material as the base of their training sessions and tapped his pool of associates to lead them. They also recruited heavily among organizational development practitioners around the West Coast. For his part, Krone tried to discourage Clark and Assum from creating this type of project in the first place. As a packaged attempt to change a large, complex company in a mechanical, rote, one-size-fits-all fashion, it was doomed to failure. As the pioneers of organizational development had learned to their cost in the 1960s, it takes a long time to train someone skilled enough to help a team of people rethink their assumptions or improve the consciousness of a workplace. But Clark and Assum had no choice if they wanted the job. The top PacBell executives, now that they accepted the idea of change, insisted that it roll out as quickly as possible. Assum later explained to Michael Brower, another Krone colleague, that he and Clark had slowed PacBell's original timetable considerably.

By 1986, the program was operating along at full steam. PacBell set up two-day "leadership development" workshops facilitated by the Network Associates trainers and crediting Krone as a source in the manuals. Assum and Clark took twenty-three thousand people (out of a workforce of sixty-seven thousand) through the workshops. They would have rolled it out further, but the workshops started to get a reputation within the company as heavy-handed, manipulative, jargon-filled, and irrelevant to the problems at hand—and expensive. (The total cost was later estimated to be $40 million, with about $15 million of that paid as fees to Network Associates. Krone, although he broke away from Assum and Clark and condemned their approach, still received a percentage of the fees as royalties.[67]) Rightly or wrongly, employees interpreted the workshops as telling them they didn't know how to think and didn't love the company, and as if that didn't raise enough hackles, the references to Gurdjieff and the underlying theme of human evolution represented a threat to some religious beliefs.

Moreover the project was moving too fast and frantically for its designers to listen to their critics and adjust accordingly. Those who disliked the program either inferred, or were told outright by their bosses, that complaints could get them fired. But Pacific Bell was a regulated utility, and it wasn't long before some staff members complained to the California Public Utilities Commission; these complaints, in turn, were leaked to the local press. A few years before, San Francisco had been suffused with cults; one of them, the People's Temple led by Jim Jones, had been responsible for the killing of a congressman and a mass suicide. It wasn't that difficult for outsiders, reading a newspaper, to believe that some kind of Gurdjieffian cult had infiltrated a major company. Front-page headlines appeared in the *San Francisco Chronicle*, with references to the "Kroning," as some employees had begun to call it. Embarrassed, the company immediately dropped the program, but the commission held hearings on it anyway and in the end ordered PacBell to charge $25 million spent on the training back to its shareholders rather than including it in the operating expenses that were covered by ratepayers' bills. A few heads rolled; one vice president who had championed the program was demoted to head what was then the relatively minor cellular telephony division—an extraordinarily fortuitous career move.[68]

Although he had played no direct role in this debacle, Charlie Krone's reputation took years to recover. (It didn't help that one of his most successful projects, at Crown Zellerbach, was halted around the same time, after the corporate raider James Goldsmith bought the company in 1985 and sold off the parts.) In many respects, the blow to Krone's reputation was undeserved; even a postmortem report produced by a local consulting firm for the Public Utilities Commission said as much. (Actually they damned him with faint praise: the Pacific Bell program wasn't mind control, they said, just "old wine in new bottles": mediocre organization development.[69]) Krone continued working with a small group of fellow researchers and consultants, and they quietly achieved further gains in companies like DuPont throughout the 1990s and 2000s. But for people familiar with management, the "Kroning" episode made it clear how difficult the task of corporate transformation could be. Resistance to change didn't come just from the power structure of the company; it was embodied in the habits and perceptions of every individual who mattered.

Soon after the "Kroning" episode, a young programmer at Pacific Bell named Scott Adams had his cartoons about a programmer named Dilbert picked up by a local syndicate, published first in the *San Francisco Chronicle* and then around the rest of the country. Whether or not he attended the leadership development sessions, Adams was clearly aware of them. Dilbert continually struggled against hypocritical bosses who used idealistic management jargon as a vehicle for manipulative controls. Despite the popularity of *Dilbert,* Scott Adams didn't leave Pacific Bell until 1995.[70] Dilbert became an ongoing chronicle of the excesses of heretical ideals—of the hypocrisies and abuses that can come to the light when a new theory of human behavior is implemented at full scale.

○

Had Pacific Bell waited a couple of years, it might have found the leadership development workshops easier to put across. By the early 1990s, the concept of transformation was enshrined as a management practice. It was typically sold as a movement away from stagnation. A CEO could no longer send out directives and expect people to obey them unquestioningly. And even the best-conceived, best-executed, top-down directives were no longer enough by themselves to guarantee success. The rapids were moving too fast; there were too many new competitors, too much interplay with potential collaborators, too many sudden problems. People at every level had to think on their feet a great deal more. The typical planning apparatus at many companies, which had often substituted for business judgment, was going the way of Shell's old Unified Planning Machinery. And in its place, for the companies that succeeded, would be some way of cultivating, rewarding, and advancing large groups of people to exercise judgment on their own.

In other words, at least on paper, it gradually became respectable for the first time in many companies to be a heretic. People had to learn to take initiative on behalf of the company. Or perhaps company leaders had recognized that they needed to cultivate the in-depth commitment of their own people; otherwise the entire operation would be stultified.

The most prominent manifestation of this new impulse was called reengineering. Like many other management fashions, it had its roots in the Harvard-MIT nexus of Cambridge, Massachusetts. Jim Champy, an MIT engineering graduate who had cofounded an information technology consulting firm called Index, invited Tom Davenport, a young sociologist, to join as a researcher; in the same building, an MIT computer science professor, Michael Hammer, maintained a small consulting firm. Champy and Davenport were engaging and bright, but Hammer was in a class by himself; he was earnest, literal minded, a bit childlike and otherworldly, and intensely contemptuous of the unnecessary impediments of mainstream bureaucracies. Like Jay Forrester before him, he had become disenchanted with computer science. He found the real-world dilemmas and opportunities at companies like Citibank and Xerox much more interesting than his academic research. He resigned his MIT professorship and began working closely with Index on joint projects, particularly with Davenport.

While studying office automation, the Index researchers shrewdly began to compile a data bank of workflow redesign anecdotes. For instance, some Ford Motor Company managers had discovered, after acquiring Mazda, that Ford had five hundred accounts payable clerks where Mazda had only a handful. The only difference was Ford's invoice process, which the company had never questioned. By cutting it, Ford eliminated three-fourths of its accounts payable staff.[71]

To Hammer, Champy, and Davenport, such stories represented the foundation of a compelling new kind of consulting practice. Hammer coined the name *reengineering* in 1987; Index adopted it after rejecting *transformation*, which sounded too touchy-feely. *Reengineering* was hard, tough, masculine, and it was a huge hit from the beginning. Hammer's first tentative presentations immediately electrified audiences. From there grew articles and books *(Reengineering the Corporation* by Hammer and Champy was the first in 1992) and lucrative project work—not just for Index but for many consulting firms that used it to make their everyday overhead reduction work seem bolder and more cutting-edge.[72]

By 1994, a $50 billion consulting industry had developed around reengineering. The early customers were information technology departments; their huge computer investments had never achieved the kind of payback they expected, and now they finally had a corporate imperative to redesign the whole organization to match the information flow of their computer systems instead of the other way around. It also appealed to those heretically minded executives who had risen to fairly high levels and now wanted to boost performance. Instead of struggling against new forms of competition or accommodating old bureaucracies, they could simply get rid of those outdated parts of the company with a virtuous rationale: They would redesign those parts freshly, starting with (as Hammer put it) "a blank sheet of paper." And this time they would get it right.

Ultimately reengineering was most seductive to those CEOs and other senior executives who sensed that their old command-and-control techniques no longer worked, especially for changing the direction of the company. But they weren't ready to give up authority and move toward a more self-managing system, as Ketchum and Dulworth had done. Reengineering gave them a way to command without the tedium of controlling; rather than tell people what to do, they could simply set up processes that, in effect, reprogrammed the whole company. In other words, reengineering promised they could get a Pelagian style of whole-hearted commitment, without having to give up their familiar Augustinian mind-set.

The day-to-day work of reengineering was process redesign: nitty-gritty exercises in rethinking the flow of work and information in a company. The method could work miracles, especially in companies split into functional stovepipes and silos, where R&D, marketing, and operations people have been isolated from one another. There *was* a lot of waste; Trist, Deming, and many others had shown that. And it was true, as both sociotechnical and quality theorists insisted, that business processes operated best when designed as a single, interrelated system. But the quality and sociotech movements invited people on the shop floor and in the back office to gradually improve their work together. To the reengineers, there wasn't time for incremental change; the frenetic pace of the business environment demanded that managers torpedo the old, wasteful, bureaucratic processes, and put the new ones in place as quickly as possible, "blank sheet of paper" or not.

Michael Hammer argued that a whole reengineering effort should take less than a year, and he offered examples in his books and speeches of creaky old hierarchical dinosaurs that suddenly became as nimble as greenfield start-ups. But most of these successes turned out to be as ephemeral as the "excellence" examples had been before them. Reengineering in practice generally meant turning over process design to teams of outside experts and information technologists, with a mandate to cut fat, particularly payroll expenses, from the corporate budget. Clients wanted results; the easiest way to measure them was staff reductions.

Tom Davenport first realized the monster he had helped create around 1994, during a consultation with Pacific Bell. Having failed to reinvent their business model with Gurdjieffian mysticism, the company was now trying to use this top-down program-the-company approach—all the while struggling to serve its high-tech market and follow the rules laid down by the state's activist Public Utilities Commission. "They announced that 10,000 people would be laid off through reengineering," Davenport later recalled. "I knew that they were nowhere near the point with their process designs where they could figure out how many people would be needed to do the work." A series of studies in the early 1990s later established that 70 percent or more of the initiatives had actually made things worse. Like T-Groups at the height of the fad cycle, reengineering projects bred confusion, delays, resentment, and screw-ups. As hundreds of jobs were eliminated, often without much subtlety or consideration, Hammer himself became an unwilling symbol for unproductive downsizing, and reengineering triggered a ferocious middle-management backlash.

About a decade later, Hammer would admit as much in an interview in the *Wall Street Journal,* Champy would apologize in an article in the Conference Board's magazine *Across the Board,* and Davenport (who was already on his next big idea, knowledge management) would write a confessional cover story for the premiere issue of *Fast Company* maga-zine.[73] All three would essentially offer the same explanation: amid the fer-vor of revolutionary change, they forgot about people. "The last thing that I would have ever imagined," Davenport later recalled, "was that people would start losing their jobs because of some ideas that I was offering."

○

Conventional wisdom, even today, says that reengineering failed because it went too far. It was too much change, too fast, with too little regard for people. But there was a case to be made that reengineering crashed because it didn't go far enough. Implicit in Michael Hammer's method, but only vaguely and occasionally voiced, was an extremely powerful heretical idea whose potential was never realized.

Both individuals and corporations resist changing their habits, and the only way to make a change stick is, in effect, to reprogram: to shift behavior, day by day, until all the people in the company are naturally operating differently. That was the essence of the Toyota Production Sys-tem and of such quiet innovations as financial literacy; bit by bit, training people to act differently, you built up a new culture. As it happened, neu-roscience research in the 1990s was discovering that the patterns of activ-ity in the human brain were far more flexible than anyone had previously thought; habitual activity literally reshaped the flow of neurons in an individual brain and made it easier to operate efficiently, with an eye toward quality.[74] In that context, a reengineering plan (or any other pro-cess design) is an algorithm. The computer is the company, the bits are people, the routines are business processes, and the operating system is the organization's culture. The goal of the plan is, effectively, to repro-gram the people, and thus make the company more capable. And since people inevitably resist being programmed against their will, it would have to happen with their full consent and participation—their collusion, in effect—because they valued the new skills and capabilities being offered to them.

Hammer, with all of the knowledge of programming methods that he had gleaned from his former profession, ignored all this in his reengineering work. Reengineering plans provided no incentives that might make people eager to consent to being reprogrammed; no stock options or guarantees of job security. And Hammer failed to talk about such elementary aspects of software engineering as debugging—the intensive work of uncovering and eliminating errors after a piece of software is released. While he wrote, in passing, that reengineering plans should be iterative—that people in a com-pany should revisit the plans in practice and eliminate problems—he also proclaimed far more loudly that "reengineering can't be carried out in small and cautious steps. It is an all-or-nothing proposition." In other words, once it was done, it was done. No revisiting. Statements like this, were, of course, what his tough-minded clients wanted to hear. They didn't have patience for iteration. But it also guaranteed that neither time nor attention was made available for fixing errors. Instead, there was enormous pressure at many sites to pretend those errors didn't exist. No wonder that working in a reengineered company often felt like living inside a piece of buggy, frustrating software, with no way to shut off the machine.

As reengineering lost its chance to apply the theoretical discipline of software design—the correspondence among simplicity, power, and elegance articulated by computer science pioneers like Edward Dijkstra and Donald Knuth—to human organizations, it also lost its claim to distinction.[75] Most likely it was Hammer's innate understanding of software elegance that led him to recognize the power of the first corporate change stories he had heard. But he seemed to have drawn back timidly from it. When asked about software elegance in the early 2000s, he sidestepped the question by arguing that companies weren't ready to be programmed, and he didn't have the theoretical base to do it: "There were hundreds of years of experimental data with the real world before Newton developed his theory; we have only a few decades of experience with process design."

The tragedy of all this was that other heretics could have helped. Anyone who knew about Lewin, for instance, could have combined reengineering with action theory—the idea of learning about a system as you try to change it—and emerged with a powerful and organic way of thinking about companies. Warren Bennis, Tom Peters, Edie Seashore, Chris Argyris, or anyone else who had ever coped with Parsival's dilemma and figured out the core of action learning could have made an enormous difference. The best of the quality and sociotechnical consultants were already operating as the reengineers could have operated. Edgar Schein was right around the corner, at MIT. But Hammer didn't seem to be aware of them or at least was not receptive to their message. Working with the heretics would mean taking on a new way of life, and not every company was prepared for that. The reengineers, like so many other management innovators, were caught in the end between the imperative to develop their theory and the need to market their work to impatient, numbers-oriented managers who needed rapid and dramatic results. Hammer's methods, for all their radical effect, had to be put in place without changing the way anybody thought, or else they wouldn't sell.

○

But there were examples of companies that took a more fundamental approach and thrived as a result. And starting in the mid-1980s, one of the most influential companies became a centerpoint for some once-heretical ideas. Before long, after being embraced by this company, they became part of the management mainstream.

For decades, General Electric had been at the forefront of conventional management thinking. The former CEO, Ralph Cordiner, had pioneered scientific management there in the 1950s; Peter Drucker had used it as his laboratory for management by objectives in the 1960s; and many contemporary portfolio management techniques had emerged there in the 1970s. GE had also been a company where the CEO invested greatly in the development of its leaders, which is why GE has often been perceived as a hothouse in which prospective CEOs can gain experience, grow, and then spread out to other companies.[76]

When Jack Welch was appointed CEO in 1981, the idea of large-scale corporate transformation was still considered countercultural at most companies. Welch had inherited one of the most respectable corporations in the world, but it was also full of stultified or uncompetitive businesses. He therefore did what many other corporate leaders would try to do in the following two decades: a massive, top-down change program. Many of the components of that change program have since become famous: the dictum that every business should be first or second in market share in its relevant markets; the idea that businesses that didn't meet this criteria would be "fixed, closed, or sold"; the ruthless discarding of many GE businesses, including its former flagship small appliance brand (indeed, Welch's own former division, GE Plastics, would ultimately be sold to a Saudi Arabian industrial company in 2007); the "vitality curve" (later known as the "rank-and-yank" system), where top performers were rewarded and the bottom 10 percent performers were axed; and the systematic discarding of bureaucratic rituals and formalities in favor of fierce executive give-and-take.[77]

These were hardly heretical ideas; indeed, they represented the numbers culture as if on steroids, buffed and strained to ruthless muscle. Rank-and-yank was particularly likely to provoke anxiety, even more among the people who stayed than among the people forced to exit. If Edwards Deming had counseled his listeners to "drive out fear," here was a company running on fear. Many GE veterans of that era recall the 1980s and early 1990s as a time when people felt pushed beyond their limits, worked to the maximum, constantly on the road, and continually worried about being fired or burning out, especially after they reached age forty.[78]

But while many companies that copied Welch's approach crashed and failed, the methods basically succeeded at GE, for Jack Welch himself was a particularly skillful Welchist. The single most vital part of the Welch revolution—the component that made his ideas comprehensible and palatable to people throughout the company—was an in-depth attention to cultivating high-quality managerial talent. This was both symbolized and exemplified by the training program called Work-Out, instilled throughout the company. And while the rest of the company was Augustinian and numbers based in the extreme, Work-Out was perhaps the most humanist large-scale program ever attempted in corporate America.

GE drew on a small army of external consultants to design and deliver Work-Out, including such well-known academics as Noel Tichy and David Ulrich at the University of Michigan and Harvard's Todd Jick, as well as management authors such as Steven Kerr, currently the chief learning officer at the Goldman Sachs Group. Most of them based their consulting practice on the program after leaving GE. The chief architect was Jim Baughman, a Harvard Business School professor who left to become Welch's first head of the Crotonville Executive Learning Center, the retreat in Westchester County where GE had been training its senior leaders since the 1950s. Baughman later called Work-Out "the most successful program I saw in 40 years of practice"; certainly it was the most influential.

The Work-Out initiative began as a natural outgrowth of GE's newly revitalized conference center at Crotonville. The center had been a corporate nexus in the 1950s, but it had been relatively neglected since then. Welch invested billions of dollars in remodeling both the facilities and the curriculum, and much of his own time talking up its significance. He thus sent a signal to the entire workforce that management learning was now not just a frill but a coveted prerequisite and central corporate value.

At the heart of Crotonville, famously, was "the pit," an amphitheater-style classroom where the chairman engaged in candid give-and-take once every two weeks with the hundred or so managers in residence at that moment, exhorting them to take initiative and (as Jim Baughman recalls it) "get with the program," that is, emulate Welch's own rough-and-tumble style of fierce and open proactivity. But rank-and-file GE managers didn't find it easy to do so. Both in the pit and during plant visits, they complained that their bosses, their bosses' bosses, and mountains of rules, some several decades old, shackled them. "We're not experiencing openness," they told Welch. "We don't have enough voice in the direction of our unit or department."

During a helicopter ride late in 1987, Welch and Baughman decided to create a series of town meeting–style events that would bring "the spirit of the pit" through the company and jettison the bureaucratic shackles. They'd call it Work-Out, as a pun on the toughening and slimming process that would (they imagined) drive the nonessential work out of the system. Anything would be up for grabs: communications ("Is this report really necessary?"), decision rights ("Does this really need to be approved by so many people?"), meetings, metrics, and policies. What could they get rid of? What could they streamline? And what could they think about more creatively? To design the sessions, they convened a group of about twenty outside consultants who had all worked with GE before. Then, in a meeting at a hotel near New York's LaGuardia airport, Welch laid out his three key principles:

○ All Work-Out sessions would involve large cross-functional and cross-level groups, of forty-five to one hundred people each, to provide the kind of combustive diversity that you don't get from intact teams.

○ All sessions would be led by a senior executive leader, who had to not just give his or her blessing but take part wholeheartedly.

○ Most controversial, that leader had to say yes or no during that session to every idea presented there. Taking it under advisement for study was not an option. Besides saving time and avoiding bureaucracy, this had the effect of forcing executives to pay attention; they were visibly on the spot throughout the session, and therefore just about every decision they made would be remembered.

Every GE business had its own Work-Out flavor, but they all took on first the "low-hanging fruit" of unnecessary reports, approvals, and meetings first. The nuclear business eliminated tedious Nuclear Regulatory Commission (NRC) compliance rules that had been slavishly followed for years. Upon examination, it turned out those weren't NRC rules at all; GE had imposed them on itself.

Welch, who wanted to avoid any semblance of formality, discouraged the Work-Out designers from keeping elaborate records. Thus, no one ever knew how many people went through Work-Out sessions. But they did track the results of decisions made there. According to Steve Kerr, all but 9 percent of the approved ideas were followed through—a record probably better than that of any other process in the company. There were other indicators of Work-Out's positive effects, such as the number of midlevel managers and even union workers who spoke up at these sessions, took charge of implementing changes they suggested, and rode that success to a more vibrant career. Senior managers' behavior visibly changed too.

"We never intended Work-Out to be an assessment technique," Kerr said later, "but when you watched managers browbeating their people in these public sessions, you could see how dreadful they were to work for. Other managers, who hadn't really been noticed, suddenly shone when a Work-Out session put them on the spot."

In 1989, a team at GE'S NBC media division proudly unveiled a video satirizing its own efforts to reduce expense reports—a parody of those old 1950s "how a bill becomes a law" short documentaries—to the Work-Out design team. "I happened to look across the table at Welch," recalls Ron Ashkenas. "He was the only one not laughing. When the lights came on, he pounded the table. He said GE wasn't just paying us to fix their expense reports. Why couldn't we use Work-Out to fix their problems with product development or customer service?"

Over the next ten years, GE expanded Work-Out's scope and scale. They tackled deeper business issues; then they tackled strategic questions. They started sending executives outside the company to look for ideas from elsewhere to emulate. For instance, Wal-Mart had a regular practice where senior sales managers met every Friday night comparing notes about what they had seen the previous week. GE copied the practice with weekly teleconferences of people from around the world who highlighted major themes they'd seen in, say, Latin American markets or Asian technologies. They raised their skills at process mapping and began plotting with senior leaders on the step-by-step moves they'd need to make to get a major change adopted. "In one exercise, the leaders identified all the key stakeholders who must be on board," recalled Jacquie Vierling-Huang, a Work-Out manager, in 1999. "Then they had to analyze the list: 'How much does each stakeholder support this idea today? And why? Where do they need to be? What's our plan for leading them in the right direction?'"[79]

Gradually they brought in customers, suppliers, and subsidiaries overseas, in, for example, China. By the mid-1990s, Work-Out was a perk routinely offered to customers and a unique source of competitive advantage for GE. By the time Welch left in 2002, the Work-Out process was woven into day-to-day practice. When GE businesses hit any kind of bureaucratic snag or market uncertainty, it was second nature for the senior manager in charge to say, "Let's do a Work-Out on that."

Team-building exercises were correspondingly fewer, but the rhythm of group dynamics was still audible. In some ways, it was as if the spirit of the original T-Groups had suffused the day-to-day practice of the company. It probably took a decade for this to happen, but once it had happened, it changed the atmosphere of the place and made up for much of the stress that people had felt in the decades before.

———————— o ————————

"New truths," wrote Thomas Huxley, "begin as heresies."[80] He was defending Charles Darwin's theory of natural selection. But the same principle is true today, in the world of management thinking. The most effective management ideas follow a life cycle—from heresy to outlier (championed by a small group of people) to ingrained practice to conventional wisdom. In the process, if they are genuinely powerful management ideas, they distinguish the organizations that adopt them.

It is not a coincidence that companies like Toyota, General Electric, Procter & Gamble, and Shell have acquired their longevity. Although they have each had their share of missteps and problems, they have one thing in common: a tradition of making some space for the heretical ideas that emerge within them, particularly those that recognize the value of vernacular spirit and provide a way for that spirit to emerge, even in the steel and glass skyscrapers of headquarters.

One could argue that a heretical idea won't succeed unless it starts at the top, with a CEO like Welch. But having support at the top is not enough in itself. Warren Bennis proved as much at the University of Cincinnati, and some operations, like Topeka's dog food plant, endure even when the corporate governance changes. The reasons that some heretics succeeded, even as most failed, are still not fully clear. But we can guess, pretty well, at some of the lessons from the record of countercultural ideas:

o Like Kurt Lewin, Lee Bradford, Ron Lippitt, and Ken Benne, the founders of National Training Laboratories, they would operate self-consciously, paying attention not just to the way they think but to the hidden rhythms of the conversations they hold.

o Like Douglas McGregor, they would continually convene and synthesize, drawing people together and seeking to pull their mutual understanding into a framework as simple as theory X and theory Y.

o Like Robert Blake and Jane Mouton, they would not be satisfied with building morale and cohesion; they would seek to understand and change the structures of power, authority, and performance.

o Like Eric Trist, they would persevere with patience, despite their own setbacks and self-doubt, seeking allies every step of the way, and taking comfort in the fact that they were not alone.

○ Like Charles Krone and his colleagues at P&G, they wouldn't be satisfied with merely improving operations; they would seek a path of the deepest possible insight, wherever that led them.

○ Like Lyman Ketchum and Ed Dulworth, and the other creators of Topeka, they would scour the world for examples and then craft a place, out on the prairie if need be, where they could prove their case. (But they would be aware, as Ketchum and Dulworth gradually came to understand, that mere success is not enough; one must anticipate the fact that people don't like to be challenged by the success of others.)

○ Like Saul Alinsky and those who hired him in Rochester, they would learn to deploy outrageous drama and community spirit in the service of a higher cause.

○ Like John Mulder, they would embody the basic decency that an organization can muster when called on.

○ Like Franklin Florence and the leaders of FIGHT, FIGHTON, and Eltrex, they would allow their plans to adapt as circumstances changed and find sustainable success in the process.

○ Like the organizers of Campaign GM, they would follow through.

○ Like Herman Kahn, they would make thinking the unthinkable entertaining without losing sight of its ultimate significance.

○ Like Pierre Wack, Ted Newland, and the scenario planners of Royal Dutch/Shell, they would rigorously train themselves to see the world more clearly and foster clarity in the thinking of others.

○ Like Willis Harman, they would recognize the interplay of faith and reason, of emotion and rationality, of the spirit of the healer and the spirit of the engineer and give voice to the synthesis.

○ Like Jay Forrester, they would explore the hidden dynamics of the world and not flinch from the implications.

○ Like Edie Seashore, they would dedicate themselves to openness and recognize that some solutions are fiercely radical.

○ Like Chris Argyris, they would dedicate themselves to solving the unsolvable problems of collective humanity by cultivating real-time awareness of their own (and everyone else's) assumptions and conclusions.

○ Like Warren Bennis, they would try to change the world, knowing but not accepting imperfection, and relishing free will.

○ Like Paul Hawken, they would take entrepreneurial risks, take stands on principle, and take advantage of the synergies between their risks and their principles.

○ Like Arnold Mitchell, Marie Spengler, and Duane Elgin, they would find a way to communicate the heretical message, knowing that even if their audience didn't believe them, it would make a difference eventually.

○ Like Amory Lovins, they would marshal their enemies' numbers to build an argument against them, and they would push voluntary simplicity, not for consumers but for producers.

○ Like Bob Hayes and Bill Abernathy, they would represent the forgotten functions of business.

○ Like Tom Peters, they would recapture the forgotten passion of business.

○ Like W. Edwards Deming (and Henry Ford before him), they would hold to constancy of purpose: the knowledge that if you seek to exalt your employees, your customers, and yourself, you will more than incidentally make money.

○ Like Tom Johnson, they would seek a deeper, but more reliable, explanation of corporate success.

○ And like Jack Welch, if they could, they would put that deeper understanding into action.

And there are some things they might do that heretics do too infrequently. They would cultivate patience and not shortchange their efforts by expecting them to show results too fast. (As the late Bill O'Brien, CEO of Hanover Insurance, used to say, they wouldn't "pull up the radishes to see how fast they were growing.") They would learn to intervene in larger organizations, which is as much a body of skill and practice as intervening surgically in a human body. They would build their own equity outside the organization—their reputation, their relationships, their financial equity, their skills—so they would not be as vulnerable and could express their opinions without fear.

And when they saw a truth that contradicted the conventional wisdom of the organization, they would find a way to remain loyal to both the organization and to the truth.

A surprisingly large number of businesspeople seem to find themselves in that position today.

○

You might believe that the purpose of corporations is power, pure and simple; they are as deliberately totalitarian as the state in George Orwell's *1984*.[81] Or perhaps you believe that the purpose of corporations is return on investment—the accumulation of wealth for shareholders and the use of that measure as a score of managers' performance. Either view suggests that corporations are dangerous, psychopathic structures, cut off from any sense of purpose that will allow them to survive in the long run.

Consider the dangers, in a turbulent environment, where transactions are instantaneous, of the view that corporations exist primarily to provide ROI.[82] To be sure, ROI is important—as a signal of a company's effectiveness and its ability to survive. But a company focused solely on ROI has no purpose except expediency. It sends an implicit message to customers: "We depend on you merely for our revenues. We're willing to make a buck off your back in any way we can." They sour relationships with employees by letting them know that any rhetoric about "all being in this together" will be empty rhetoric. Exploiting the resources of the company for narrow and immediate ends drains away the vernacular spirit that nurtures the people of the firm.

Shareholders should also be wary of a company that puts its purpose solely in their hands. When a company sends the message, through its messages to stock analysts, that it will do anything necessary for short-term capital (typically meaning that it will slash costs and lay people off frantically), it ensures that the capital it raises *will* be short term—ready to switch to any other company that promises to slash costs more. Sooner or later a company that is built around this purpose will falter. Its competitive advantage will wither away, since any enterprise can dedicate itself to returning investment on capital merely by reinvesting it.

Finally, the belief that the purpose of a corporation is ROI is the root cause of excessive legislation. If a company does not build up its ethical capability—if it is fundamentally irresponsible to its employees, customers, and community—then government will feel obliged to set enough rules to rein the companies in. The company's ability to act with impunity, like that of any irresponsible creature, will be increasingly limited.[83]

Any heretic who tries to argue this case—even the CEO—will face a difficult battle. Every force associated with the corporation, even the victims of short-term policies, will line up to support the rhetoric of ROI as the ultimate purpose of the firm. The compelling value of simply keeping score, to try to stay in the game and survive at all costs, will overwhelm all other concerns. That is why you cannot make any long-lasting change in a corporation without an alternative image of what its purpose should be.

o

If not the accumulation of power or return on investment, then what purpose should a corporation have? What are corporations for?

It might seem ridiculous at first to answer that question by saying, "They are here to remake the world." But that has been their purpose all along, ever since the days of monasteries, ecclesiastical universities, and joint-stock companies. A corporation has always been an artificial vehicle, with powers bestowed on it by the state, which could act independently, through which men and women could wreak large-scale change at little risk to themselves.

Corporations have become powerful because they work. They work because of the power of large-scale business methods. As Peter Drucker noted, most of the outside protest against corporations exists not because they are failures but because they are successful. We who are their neighbors, or who consume their products, or who live in their world want them to act with similar success on behalf of the whole of humankind.

Without corporations, no efforts to make the world better can succeed because corporations are responsible for infrastructure—not just the networks of telecommunications and transportation, but the distribution, commerce, energy, and financial infrastructures that determine the quality of life in general, inside and outside the commercial world. Without corporations, no effort to solve the greenhouse gas problem will succeed, because corporations determine both how much pollution goes in the air and how much technology exists to mitigate it. Without corporations, globalization doesn't exist, and without corporations, the benefits and pains of globalization cannot be distributed more equitably.

But corporations can't realize any of this unfulfilled potential with the prevailing management culture—the culture of the numbers. That is why the restoration of vernacular spirit inside corporations is so essential—and probably inevitable. Many people enter corporate life as engineers or analysts, insecure about human relationships, choosing to work in a place where they can avoid the fracas of conflict and the uncertainty of the streets. Then they discover that human interaction is all too prevalent in corporations; it is simply stylized, routinized, encapsulated in numbers that can be aggregated and scaled. But it doesn't go away. Even in the most constricting corporate structure, people love, hate, aspire, and despair. And to the extent that a company ignores that simmering evolution, it will not serve its communities, its shareholders, its customers, or its own employees. If companies exist to build wealth, they can do so only by building a more effective, more intelligent community than anyone else has built.

People are needed to say all this inside corporate walls. And fortunately those who take on that role may be more appreciated, and more listened to, than they have been in the past. The power of the numbers has diminished; even analysts and M.B.A.s recognize that the exclusive knowledge of the conventional managerial priesthood is no longer enough. The power of financial control is also evaporating; too many companies have lost their power by pursuing only short-term results. And a growing number of large and small businesses are recognizing that their success depends, as Henry Ford noted, on doing something besides making money.

In late 2007, *strategy+business* published "My Unfashionable Legacy," an article by Ralph Sink, a long-time sociotechnically oriented manager and an associate of Charlie Krone. "The last few years have been bittersweet for people like me, pioneers of high-performance systems with decades of experience," Sink wrote. "Despite [our successes], the concept is less fashionable. . . . Some leaders of the field, including Eric Trist and Fred Emery, have passed away. Others, like Charles Krone, are retired or semiretired. Some companies that once made major commitments to high-performance systems have slid back to authoritarian management, even if it leads to decreased productivity. The next generation of managers, particularly on the operations and shop-floor side, don't always have the skills and training to design, create and lead high-performance systems, and there's a real danger that this knowledge could be lost entirely." Then he went on to describe his own experience at DuPont and at a smaller manufacturer, CPFilms, and the way that had shaped his thinking.[84]

Sink received a number of letters after the article appeared. One of the first came from P. V. Kannan, the cofounder of 24/7, an India- and Silicon-Valley-based global call center outsourcing giant. "We have over 6000 employees worldwide," wrote Kannan, "and we are doing a lot of what Ralph Sink describes, although it is not 100% implemented. I sent this article to every operations manager and we are making it part of our new year plans."[85]

There may be more CEOs emerging like Kannan, from around the world, with a greater commitment to high performance. There may be more companies reconsidering, redeveloping, reinventing their purpose away from merely making money. These companies will not be in the majority, but they will be the companies that thrive, take over others, and navigate the rapids to come.

These days, the greatest asset that heretics have is that there are so many of them. They exist in every organization, balancing the imperative to do good works with the imperative to keep their jobs and keep earning a living. Their greatest dream is to bring their work lives in tune with their personal hopes and dreams. Perhaps a corporation exists, in the end, precisely for its heretics. Perhaps its purpose in the long run is to help people expand their souls and capabilities by providing venues within which people can try things on a large scale—to succeed and fail and thereby change the world.

BIBLIOGRAPHY

IT WOULD TAKE A FULL-SIZED VOLUME to list the written sources I perused in researching this book. This bibliography, with brief annotations, represents my informal guide to the books that spurred me on or changed my thinking, and the sources I think readers who choose to follow up might find most useful.

Alinsky, Saul. *Rules for Radicals*. New York: Random House, 1971. An autobiography/manifesto in which Alinsky's voice comes through terrifically strong. Makes you wish you had known him.

Argyris, Chris. *Personality and Organization*. New York: HarperCollins, 1957. How organizations infantilize or eject the people who work for them.

Argyris, Chris. "Some Causes of Organizational Ineffectiveness Within the Department of State." Center for International Systems Research Occasional Paper 2. Washington, D.C.: Department of State, 1966. If this booklet had a mouth, butter would not melt in it.

Argyris, Chris. *Flawed Advice and the Management Trap: How Managers Can Know When They're Getting Good Advice and When They're Not*. New York: Oxford University Press, 2000. Eye-opening introduction to the perils of managerial game playing and its relationship to theories in use.

Argyris, Chris, with Harrison, Roger. *Interpersonal Competence and Organizational Effectiveness*. Homewood, Ill.: Dorsey Press/Richard D. Irwin, 1962. Argyris explores (and reproduces dialogue from) high-level management teams in IBM in the mid-1960s.

Argyris, Chris, and Schön, Donald. *Theory in Practice: Increasing Organizational Effectiveness*. San Francisco: Jossey-Bass, 1974. The explanation of theories-in-use versus espoused theories and how they affect managers' learning.

Back, Kurt. *Beyond Words*. New York: Russell Sage Foundation, 1972. A full, in-depth history of the National Training Laboratories, encounter groups, and all the dilemmas and conundrums that emerge as people try to put them into practice.

Bedein, Arthur G. *Management Laureates: A Collection of Autobiographical Essays*. Greenwich, Conn.: JAI Press, 1991. Chris Argyris, Robert Blake, and Jay Forrester wrote autobiographical essays for this book.

Bennett, J. G. *Is There "Life" on Earth? An Introduction to Gurdjieff*. New York: Stonehill, 1973. The most accessible introduction for novices (like myself).

Bennis, Warren. *The Unconscious Conspiracy: Why Leaders Can't Lead*. New York: AMACOM, 1976. Essays written during the time of student protest, Watergate, and Bennis's presidency at the University of Cincinnati. Fascinating glimpses of his personality and priorities.

Bennis, Warren. *An Invented Life, Reflections on Leadership and Change*. Reading, Mass.: Addison-Wesley, 1993. I appreciate Bennis's writings about himself, particularly in this retrospective collection of his most powerful essays.

Bennis, Warren. *Beyond Bureaucracy: Essays on the Development and Evolution of Human Organization*. San Francisco: Jossey-Bass, 1993. Revised version of a 1966 book of essays *(Changing Organizations)* that contains "Democracy Is Inevitable" and close observations of Chris Argyris, Robert Blake, Herb Shepard, and others.

Bennis, W., Benne, K., and Chin, R. (eds.). *The Planning of Change*, 3rd ed. New York: Holt, 1976. One of the nice things about these collections of early organization development articles is the strange feeling of anarchy they evoke; you can see Bennis and Chin creating the first texts of their field (of organization development) and reveling in the freedom to do so.

Berry, Wendell. *What Are People For?* Berkeley, Calif.: North Point Press, 1990. Cogent essays that argue against the premise of heretic—that corporate reform is a worthy activity. Large, remote enterprises, Berry says poetically, are inherently corrupt.

Blake, Robert, and Mouton, Jane Srygley. *Corporate Excellence Through Grid Organization Development: A Systems Approach*. Houston: Gulf Publishing, 1968. An overview to the managerial grid system that shows how it is supposed to work when followed all the way to the end.

Blake, Robert, and Mouton, Jane Srygley. *Diary of an OD Man*. Houston: Gulf Publishing, 1976. A wonderful memoir of two years of harrowing consultation at the Bayway refinery.

Bradford, Leland P. *National Training Laboratories: Its History, 1947–1970*. Bethel, Me.: NTL Institute for Applied Behavioral Science, 1974. Bradford's memoirs are a rich vein of ore about the man and the institution; the book also is a mini-archive in itself, including many of the pivotal documents in NTL's history. Whenever I describe how NTLers saw things, particularly in the early years, I am probably relying on something from this book.

Bradford, Leland P., Gibb, Jack R., and Benne, Kenneth D. (eds.). *T-Group Theory and Laboratory Method*. Hoboken, N.J.: Wiley, 1964. Nitty-gritty T-Group practice, almost enough to run one as it was run in the late 1950s.

Brand, Stewart (ed.). "The New Class." *CoEvolution Quarterly,* Spring 1977, p. 8. A meeting transcript with Herman Kahn, Amory Lovins, and then-governor Edmund G. Brown. This conversation between two prodigies (three, if you count Jerry Brown) still rings with insight two decades later.

Braudel, Fernand. *The Wheels of Commerce* (Vol. 2) and *The Perspective of the World* (Vol. 3), from *Civilization and Capitalism, 15th–18th Century,* trans. Siân Reynolds. Berkeley: University of California Press, 1967–1983. These were the two more useful volumes, for my purposes, of Braudel's classic three-volume history of the age when vernacular culture first faced off against the predecessors of industrial culture. Others seem to read these books front to back; I dive into them and surface several hours later, having gone back in time.

Brimm, Michael. *Analytical Perspectives in Organizational Behavior: A Study of an Organizational Innovation.* Cambridge, Mass.: Harvard University, School of Business, Department of Business Administration, 1975. A wonderfully written in-depth guide to day-to-day life at the Topeka plant. It contains both a Marxist and a sociotechnical critique. Brimm was trying to show how a researcher's point of view influences the conclusions.

Brown, Juanita. "Change, Challenge, and Community: Walking the Lifework Path," and "Si, Se Puede—Yes It Can Be Done! Merging the Best of Two Worlds." Mill Valley, Calif.: Whole Systems Associates, 1995. Two beautifully written essays describing how Alinsky-style techniques translate into modern corporate practice.

Callenbach, Ernest. *Ecotopia: The Notebooks and Reports of William Weston.* New York: Bantam, 1975. Originally a news report about sewage, this became one of the few viable postwar utopian novels. It portrays a society much like the dreams of Californians in the 1970s: the internal combustion engine was outlawed and babbling brooks flowed down San Francisco's Market Street. *Ecotopia*'s most engaging quality is the portrait that Callenbach provides of the golden young people of the counterculture, living the vernacular spirit that American culture had beaten down. I believe that a few hours with this novel would be worthwhile for any manager, particularly the chapter, near the end, where Callenbach (a former organization development consultant) describes Ecotopian corporations—collaborative enterprises owned by the participants.

Campbell, Joseph. *In Search of the Holy Grail: The Parzival Legend.* St. Paul, Minn.: HighBridge Productions, 1989, cassette recording; and *Reflections on the Art of Living: A Joseph Campbell Companion,* selected and edited by Diane K. Osbon. New York: HarperCollins, 1991. My version of Parzival borrows from the explications of Joseph Campbell. Campbell has written and spoken several versions of this story; these are not the most scholarly, but they are the most evocative.

Christie-Murray, David. *A History of Heresy*. London: New English Library, 1976. Probably the most complete overview; a Baedeker of everyone who challenged the ideas of the Christian church from within.

Cohen, Peter. *The Gospel According to the Harvard Business School*. New York: Doubleday, 1973. Diary of a sorcerer-in-training, rife with anecdotes, angst, student protest, and soul searching.

Cohen, Sam. "Smartest Guy in the Army." *Army Magazine*, Jan. 1984, p. 35. A short, thoroughly engaging profile of Herman Kahn by one of his oldest and closest friends.

Cohn, Norman. *The Pursuit of the Millennium: Revolutionary Millenarians and Mystical Anarchists of the Middle Ages*. New York: Oxford University Press, 1981. After being swept up in Cohn's dramatic account of waves of "free spirits," beguines, proto-anarchists, true believers, and flagellants, I saw echoes of them all in our time.

Collier, Peter, and Horowitz, David. *The Fords: An American Epic*. New York: Summit Books, 1987. Nice group biography with lots of rich detail about the Fords and their company. Lots of heresy stories.

Cross, Elsie Y., Katz, Judith H., Miller, F. A., and Seashore, Edith W. *The Promise of Diversity*. New York: NTL Institute/Irwin, 1994. Forty authors talking directly to the reader about their diversity work. I have found no better overview, and I base most of what I wrote about diversity in Chapter Seven on reactions to points made in this book.

Crystal, Graef S. *In Search of Excess*. New York: Norton, 1991. The best book extant on corporate corruption by someone who understands it from the inside out—a compensation consultant who can write, and who turned defector.

Davis, John P. *Corporations*. New York: Capricorn Books, 1961. Originally published in 1897, this book traces the corporation back to the monastery and on into the ecclesiastical university and beyond. I have a great affection for this book, as if Davis were a beloved former professor.

Davis, Louis E., Cherns, Albert B., and Associates. *The Quality of Working Life*. New York: Free Press, 1975. Like Zager and Rosow's *The Innovative Organization: Productivity Programs in Action* (see below), a collection of key papers in the quality of working life movement.

Deming, W. Edwards. *Out of the Crisis*. Cambridge, Mass.: MIT Press, 2000. Oracular, disjointed, wise, idiosyncratic, almost biblical in tone. A work of art.

Dobyns, Lloyd, and Crawford-Mason, Clare. *Quality or Else*. Boston: Houghton Mifflin, 1991. Deming's life and work by the creators of the documentary that opened American awareness to him.

Drucker, Peter. *The Practice of Management*. New York: HarperCollins, 1954. I taught myself the content of conventional management with this book, much as managers probably did when it first came out.

Drucker, Peter. *Adventures of a Bystander*. New York: HarperCollins, 1978. A wonderful, inspiring book of portraits that gives face and voice to the twentieth century.

Drucker, Peter. *The New Realities*. New York: HarperCollins, 1989. I borrowed gratefully from Drucker's description of the "great divide" that struck society around 1973. Much of the curiosity that fed my research stemmed from a desire to fill in the gaps of the story told here.

Editors of *Institutional Investor*. *The Way It Was: An Oral History of Finance, 1967–1987*. New York: Morrow, 1988. Exactly what the subtitle says, with no attempt to provide Cliffs Notes for novices. Great glimpse of an alien culture.

Elgin, Duane. *Voluntary Simplicity*. New York: Morrow, 1981. Portrait of the vernacular undertow.

Emery, F. E. (ed.). *Systems Thinking: Selected Readings*. New York: Penguin, 1969. A series of influential papers from the late 1960s in which a sociotechnical pioneer applies principles from biology and cybernetics to organizations.

Fairtlough, Gerard. *Creative Compartments: A Design for Future Organization*. London: Adamantine Press, 1994. A Shell veteran and colleague of Pierre Wack explains three key forms of corporate governance: market, clan, and hierarchy.

Fisher, Lawrence. "The Prophet of Unintended Consequences." *strategy+business,* Fall 2005, http://www.strategy-business.com. An in-depth profile of Jay Forrester, with links to his autobiographical papers.

Fligstein, Neil. *The Transformation of Corporate Control*. Cambridge, Mass.: Harvard University Press, 1990. A remarkably insightful contemporary corporate history, analyzing the changing impact of three great subcultures—manufacturing/engineering, marketing, and finance—on the prevailing corporate culture. A brilliant history of the numbers culture that the heretics sought to balance.

Forrester, Jay. *Industrial Dynamics*. Cambridge, Mass.: MIT Press, 1961. Most accessible (to me) of Forrester's books, and not just an introduction to systems modeling but also to management thinking.

Friedman, Milton. "A Friedman Doctrine: The Social Responsibility of Business Is to Increase Its Profits." *New York Times Magazine,* Oct. 4, 1970.

Fuller, R. Buckminster. *Everything I Know: Forty-Two Hours with Buckminster Fuller*. Santa Barbara, Calif.: Buckminster Fuller Institute, Jan. 20, 1975.

Listening to these tapes clarified my understanding dramatically. People say Fuller is hard to follow in audio, but I hung on effortlessly, riveted.

Fuller, R. Buckminster. *A Grunch of Giants*. New York: St. Martin's Press, Buckminster Fuller Institute, 1995. One of Fuller's last books, it is a polemic venting against the banker, pirates, and corporations and how they distorted civilization.

Gabor, Andrea. *The Capitalist Philosophers*. New York: Times Business, 2000. A tour de force evocation of the history of management thinking— mainstream and counterculture. Includes many, including Peter Senge, Herbert Simon, Alfred D. Chandler, and Abraham Maslow, who are underrepresented in this volume, plus much more on Deming.

Gelber, Steven M., and Cook, Martin L. *Saving the Earth: The History of a Middle-Class Millenarian Movement*. Berkeley: University of California Press, 1990. Tells what happened to the Sequoia Seminars (later, the Beyond War Foundation) before, during, and after their intersection with Willis Harman.

Geneen, Harold, with Moscow, Alvin. *Managing*. New York: Doubleday, 1984. I did not understand the "numbers" until I read this book. Geneen declined to be interviewed for *The Age of Heretics*.

Geohegan, Thomas. *Whose Side Are You On? (Trying to Be for Labor When It's Flat on Its Back)*. New York: Farrar, Strauss, Giroux, 1991. My favorite guide to the labor movement, written by a street poet in labor union lawyer's clothing, full of regrets and howling outrage and sensible political proposals that, alas, will never be followed.

Gibson, Wendell B. *SRI: The Founding Years (A Significant Step at the Golden Time)*. Los Altos, Calif.: Publishing Services Center, 1980. A kind of yearbook that gives a strong impression of the Stanford Research Institute as it was and later yearned to be.

Gregg, Richard. "Voluntary Simplicity." *CoEvolution Quarterly*, Summer 1977, p. 20; adapted from an earlier version in *Visva-Bharati Quarterly*, Aug. 1936. The original statement that Duane Elgin of the Stanford Research Institute found.

Grichnik, Kaj, and Winkler, Conrad. *Make or Break: How Manufacturers Can Leap from Decline to Revitalization*. New York: McGraw-Hill, 2008. Jobs aren't draining from the United States to China, but rather from poorly managed companies to companies managed on heretical principles.

Halberstam, David. *The Reckoning*. New York: Morrow, 1986. Intertwined history of the decline of the U.S. auto industry, the rise of the Nader counterculture, and the emergence of Japan. W. Edwards Deming said that Halberstam was a "great man!" for writing this book.

Hamilton, Adrian. *The Price of Power*. London: Rainbird, 1986. Documentary source of oil industry history, admired by Shell scenario planners.

Handy, Charles. *The Age of Unreason*. London: Business Books, 1989. Views of the organization of the future, described in the style your uncle might use during a long car ride to a job interview.

Harman, Willis, and others. *Changing Images of Man*. Policy Research Report 4. Dayton, Ohio: Charles F. Kettering Foundation, May 1974. Republished in 1982, London: Pergamon Press. Currently online in various places, including http://www.skilluminati.com/research/entry/scientists_on_acid_the_story_behind_changing_images_of_man/. The great millenarian manifesto.

Havener, Cliff, with Thorpe, Margaret. *Discovering the Lost Spirit of Business*. Forest Lake, Minn.: Growth Resource Group, 1994. Havener is the former General Foods manager who proposed the package redesign for Biscuits and Bits, and shortly after left the company.

Hawken, Paul. *The Ecology of Commerce: A Declaration of Sustainability*. New York: HarperBusiness, 1993. Hawken begins to envision a "restorative economy," and thus articulates—for the first time— the ecologist's view of what the value of large mainstream corporations can be.

Hawken, Paul, Ogilvy, James, and Schwartz, Peter. *Seven Tomorrows: Towards a Voluntary History*. New York: Bantam, 1982. Three of the most influential futurists active today, together in their first published work.

Hayes, Robert H., and Abernathy, William J. "Managing Our Way to Economic Decline." *Harvard Business Review*, July-Aug. 1980. A still-significant in-depth warning about the dangers of numbers-based management.

Heilbroner, Robert. *The Worldly Philosophers: The Lives, Times, and Ideas of the Great Economic Thinkers*, 6th ed. New York: Simon & Schuster, 1986. A wonderful history of economic thinking, whose first chapter deeply influenced Chapter One.

Helgesen, Sally. "Masters of the Breakthrough Moment." *strategy+business*, Winter 2006, http://www.strategy-business.com. Rollicking profile of the "godparents of group dynamics," Edie and Charlie Seashore.

Heller, Joseph. *Something Happened*. New York: Knopf, 1974. Artist's-eye view of the pathologies, power plays, and heartbreak of the world of the numbers.

Hirsch, Jerrold. "A History of the NTL Institute for Applied Behavioral Science, 1947–1986." Unpublished Ed.D. dissertation, Boston University, 1986. A great, readable dissertation, where I first learned that National Training Lab's story was a story worth telling.

Hoopes, James. *False Prophets*. New York: Perseus, 2003. In-depth view of Deming's time in Japan, plus many other management pioneers (Mary Parker Follett, Elton Mayo, Chester Barnard, Peter Drucker) not emphasized in this book. Hoopes regards them as apologists for abusive management power.

Horwitt, Sanford. *Let Them Call Me Rebel*. New York: Knopf, 1989. An incisive, compassionate biography of Saul Alinsky by an associate/writer/journalist.

Hunt, Morton. *The Story of Psychology*. New York: Doubleday. The reference I used for basic information about psychologists.

Illich, Ivan. *Shadow Work*. Salem, N.H.: Marion Boyars, 1981. Illich's surveys of the shadow side of industrial culture are the greatest antidotes I know to the corporate/professional mind-set. This book contains his essay "Vernacular Values," a history of the centuries-old battle between "subsistence," preeconomic, preindustrial life, and the urge to control and professionalize all human activity.

Johnson, H. Thomas. *Relevance Regained*. New York: Free Press, 1992. A heretic steps out on the limb, renouncing his old beliefs (in the numbers culture).

Johnson, H. Thomas, and Kaplan, Robert S. *Relevance Lost: The Rise and Fall of Management Accounting*. Boston: Harvard Business School Press, 1991. Building on historian Alfred Chandler, Johnson and Kaplan get to the bottom of the story of the numbers—how they evolved and how they eventually deceived the managers who depended on them. Kaplan used this book to springboard activity-based cost management, which Johnson later denounced.

Jones, Brenda, and Brazzel, Michael (eds.). *The NTL Handbook of Organization Development and Change*. San Francisco: Pfeiffer/Jossey-Bass, 2006. A comprehensive guide to organization development practice, starting with a concise evocation of Lewin's ideas and going forward.

Kahn, Herman. *On Thermonuclear War*. Princeton, N.J.: Princeton University Press, 1960. In his inimitable lecture style, the "thinker of unthinkables" presents a range of scenarios for disasters that never happened.

Kahn, Herman (ed.). *The Future of the Corporation*. New York: Mason & Lipscomb, 1974. This conference proceedings was Kahn's only direct statement on corporations as entities, and he doesn't have much to say. But the people he invites do—particularly Peter Drucker on the responsibility of managers to the world at large.

Kahn, Herman. *World Economic Development: 1979 and Beyond*. Boulder, Colo.: Herman Kahn, 1979. Written four years before his death, it weaves together the arguments from all of Kahn's books and provides the most accessible framework to his utopian futures and the facts behind his reasoning. Kahn, Herman, and Weiner, Anthony J. *The Year 2000*. New York: Macmillan, 1968. Kahn, Herman, and Bruce-Briggs, Barry. *Things to Come (Thinking About the Seventies and Eighties)*. New York: Macmillan, 1972. Kahn, Herman, Brown, William, and Martel, Leon. *The Next 200 Years*. New York: Morrow, 1976. Herman Kahn's trilogy of glances ahead, each with a different coauthor.

Kanter, Donald L., and Mirvis, Philip H. *The Cynical Americans: Living and Working in an Age of Discontent and Disillusion*. San Francisco: Jossey-Bass, 1989. The legacy of heretics, says this book, is shattered expectations and defeated idealism. Nowhere to go but up.

Kaplan, Fred. *The Wizards of Armageddon*. New York: Simon & Schuster, 1983. Authoritative, nicely written history of the RAND corporation and nuclear strategists.

Keller, Maryann. *Rude Awakening*. New York: Morrow, 1989. One of the most eloquent writers on the automobile industry.

Ketchum, Lyman D., and Trist, Eric. *All Teams Are Not Created Equal*. Thousand Oaks, Calif.: Sage, 1992. How (and how not) to create a "Topeka" of your own, by two key heretics in Chapter Three.

Kilian, Cecelia. *The World of W. Edwards Deming*. Washington, D.C.: CEE Press Books, George Washington University, 1988. Deming's long-standing secretary assembled this invaluable compendium of notes, papers, and observations.

Kleiner, A. "Revisiting Reengineering," Third Quarter 2000; "Strike Up the Brand," Second Quarter 2001; "What Are the Measures That Matter?" First Quarter 2002; "Apocalypse 2010," Fourth Quarter 2002; "The Man Who Saw The Future," Spring 2003; "GE's Next Workout," Winter 2003; "Beware the Product Death Cycle," Spring 2005; and "Leaning Toward Utopia," Summer 2005. All are in *strategy+business*, http://www.strategy-business.com. For five years I wrote the "Culture and Change" column for this magazine (which I now edit); parts of this book's second edition were first aired in the columns and articles cited here.

Kleiner, Art. *Who Really Matters: The Core Group Theory of Power, Privilege, and Success*. New York: Doubleday, 2003. How to be an effective heretic when you aren't granted reward and recognition commensurate with your contribution.

Krone, Charles G. "Open Systems Redesign." In W. Warner Burke (ed.), *Contemporary OD: Conceptual Orientations and Interventions*. La Jolla, Calif.: University Associates, 1975. Charlie Krone's main published effort to explain the system that he and his colleagues had developed at Lima, Ohio.

Kuhn, Thomas. *Structure of Scientific Revolutions*. Chicago: University of
Chicago Press, 1970. Origin of the idea of a paradigm shift, describing
how new ideas spread in scientific communities and very loosely adapted
by many heretics to talk about new ideas in business.

Kushi, Aveline, with Jack, Alex. *Aveline: The Life and Dream of the Woman
Behind Macrobiotics Today*. Tokyo and New York: Japan Publications,
1988. Straightforward autobiography by Paul Hawken's ex-partner (who
mentions him once).

Lee, Martin A., and Shlain, Bruce. *Acid Dreams*. New York: Grove Press, 1985.
Classic story of the early days of LSD, full of colorful characters like Al
Hubbard.

Lewin, Kurt. *A Dynamic Theory of Personality: Selected Papers*. New York:
McGraw-Hill, 1935. Back to the source.

Lippitt, Ronald. *Training in Community Relations*. New York: HarperCollins,
1949. Nearly all the direct description of the Connecticut Workshop,
including all of the dialogue I used, comes from Ron Lippitt's authoritative
write-up.

Lippitt, R., and White, R. K. *Autocracy and Democracy: An Experimental
Inquiry*. New York: HarperCollins, 1960. This is the story of the "boys'
club" experiments in which Lewin, Lippitt, and White demonstrated how
completely organizational structure determines behavior. They knew
how to conduct an experiment in those days.

Lovins, Amory B. "Energy Strategy: The Road Not Taken?" *Foreign Affairs*,
Oct. 1976. This was expanded later into Amory Lovins, *Soft Energy
Paths: Toward a Durable Peace*, San Francisco: Friends of the Earth
International, 1977. Influential analysis of the choice the United States
faced (and faces) for its energy grid.

Maccoby, Michael. *The Gamesman*. New York: Simon & Schuster, 1976. A
fascinating anthropological study of managerial players.

Manchester, William. *The Glory and the Dream*. Boston: Little, Brown, 1972.
This history of the United States from Roosevelt's era to Nixon's inspired
the form of *The Age of Heretics*. I can think of no better model for a
comprehensive history.

Mansbridge, Jane J. *Beyond Adversarial Democracy*. Chicago: University of
Chicago Press, 1983. Shows how NTL-inspired modes of governance and
conversation actually operated in a real-life counterculture "help-line,"
and leaps from there to compelling insights about how to create political
organizations that engage constituents.

Marrow, Alfred. *The Practical Theorist: The Life and Work of Kurt Lewin*.
New York: Basic Books, 1969. A loving history by a student and
collaborator.

Marrow, Alfred. *Making Waves in Foggy Bottom*. Washington, D.C.: National Training Laboratories, 1974. A brief, to-the-point narrative history of the fateful State Department intervention that demonstrated (to people like Chris Argyris) the political backlash that could strike a Pelagian effort to change government.

McGill, Michael. *American Business and the Quick Fix*. New York: Henry Holt, 1988. Acerbic survey of forty years of management fads, notable for the way it portrays business's love-hate relationship with the "numbers."

McGregor, Douglas. *The Human Side of Enterprise*. New York: McGraw-Hill, 1985. The classic exposition of Theory Y (Pelagian) management.

Meadows, Donella H., Meadows, Dennis L., and Randers, Jørgen. *Beyond the Limits*. Post Mills, Vt.: Chelsea Green Publishing Company, 1992. Twentieth anniversary recap of *Limits to Growth*. The authors, all three of whom were around at the beginning, had a chance to consider the implications over time.

Meadows, Donella H., Meadows, Dennis L., Randers, Jørgen, and Behrens, William W. III. *The Limits to Growth*. Washington, D.C.: Potomac Associates, 1972. See Chapter Six.

Michael, Donald N. *On Learning to Plan—and Planning to Learn*. Alexandria, Va.: Miles River Press, 1996. Michael's explication of the ways in which planners can effectively set themselves up as nonexperts—if they can only see past their own predilections. A lodestar for judgment.

Mintzburg, Henry. *The Rise and Fall of Strategic Planning: Reconceiving Roles for Planning, Plans, Planners*. New York: Free Press, 1994. As Tom Peters says: "A shockingly, tightly ordered, tightly argued 25 years of the history of the ups and downs of strategic planning around the world." Depicts strategic planning as a vain desire for control of the uncontrollable. Mintzburg is an authoritative advocate of intuitive management. Like its subject, this book is a bit forbidding to outsiders.

Moore, James. *Gurdjieff: The Anatomy of a Myth*. Rockport, Mass.: Element Books, 1991. A well-written biography.

Moskowitz, Milton (ed.). *Business and Society: A Biweekly Report on Business and Social Responsibility*. Collected issues from July 2, 1968, to Dec. 27, 1974. This newsletter summed up just about everything going on in social responsibility with indefatigable passion and commitment.

Moskowitz, Milton, Levering, Robert, and Katz, Michael. *Everybody's Business: The Irreverent Guide to Corporate America*. New York: Doubleday/Currency, 1990; and Moskowitz, Milton. *The Global Marketplace*. New York: Macmillan, 1987. Engaging field guides to the histories and personalities of large mainstream corporations. Probably the most dog-eared, tattered, well-used books in my office.

Mowrey, Marc, and Redmond, Tim. *Not in Our Backyard: The People and Events That Shaped America's Modern Environmental Movement.* New York: Morrow, 1993. Compelling stories of the people in the modern environmental movement.

Nigg, Walter. *The Heretics*, ed. and trans. Richard and Clara Winston. New York: Knopf, 1962. Nigg was a minister and professor at the University of Zurich who conceived of his subjects, medieval heretics, as mythic creatures adrift amid the clash of colossal forces.

O'Toole, James, and Lawler, Edward E. III. *The New American Workplace.* New York: Palgrave Macmillan, 2006. A look back and a look forward (as an update of a 1972 report) on the quality of working life.

Pascale, Richard Tanner. *Managing on the Edge: How the Smartest Companies Use Conflict to Stay Ahead.* New York: Touchstone, 1990. Clearest indictment of American management on its own terms because it combines detailed reporting (Ford, GE, GM, Honda) with a solid understanding of "the fallacy of straight-line thinking."

Perez, Carlota. *Technological Revolutions and Financial Capital.* Cheltenham, U.K.: Edward Elgar, 2002. The context for industrial-age heresy is the need to keep moving corporations (and governments) toward what Perez calls the "Golden Age."

Peters, Thomas J., and Waterman, Robert H. Jr. *In Search of Excellence.* New York: HarperCollins, 1982. Less a book than an event, this is still a very good book. See Chapter Nine.

Phillips, Michael. *The Seven Laws of Money.* New York: Random House, 1974. The great counterculture money book; with great zest, good humor, and Taoist wisdom, Phillips describes the ways to think about one's life with money.

Rees, B. R. *Pelagius: A Reluctant Heretic.* Suffolk, U.K.: Boydell Press, 1988. Biography of the British monk and his influence through the centuries.

Richardson, George. *Feedback Thought in Social Science and Systems Theory.* Philadelphia: University of Pennsylvania Press, 1991. Very technical, very engrossing history of all the strands of systems thinking and how they moved from engineering and cybernetics into politics and organizational change. I admire the depth of research and skill of distinction that went into this book.

Robinson, Jeffrey. *Yamani: The Inside Story.* London: Simon & Schuster, 1988. A British potboiler in that great Fleet Street style.

Rosenzweig, Phil. *The Halo Effect.* New York: Free Press, 2007. How much management wisdom can be trusted? Not that much. A brilliant dissection and a starting point for future research.

Russell, Jeffrey Burton. *Dissent and Order in the Middle Ages.* New York: Twayne/Macmillan, 1992. A slim, elegant, thoroughly engrossing book that makes sense of the heretics' struggle, gives them a historical context, and draws readers into their story.

Sampson, Anthony. *The Seven Sisters: The Great Oil Companies and the World They Shaped*. New York: Viking Press, 1975. Amazing feat to be so thorough and readable on such a big topic so soon after the crisis happened.

Schein, Edgar H. *Organizational Psychology*. Upper Saddle River, N.J.: Prentice Hall, 1980. Very solid, concise, and thoughtful overview of the theories of organizational behavior and the people who developed them.

Schein, Edgar H. *Process Consultation*. Reading, Mass.: Addison-Wesley, 1987. "But what do organizational change agents actually *do?*" This is the manual that most of them read—a guide for professionals to wielding the power of conventional organization development, at its best, without doing damage.

Schoenberg, Robert J. *Geneen*. New York: Warner Books, 1985. Fascinating, in-depth journalistic biography.

Schwartz, Peter. *The Art of the Long View*. New York: Doubleday, 1991. Scenario practice as Wack and Newland practiced it and as it evolved further at Shell and elsewhere, codified and described by a leader of the field with roots in Stanford Research Institute and Shell. I was a consulting editor on this book. I refer people here when they want to practice developing scenarios.

Seashore, Charles, Seashore, Edie, and Weinberg, Gerald M. *What Did You Say? The Art of Giving and Receiving Feedback*. North Attleborough, Mass.: Douglas Charles Press, 1992. You too can learn what they do in T-Groups and National Training Laboratories skill sessions. A matter-of-fact book of conversational skill building by three of the most influential people in the field.

Senge, Peter. *The Fifth Discipline*. New York: Doubleday, 1990. The preeminent manifesto of the learning organization movement, newly updated. This book lays out five bodies of activity that are necessary for transforming organizational life. Provides introductions to the ideas of Chris Argyris, Jay Forrester, and the organizational change movement. I conceived of *The Age of Heretics* while working as a consulting editor on *The Fifth Discipline* and wondering about the roots of its practices.

Senge, Peter, Kleiner, Art, Roberts, Charlotte, Ross, Rick, and Smith, Bryan. *The Fifth Discipline Fieldbook*. New York: Doubleday, 1994. Five authors and seventy contributors (including me) present recipes for practice, intended to bootstrap readers out of the need for recipes. This is a good place to go to follow up on Saul Alinsky (organizations as communities), Chris Argyris, systems thinking, shared vision, and more.

Senge, Peter, Kleiner, Art, Roberts, Charlotte, Ross, Rick, Roth, George, and
    Smith, Bryan. *The Dance of Change*. New York: Doubleday, 1999. A
    fieldbook applying organizational learning to large-scale systems change,
    with a particularly valuable article by Jacquie Vierling-Huang about GE's
    Work-Out.

Sethi, S. Prakash. *Business Corporations and the Black Man*. Scranton, Pa.:
    Chandler, 1970. I depended heavily on this for detail and context on the
    Kodak-FIGHT story.

Sethi, S. Prakash. *Up Against the Corporate Wall: Modern Corporations and
    the Social Issues of the Seventies*. Upper Saddle River, N.J.: Prentice Hall,
    1971. Sethi was watching, seemingly, at every crisis where corporations
    fought the public, including PG&E's notorious Bodega Bay nuclear plant
    battle (it lost), the first surgeon general's antismoking campaign, the
    Eastman Kodak-FIGHT story, Dow's fights with anti-napalm student
    protests, and Campaign GM. He conveys the sensibilities of all sides with
    thoroughness.

Shorris, Earl. *Scenes from Corporate Life*. New York: Penguin, 1984. Shorris
    musters stories and political analysis to show that organizations are
    inherently totalitarian. Some of his stories are heartbreaking—for
    instance, the floor polish marketing director who sees his destiny soar and
    then crash, all because they cut a few pennies per bottle from the
    production budget and inadvertently created a floor wax that turned to
    coarse gray film in cold weather.

Sloan, Alfred P. *My Years with General Motors*. New York: Doubleday, 1990.
    Robert Blake's favorite management book. I had not understood, until
    reading this, the drive, vigor, farsightedness, and incredible discipline of
    the pioneering industrial mind.

Sternberg, Elaine. *Just Business: Business Ethics in Action*. Boston: Little,
    Brown, 1994. A terrific hard-headed book on the purpose of business and
    why simply "returning investment to shareholders" is not sufficient—
    because it doesn't protect the shareholders! It also contains the most
    cogent arguments against social responsibility and stakeholder theory, and
    for business ethics and whistle-blowing, that I have seen.

Stolaroff, Myron J. *Thanatos to Eros: Thirty-Five Years of Psychedelic
    Exploration*. Berlin: Verlag für Wissenschaft und Bildung, 1994. Heartfelt
    personal autobiography of one manager's experience with psychedelics,
    extrasensory perception, and personal growth.

Sunter, Clem. *The World and South Africa in the 1990s*. Cape Town: Human &
    Rousseau, 1987. Evocation of high and low roads for the world's most
    dramatic emergence from autocracy to democracy.

Talner, Lauren. *The Origins of Shareholder Activism*. Washington, D.C.: Investor Responsibility Research Center, 1983. The full story.

Tuchman, Barbara. *A Distant Mirror*. New York: Random House, 1978. Tuchman holds up a sharp mirror to the plague-ridden fourteenth century.

Vaill, Peter B. *Managing as a Performing Art*. San Francisco: Jossey-Bass, 1989. Very nice collection of heretical essays, all about learning to make better distinctions among abstractions of management theory and practice.

Ventura, Michael. *Shadow Dancing in the U.S.A.* Los Angeles: Jeremy Tarcher, 1985. Contains "Hear the Long Snake Moan," an essay about the slavery/ African/Irish/voodoo/jazz roots of the counterculture, and several other fine essays.

Vogel, David. *Lobbying the Corporation: Citizen Challenges to Business Authority*. New York: Basic Books, 1978. A spirited, comprehensive guide to the shareholder protest and corporate social responsibility movement that conveys the fervor that its members felt (and feel) and the stunned, grim resignation that the executives felt.

Von Eschenbach, Wolfram. *The Parzival of Wolfram von Eschenbach*. Trans. Edwin H. Zeydel and Bayard Quincy Morgan. Chapel Hill: University of North Carolina Studies in the Germanic Languages and Literatures, 1951. I chose this translation because it was in verse.

Vonnegut, Kurt. *Player Piano*. New York: Delacorte, 1952. Vonnegut worked at General Electric's "Works" before publishing this novel. It portrays corporate engineering culture vividly and effectively.

Wack, Pierre. "Scenarios: Uncharted Waters Ahead." *Harvard Business Review*, Sept.-Oct. 1985, and "Scenarios: Shooting the Rapids," *Harvard Business Review*, Nov.-Dec. 1985. Those interested in scenarios as useful tools should follow up with Wack's own writing. These clearly written, but dense and oracular reports reward study.

Wack, Pierre. "I Find by Experience . . ." *Harvard Business School Magazine*, 1985. A transcription of Wack's lecture to a Harvard Business School course in country analysis and scenario planning, with Pierre Wack's voice intact.

Wagner, G. A. *Business in the Public Eye: Reflections on the Ethics of Business*. Trans. Theodore Plantinga. Grand Rapids, Mich.: Wm. B. Eerdmans, 1982. Meditations on ethics by a thoughtful Shell managing director.

Wakefield, Walter L., and Evans, Austin P. *Heresies of the High Middle Ages*. New York: Columbia University Press, 1991. A book of rants, exhortations, pleadings, condemnations, and other source documents.

Walton, Richard E. "How to Counter Alienation in the Plant." *Harvard Business Review*, Nov.-Dec. 1972. The ur-article about Topeka, translating its innovative story into language aimed at conventional business academics.

Waterman, Robert. *What America Does Right.* New York: Norton, 1994.
If I were a working manager, I would get a great deal of inspiration from the examples given here.

Weaver, Paul H. *The Suicidal Corporation.* New York: Simon & Schuster, 1988. Great memoir by a former neoconservative writer whose ideals brought him to Ford at a crisis point. True to life about Ford and all other companies.

Weick, Karl. *The Social Psychology of Organizing.* Reading, Mass.: Addison-Wesley, 1969. Why work is worthwhile and how organizations can embody that intrinsic value.

Weisbord, Marv. *Productive Workplaces.* San Francisco: Jossey-Bass, 1987. The first part is a set of in-depth profiles of Frederick Taylor, Kurt Lewin, Douglas McGregor, and Eric Trist; the second part describes how Weisbord himself used their techniques and practices. One of the most valuable books in my library.

Whiteside, Thomas. *The Investigation of Ralph Nader.* New York: Arbor House, 1972. Straightforward journalistic recounting of Nader's trials with General Motors.

Whyte, William H. *The Organization Man.* New York: Simon & Schuster, 1956. Pathfinding excursion into the dark and bright sides of the corporate mentality.

Womack, James P., Jones, Daniel T., and Roos, Daniel. *The Machine That Changed the World.* New York: Rawson Associates, 1990. Evokes the lean idea from the automobile industry outward.

Wren, Daniel A. *The Evolution of Management Thought.* New York: Ronald Press, 1972. A well-written snapshot of management thought as seen in 1972. I was surprised at how often I referred to it.

Yergin, Daniel. *The Prize.* New York: Simon & Schuster, 1991. Complete and highly readable narrative history of the coevolution of the oil industry and "hydrocarbon man." I depended on it as a model and a guide to the oil crisis.

Zager, Robert, and Rosow, Michael P. (eds.). *The Innovative Organization: Productivity Programs in Action.* New York: Pergamon Press, 1982. Reports on real-world quality of working life and sociotechnical experiments, with critical details on key projects, in one fairly slim book.

NOTES

THESE NOTES LIST ALL PUBLISHED SOURCES for quotes and facts throughout this book. Any quote in *The Age of Heretics* that is not attributed with a specific source came from an interview with me. The vast majority of these interviews were conducted between 1988 and 1995, or (in parts of Chapters Eight and Nine) between 2000 and 2005. Updates and corrections may be available at http://www.ageofheretics.com.

CHAPTER ONE

1. J. P. Davis, *Corporations* (New York: Capricorn Books, 1961).

2. P. Drucker, *The Concept of the Corporation* (New York: John Day, 1972), pp. 15–21; P. Drucker, *Adventures of a Bystander* (New York: HarperCollins, 1978), pp. 264–265; G. Wise, "General Electric's Century," unpublished manuscript, 1992, p. 10; H. T. Johnson and R. S. Kaplan, *Relevance Lost* (Boston: Harvard Business School Press, 1991), pp. 110–112 and elsewhere.

3. I. Illich, "Vernacular Values," *CoEvolution Quarterly*, Summer 1980, pp. 30, 41.

4. F. Braudel, *The Wheels of Commerce* (New York: HarperCollins, 1979), pp. 120–123.

5. Illich elaborates on this point in his book *Gender* (New York: Pantheon, 1982).

6. R. Heilbroner, *The Worldly Philosophers: The Lives, Times, and Ideas of the Great Economic Thinkers*, 6th ed. (New York: Simon & Schuster, 1986), pp. 34ff.

7. Elin Smith helped me see this, partly in e-mail and partly in her article "The Vindication of Karl Marx," *Whole Earth Review*, 1992, 74, 86.

8. J. K. Galbraith, *The New Industrial State* (Boston: Houghton Mifflin, 1967), Chaps 5. and 6, particularly pp. 107–108.

9. J. B. Russell, *Witchcraft in the Middle Ages* (Ithaca, N.Y.: Cornell University Press, 1972), p. 5.

10. This story, often told by Pierre Wack, was written up by P. Schwartz, *The Art of the Long View* (New York: Doubleday/Currency, 1991), p. 120.

11. T. Johnson, "Accounting and the Rise of Remote-Control Management: Holding Firm by Losing Touch," *Accounting History,* 2002, 7(1), 9–21. Also see Johnson and Kaplan, *Relevance Lost.*

12. P. Drucker, *The Practice of Management* (New York: HarperCollins, 1954), p. 30.

13. N. Fligstein, *The Transformation of Corporate Control* (Cambridge, Mass.: Harvard University Press, 1990), p. 140.

14. G. R. Brown, "The Business That Could Not Fail," *Audacity,* Summer 1995, p. 46.

15. Johnson and Kaplan, *Relevance Lost.* The pivotal chapter of Sloan's memoir, *My Years with General Motors* (New York: Doubleday, 1990), is "The Development of Financial Controls," and it concerns his successful efforts to use Brown's formulas to get GM's famous automobile divisions (Buick, Chevrolet, Pontiac, Cadillac, and Oldsmobile) "under control." The company had been buffeted by the business turndown of 1921, and Sloan had vowed it would never happen again. It never did, because the financial controls ensured that division heads, no matter how much rivalry they felt toward each other, would not work at cross-purposes. One division would not be profligate with expenses while another was cutting pennies.

16. To use just four examples from J. K. Shim, J. G. Siegel, and A. J. Simon, *The Vest-Pocket MBA* (Upper Saddle River, N.J.: Prentice Hall, 1986).

17. See, for example, A. Ries and J. Trout, *Marketing Warfare* (New York: McGraw-Hill, 1986).

18. Alvin Toffler talks at length about this in *The Third Wave* (New York: Morrow, 1980), particularly in the chapter "The Invisible Wedge." Toffler takes a lot of his historical understanding from F. Braudel, *Capitalism and Material Life* (New York: HarperCollins, 1973).

19. This example comes from E. P. Thompson, *Customs in Common* (New York: Norton, 1991).

20. See, for example, the evocative chapter, "The Numbers," in H. Geneen with A. Moscow, *Managing* (New York: Doubleday, 1984).

21. See F. Kofman, "Double-Loop Accounting," in P. Senge and others, *The Fifth Discipline Fieldbook* (New York: Doubleday, 1994), p. 286; and D. Meador, "Measuring to Report . . . or to Learn?" in P. Senge and others, *The Dance of Change* (New York: Doubleday, 1999), p. 298.

22. B. Fuller, *A Grunch of Giants* (Santa Barbara, Calif.: Buckminster Fuller Institute, 1995), p. 2, and *Everything I Know* (Santa Barbara, Calif.: Buckminster Fuller Institute, 1975), Vol. 5, tape 27A, counter 1842.

23. Fuller, *Everything I Know.*

24. E. J. Kahn, "We Look Forward to Seeing You Next Year," *New Yorker,* June 20, 1970, p. 49.

25. G. S. Crystal, *In Search of Excess* (New York: Norton, 1991), p. 187.

26. W. H. Whyte, *City* (New York: Doubleday, 1988), pp. 291–293.

27. F. Braudel, *The Perspective of the World* (New York: HarperCollins, 1981), p. 629.

28. M. Maccoby, *The Gamesman* (New York: Simon & Schuster, 1976). Maccoby's research was based on his work on Mexican villages with Erich Fromm. See E. Fromm and M. Maccoby, *Social Character in a Mexican Village: A Sociopsychoanalytic Study* (Upper Saddle River, N.J.: Prentice Hall, 1970), which was based on E. Fromm, *Man for Himself* (New York: Holt, 1947). Illich's ideas about the value of the vernacular influenced Fromm, Maccoby, and this book.

29. Maccoby, *The Gamesman.*

30. W. Whyte, *The Organization Man* (New York: Simon & Schuster, 1956).

31. Maccoby, *The Gamesman,* p. 148.

32. This quotation and the closing story about the "hero factor" are from Doug Carmichael, a psychoanalyst who worked as one of Maccoby's researchers.

33. Maccoby, *The Gamesman,* pp. 200–201, 220–223.

CHAPTER TWO

1. B. R. Rees, *Pelagius: A Reluctant Heretic* (Suffolk, U.K.: Boydell Press, 1988); D. Christie-Murray, *A History of Heresy* (London: New English Library, 1976), pp. 87–92; and Anthony Burgess, *The Wanting Seed* (New York: Heinemann, 1962), especially the Foreword.

2. I would like to acknowledge people who were significant in the National Training Laboratories, Tavistock, and organization development history, but whose stories I do not have room to include as I would like in this chapter and Chapter Seven: Billie Alban, Alex Bavelas, Dick Beckhard, David Berlew, Lee Bolman, Harold Bridger, Werner Burke, Robert Chin, Jim Clark, Kathy Dannemiller, Morton Deutsch, Jack Glidewell, Roger

Harrison, Jerry Harvey, Robert Kahn, Rensis Likert, Gordon Lippitt, Alfred
Marrow, Elizabeth Menzies, Barry Oshry, Mickie Ritvo, Will Schutz, Herb
Shepard, Robert Tannenbaum, John Weir, Tommy Wilson, and many,
many others.

3. K. D. Benne, "The Processes of Re-Education: An Assessment of Kurt
Lewin's Views," in W. Benniss, K. Benne, and R. Chin (eds.), *The Planning
of Change,* 3rd ed. (New York: Holt, 1976), pp. 315–316.

4. The play was produced in 1948, and the movie came out in 1957. The
movie, based on a book by Richard Bissell (*Seven and a Half Cents*), was
directed by George Abbott, choreographed by Bob Fosse, and released by
Warner Brothers; it starred Doris Day and John Raitt.

5. "A person and his psychological environment, Lewin insisted, are
dynamically one field," Alfred Marrow wrote in a biography of his mentor.
"They should never be treated as separate entities. From early childhood,
social facts—especially the sense of belonging to particular groups—are
among the most fundamental determinants of the child's growing world, for
they shape his wishes and goals and what he considers right and wrong."
A. Marrow, *The Practical Theorist* (New York: Basic Books, 1969),
p. 110. Also see Kurt Lewin, *A Dynamic Theory of Personality: Selected
Papers,* trans. D. K. Adams and K. E. Zener (New York: McGraw-Hill,
1935), pp. 66ff.

6. Lewin may have been the first modern researcher to articulate the idea of
creative tension, the valuable stress that stems from simultaneous awareness
of aspiration and current reality and pulls people forward toward their
goals. See R. Fritz's "structural tension" in *The Path of Least Resistance*
(New York: Fawcett, 1989); P. Senge's "creative tension" in *The Fifth
Discipline* (New York: Doubleday, 1990), pp. 150–155; and Marrow in
The Practical Theorist, pp. 30–32.

7. Weisbord describes how Lippitt and Lewin coined the name *group
dynamics* in 1939 and how originally Lewin meant "groups of forces"
rather than "groups of people" but came to change his approach.
M. Weisbord, *Productive Workplaces* (San Francisco: Jossey-Bass, 1987),
pp. 83–84.

8. M. Hunt, *The Story of Psychology* (New York: Doubleday, 1993).

9. K. Lewin, R. Lippitt, and R. K. White, "Patterns of Aggressive Behavior
in Experimentally Created Social Climates," *Journal of Social Psychology,*
1939, *10,* 271–279. Also see R. Lippitt and R. K. White, *Autocracy and
Democracy: An Experimental Inquiry* (New York: HarperCollins, 1960).

10. Lippitt and White, *Autocracy and Democracy,* p. 25.

11. This statement of Benne's mistrust is adapted from a line written in
    J. Hirsch, "A History of the NTL Institute for Applied Behavioral Science,
    1947–1986" (unpublished Ed.D. dissertation, Boston University, 1986).

12. R. Lippitt, *Training in Community Relations* (New York: HarperCollins,
    1949), p. 116.

13. L. P. Bradford, *National Training Laboratories: Its History, 1947–1970*
    (Bethel, Me.: NTL Institute for Applied Behavioral Science, 1974), p. 48.

14. Bradford, *National Training Laboratories,* p. 81.

15. "Research Center for Group Dynamics," Institute for Social Research,
    University of Michigan, Mar. 22, 2008, http://www.rcgd.isr.umich.edu/
    history/.

16. Bradford, *National Training Laboratories,* p. 167.

17. Bradford, *National Training Laboratories,* p. 73.

18. David Bradford, son of Leland, to the author, 1994.

19. Some of this sequence comes from L. P. Bradford, "Trainer-Intervention:
    Case Episodes," in L. P. Bradford, J. R. Gibb, and K. D. Benne (eds.),
    T-Group Theory and Laboratory Method (Hoboken, N.J.: Wiley, 1964),
    p. 136. I also drew from S. Klaw, "Two Weeks in a T-Group," *Fortune,*
    Aug. 1961; A. Friendly, "Where Bosses Let Down Their Hair," *Washington
    Post,* Nov. 27, 1966; and "What Makes a Small Group Tick," *Business
    Week,* Aug. 13, 1955.

20. These lectures would cover, for example, the theories of Wilfred Bion,
    Jacob Moreno, and Eric Trist. Much of the group dynamics work at NTL
    was deeply influenced by the Tavistock Institute of Human Relations.
    See M. Weisbord, *Productive Workplaces* (San Francisco: Jossey-Bass,
    1987), pp. 146–149; and K. Back, *Beyond Words* (New York: Russell Sage
    Foundation, 1972), pp. 62–64.

21. C. Seashore, E. Seashore, and G. M. Weinberg, *What Did You Say? The Art
    of Giving and Receiving FeedBack* (North Attleborough, Mass.: Douglas
    Charles Press, 1992), pp. 4–11.

22. There are many different versions of this story, with many people credited.
    Sometimes it's newsprint from a print shop. In one version, it was a butcher
    shop and the paper was butcher paper; in another, it was the *Bethel Citizen.*
    Weisbord, *Productive Workplaces,* p. 100, says it actually happened at the
    Connecticut Workshop in 1946.

23. Excerpt from Maslow's journal in his *Abraham H. Maslow: A Memorial
    Volume,* compiled with the assistance of B. G. Maslow (Belmont, Calif.:
    Wadsworth, 1972), p. 92. Maslow labeled T-Groups a "peak experience"

on p. 52 of the same book. Carl Rogers wrote similarly about T-Groups in *Carl Rogers on Encounter Groups* (New York: Harrow Books, 1970).

24. A. Gabor, *The Capitalist Philosophers: The Geniuses of Modern Business— Their Lives, Times and Ideas* (New York: Times Books, 2000), Chap. 6.

25. Friendly, "What Makes a Small Group Tick."

26. C. Crockett and R. Boyer. "An O.D. Expert in the Cat Bird's Seat," *Journal of Higher Education* (Ohio State University), 1972, p. 395. This was an interview with Warren Bennis.

27. Friendly, "Where Bosses Let Down Their Hair."

28. J. Luft and H. Ingham, "The Johari Window, a Graphic Model of Interpersonal Awareness," in *Proceedings of the Western Training Laboratory in Group Development* (Los Angeles: UCLA, 1955). Also see "Johari Window," retrieved Mar. 2008 from Wikipedia, http://en.wikipedia .org/wiki/Johari_Window.

29. D. McGregor, *The Human Side of Enterprise, Annotated Edition* (New York: McGraw-Hill, 2005) pp. 345, 352.

30. Warren Bennis suggested this point.

31. Some of this charge is represented in C. Hampden-Turner, "An Existential 'Learning Theory' and the Integration of T-Group Research," in R. T. Golembiewski and A. Blumberg, *Sensitivity Training and the Laboratory Approach* (Itasca, Ill.: F. E. Peacock, 1970). It also appears in Rogers, *Carl Rogers on Encounter Groups.* William H. Whyte opened *The Organization Man* with an attack on the leaderless groups of NTL on p. 54.

32. E. H. Schein, *Brainwashing* (Cambridge, Mass.: Center for International Studies, MIT, 1961).

33. Schein, *Brainwashing;* Schein, "The Academic as Artist: Personal and Professional Roots" (unpublished paper, Oct. 1990); and Schein, "Management Development as a Process of Influence," *Industrial Management Review,* May 1961.

34. Schein, "Management Development as a Process of Influence."

35. "Bayway Refinery," Wikipedia, retrieved Dec. 23, 2007, from http:// en.wikipedia.org/wiki/Bayway_Refinery.

36. Standard Oil of New Jersey, descended directly from John D. Rockefeller's original oil company, had a surfeit of names. Its chief brand, sold in the East, was Esso, named after the letters "S" and "O." Antitrust suits had forced it to use the brand names *Enco and Humble* elsewhere. Its own managers called it Esso, while oilmen at other companies called it Jersey. In 1972, all these identities were gathered together under the name Exxon.

37. See, for example, T. Geohegan, *Whose Side Are You On? (Trying to Be for Labor When It's Flat on Its Back)* (New York: Farrar, Strauss, Giroux, 1991), pp. 52–53.

38. I. L. Neill Hicks, "Forgotten Voices: Women in Organizational Development and Human Resource Development" (unpublished doctoral dissertation, University of Texas at Austin, 1991), University Microfilms 9128249, pp. 65–86.

39. R. Blake and J. S. Mouton, *Diary of an OD Man* (Houston: Gulf Publishing, 1976).

40. This episode takes place in Chapter Eight in "Headquarters Intervenes," in Blake and Mouton, *Diary of an OD Man,* p. 63.

41. Blake and Mouton, *Diary of an OD Man,* p. 10.

42. R. Blake and J. S. Mouton, *The Managerial Grid* (Houston: Gulf Publishing, 1964), p. 10.

43. All of this comes from R. Blake and J. S. Mouton, *Corporate Excellence Through Grid Organization Development: A Systems Approach* (Houston: Gulf Publishing, 1968).

44. R. R. Blake, "Memories of HRD," *Training and Development,* Mar. 1995.

45. J. W. Pfeiffer and J. E. Jones, *Structured Experiences for Human Relations Training,* Vol. 1 (Tucson, Ariz.: University Associates, 1969).

CHAPTER THREE

1. Tavistock was a complex organization, composed of a psychiatric clinic (associated with the British Health Service) and a separate but related research institute. Two influential psychoanalytic figures at Tavistock were Melanie Klein and Wilfred Bion. See M. Weisbord, *Productive Workplaces* (San Francisco: Jossey-Bass, 1987); and H. V. Dicks, *Fifty Years of the Tavistock Clinic* (London: Routledge & Kegan Paul, 1970).

2. E. H. Schein, *Organizational Psychology,* 3rd ed. (Upper Saddle River, N.J.: Prentice Hall, 1980), pp. 60–61.

3. The concept of open systems came primarily from the work of Eric Trist. See Trist, *The Evolution of Socio-Technical Systems* (Toronto: Ontario Quality of Working Life Centre, 1981), and "Culture as a Psycho-Social Process," paper T.1059, revised 1967 (for the celebration book for Sir Frederic Bartlett's Eightieth Birthday); Weisbord, *Productive Workplaces*; F. E. Emery and E. L. Trist, "Socio-Technical Systems," in C. W. Churchman and M. Verhulst (eds.), *Management Science, Models and Techniques* (New York: Pergamon, 1960), pp. 83–97.

4. The stories linking self-managing work teams to anti-Nazi resistance are generally credited to Norwegian sociotechnical pioneer Einar Thorsrud. See Weisbord, *Productive Workplaces,* p. 165. One knowledgeable source, Max Elden, discounts the story as I have told it here.

5. The resulting paper was Emery and Trist, "The Causal Texture of Organizational Environments," *Human Relations,* 1965, *18,* 21–32.

6. L. von Bertalanffy, "The Theory of Open Systems in Physics and Biology," *Science,* 1950, *3,* 23–29. Also see D. Katz and R. L. Kahn, *The Social Psychology of Organizations* (Hoboken, N.J.: Wiley, 1966), pp. 14–29. The ovum example comes from Katz and Kahn. (They talked specifically about sea urchin ova.)

7. Weisbord, *Productive Workplaces.*

8. D. A. Wren, *The Evolution of Management Thought* (New York: Ronald Press, 1972), p. 127.

9. The story that follows is partly based on, and complementary to, the story told in R. Waterman, *What America Does Right* (New York: Norton, 1994), pp. 36ff.

10. At least four people, in various versions of the story, are credited with introducing sociotechnical techniques into P&G: Charles Eberle, Dave Swanson, Phil Willard, and John Anderson. In crediting McGregor with helping design the Augusta plant, I am choosing to follow the account given by Waterman. Others in P&G say that McGregor did little more than make speeches. It is certain that Dick Beckhard, who worked closely with McGregor and taught with him at MIT, was closely involved in consulting on the design of Mehoopany.

11. The quote about "navel examining" comes from Charles Eberle, who managed the Sacramento plant in the early 1960s. He later promoted the technician system throughout Procter's international system.

12. This happened, almost verbatim in 1973, to someone I interviewed.

13. Waterman, *What America Does Right,* p. 47.

14. D. Jenkins, *Job Power: Blue and White Collar Democracy* (New York: Doubleday, 1973). Also, correspondence from Michael Brower in 1995 and 2007–2008.

15. Many people associated with the T-Group movement had settled at UCLA. Among them were Robert Tannenbaum, Jim Clark, Richard Walton, and some prominent psychologists, including Carl Roberts and Abraham Maslow, who were exploring the idea of humanizing business. Finally, there was a large sociotechnical contingent there, spearheaded by an

organizational sciences professor named Lou Davis, who brought Eric Trist in from the Tavistock Institute in 1966. The organization development and sociotechnical movements, once linked through Trist's friendship with McGregor, had now fallen apart, but when the P&G contingent arrived at UCLA with curiosity about both schools of thought, the two groups of professors (whose officers were down the hall from each other) discovered they had much to talk about.

16. J. G. Bennett, *Is There "Life" on Earth? An Introduction to Gurdjieff* (New York: Stonehill, 1973), p. 77.

17. C. G. Krone, "Open Systems Redesign," in W. W. Burke (ed.), *Contemporary OD: Conceptual Orientations and Interventions* (La Jolla, Calif.: University Associates, 1975), pp. 364ff; "Seminar by Charles Krone of the International Development Organization," *Massachusetts Quality of Working Life Center Newsletter,* June 1977, p. 6; Waterman, *What America Does Right,* p. 64.

18. "Seminar by Charles Krone," p. 6.

19. Krone, "Open Systems Redesign," p. 366. Social psychologist Karl Weick describes a theory similar to Krone's flower theory. The most satisfying thing any of us can get out of work, he said, is not money but "the removal of equivocality." A pile of component chemicals is highly "equivocal"; it can be made into many different products. It's satisfying to make that lump more specific by turning it into detergent, and more satisfying still to make a bottled product, from start to finish, continually improving the process for yourself. That's why mechanized processes dehumanize and why workers seek money in compensation. See K. Weick, *The Social Psychology of Organizing* (Reading, Mass.: Addison-Wesley, 1969), pp. 75–76.

20. See, for example, K. Grichnik and C. Winkler, *Make or Break: How Manufacturers Can Leap from Decline to Revitalization* (New York: McGraw-Hill, 2008), pp. 7–8.

21. L. Ketchum, "A Case Study of Diffusion," in L. E. Davis, A. B. Cherns, and Associates, *The Quality of Working Life* (New York: Free Press, 1975), p. 140.

22. "If we want workers to work . . . willingly and well, we must give them the right to think. . . . We must welcome the expression of their thinking and let management decisions be influenced by it. We must even delegate some decisions directly to the workers; for instance, decisions on all phases of safety, on some or all phases of house rules and discipline, on many phases of technological changes. . . . There must be an increasing supply of the facts, which have been the exclusive property of management because only

management needed them for its thinking." A. R. Heron, *Why Men Work* (Stanford, Calif.: Stanford University Press, 1948), p. 175.

23. The champion of the study, Jack Shipman of the Post division's market research department, was given the same treatment for his career that Lyman Ketchum got.

24. This story is told in C. Havener with M. Thorpe, *Discovering the Lost Spirit of Business* (Forest Lake, Minn.: Growth Resource Group, 1994), pp. 30–41. Havener is the former General Foods manager who proposed the package redesign for Biscuits and Bits shortly before he left the company.

25. They were advised in this by Dick Walton.

26. The planning group included Ketchum, Dulworth, Don Lafond (see later in the chapter), Robert Mech, and Phil Simshauser. Mech and Simshauser took jobs at Topeka as managers.

27. "Topeka Organization and Systems Development," internal General Foods document, Oct. 24, 1969.

28. Other key corporate champions at GF were Art Larkin and Ross Barzelay.

29. J. Stone, letter to the author, 1994.

30. D. Jenkins, "Democracy in the Factory: A Report on the Movement to Abolish the Organization Chart," *Atlantic Monthly,* Apr. 1973, p. 78.

31. M. Brimm, *Analytical Perspectives in Organizational Behavior: A Study of an Organizational Innovation* (Cambridge, Mass.: Harvard University, School of Business, Department of Business Administration, 1975), p. V-7.

32. Brimm, *Analytical Perspectives in Organizational Behavior,* p. V-5.

33. Brimm, *Analytical Perspectives in Organizational Behavior,* p. V-31.

34. Brimm, *Analytical Perspectives in Organizational Behavior,* p. V-51.

35. Brimm, *Analytical Perspectives in Organizational Behavior,* p. V-53.

36. Brimm, *Analytical Perspectives in Organizational Behavior,* p. X-5.

37. Brimm, *Analytical Perspectives in Organizational Behavior,* p. V-53.

38. Brimm, *Analytical Perspectives in Organizational Behavior,* p. VII-17.

39. K. Bradsher, "Donald F. Ephlin, 74; Helped U.A.W. Fashion Saturn Agreement," *New York Times,* June 3, 2000; J. O'Toole and E. E. Lawler III, *The New American Workplace* (New York: Palgrave Macmillan, 2006), p. 172.

40. L. Ketchum and E. Trist, *All Teams Are Not Created Equal* (Thousand Oaks, Calif.: Sage, 1992).

41. R. Walton, "How to Counter Alienation in the Plant," *Harvard Business Review,* Nov.-Dec. 1972, pp. 70ff; particularly see pp. 71–74. Also see Special Task Force to the Secretary of Health, Education and Welfare, *Work in America* (Cambridge, Mass.: MIT Press, 1973).

42. "The Job Blahs: Who Wants to Work?" *Newsweek,* Mar. 26, 1973; "Productivity: The New Stakhanovites," *Time,* Feb. 12, 1973.

43. Jenkins, *Job Power,* p. 103.

44. A. Kleiner, "Management Bites Dog Food Factory," *Fast Company,* June 1996, http://www.fastcompany.com/magazine/03/ideas.html.

45. M. Hooper, "Del Monte Picks Topeka to Expand: Distribution Center Will Create 80 Jobs," *Capital-Journal,* Oct. 30, 2007, http://cjonline.com/stories/103007/bre_delmonte.shtml; A. Cohen, "Building a Company of Leaders," *Leader to Leader,* Spring 2004.

CHAPTER FOUR

1. The heretic's speech is adapted from "A Vindication of the Church of God," circa 1250, in "The Catharist Church and Its Interpretation of the Lord's Prayer," in W. L. Wakefield and A. P. Evans, *Heresies of the High Middle Ages* (New York: Columbia University Press, 1991), pp. 592ff.

2. This line comes from "A Debate Between Catholics and Heretics," in Wakefield and Evans, *Heresies of the High Middle Ages,* p. 189.

3. Some of this material is influenced by J. Campbell, *In Search of the Holy Grail* (St. Paul, Minn.: HighBridge Productions, 1990) (cassette recording).

4. P. Collier and D. Horowitz, *The Fords* (New York: Summit Books, 1987), pp. 62–63.

5. R. S. Tedlow, *Giants of Enterprise: Seven Business Innovators and the Empires They Built* (New York: HarperBusiness, 2001), pp. 119–120; P. Collier and D. Horowitz, *The Fords: An American Epic* (New York: Summit Books, 1987), p. 83; A. Kleiner, *Who Really Matters* (New York: Doubleday, 2003), pp. 200–201; A. Kleiner, "Apocalypse 2010?" *strategy+business,* Fourth Quarter 2002.

6. N. Mourkogiannis, *The Starting Point of Great Companies* (New York: Palgrave, 2006), p. 95.

7. V. S. Clyne offers this definition of corporate purpose: "A corporation's purpose is to maximize shareholder wealth, defined as the present discounted value of all future profits. In other words, the longer a

shareholder has to wait for future profits, the less they are worth." Clyne to the author, 1992.

8. I acknowledge that this inquiry is the basis of stakeholder theory, as set out in R. E. Freeman, *Strategic Management: A Stakeholder Approach* (New York: Pitman, 1984). I have not written about stakeholder theory in this book because it seems like a nonheretical way of evading the issues raised in corporate responsibility. I buy the arguments made by E. Sternberg, *Just Business: Business Ethics in Action* (Boston: Little, Brown, 1994), pp. 51–53.

9. M. Kelly, *The Divine Right of Capital: Dethroning the Corporate Aristocracy* (San Francisco: Berrett-Koehler, 2001).

10. M. Moskowitz, R. Levering, and M. Katz, *Everybody's Business: The Irreverent Guide to Corporate America* (New York: HarperCollins, 1980).

11. A. L. Whitaker, "Anatomy of a Riot," *Crisis,* Jan. 1965, pp. 20–25.

12. S. Sethi, *Business Corporations and the Black Man* (Scranton, Pa.: Chandler, 1970), pp. 67–68.

13. S. Horwitt, *Let Them Call Me Rebel* (New York: Knopf, 1989), p. 456.

14. Horwitt, *Let Them Call Me Rebel*, p. 453.

15. Horwitt, *Let Them Call Me Rebel*, pp. 451–452.

16. Alinsky, *Rules for Radicals* (New York: Random House, 1971), p. 91.

17. Horwitt, *Let Them Call Me Rebel*, p. 457.

18. Alinsky, *Rules for Radicals*, p. 138.

19. Horwitt, *Let Them Call Me Rebel*, p. 465.

20. Having picked the acronym, they selected its component rhetorical parts: "Freedom, Integration, Honor, God, Today." "God" was Alinsky's own last-minute suggestion, and "Integration" was later changed to "Independence." Horwitt, *Let Them Call Me Rebel*, p. 461.

21. Sethi, *Business Corporations and the Black Man*, p. 76.

22. Alinsky, *Rules for Radicals*, p. 102.

23. Sethi, *Business Corporations and the Black Man*, p. 52.

24. Horwitt, *Let Them Call Me Rebel*, p. 489.

25. Much of this comes from Sethi, *Business Corporations and the Black Man*, pp. 11–12, 26–27.

26. Sethi, *Business Corporations and the Black Man*, p. 50.

27. Horwitt, *Let Them Call Me Rebel*, p. 492; Sethi, *Business Corporations and the Black Man*, p. 35; R. Beardwood, "The Southern Roots of the Urban Crisis," *Fortune,* Aug. 1968; R.D.G. Wadhwani, "Kodak, Fight

and the Definition of Civil Rights in Rochester, New York 1966–1967,"
   Historian, 1997, 60(1), 59–75.

28. Sethi, *Business Corporations and the Black Man.*

29. Sethi, *Business Corporations and the Black Man,* p. 35.

30. Gilbert is quoted in L. Talner, *The Origins of Shareholder Activism*
   (Washington, D.C.: Investor Responsibility Research Center, 1983), p. 5.

31. Alinsky, *Rules for Radicals,* p. 178.

32. P. Drucker, *The Unseen Revolution: How Pension Fund Socialism Came to
   America* (New York: HarperCollins, 1976). This book, incidentally, was the
   most visible unfulfilled prediction that Peter Drucker made: he predicted
   that pension funds as corporate investors would alter the relationship
   between management and labor. In the end, the prevalence of pension fund
   investment has diffused ownership and made it more difficult for either
   managers or shareholders to take control of an enterprise. It has been a
   great force for the status quo.

33. F. Norris, "As Magellan Makes Big Bets, the Risks Rise," *New York Times,*
   Dec. 11, 1994, p. 3:1.

34. English was interviewed in Editors of Institutional Investor, *The Way It Was:
   An Oral History of Finance, 1967–1987* (New York: Morrow, 1988), p. 33.

35. See, for instance, R. Sobel, *The Rise and Fall of the Conglomerate Kings*
   (New York: Stein & Day, 1984).

36. S. P. Sethi, *Up Against the Corporate Wall: Modern Corporations and
   the Social Issues of the Seventies* (Upper Saddle River, N.J.: Prentice Hall,
   1971), p. 124, quoting John Kifner, "Twenty-One Churches Withhold
   Proxies to Fight Kodak Rights Policies," *New York Times,* Apr. 7, 1967.

37. Horwitt, *Let Them Call Me Rebel,* p. 498. Also Alinsky, *Rules for Radicals,*
   p. 173.

38. Sethi, *Up Against the Corporate Wall,* p. 126.

39. J. Aroune, "Eltrex: Born of Diversity," Apr. 16, 2006, RNews.com,
   http://www.rnews.com/Story_2004.cfm?ID=36928&rnews_story_
   type=17&category=10; "Xerox Claims World-Class Supplier Diversity
   Status," *Diversity/Careers in Engineering and Technology,* Feb.–Mar. 2005,
   http://www.diversitycareers.com/articles/pro/05-febmar/sd_xerox.htm.

40. Alinsky, *Rules for Radicals,* p. 175.

41. D. Nasaw, *Andrew Carnegie* (New York: Penguin, 2006).

42. S. Melman, *The Defense Economy* (New York: Praeger, 1971); S. Melman,
   Pentagon Capitalism (New York: McGraw-Hill, 1967).

43. Collier and Horowitz, *The Fords,* pp. 276–278, 309–310.

44. "Mister Ford: They Never Call Him Henry," *Time,* July 20, 1970, p. 67;
D. Halberstam, *The Reckoning* (New York: Morrow, 1986), p. 192;
B. Herndon, *Ford: An Unconventional Biography of the Men and Their
Times* (New York: Weybright and Talley, 1969), p. 24; W. Serrin,
"At Ford Everyone Knows Who Is the Boss," *New York Times Magazine,*
Oct. 19, 1969.

45. Collier and Horowitz, *The Fords,* p. 332.

46. M. Moskowitz, *Business and Society,* July 30, 1968; see also Collier and
Horowitz, *The Fords,* p. 334.

47. Most of this is from "The Executive as Social Activist," *Time,* July 20, 1970.

48. *Business and Society,* Jan. 7, 1969.

49. *Business and Society,* Oct. 22, Dec. 3, 1968.

50. *Business and Society,* Apr. 8, 1969.

51. *Business and Society,* Nov. 25, 1969, Oct. 14, 1969, p. 1.

52. Henry Ford II, speech at Vanderbilt University, 1969.

53. Collier and Horowitz, *The Fords,* tell several such stories—one, in
particular, about the battle over embracing or fighting safety standards.

54. D. Vogel, *Lobbying the Corporation: Citizen Challenges to Business
Authority* (New York: Basic Books, 1978), pp. 48–55.

55. "Nader Panel Rebuffed by GM on Plea to List Customer Demands," *Wall
Street Journal,* Mar. 6, 1970, p. 14.

56. D. L. Kanter and P. Mirvis, *The Cynical Americans: Living and Working in
an Age of Discontent and Disillusion* (San Francisco: Jossey-Bass, 1989),
p. 113; B. Kremen, "Lordstown—Searching for a Better Way of Work,"
New York Times, Sept. 9, 1973, 3:1.

57. B. Tuchman, *The March of Folly: From Troy to Vietnam* (New York:
Knopf, 1984), p. 62.

58. D. Cordtz, "Henry Ford, Superstar," *Fortune,* May 1973, p. 285.

59. T. Whiteside, *The Investigation of Ralph Nader* (New York: Arbor House,
1972), p. 9.

60. Whiteside, *The Investigation of Ralph Nader,* pp. 25–29, 164.

61. P. F. Drucker, *The Age of Discontinuity* (New York: HarperCollins, 1967),
pp. 203–204.

62. Talner, *The Origins of Shareholder Activism,* p. 14.

63. D. E. Schwartz, "The Public-Interest Proxy Contest: Reflections on
Campaign GM," *Michigan Law Review,* Jan. 1971, p. 426.

64. H. Henderson, "Should Business Tackle Society's Problems?" *Harvard Business Review,* 1968, 46(4).

65. E. J. Kahn, Jr., "We Look Forward to Seeing You Next Year," *New Yorker,* June 20, 1970, p. 40.

66. Talner, *The Origins of Shareholder Activism,* p. 20.

67. Kahn, "We Look Forward to Seeing You Next Year," p. 42.

68. M. Moskowitz, *Business and Society,* Jan. 7, 1969, pp. 2–3.

69. Vogel, *Lobbying the Corporation,* p. 176.

70. Milton Friedman, "The Social Responsibility of Business Is to Increase Its Profits," *New York Times Magazine,* Oct. 4, 1970, p. 32.

71. M. Moskowitz, *Business and Society,* May 23, 1972, p. 1.

72. Horwitt, *Let Them Call Me Rebel,* p. 533.

73. Alinsky, *Rules for Radicals,* pp. 190–196.

74. For example, J. Gilmore and J. Pine, "The End of Corporate Social Responsibility," *Harvard Business Online,* Dec. 26, 2007, http:// conversationstarter.hbsp.com/2007/12/the_end_of_corporate_social_ re.html?cm_mmc=npv-_-hbopostcard-_-Dec2007-_-TheYearAhead.

75. J. Brown, "Change, Challenge, and Community," privately circulated paper, 1994, p. 7. Fred Ross and Ed Chambers, two of Alinsky's longtime associates, have also commented on this.

76. J. Brown, "Si, Se Puede—Yes, It Can Be Done!" privately circulated paper, 1994; J. Brown and D. Isaacs, *The World Café* (San Francisco: Berrett-Koehler, 2005).

CHAPTER FIVE

1. K. Krabbenhoft, "Reading the Mystics: Allegories of Body, Garden and Temple in the Classical Literature of Western Mysticism," unpublished manuscript, 1989.

2. *A History of the Royal Dutch/Shell Group of Companies* (London: Royal Dutch/Shell Group Public Affairs, 1988).

3. D. Wade, taped interview with T. Newland, May 13, 1994, Cybard, France; untitled internal document for Shell Group Planning, p. 1.

4. In 1966, the Seven Sisters sold 90 percent of the world's petroleum. Three were remnants of the old John D. Rockefeller monopoly: Standard Oil of New Jersey (Esso, Enco), Standard Oil of California (Chevron), and Mobil. Two were large companies with roots in Texas: Texaco and Gulf. A sixth company, British Petroleum, owed its heritage to the long-standing

relationship between Britain and Persia (it was previously called Anglo-Iranian). Royal Dutch/Shell was the seventh.

5. "The Seventh Sister," *Forbes*, Nov. 15, 1972.

6. P.D.S. Hadfield, "From Scenarios to Strategy," presented at Top Management Forum, Managing in the 1990s: Crafting and Implementing Strategy in a Changing Global Environment, Paris, June 13–14, 1990.

7. A. Hamilton, *The Price of Power* (London: Rainbird, 1986). See also D. Yergin, *The Prize* (New York: Simon & Schuster, 1991). On the Six-Day War, see A. Sampson, *The Seven Sisters: The Great Oil Companies and the World They Shaped* (New York: Viking Press, 1975).

8. Yergin, *The Prize*, pp. 65–69.

9. H. Higdon, *The Business Healer* (New York: Random House, 1969), pp. 48, 134.

10. P. W. Beck, "Strategic Planning in the Royal Dutch/Shell Group" (paper presented to the Conference on Corporate Strategic Planning, Institute of Management Science, New Orleans, 1977). "Royal Dutch Shell," Wikipedia, retrieved Mar. 2008 from www.//en.wikipedia.org/wiki/Royal_Dutch/Shell#Businesses.

11. H. Kahn, *On Thermonuclear War* (Princeton, N.J.: Princeton University Press, 1960), p. 19.

12. J. R. Newman, "This Is . . ." (review of *On Thermonuclear War*), *Scientific American*, Mar. 1961; F. Kaplan, *The Wizards of Armageddon* (New York: Simon & Schuster, 1983), p. 228; S. Ghamari-Tabrizi, *The Worlds of Herman Kahn: The Intuitive Science of Thermonuclear War* (Cambridge, Mass.: Harvard University Press, 2005), pp. 288–291.

13. W. A. McWhirter, "I Am One of the Ten Most Famous Obscure Americans," *Life*, Dec. 6, 1968; also see Kaplan, *The Wizards of Armageddon*, pp. 57, 61, 220.

14. Wade, taped interview with Newland, 1994, p. 8.

15. An alternative history for the term has it coming from military uses, through the Office of Strategic Services to RAND. I prefer this story, which comes directly from an interview with Leo Rosten.

16. H. Kahn and A. J. Weiner, *The Year 2000* (New York: Macmillan, 1968), Chap. 4.

17. Tony Weiner phrased this point in *The Year 2000* this way: "Our own Standard World, adumbrated throughout the volume, reflects our own expectations, of course, and we have tried to make these explicit as much as possible" (p. 8).

18. "Herman Kahn's Thinkable Future," *Business Week,* Mar. 11, 1967, p. 116.

19. Kahn, *The Year 2000,* p. 137; E. Parker, *Objectif 10% de Croissance* (Paris: Criterion, 1993).

20. H. J. Alkema and E. V. Newland, "Increased Efficiency of the Use of Energy Resources" (paper presented at the Institute of Petroleum Summer Meeting, Harrogate, U.K., June 5–8, 1973).

21. *International Petroleum Monthly: OECD Countries and World Petroleum (Oil) Demand, 1970–2006,* Nov. 2007.

22. In the 1980s, Rothschild would be accused by Tory backbenchers—but never with substantiation or much credibility—of being a member of Kim Philby's spy ring. See "Lord Rothschild: Biotechnologist and Businessman," *Financial Times,* Mar. 22, 1990, p. 11.

23. Wade, taped interview with Newland, 1994, pp. 2–3.

24. Wade, taped interview with Newland, 1994, p. 3.

25. P. Wack, untitled and undated memoir, dictated to Eve Wack, University of Oxford, Pierre Wack library.

26. Wack, untitled and undated memoir.

27. G. I. Gurdjieff, *Meetings with Remarkable Men* (New York: Dutton, 1963).

28. Wack, untitled and undated memoir.

29. Wack, untitled and undated memoir.

30. In 1986, Bénard would become co-chairman of the Channel Tunnel Project to link France and England. He published the first serious article on scenario planning in the *Harvard Business Review:* "World Oil and Cold Reality," Nov.–Dec. 1980, p. 91.

31. In this narrative, I have not been able to give full credit to the significant contributions of some members of the Planning Department: Cor Kuiken, Harry Beckers, Doug Wade, Gareth Price, Napier Collyns, Graham Galer, and others. As Jimmy Davidson wrote to the author, "It would be grossly unfair . . . to give the impression that everything flowed from Wack and Newland, or that they were the [sole] leaders." This is also a good place to acknowledge Karel Swart, a managing director whose support was critical to Shell's scenario planning team.

32. Hamilton, *The Price of Power,* p. 100; Sampson, *The Seven Sisters,* pp. 274–285; Yergin, *The Prize,* pp. 583–585.

33. Gerrit Wagner, Karel Swart, and André Bénard are three managing directors about whom I can say this with assurance, based on interviews with them.

34. Pierre Wack's exact words are forever lost, but these, taken from a speech given years later and from Gerrit Wagner's and his own recollections, are similar to what he said that September morning. The speech was: "I Find by Experience . . . ," *Harvard Business School Magazine,* 1985. Another version of this speech saw print as Wack, "Scenarios: The Gentle Art of Re-Perceiving Reality: One Thing or Two Learned While Developing Planning Scenarios for Royal Dutch/Shell," Harvard Business School Working Paper 9–785–042, 1984. Also see "Scenarios: Uncharted Waters Ahead," *Harvard Business Review,* Sept.-Oct. 1985.

35. Yergin, *The Prize,* pp. 594–595.

36. Group Planning, "Scenarios for 1973 Planning Cycle," 1973, p. 10.

37. Wack, "Scenarios: The Gentle Art of Re-Perceiving Reality," p. 28.

38. Group Planning, "Scenarios for 1973 Planning Cycle," p. 12.

39. G. Wagner to P. Wack, Sept. 24, 1985.

40. Group Planning, "Scenarios for 1973 Planning Cycle," p. 24.

41. Originally the planners had wanted to suggest a price of twelve dollars but moved it down to ten dollars before the presentation.

42. U.S. Energy Information Administration, *Annual Energy Review 2006* (Washington, D.C.: USEIA, 2007), http://www.eia.doe.gov/aer/.

43. This section is derived from interviews with Wack, Newland, and Group Planning staff members. Also see Yergin, *The Prize,* p. 432.

44. G. Clarke, "What Went Wrong?" *Time,* Dec. 10, 1973, p. 49.

45. Wagner to Wack, Sept. 24, 1985.

46. M. Heikal, *The Road to Ramandan* (London: Collins, 1975), quoted in Yergin, *The Prize,* p. 597.

47. J. Robinson, *Yamani: The Inside Story* (London: Simon & Schuster, 1988), pp. 146–148.

48. The "lime and Coke" story is told in Yergin, *The Prize,* p. 602, and Sampson, *The Seven Sisters,* p. 18. My account is based on comments from André Bénard, who showed Sampson his original notes of the meeting but disputes some of that version. (The man in his pajamas, Bénard says, came from Iraq, not Kuwait, and Yamani never placed a call to Baghdad.) The detail of the dates from Saudi Arabia is described here for the first time. Thanks to Bénard, it's my own contribution to the record about "one of the most critical encounters in the history of oil," as Sampson puts it.

CHAPTER SIX

1. This account comes from several sources, but I relied most heavily on W. Nigg, *The Heretics,* ed. and trans. R. Winston and C. Winston (New York: Knopf, 1962), p. 158. I also used the account of Abélard in W. Durant and A. Durant, *The Age of Faith* (New York: MJF Books, 1950); and E. Gilson, *Héloïse and Abélard,* trans. L. K. Shook (Ann Arbor: University of Michigan Press, 1963).

2. R. E. Shannon, "Operations Research and Mathematical Modelling," in L. R. Bittel (ed.), *Encyclopedia of Professional Management* (New York: McGraw-Hill, 1978).

3. D. A. Wren, *The Evolution of Management Thought* (New York: Ronald Press, 1972). Also see the entries on operations research (written by Russell L. Ackoff) and systems engineering (written by H. W. Bode) in *Encyclopaedia Britannica* (Chicago: University of Chicago, 1980).

4. S. M. Gelber and M. L. Cook, *Saving the Earth: The History of a Middle-Class Millenarian Movement* (Berkeley: University of California Press, 1990), pp. 64–74.

5. This was part of the international "Jesus as Teacher" movement; see Gelber and Cook, *Saving the Earth*; M. J. Stolaroff, *Thanatos to Eros: Thirty-Five Years of Psychedelic Exploration* (Berlin: Verlag für Wissenschaft und Bildung, 1994).

6. A. Huxley, *Brave New World* (London: Chatto and Windus, 1932); Huxley, *The Doors of Perception and Heaven and Hell* (New York: HarperCollins, 1954).

7. M. A. Lee and B. Shlain, *Acid Dreams* (New York: Grove Press, 1985); details about Leary and Hubbard come from pp. 6–19, 87–88, 96, 117.

8. Lee and Shlain, *Acid Dreams,* pp. 48–51; Gelber and Cook, *Saving the Earth,* pp. 79–86.

9. Lee and Shlain, *Acid Dreams,* p. 198.

10. Stolaroff, *Thanatos to Eros.*

11. The Sequoia Seminars later became known as the Beyond War Foundation.

12. W. H. Auden, "The Labyrinth," in E. Mendelson (ed.), *Collected Poems* (New York: Random House, 1976), p. 9.

13. Lee and Shlain, *Acid Dreams,* p. 18n.

14. W. B. Gibson, *SRI: The Founding Years (A Significant Step at the Golden Time)* (Los Altos, Calif.: Publishing Services Center, 1980), p. 5.

15. Gibson, *SRI,* p. 184.

16. Gibson, *SRI,* pp. 88, 99, 100, 102, 108; B. Royce, "A History of Strategic Management Planning at SRI," internal SRI report, 1985.

17. "SRI Pulls Hard on the Growth Reins," *Business Week,* Mar. 25, 1967, p. 106.

18. Other advisers to Gideonse and his project included Syracuse University futurist Michael Marien and Don Michael, then at the University of Michigan.

19. R. Rhyne, "Projecting Whole-Body Future Patterns—The Field Anomaly Relaxation (FAR) Method" (Menlo Park, Calif.: Stanford Research Institute Educational Policy Research Center, 1969).

20. O. W. Markley, "Alternative Futures: Contexts in Which Social Indicators Must Work," EPRC Research Note 6747–11, Feb. 1971, supported by National Center for Educational Research and Development, prepared for a session on social indicators for the American Statistical Association, Detroit, Dec. 27–30, 1970, contract OEC-1-7–071013–4274, pp. 3–6.The five futures were: "New Society," "Status Quo Extended," "Imprudent Optimism," "Excessive Reprivatization," and "Violence Escalated."

21. Educational Policy Research Center, "Progress Report, June 1, 1971–Sept. 1, 1971," contract OEC-1-7–071013–4274.

22. O. Markley, "The Omniverse Center for Cultural Development, and Other Noetic Technologies for Global Consciousness and Personal/Planetary Transformation" (paper presented at Open Heart, Open Mind: Fourth Annual Conference of the Institute of Noetic Sciences, San Diego, Calif., July 17, 1995).

23. J. Forrester, "From the Ranch to System Dynamics: An Autobiography," in A. G. Bedein, *Management Laureates: A Collection of Autobiographical Essays* (Greenwich, Conn.: JAI Press, 1991).

24. Forrester, "From the Ranch to System Dynamics," p. 14.; L. Fisher, "The Prophet of Unintended Consequences," *strategy+business,* Fall 2005.

25. L. Runyan "Forty Years on the Frontier (History of Computing)," *Datamation,* Mar. 15, 1991, p. 34.

26. D. Warsh, "Reaping the Whirlwind," *Boston Globe,* Aug. 10, 1986, p. 79.

27. Forrester, "From the Ranch to System Dynamics," p. 14.

28. This story has been described to the author in two ways: once (by Forrester) as being about General Electric, the other (by Dennis Meadows)

as being about Sprague Electric, makers of electrical components such as resistors and capacitors.

29. G. Richardson, *Feedback Thought in Social Science and Systems Theory* (Philadelphia: University of Pennsylvania Press, 1991); P. Senge, *The Fifth Discipline* (New York: Doubleday, 1990), pp. 73–79.

30. These numbers come not from General Electric's actual experience but from Forrester's computer simulation of their case.

31. Adapted from J. Forrester, *Industrial Dynamics* (Waltham, Mass.: Pegasus Communications, 1961); Fisher, "The Prophet of Unintended Consequences."

32. Senge, *The Fifth Discipline*, pp. 40–42.

33. Fisher, "The Prophet of Unintended Consequences."

34. For more on this, see J. Sterman, *Beyond Training Wheels*, in P. Senge and others (eds.), *The Fifth Discipline Fieldbook* (New York: Doubleday/ Currency, 1994), p. 177; and Fisher, "The Prophet of Unintended Consequences."

35. J. Forrester, "A New Concept of Corporate Design," *Industrial Management Review*, 1965, 7, 5; J. Forrester, "Reconsidering 'A New Corporate Design,'" unpublished manuscript, 1993.

36. Conversation with Peter Senge, referring to reviews of *Industrial Dynamics* by University of Chicago physicist John Platt.

37. C. Sterling, "Club of Rome Tackles the Planet's 'Problématique,'" *Washington Post*, Mar. 2, 1972, p. A18; P. O'Keefe, "A Warning on Man's Big Problem," *Washington Evening Star*, Mar. 2, 1972, p. A3.

38. The model is described in full in J. W. Forrester, *World Dynamics* (Cambridge, Mass.: Wright-Allen Press, 1971).

39. D. L. Meadows, *Dynamics of Commodity Production Cycles* (Cambridge, Mass.: Wright-Allen Press, 1970). The other members of the team were Jørgen Randers and William W. Behrens III.

40. D. E. Meadows, J. Randers, and W. W. Behrens, *The Limits to Growth* (Washington, D.C.: Potomac Associates, 1972), pp. 129, 140.

41. A. Kleiner, "Flexing Their Mussels," *Garbage*, 1992, pp. 4, 48.

42. P. Passell, M. Roberts, and L. Ross, review of *The Limits to Growth, World Dynamics,* and *Urban Dynamics*, *New York Times Book Review*, Apr. 2, 1972, p. 1.

43. J. Pournelle, "Computing at Chaos Manor: The Hunt for Bad Sectors," *Byte*, June 1, 1989, p. 119.

CHAPTER SEVEN

1. "Trevrezent as Parzival's Rival?" in U. Hoffman (ed.), *Wolfram's Parzival: Five Essays,* with an Introduction by H. J. Weigand (Ithaca, N.Y.: Cornell University Press, 1969), pp. 149–151.

2. "Woe's me that he did not inquire! For him I still feel sorrow dire," in *The Parzival of Wolfram von Eschenbach,* trans. E. H. Zeydel and B. Q. Morgan (Chapel Hill: University of North Carolina Studies in the Germanic Languages and Literatures, 1951), p. 127, book 5, verse 240, line 3. The question is finally posed much later: "What afflicts thee, uncle dear?" (p. 328, book 16, verse 795, line 29).

3. "Abandon boorish breeding. From too much questioning refrain." In *The Parzival of Wolfram von Eschenbach,* p. 89, book 3, verse 171, lines 17–18.

4. My rendition of Parzival owes a tremendous amount to the explications of Joseph Campbell. I found two Campbell renditions of this story: *Reflections on the Art of Living* (New York: HarperCollins, 1991) and *In Search of the Holy Grail* (St. Paul, Minn.: HighBridge Productions, 1989, 1990).

5. E. H. Schein, *Process Consultation: Its Role in Organizational Development* (Reading, Mass.: Addison-Wesley, 1969).

6. "The [conventional academic] group dynamics research was very static in its emphasis on experiments, and the classic Sherif studies on intergroup conflict studied outcomes more than process. What I think I and others have argued for, all these years, is more careful attention to the ongoing dynamics of what went on between people and in groups, and the moment-to-moment consequences of small bits of behavior." E. Schein to the author, June 1995.

7. These details come from M. R. Weisbord, "Team Work: Building Productive Relationships," in W. B. Reddy and K. Jamison (eds.), *Team Building: Blueprints for Productivity and Satisfaction* (Washington, D.C.: NTL Institute, 1988). It was adapted in turn from M. Weisbord, *Productive Workplaces* (San Francisco: Jossey-Bass, 1987). The questions "on a scale of 1 to 5" come from R. Harrison, "Role Negotiations," in W. Burke and H. Hornstein (eds.), *The Social Technology of Organization Development* (Fairfax, Va.: NTL Institute/Learning Resources, 1972).

8. S. Helgesen, "Masters of the Breakthrough Moment," *strategy+business,* Winter 2006.

9. Helgesen, "Masters of the Breakthrough Moment."

10. The date 1957 is suggested by Robert Blake, who describes the first pivotal clash between the "power and authority" people and the "morale

and cohesion" people at NTL as occurring that year. Gradually the morale and cohesion people shifted West. R. R. Blake, "Memories of HRD," *Training and Development,* Mar. 1995.

11. J. A. Byrne, "Executives Latch on to Any Management Idea That Looks Like a Quick Fix," *Business Week,* Jan. 20, 1986, p. 52.

12. This lemon game was invented by Jon Klee, a member of the NTL staff.

13. P. Drucker, *Concept of the Corporation* (New York: John Day Company, 1946).

14. See, for instance, P. Drucker, *The Practice of Management* (New York: HarperCollins, 1954).

15. Drucker, *The Practice of Management.*

16. Odiorne's own description of his system comes from "Objectives, Management by," in *The Encyclopedia of Professional Management* (New York: McGraw-Hill, 1987), pp. 781–787. I also used G. Odiorne, "The Trouble with Sensitivity Training," *Training Director's Journal,* 1963.

17. The MBO system was originally conceived by Peter Drucker, using the ideas of Douglas McGregor, Ron Lippitt, and others. Odiorne expanded on Drucker's ideas and developed the "MBO" package, which persists in many companies today. Odiorne describes his system concisely in "Objectives, Management by," pp. 781–787. Also see G. Odiorne, *The Human Side of Management: Management by Integration and Self-Control* (Lexington, Mass.: Lexington Books/University Associates, 1987), p. xii.

18. For his argument, see Odiorne, "The Trouble with Sensitivity Training."

19. "Yourself as Others See You," *Business Week,* Mar. 16, 1963.

20. C. Argyris, "On the Future of Laboratory Education," *Journal of Applied Behavioral Science,* 1967, *3,* 153–183; C. Argyris, "T-Groups for Organizational Effectiveness," *Harvard Business Review,* 1964, *42,* 60–74; C. Argyris, with R. Harrison, *Interpersonal Competence and Organizational Effectiveness* (Homewood, Ill.: Dorsey Press/Richard D. Irwin, 1962), pp. 232–233, 250–254.

21. This story was recounted by Argyris. I couldn't check it with Odiorne, who had passed away.

22. C. Argyris, "Looking Backward and Inward in Order to Contribute to the Future," in A. Bedein (ed.), *Management Laureates: A Collection of Autobiographical Essays* (Greenwich, Conn.: JAI Press, 1992), Vol. 1, pp. 43–64.

23. Argyris, "Looking Backward and Inward in Order to Contribute to the Future."

24. Argyris, "Looking Backward and Inward in Order to Contribute to the Future"; C. Argyris, *Management and Organizational Development: The Path from XA to YB* (New York: McGraw-Hill, 1971), p. 120.

25. W. Bennis, afterword to A. Marrow, *Making Waves in Foggy Bottom* (Washington, D.C.: National Training Laboratories, 1974), p. 77.

26. C. Argyris, "Some Causes of Organizational Ineffectiveness Within the Department of State" (Washington, D.C.: Department of State, 1966).

27. Marrow, *Making Waves in Foggy Bottom,* pp. xiii, 3, 7.

28. This episode is based on a training session I witnessed in 1993; OD veterans have commented that it is representative of problematic interventions since the 1960s.

29. K. Back, *Beyond Words* (New York: Russell Sage Foundation, 1972), pp. 220–221.

30. L. P. Bradford, *National Training Laboratories: Its History, 1947–1970* (Bethel, Me.: NTL Institute for Applied Behavioral Science, 1974), p. 178.

31. J. Hirsch, "A History of the NTL Institute for Applied Behavioral Science, 1947–1986" (unpublished Ed.D. dissertation, Boston University, 1986), p. 88.

32. W. Bennis, *An Invented Life* (Reading, Mass.: Addison-Wesley, 1993).

33. W. Bennis and P. Slater, "Democracy Is Inevitable," *Harvard Business Review,* Apr. 1964.

34. "NTL Executive Committee Meeting," Mar. 16, 1969, in Bradford, *National Training Laboratories,* pp. 341–342.

35. David Bradford suggested this point in a letter to the author, 1995.

36. Bradford, *National Training Laboratories.*

37. Jane Howard, "Inhibitions Thrown to the Gentle Winds," *Life,* July 12, 1968.

38. This figure comes from my interview with Warren Bennis. In *National Training Laboratories* (p. 185), Lee Bradford writes that he received pledges for the full $1 million.

39. Hirsch, "A History of the NTL Institute for Applied Behavioral Science, 1947–1986," p. 89.

40. W. Bennis, "Development of a Dream: A New International University for Social Change" (speech given at NTL board meeting, Nov. 13–14, 1969), in Bradford, *National Training Laboratories,* p. 346.

41. Hirsch, "A History of the NTL Institute for Applied Behavioral Science, 1947–1986," pp. 85–86.

42. Hirsch, "A History of the NTL Institute for Applied Behavioral Science, 1947–1986," p. 95.

43. B. L. Harragan, *Games Mother Never Taught You* (New York: Warner Books, 1977).

44. Some of this story comes from F. A. Miller, "Forks in the Road: Critical Issues on the Path to Diversity," in E. Y. Cross, J. H. Katz, F. A. Miller, and E. W. Seashore, *The Promise of Diversity* (New York: NTL Institute/ Irwin, 1994). Also see A. Kleiner, "Diversity and Its Discontents," *strategy+business,* Spring 2004.

45. C. C. Swanger, "Perspectives on the History of Ameliorating Oppression and Supporting Diversity in United States Organizations," in Cross, Katz, Miller, and Seashore, *The Promise of Diversity,* pp. 13–14; S. Kleinfield, *The Biggest Company on Earth* (New York: Holt, 1981), pp. 205–206.

46. C. N. Seashore and B. R. Fletcher, "The White Male Category at the Intersection of Race and Gender," in Cross, Katz, Miller, and Seashore, *The Promise of Diversity,* p. 157.

47. Hirsch, "A History of the NTL Institute for Applied Behavioral Science, 1947–1986," p. 109.

48. See, for example, M. Chesler, "Organizational Development Is Not the Same as Multicultural Organizational Development," in Cross, Katz, Miller, and Seashore, *The Promise of Diversity,* p. 240; Kleiner, "Diversity and Its Discontents."

49. Argyris with Harrison, *Interpersonal Competence and Organizational Effectiveness,* p. 5.

50. C. Argyris, "Teaching Smart People How to Learn," *Harvard Business Review,* May-June 1991; Argyris, "Skilled Incompetence," *Harvard Business Review,* Sept. 1986; Argyris and D. Schön, *Theory in Practice: Increasing Organizational Effectiveness* (San Francisco: Jossey-Bass, 1974), pp. 3–4; D. A. Schön, *The Reflective Practitioner: How Professionals Think in Action* (New York: Basic Books, 1983); Argyris, *Overcoming Organizational Defenses* (Needham Heights, Mass.: Allyn & Bacon, 1990); Argyris, *Flawed Advice and the Management Trap* (New York: Oxford University Press, 2000).

51. For more on this, see R. Putnam, "Conversational Recipes," and P. McArthur, "Opening Lines," in P. Senge and others, *The Fifth Discipline Fieldbook* (New York: Doubleday/Currency, 1994).

52. For some examples, see Senge and others, *The Fifth Discipline Fieldbook,* particularly, "Skillful Discussion at Intel," p. 392; "Creating a Learning

Lab—and Making It Work," p. 554; "The Ladder of Inference," p. 242; and "The Left-Hand Column," p. 246.

53. R. L. Gordon, "Warren Bennis: New President Looks Beyond U.C. Campus," *Cincinnati,* Nov. 1971, p. 32.

54. R. Davis, "UC's New First Lady Arrives," *Cincinnati Enquirer,* Sept. 1, 1971.

55. M. Edinberg, "Dr. Bennis's Open Office Hours," social psychology paper for L. Lansky's class, University of Cincinnati, Dec. 13, 1971.

56. Some of this story is told in W. Bennis, *The Unconscious Conspiracy* (New York: AMACOM, 1976).

57. W. Bennis, "Reflections on Six Impatient Years," *Cincinnati Horizons,* June 1977; N. Foy, "Bennis Breaks Out of His Ivory Tower," *London Times,* Aug. 20, 1973, p. 20.

58. W. Bennis, "Only Connect" (speech at American Group Psychologists Association annual meeting, New York, Feb. 18, 1974).

59. S. Yohe, "UC Money Crisis May Mean End to Some Programs," *Cincinnati Post,* Apr. 19, 1973.

60. W. Bennis and B. Nanus, *Leaders* (New York: HarperCollins, 1985).

61. Commencement address, University of Cincinnati, Aug. 26, 1977.

CHAPTER EIGHT

1. N. Cohn, *The Pursuit of the Millennium: Revolutionary Millenarians and Mystical Anarchists of the Middle Ages* (New York: Oxford University Press, 1970); M. Lambert, *Medieval Heresy: Popular Movements from Bogomil to Hus* (New York: Holmes & Meier, 1976).

2. J. Mitchell, "For Free," *Ladies of the Canyon* (Reprise, 1970).

3. H. Kahn, "Forces for Change," in Kahn, *The Future of the Corporation* (New York: Mason & Lipscomb, 1974).

4. B. Henry, screenplay, *The Graduate,* 1967, http://www.geocities.com/ Hollywood/8200/graduate.html; G. Wise, "General Electric's Century: A History of the General Electric Company from Its Origins to 1986," unpublished manuscript, n.d.; N. Tichy and S. Sherman, *Control Your Destiny or Someone Else Will* (New York: HarperCollins, 2005).

5. Jerry Della Femina, "What's The Ugliest Part of Your Body?" campaign for Pretty Feet; also see Della Femina, *From Those Wonderful Folks Who Gave You Pearl Harbor* (New York: Pocket Books, 1971).

6. WELL computer network, news conference, topic 877: "Bill Graham Dead?" post 207 by Phil Catalfo, Nov. 1, 1991; quoting an appearance by Bill Graham on the radio show *Fresh Air* by Terry Gross; also see C. Perry, *The Haight-Ashbury: A History* (New York: Random House, 1984).

7. The UC Berkeley student was Lynne Hall, who later became a management consultant.

8. B. L. Harragan, *Games Mother Never Taught You* (New York: Warner Books, 1977), p. 305.

9. F. Braudel, *Capitalism and Material Life* (New York: HarperCollins, 1973), p. 59.

10. Michael Philips, Stewart Brand, in conversations; A. Kleiner, "Renegades of Retail," *San Francisco Bay Guardian*, Oct. 15, 1986.

11. P. DiMaggio, *The Hitchhiker's Field Manual* (New York: Macmillan, 1993), p. 161.

12. A. Kushi with A. Jack, *Aveline: The Life and Dream of the Woman Behind Macrobiotics Today* (Tokyo and New York: Japan Publications, 1988), pp. 185–186.

13. R. W. Eivers, "From Alternative to Big Business: The Story Behind Erewhon's Unionization," *New Age Journal*, Nov. 1978. Also see "Erewhon: High Hopes, High Standards—and Low Profits," *New Age Journal*, July 1982, and interviews with the Kushis in Editors of East West, *Meetings with Remarkable Men and Women* (Brookline, Mass.: East West Health Books, 1989).

14. P. Hawken, *Growing a Business* (New York: Simon & Schuster, 1987), p. 48.

15. Ram Dass, *Be Here Now* (San Cristobal, N.M.: Lama Foundation, 1971).

16. Hawken, *Growing a Business*, p. 140.

17. D. S. Elgin, D. C. MacMichael, and P. Schwartz, *Alternative Futures for Environmental Policy Planning, 1975–2000* (Stanford, Calif.: Stanford Research Institute, Center for the Study of Social Policy, Oct. 1975).

18. Norman MacEachron of SRI International introduced the paradigm idea to the futures group there. This passage was influenced by Don Michael's analysis, in conversation, of the evolution of the paradigm idea. Also see T. Kuhn, Postscript to *Structure of Scientific Revolutions* (Chicago: University of Chicago Press, 1970), p. 177

19. W. Harman and others, *Changing Images of Man* (Dayton, Ohio: Charles F. Kettering Foundation, May 1974), p. 187

20. Harman and others, *Changing Images of Man*, p. 58.

21. Harman and others, *Changing Images of Man*, p. 4.

22. Harman and others, *Changing Images of Man*, p. 75.

23. Harman and others, *Changing Images of Man*, pp. 149, 258.

24. J. Campbell, with B. Moyers, *The Power of Myth* (New York: Doubleday, 1988), pp. 5, 117.

25. O. W. Markley, "The New Image of Man," *New York Times*, Dec. 16, 1974.

26. P. Hawken, J. Ogilvy, and P. Schwartz, *Seven Tomorrows: Towards a Voluntary History* (New York: Bantam Books, 1982).

27. See, for example, P. Hawken, *Blessed Unrest: How the Largest Movement in the World Came into Being and Why No One Saw It Coming* (New York: Viking, 2007); *The Ecology of Commerce* (New York: HarperBusiness, 1993); and, with A. Lovins and L. H. Lovins, *Natural Capitalism: Creating the Next Industrial Revolution* (New York: Back Bay Books, 2000). Also see P. Schwartz, *The Art of the Long View* (New York: Doubleday, 1991); and J. Ogilvy, *Multidimensional Man* (New York: Oxford University Press, 1977), and *Living Without a Goal* (New York: Doubleday, 1995). Schwartz and Ogilvy would later become partners, with Napier Collyns, Stewart Brand, and Lawrence Wilkinson, in Global Business Network. See A. Kleiner, *Consequential Heresies: How 'Thinking the Unthinkable' Changed Royal Dutch/Shell* (San Francisco: Global Business Network, 1989).

28. R. Gregg, "Voluntary Simplicity," *Visva-Bharati Quarterly*, Aug. 1936.

29. D. Elgin and others, "The Impact of Sociocultural Changes upon the Automobile Industry, 1975 to 2000," in *Long-Term Outlook for the United States Auto Industry* (Stanford, Calif.: Stanford Research Institute, Nov. 1975).

30. Elgin and others, "The Impact of Sociocultural Changes upon the Automobile Industry, 1975 to 2000."

31. P. Collier and D. Horowitz, *The Fords: An American Epic* (New York: Summit Books, 1987), pp. 379–381.

32. B. Herndon, *Ford: An Unconventional Biography of the Men and Their Times* (New York: Weybright and Talley, 1969), p. 24; W. Serrin, "At Ford Everyone Knows Who Is the Boss," *New York Times Magazine*, Oct. 19, 1969.

33. D. Cordtz, "Henry Ford, Superstar," *Fortune*, May 1973, p. 191.

34. Elgin and others, "The Impact of Sociocultural Changes upon the Automobile Industry, 1975 to 2000."

35. D. Elgin and A. Mitchell, "Voluntary Simplicity," *CoEvolution Quarterly*, Summer 1977, p. 6.

36. Recalled by former franchise owner Mirick Friend, quoted in A. Kleiner, "Theatre of the McServed," *Garbage*, Sept.–Oct. 1991, p. 53, http://www .well.com/~art/McDon.html.

37. Elgin's book became *Voluntary Simplicity: Toward a Way of Life That Is Outwardly Simple, Inwardly Rich* (New York: Morrow, 1981).

38. R. D. Michman, *Lifestyle Market Segmentation* (New York: Praeger, 1991), pp. 60ff.

39. H. Kahn, W. Brown, and L. Martel, *The Next 200 Years* (New York: Morrow, 1976).

40. H. Kahn, *The Prospects for Mankind One and a Year 2000 Ideology* (Croton-on-Hudson, N.Y.: Hudson Institute, Aug. 1, 1972), p. 4-D.

41. H. Kahn, J. Brown, and A. Lovins, "The New Class," *CoEvolution Quarterly*, Spring 1977, p. 9.

42. H. Kahn and B. Bruce-Briggs, *Things to Come: Thinking About the Seventies and Eighties* (New York: Macmillan, 1972), pp. 30, 44.

43. Kahn, Brown, and Lovins, "The New Class," p. 8.

44. Kahn and Bruce-Briggs, *Things to Come*, p. 60.

45. Kahn and Bruce-Briggs, *Things to Come*, p. 219.

46. Kahn, Brown, and Martel, *The Next 200 Years*, p. 164.

47. H. Kahn, *World Economic Development* (Boulder, Colo.: Herman Kahn, 1979).

48. Kahn, Brown, and Lovins, "The New Class," p. 8

49. Kahn, Brown, and Lovins, "The New Class," pp. 11, 17.

50. M. Mintz and J. S. Cohen, *America, Inc.: Who Owns and Operates the United States* (New York: Dial Press, 1971).

51. G. A. Wagner, *Business in the Public Eye: Reflections on the Ethics of Business*, trans. T. Plantinga (Grand Rapids, Mich.: Wm. B. Eerdmans, 1982), p. 117.

52. "Royal Dutch/Shell Group of Companies Statement of Business Principles," reprinted in Wagner, *Business in the Public Eye*, pp. 121ff.

53. Kleiner, "The Man Who Saw the Future."

54. D. Wade, taped interview with T. Newland, May 13, 1994, Cybard, France, p. 8.

55. Kahn, *World Economic Development*, pp. 285–288.

56. H. DuMoulin and J. Eyre, "Energy Scenarios: A Learning Process," *Energy Economics,* Apr. 1979, p. 78.

57. DuMoulin and Eyre, "Energy Scenarios," p. 78.

58. DuMoulin and Eyre, "Energy Scenarios," p. 77.

59. Many of the details about Amory Lovins come from C. Brown, "High Priest of the Low-Flow Shower Heads," *Outside Magazine,* Nov. 1991, p. 58. Also J. R. Emshwiller, "Amory Lovins Presses Radical Alternatives for Fueling the Nation," *Wall Street Journal,* Mar. 16, 1981, p. 1.

60. Introduction to Lovins's article in *Not Man Apart, Friends of the Earth,* Autumn 1976. The "butter with a chainsaw" line, often attributed to Lovins, was first said by Doug Kelbaugh, a professor at the University of Washington. Brown, "High Priest of the Low-Flow Shower Heads," p. 60.

61. A. B. Lovins, "Energy Strategy: The Road Not Taken?" *Foreign Affairs,* Oct. 1976. Also see A. B. Lovins, *An Historical Footnote* (Snowmass, Colo.: Rocky Mountain Institute, 1991).

62. Lovins, "Energy Strategy."

63. Kahn, Brown, and Lovins, "The New Class," p. 22.

64. "Setting Business Straight on Energy Priorities," interview with Amory Lovins by S. G. Michaud and D. Ediger, *Business Week,* Dec. 5, 1977.

65. This is a paraphrase of a speech made by Carl Goldstein, assistant vice president of the Atomic Industrial Forum, at the AIF-SVA International Workshop, "Nuclear Power and the Public," Geneva, Switzerland, Sept. 26–29, 1977.

66. "Lapp vs. Lovins," in H. Nash (ed.), *The Energy Controversy: Soft Path Questions and Answers, by Amory Lovins and His Critics* (San Francisco: Friends of the Earth, 1979), pp. 93–94.

67. D. Foster, "The Calculator Kid," *Mother Jones,* Feb.–Mar. 1978, p. 49.

68. P. Wack, "Scenarios: The Gentle Art of Reperceiving," *Harvard Business Review,* Sept.–Oct. 1985; "Scenarios, Uncharted Waters Ahead," *Harvard Business Review,* Sept.–Oct. 1985; "Scenarios: Shooting the Rapids," *Harvard Business Review,* Nov.–Dec. 1985. Also see A. de Geus, "Planning as Learning," *Harvard Business Review,* Mar.–Apr. 1988.

69. Senge, *The Fifth Discipline.*

70. Kleiner, "Consequential Heresies."

71. M. de Kuijper, "Profit Power," manuscript in process.

72. G. Galer, "Scenarios of Change in South Africa," *Round Table,* 2004, 93(375), 369–383; Galer, "South Africa: Scenarios of the Future as Apartheid Was Ending" (Canterbury, U.K.: University of Kent, 2003).

73. C. Sunter, *The World and South Africa in the 1990s* (Cape Town: Human and Rousseau and Tafelberg, 1987), p. 94.

74. Sunter, *The World and South Africa in the 1990s*.

75. Galer, "Scenarios of Change in South Africa"; P. Waldmeir, *Anatomy of a Miracle: The End of Apartheid and the Birth of the New South Africa* (London: Viking, 1997), p. 71; S. Chan and V. Jabri (eds.), *Mediation in Southern Africa* (London: Macmillan, 1993), p. 172.

76. A. Kahane, *Solving Tough Problems: An Open Way of Talking, Listening, and Creating New Realities* (San Francisco: Berrett-Koehler, 2004); Kahane, "Learning from MontFleur," in *Scenario Thinking: Concepts and Approaches* (Emeryville, Calif.: Global Business Network, 1996); C. Sunter, *The New Century: Quest for the High Road* (Cape Town: Human and Rousseau, 1992), *The High Road: Where Are We Now?* (Cape Town: Human and Rousseau and Tafelberg, 1996), and, with C. Ilbury, *The Mind of a Fox: Scenario Planning in Action* (Cape Town: Human and Rousseau and Tafelberg, 2001).

CHAPTER NINE

1. B. Tuchman, *A Distant Mirror* (New York: Random House, 1978), pp. 43ff.

2. Tuchman, *A Distant Mirror*, p. 34.

3. F. E. Emery and E. L. Trist, "The Causal Texture of Organisational Environments," *Human Relations*, 1967, *20*, 199–237; H. Kahn, W. Brown, and L. Martel, *The Next 200 Years* (New York: Morrow, 1976); A. Toffler, *Future Shock* (New York: Random House, 1970); P. Vaill, *Managing as a Performing Art* (San Francisco: Jossey-Bass, 1989).

4. P. Wack, "Scenarios: Shooting the Rapids," *Harvard Business Review,* Nov.–Dec. 1985.

5. "Big Oil—Under Pressure," *Newsweek,* Dec. 17, 1973, p. 79; D. Yergin, *The Prize* (New York: Simon & Schuster, 1991).

6. "Big Oil—Under Pressure," p. 79.

7. R. Sherrill, *The Oil Follies of 1970–1980* (New York: Anchor/Doubleday, 1983), p. 217.

8. R. L. Heilbroner, "Controlling the Corporation," in Heilbroner and others (eds.), *In the Name of Profits* (New York: Doubleday, 1972), p. 192. Heilbroner cites the *Wall Street Journal,* Feb. 11, 1971.

9. R. Mokhiber, *Corporate Crime and Violence* (San Francisco: Sierra Club Books, 1988), pp. 163–170.

10. F. D. Sturdivant, *The Corporate Social Challenge: Cases and Commentaries,* 3rd ed. (Homewood, Ill.: Irwin, 1985), pp. 127–129.

11. Leonard L. Silk and David D. Vogel, *Ethics and Profits: The Crisis of Confidence in American Business* (New York: Simon & Schuster, 1976), p. 178.

12. Silk and Vogel, *Ethics and Profits,* pp. 117, 221.

13. B. D. Henderson, *The First Ten Years—Remembered, or How BCG Became a Group* (Boston: Boston Consulting Group, 1973), pp. 3–4.

14. M. Rothschild, *Bionomics: The Inevitability of Capitalism* (New York: Holt, 1990), pp. 178–179. The factory manager who discovered the curve was Theodore P. Wright.

15. B. D. Henderson, *Henderson on Corporate Strategy* (Cambridge, Mass.: Abt Books, 1979), p. 82.

16. "The World of 1976: A Time of Healing, a Return to Growth," slides by Lawrence Wilkinson, Global Business Network, Emeryville, Calif.

17. N. Fligstein, *The Transformation of Corporate Control* (Cambridge, Mass.: Harvard University Press, 1990), particularly Chaps. 7 and 8.

18. Office of Technology Assessment Project Staff, *Technology and the American Economic Transition: Choices for the Future* (Washington, D.C.: U.S. Office of Technology Assessment, 1988), p. 175.

19. R. Reich and J. D. Donahue, *New Deals: The Chrysler Renewal and the American System* (New York: Viking/Penguin, 1985), p. 90.

20. P. H. Weaver, *The Suicidal Corporation* (New York: Simon & Schuster, 1988), pp. 84–85.

21. M. Keller, *Rude Awakening* (New York: Morrow, 1989), p. 68.

22. R. T. Pascale, *Managing on the Edge: How the Smartest Companies Use Conflict to Stay Ahead* (New York: Touchstone, 1990), pp. 18–19; H. Mintzburg, *The Rise and Fall of Strategic Planning: Reconceiving Roles for Planning, Plans, Planners* (New York: Free Press, 1994), p. 103.

23. L. Wayne, "Management Gospel Gone Wrong," *New York Times,* May 30, 1982, 3:1; R. H. Hayes and W. J. Abernathy, "Managing Our Way to Economic Decline," *Harvard Business Review,* July–Aug. 1980.

24. Quoted in A. Gabor, "Lessons for Business Schools," *strategy+business,* Spring 2008, p. 114.

25. This is from a letter to Peter Vaill.

26. T. J. Peters and R. H. Waterman, *In Search of Excellence* (New York: HarperCollins, 1982), p. viii. Peters is referring specifically to Gene Webb and Hal Leavitt, as well as to Karl Weick at Cornell (later Michigan) and Herb Simon at Carnegie-Mellon.

27. Peters and Waterman, *In Search of Excellence,* p. 10.

28. Peters, "Tom Peters' True Confessions," *Fast Company,* Dec. 2001, p. 81, quoted in P. Rosenzweig, *The Halo Effect . . . and the Eight Other Business Delusions That Deceive Managers* (New York: Free Press, 2007), p. 84.

29. Peters and Waterman, *In Search of Excellence,* pp. 127, 132, 150.

30. Waterman, *What America Does Right.*

31. Peters and Waterman, *In Search of Excellence,* pp. 286–287.

32. See, for instance, "Who's Excellent Now?" *Business Week,* Nov. 5, 1984, pp. 76–88; D. Carroll, "A Disappointing Search for Excellence," *Harvard Business Review,* 1983, *61,* 78–88; or the most in-depth survey, A. Ghosh, *Redefining Excellence* (New York: Praeger, 1990).

33. Rosenzweig, *The Halo Effect,* pp. 88–95.

34. H. T. Johnson and R. S. Kaplan, *Relevance Lost* (Boston: Harvard Business School Press, 1991), p. 183

35. Johnson and Kaplan, *Relevance Lost,* p. 187.

36. Paul R. Carlile and Clayton M. Christensen, "Practice and Malpractice in Management Research," Jan. 6, 2005, circulated paper, version 6.0, p. 13.

37. A. Kleiner, "What Are the Measures That Matter?" *strategy+business,* First Quarter 2002, http://www.strategy-business.com/press/article/11409.

38. M. Walton, *The Deming Management Method* (New York: Dodd, Mead, 1986), p. 7.

39. J. Hoopes, *False Prophets* (New York: Da Capo Press, 2003), p. 214; J. Dowd, "How the Japanese Learned to Compete," *Asia Times,* Oct. 27, 2006.

40. Hoopes, *False Prophets,* p. 210.

41. "Toyota Vision and Philosophy," retrieved January 2008 from http://www .toyota.co.jp/en/vision/traditions/sep_oct_05.html.

42. J. P. Womack, D. T. Jones, and D. Roos, *The Machine That Changed The World* (New York: Rawson Associates, 1990), pp. 55–56; J. P. Womack and D. T. Jones, *How the World Has Changed Since* The Machine That Changed the World (Brookline, Mass.: Lean Enterprise Institute, 2001), pp. 11–12; A. Kleiner, "Leaning Toward Utopia," *strategy+business,* Summer 2005.

43. L. Dobyns and R. Frank, *If Japan Can, Why Can't We?* (New York: NBC News Documentary, June 24, 1980); C. C. Mason and L. Dobyns, *Quality or Else: The Revolution in World Business* (Boston: Houghton Mifflin, 1991).

44. C. S. Kilian, *The World of W. Edwards Deming* (Washington D.C.: CEE Press Books, 1988), pp. 236ff., 261ff.

45. This seminar was conducted at Montreal in 1991; I was present.

46. The anecdote is from an interview. Also see A. Gabor, *The Capitalist Philosophers: The Geniuses of Modern Business—Their Lives, Times and Ideas* (New York: Times Books, 2000), p. 194; A. Gabor, *The Man Who Discovered Quality* (New York: Crown, 1990).

47. W. E. Deming, *Out of the Crisis* (Cambridge, Mass.: Massachusetts Institute of Technology Center for Advanced Engineering Study, 1986), p. 78.

48. Deming, *Out of the Crisis.*

49. A. Kleiner, "The Battle for the Soul of Corporate America: Hammerism Battles Demingism," *Wired,* Aug. 1995.

50. C. C. Mason and L. Dobyns, *Application of the New Philosophy,* Vol. 6 of the Deming Library video series (Chicago: Films, Incorporated, 1988).

51. Kleiner, "Leaning Toward Utopia."

52. P. Crosby, *Quality Is Free: The Art of Making Quality Certain* (New York: McGraw-Hill, 1979); T. J. Peters and N. Austin, *A Passion for Excellence: The Leadership Difference* (New York: Random House, 1985); T. J. Peters, *Thriving on Chaos: Handbook for a Management Revolution* (New York: Knopf, 1987).

53. Peters, *Thriving on Chaos,* p. 390; Dave Rogers, "Answer to Big Three's 'Black October' Are People, Says Pat Carrigan," *MyBayCity.com,* Nov. 13, 2005, http://mybaycity.mmcctech.net/scripts/Article_View.cfm?ArticleID=93 4&NewspaperID=310.

54. R. M. Kanter, *The Change Masters* (New York: Free Press, 1985), and *When Giants Learn to Dance* (New York: Free Press, 1990).

55. A. de Geus, "Planning as Learning," *Harvard Business Review,* Mar.–Apr. 1988.

56. A. Kleiner, "Jack Stack's Story Is an Open Book," *strategy+business,* Third Quarter 2001; J. Stack and B. Burlingham, *A Stake in the Outcome: Building a Culture of Ownership for the Longterm Success of Your Business* (New York: Doubleday, 2002),

57. W. E. Deming, *The New Economics for Industry, Government, Education* (Cambridge, Mass.: MIT Press, 1993).

58. H. T. Johnson and A. Broms, *Profit Beyond Measure: Extraordinary Results Through Attention to Work and People* (New York: Free Press, 2000); H. T. Johnson, "Moving Upstream from Measurement," in P. Senge and others, *The Dance of Change* (New York: Doubleday, 1999), p. 291.

59. Johnson, "Moving Upstream from Measurement."

60. Kleiner, "What Are the Measures That Matter?"; H. T. Johnson, "It's Time to Stop Overselling Activity-Based Concepts," *Management Accounting,* 1992, *74,* 26–34.

61. C. Argyris and R. Kaplan, "Implementing New Knowledge: The Case of Activity Based Costing," *Accounting Horizons,* Sept. 1994.

62. H. T. Johnson, *Relevance Regained: From Top-Down Control to Bottom-Up Empowerment* (New York: Free Press, 1992); R. Kaplan and R. Cooper, *Cost and Effect: Using Integrated Cost Systems to Drive Profitability and Performance* (Cambridge, Mass.: Harvard Business School Press, 1997).

63. R. S. Kaplan and D. P. Norton, *The Balanced Scorecard: Translating Strategy into Action* (Cambridge, Mass.: Harvard Business School Press, 1996).

64. H. T. Johnson, "Management by Financial Targets Isn't Lean," *Manufacturing Engineering,* Dec. 1, 2007.

65. R. Sink, "My Unfashionable Legacy," *strategy+business,* Autumn 2007.

66. A. Kleiner, "PacBell: The New Octopus," *San Francisco Bay Guardian,* Mar. 19, 1986.

67. K. Pender, "PacBell 'Kroning'—Figures Soar," *San Francisco Chronicle,* Mar. 27, 1987.

68. A. Clardy, "Case Report: Kroning at Pac Bell" (Towson, Md.: Towson University, 2004), http://pages.towson.edu/aclardy/ WORKING%20PAPERS.htm; J. Ciulla, "Leadership and the Problem of Bogus Empowerment," in J. Ciulla (ed.), *Ethics: The Heart of Leadership* (Westport, Conn.: Greenwood Press, 2004); K. Pender, "Pac Bell's New Way to Think," *San Francisco Chronicle,* Mar. 23, 1987.

69. Clardy, "Case Report: Kroning at Pac Bell"; Pender, "Pac Bell's New Way To Think"; Pender, "PacBell 'Kroning'—Figures Soar"; K. Pender, "PUC Staff Assails PacBell Training," *San Francisco Chronicle,* June 11, 1987; K. Pender, "Pac Bell Stops Kroning," *San Francisco Chronicle,* June 16, 1987.

70. S. Adams, "The Scoop on Pacific Bell," 2001, http://www.dilbert.com.

71. M. Hammer and J. Champy, *Reengineering the Corporation: A Manifesto for Business Revolution* (New York: HarperCollins, 1993), p. 43.

72. Hammer and Champy, *Reengineering the Corporation;* M. Hammer, *Beyond Reengineering: How the Process-Centered Organization Is Changing Our Work and Our Lives* (New York: HarperCollins, 1997); J. Champy, *Reengineering Management: Mandate for New Leadership* (New York: HarperCollins, 1995); T. Davenport, *Process Innovation: Reengineering*

Work Through Information Technology (New York: McGraw-Hill, 1992); T. Davenport, *Mission Critical: Realizing the Promise of Enterprise Systems* (Cambridge, Mass.: Harvard Business School Press, 2000).

73. H. Lancaster, "Reengineering Authors Reconsider Reengineering," *Wall Street Journal,* Jan. 17, 1995. Also see J. B. White, "Next Big Thing: Re-Engineering Gurus Take Steps to Remodel Their Stalling Vehicles," *Wall Street Journal,* Nov. 26, 1996; J. Micklethwait, *The Witch Doctors* (New York: Times Business, 1996), p. 37; T. H. Davenport, "The Fad That Forgot People," *Fast Company,* Oct. 1995.

74. D. Rock and J. Schwartz, "The Neuroscience of Leadership," *strategy+business,* Summer 2006.

75. E. W. Dijkstra, *A Discipline of Programming* (Upper Saddle River, N.J.: Prentice Hall, 1976), and *Selected Writings on Computing: A Personal Perspective* (New York: Springer-Verlag, 1982); D. Knuth, *The Art of Computer Programming* (Reading, Mass.: Addison-Wesley, 1997–1998).

76. N. Tichy and S. Sherman, *Control Your Destiny or Someone Else Will* (New York: HarperCollins, 2005).

77. A. Kleiner, "GE's Next Work-Out," *strategy+business,* Winter 2003; J. Welch with J. A. Byrne, *Straight from the Gut* (New York: Business Plus, 2001), Chap. 11.

78. A. Kleiner, *Who Really Matters* (New York: Doubleday, 2003), Chap. 10.

79. J. Vierling-Huang, "Culture Change at General Electric," in Senge and others, *Dance of Change,* p. 80.

80. T. H. Huxley, "New Truths Begin as Heresies and End as Superstitions," *Collected Essays [1894]* (Westport, Conn.: Greenwood Press, 1968), p. 156.

81. See, for example, E. Shorris, *Scenes from Corporate Life* (New York: Penguin, 1984).

82. This segment derives from several sources: B. Smith, published in *The Lost Chapters of the Fifth Discipline Fieldbook* (Oxford, Ohio: Fifth Discipline Fieldbook Project, 1994), and then in *Systems Thinker,* 1995, 6(3); N. Mourkogiannis, *Purpose: The Starting Point of Great Companies* (New York: Palgrave, 2006); S. Wheeler, W. McFarland, and A. Kleiner, "A Blueprint for Strategic Leadership," *strategy+business,* Winter 2007.

83. This point borrows from a statement made by Libbi Lepow on the River computer network (*Inquiry,* Sept. 1995).

84. Sink, "My Unfashionable Legacy."

85. P. V. Kannan, letter to the editor, *strategy+business,* Spring 2008.

ACKNOWLEDGMENTS

FOUR EDITORS HAVE OVERSEEN THIS BOOK. The first was Harriet Rubin at Doubleday/Currency. It emerged from a series of articles she commissioned me to do in 1989. Roger Scholl at Doubleday took over the book around the time of its publication in 1996. At Jossey-Bass/Wiley, Neil Maillet devoted himself to developing a new edition for the book; then Rebecca Browning, its current editor, brought it to fruition. A writer (especially of a complex book like this one) could not ask for more enthusiastic, dedicated, professional, and admirable oversight.

I am also immensely gratified by the interest that Warren Bennis has shown in this new edition and by the support he has given it. It isn't easy for a character in a book to become an advocate of it, and his grace, perspective, clarity of thought, and mentorship for others provide a model that I hope to emulate throughout my life.

Joe Spieler, literary agent, has been a friend and business partner since 1986. His support, suggestions, and insight were crucial to making this book real.

Janis Dutton was an ongoing conscience, as well as a research administrator, during the book's early stages. Eric Brush, Max Stoltenberg, Chris Haymaker, Benjamin Florer, and Tom Fritsch also provided research help back then. Later I benefited greatly from the help of Maggie Piper and Emily Freidberg.

Work on the second edition took place while I was a principal at Booz Allen Hamilton (and subsequently Booz & Company) and the editor-in-chief of *strategy+business,* its quarterly magazine. I could not have done it without the support and encouragement of a large number of people. I particularly thank those who had something to do with it directly: Virginia Brosnan, Mark Fortier, Jonathan Gage, Sal Bianco, Lawrence Fisher, Nancy Hardwick, Sally Helgesen, Marie Lerch, Walt McFarland, and Steven Wheeler. The second edition also drew substantially on articles I wrote as a columnist for *strategy+business* between 2000 and 2005; during that time, I benefited greatly from the editorial and collegial support of Randall Rothenberg, Ann Graham, Cindie Baker, Victoria Beliveau, and others.

Finally, the book benefited in a variety of ways from my membership in such a strong team at s+b, including Amy Bernstein, Melissa Cavanaugh, Bridget Finn, Laura Geller, Elizabeth Johnson, Ted Kinni, Jeff Rothfeder, Judy Russo, Alan Shapiro, and others; and from the example of colleagues at both "Booz" firms, colleagues such as Viren Doshi, Kaj Grichnik, Barry Jaruzelski, Ed Landry, Fernando Napolitano, Karim Sabbagh, Chris Vollmer, Conrad Winkler; Art Fritzson, Mark Gerencser, Chris Kelly, Reggie Van Lee, and Dov Zakheim; Susan Balding, Michael Bulger, Jodie Collins, Adrienne Crowther, Michael Delurey, Georgina Grenon, Lisa Mitchell, Kate Pinkerton, Andrew Sambrook, Ilona Steffen, Emma van Rooyen, and many, many others.

At Jossey-Bass/Wiley, this book benefited from the time and involvement of Angela Bole, Amie Wong, Erin Kelly, Gayle Mak, and Mark Karmendy. And it still bears the imprint of conversations with Janet Coleman, Lauren Osborne, Michael Ianozzi, and Laurel Cook at Doubleday. Tape transcriptions were a key part of this book's research. These were handled (with savoir faire, dignity, and aplomb) by a series of colleagues: Sharon Lee Harkey and Purple Shark Transcriptions; Judi Webb; Ronna Herman; Esther Shear; and Laura Tawater.

I wish to single out several people for the time they spent guiding me through the unfamiliar terrain of the material here.

Napier Collyns saw the potential value of this book from its earliest stages to its current revised incarnation and has been a constant source of perspective, cheer, and insight. Without Napier's help, the sections on Royal Dutch/Shell could never have been researched, and much of the rest of the book would lack verve. His and Pat Collyns's support gave me the confidence to continue even during bleak moments. Napier has probably never been acknowledged in print for his role as a godparent to significant books, including *The Fifth Discipline* by Peter Senge, *The Art of the Long View* by Peter Schwartz, *Living Without a Goal* by Jay Ogilvy, and *The Prize* by Daniel Yergin. This book is a definite addition to the list.

Donald N. Michael, social psychologist and author, was a key influence and good friend throughout my research on the first edition, continually prompting me toward thoughtfulness, comprehensiveness, and rigor. He has also been a colleague, counselor, collaborator, and mentor to many of the people and events described in this book. He counseled Warren Bennis about the NTL presidency; he oversaw Willis Harman's project for Hendrik Gideonse; he was one of Pierre Wack's remarkable people; he is a member of the Club of Rome; and he was a colleague of Eric Trist. In early drafts, Don's name kept popping up; ultimately I was forced to remove most of the references for simplicity, but that does not diminish his significance. Don passed away in 2000 and is greatly missed.

Dick Beckhard's name was also cut for the sake of narrative simplicity. Any comprehensive history would include him as a key innovator and cofounder of organizational development (beginning in the early 1950s), as well as a close associate of Douglas McGregor, a professor in the MIT organizational behavior program, and an ongoing mentor and guide to many people in the field. (For example, he employed Edie Seashore during the early 1960s.) He provided a living link between the "change agentry" of the 1950s and 1960s and the "learning organization" work of the 1980s and 1990s. He also took great pains to help me better understand the NTL, P&G, and General Foods histories. Dick, who passed away in 1999, is still greatly beloved and remembered.

Milt Moskowitz introduced me to the subject of corporate social responsibility, which no one else knows better. He edited the newsletter *Business and Society* in the 1960s and early 1970s. In more recent times, he has become known as the instigator of the *Everybody's Business* series of almanacs, on which I depended during my research, and he is currently known as the co-creator of *Fortune*'s "100 Best Places to Work" series.

My *Fifth Discipline Fieldbook* and MIT learning history colleagues— Charlotte Roberts, Rick Ross, Peter Senge, Bryan Smith, Michael Goodman, Nina Kruschwitz, George Roth, Nelda Cambron-McCabe, Janis Dutton, and Tim Lucas—all made a point of helping me understand and express the value of corporate heresy. Martin Elton, Will McWhinney, Ken Wessel, Tom Gilmore, Beulah Trist, Mary Wilson, Ralph Sink, Michael Jaliman, and Michael Brower went far out of their way to help me understand the sociotechnical/open systems body of work—the work of Eric Trist, Charles Krone, and others. Diana Smith, Grady McGonagill, Bill Joiner, and Robert Putnam welcomed me into a better understanding of Chris Argyris's work and the theory of action in practice. Bill Isaacs, Kelvy Bird, and Skip Griffin of Dialogos provided a great and skillful friendship that forever changed my view of heresy and humanity. Lawrence Wilkinson, Doug Carmichael, V. Shannon Clyne, and Tom Johnson showed me what a corporation was. Clare Crawford-Mason, author of *Quality or Else,* introduced me to the quality movement and deepened my knowledge of the corporate change terrain. James C. Davidson went over the facts about Royal Dutch/Shell with me repeatedly; without our correspondence, that section would be far more awry. Phil Mirvis, on a parallel track, made me feel I wasn't alone. David Bradford contributed photographs to this book, and insights and knowledge about NTL. Ed Dulworth and Lyman Ketchum worked persistently to articulate their story.

Marc Sarkady provided a vital sense of the linkage between seemingly unrelated areas of the terrain. Louis van der Merwe embodied perception and passion as a guide to the South Africa story and to organizational heresy in general. Pierre Wack and Ted Newland hosted me and contributed generously of their time and insight. Edie and Charlie Seashore also hosted me and took a strong and valued interest in the project, as did Ed Schein. Oliver Markley served as a Dantean guide to the caverns and byways of futures research. Ken Krabbenhoft shared his knowledge of mysticism and his passion for understanding religious practice. J. Baldwin broke into his own book schedule for a critically important talk with me about the counterculture. Larry Frascella, in a conversation in 1989, showed me that there would be an audience for this book.

The information in this book was drawn from interviews and correspondence with a large number of people. In many cases, their interest, encouragement, and extra effort meant a great deal to me personally. They include Billie Alban, Hank Alkema, Jackie De Moss Allen, Michael Allen, Brad Allenby, Roy Anderson, Chris Argyris, Michael Assum, Douglas Augstrom, Nancy Badore, Edward Baker, Paul Banas, Joan Bavaria, Peter Beck, André Bénard, Warren Bennis, Dave Berlew, Robert Blake, Auriol Blandy, Peter Block, Irving Bluestone, Lee Bolman, Joan Bragan, Ren Beck, Bill Brenneman, Mike Brimm, Juanita Brown and David Isaacs, Barry Bruce-Briggs, Rinaldo Brutoco, Jim Burch, Frank Burns, Ernest Callenbach, Bill Campbell, Pat Carrigan, Stanley Carson, John Catenacci, Tom Chappell, Dan Ciampa, Liane Clorfene-Casten, Nancy Cole, Eliza Collins, Nancy Couch, Bob Craig, Philip Crosby, Kathy Dannemiller, Kathy Davis, Arie de Geus, Leslie Deighton, Chris Desser, Tim Devinney, Joe Doyle, Hans Dumoulin, Betty Duval, Amy Edmundson, Max Elden, Duane Elgin, Don Ephelin, Werner Erhard, Mitchell Fein, John Filer, Jeffrey Fine, Larry Fink, Franklin Florence, Jay Forrester, Michael Foster, Susan Frank, Winston Franklin, Milton Friedman, Shelley Gallup, Robert Gass, Jeffrey Gates, Clark Gellings, Peter Gibb, Hendrik Gideonse, Larry Good, Ian Graham-Bryce, Charles Grantham, Michael Gruber, Lynne Hall, Harold Haller, Robert Hargrove, Willis Harman, Sidney Harmon, Jim Harney, Betty Harragan, Roger Harrison, Jerry Harvey, Cliff Havener, Paul Hawken, Denis Hayes, Sally Helgesen, Hazel Henderson, Ed Henneman, Jim Henry, Harvey Hornstein, Mark Horowitz, Sanford Horwitt, Thomas Hout, Bill Joiner, Walter Jolson, Jane Kahn, Mark Kamin, Rosabeth Moss Kanter, Jeff Kaplan, Charlie Kiefer, Lisa Kimball, Jim Knight, Frank Kontely, Don LaFond, Dutch Landen, Jeff Litwin, Paul and Janice Long, Amory Lovins, Vic Lowe, Michael Maccoby, Bruce MacDonald, Jane Mansbridge, Alice Tepper Marlin, Leon Martel, Mike McCurdy,

Norm McEachron, Jack McKittrick, Dana Meadows, Dennis Meadows, Douglas Merchant, D. R. Miller, Frederick Miller, Kelly Blake Morgan, Laura Nash, Thomas Naylor, Larry Nichols, Barry Oshry, Michael Owen-Jones, Ken Oye, Richard Pascale, Bill Paul, Claude and Sandy Pelanne, Myron Peskin, Stanley Peterfreund, Tom Peters, Neil Pickett, Darryl Poole, Elsa Porter, Don Povejsio, Gareth Price, Wendy Pritchard, Robert Putnam, Rafael Ramirez, Dick Raymond, Charles Reed, Jim Richard, Margaret Rioch, Mickie Ritvo, Vickie Robin, Jeremy Robinson, Sylvan Robinson, Alan Rodda, Joe Roeber, Mitch Rofsky, Steven Roselle, Leo Rosten, Joel Schatz, Peter Scholtes, Peter Schwartz, Robert Schwartz, Will Shutz, Eric Siegel, Wayne Silby, Herm Simon, Mary Sinclair, Max Singer, R.G.H. Siu, Diana Smith, J. Andy Smith, Benson Snyder, Basil South, Marie Spengler, Carl Spitzer, Lowell Steel, Karen Stephenson, David Sternlight, Myron Stolaroff, Jim Stone, Harris Sussman, Karel Swart, Lee Swenson, Norman Thomas, Noel Tichy, Bill Torbert, Jack Trainor, Hugh Tranum and Sam Nalbone, Beulah Trist, Alexander Trowbridge, Peggy Umanzio, Peter Vaill, Kees van der Heijden, Bill Veltrop, Doug Wade, Gerrit Wagner, Tom Wagner, Richard Walton, Robert Waterman, Paul Weaver, Anthony Weiner, Edith Weiner, Marvin Weisbord, Margaret Wheatley, Dr. Norman White, Ian Wilson, Brian Yost, Rene D. Zentner, Sam Zimmerman, and many others.

Some critical conversations took place during the preparation of the second edition, or between the two editions. I thank Joseph Balazs, Michael Brower, Alfred Chandler Jr., Ram Charan, Michael Chender, Jim Collins, Ed Dulworth, Mike Dulworth, Tom Ehrenfeld, Chris Ertel, Andrea Gabor, R. Gopalakrishnan, Skip Griffin, Charles Hampden-Turner, Tom Igoe, Bill Isaacs, David Isenberg, Elliot Jaques, P. V. Kannan, A. J. Lafley, Nikos Mourkogiannis, Vincent Potenza, Hal Richman, Al Ringleb, David Rock, David and Trudy Sable, Carol Sanford, Michael Schrage, Jeffrey Schwartz, Clay Shirky, Sue Simington, George Smart, Mary Stacey, Mark Stahlman, Fons Trompenaars, Lavinia Weissman, Jim Womack, and many others.

I am very grateful for the help, guidance, and friendship (or all of the above) that the following people have rendered to this project: George Agudow, Steve Baer, Linda Baston, Hilary Bradbury, Stewart Brand, John Brockman, Rinker Buck, David Burnor, Red Burns, William Calvin, Brian Clough, Ferris Cook, Sheryl Erickson, Chris Ertel, Jim and Marylin Evers, David Ferguson, Alan Fertziger, Larry Fisher, Graham Galer, Lorrie Gallagher, Tracy Goss, Alan Gussow, Ed Hamell, Tom Hargadon, Sally Helgesen, Anne Herbert, Sue Miller Hurst, Jody Isaacs, Peter and Trudy Johnson-Lenz, Adam Kahane, David Kantor, Lisa Kimball and John Cooney, Bryan Kreutzer, Bill Leigh, Steven Levy, Nan Lux, Pamela

McCorduck, Gregory Meyding, Irving Mintzer and Amber Leonard, Jacqueline Mouton, Marc Mowrey, Nancy Murphy, Kathleen O'Neill, James O'Toole, Ryan Phelan, Michael Phillips, Patricia Poore and Bill Breen of *Garbage,* Ruthann Prange, Tim Redmond, Howard Rheingold, Alan Richardson, Hank Roberts, Joyce Ross, Harry Schessel, Dan Simpson, Ellen and Bruce Singleton, John Sumser, Lee Swenson, Robert Tannenbaum, Ann Thomas, Langg Tomura, Martin Turchin, John Wallis, Alan Webber and Bill Taylor of *Fast Company,* Bob Weber and Dave Mason and others of Northeast Consulting Resources, Fred Weiderhold, Diane Weston, Linda Zarytski, and (again) many others.

I benefited from aid from BNA films, the University of Cincinnati Rare Documents Library (Kevin Grace), Block Petrella Weisbord, the Buckminster Fuller Institute, *Processed World Magazine,* the River inquiry conference, the WELL writer's conference (Thaisa Frank, Joe Flower, and many others), the New York University Interactive Telecommunications Program, many people at CoOp America, the Wayne State University Archives of Labor and Urban Affairs (Thomas Featherstone), the NTL Archives at the University of Akron, Antiochiana at the Antioch College Library (Nina Myatt), the MIT Museum, the MIT Center for Organizational Learning, Global Business Network, the Institute for Noetic Sciences, Point Foundation and the *Whole Earth Catalog,* and libraries at Miami University, New York University, the Work Research (ACAS, British Government), the University of Cincinnati, MIT, the University of Dayton, Harvard Business School, George Washington University, Columbia University, the OD Network, the Shambhala Institute for Authentic Leadership (whose program each summer in Halifax, Nova Scotia, represents a great example of training for effective heretics), and Oxford University's Said Business School (home of the new Pierre Wack memorial library).

I want to acknowledge several people whom I interviewed or talked with about this project who have passed away since but remain present in my thoughts: W. Edwards Deming, Ivan Illich, Tom Mandel, David Miller, Calvin Pava, Joseph Smith, Carol Townsend, Eric Trist, and William C. Williams. And since the publication of the first edition: Richard Beckhard, Kathy Dannemiller, Gerard Fairtlough, Cliff Havener, Will McWhinney, Don Michael, and Pierre Wack.

My parents, Julius Kleiner and Irene Slovak Kleiner, have been a longstanding source of help, guidance, and encouragement. I also thank Edward Kleiner for his understanding and support, and I remain grateful to the memory of Regina Weisman, Max Kleiner, Herbert Florer Jr., and Calvin Heusser. I express much appreciation and gratitude to Linda Heusser, Benjamin Florer, Herb Florer III, and Tami Florer.

Finally, I acknowledge gratitude, admiration, and love for my wife, Faith Florer. This book was a central part of her life for at least six years, and in a thousand great and small ways, she has shown how much she cares about the quality of the work and the happiness of its author. I also thank our children—Frances, Elizabeth, and Constance—for their patience, interest, and love. They were all born between the publication of the first and second edition of this book. They have made the life of this father, writer, and editor far richer than it would otherwise have been.

ABOUT THE AUTHOR

ART KLEINER is the editor-in-chief of *strategy+business* (http://www .strategy-business.com), a quarterly management magazine for executives and senior decision makers, published by Booz & Company. His other published works include the critically acclaimed book *Who Really Matters: The Core Group Theory of Power, Privilege and Success* (2003) and the best-selling *Fifth Discipline Fieldbook* series (for which he was editorial director and coauthor with Peter Senge and others). A former editor of the *Whole Earth Catalog*, Kleiner helped found the WELL computer network and teaches scenario planning at New York University's Interactive Telecommunications Program. He also was a codesigner (with George Roth) of the Learning History series from the MIT Center for Organizational Learning. Kleiner is a long-standing writer, educator, and consultant on management thinking, organizational change, technology and media, and leadership. His articles have appeared in a variety of publications, including *Wired, Fast Company*, the *Harvard Business Review*, the *New York Times Magazine*, and www.artkleiner.com.

INDEX